PERILS OF
THE PORT OF
NEW YORK

Captain Robert W. Carle

PERILS OF
THE PORT OF
NEW YORK

Maritime Disasters from Sandy Hook to Execution Rocks

JEANNETTE EDWARDS RATTRAY

Illustrated with map, charts and photographs

Dodd, Mead & Company, New York

ISBN: 0-396-06790-5
Library of Congress Catalog Card Number: 72-12441
Printed in the United States of America

ACKNOWLEDGMENTS

S. Kip Farrington, Jr., has read the manuscript for this book and given invaluable advice. Many others have given information and discussed various points. Among them are: Werner Bamberger, Mrs. Emily Barto, Mrs. Amy Osborn Bassford, Miss Helen P. Bolman, Frank O. Braynard, Howard I. Chappelle, Mrs. Frank Dayton, Dwight B. Demeritt, Jr., Charles Dunn, Dr. and Mrs. George W. Fish, Captain Edmund W. Florimont, Captain William C. Hall, Walter Hamshar, Miss Russella Hazard, George Hermann, James J. Heslin, Arthur L. Hodges, George Horne, Captain Eugene E. Kenny, Edward R. King, Mrs. Betty Kuss, Mrs. Celia Lambert, Captain Albert Larsen, John L. Lochhead, Don Marchese, Clarence E. Meek, Captain W. A. Mitchell, William C. North, Louis P. Pearsall, Captain Jay Porter, Everett Rattray, Miss Anna Sackmann, Frederick P. Schmitt, William Seabrook, Captain George Seeth, Murray Seliger, Edward J. Shean, Captain William W. Sherwood, Captain William F. Smith, Lieutenant W. N. Smith, USCG, Peter Stanford, Captain Joseph Sweeney, Captain James H. Thombs, Paul Van Wicklen, Joseph Vath, Stanley Warren, John Wieting, William D. Wilkinson, Mr. and Mrs. James Wilson.

Flaunt out, O sea, your separate flags of nations!

Flaunt out visible as ever the various ship-signals! But do you reserve especially for yourself and for the soul of man one flag above all the rest,

A spiritual woven signal for all nations, emblem of man elate above death,

Token of all brave captains and all intrepid sailors and mates,

And all that went down doing their duty,

A pennant universal, subtly waving all time, o'er all brave sailors,

All seas, all ships.

—Walt Whitman, "Song for All Seas, All Ships"

FOREWORD

The day after the 1938 hurricane, George Carter of Center Moriches, Long Island, and Dr. George W. Fish of New York were walking the beach on Fire Island—that long, narrow strip of sand that stretches from a point off West Islip to Southampton on Long Island's south shore. They were looking for their gunning shanty, which had been blown off its foundation by the storm. The Coast Guard station at Moriches had been washed away. The men saw something lying in the sand. It was a set of logbooks, kept in the Moriches station when it was in the Life Saving Service, 1875–1915.

Before turning over the logbooks to the Coast Guard, they had twenty-one pages of notes on shipwrecks of that area typed from them. Their friend and gunning companion, Dr. David Edwards of East Hampton, knowing my passion for Long Island history and especially history concerning the sea, brought me the notes.

These were the starting point for the book *Ship Ashore! A Record of Maritime Disasters off Montauk and Eastern Long Island, 1640–1955*. That was a natural, growing up as I did within sight and sound of the sea on the eastern end of Long Island. Nautical tales were an inheritance.

My father and two of his brothers held their master's papers by the time they were twenty-one. Grandfather had sailed around Cape Horn, up into the Arctic and down into the South Seas on whaleships for eighteen years before he married. In his time at least one young man in every family on Long Island went to sea.

After collecting notes of eastern Long Island shipwrecks, friends began

From a map of the Province of New York, published in London in 1779, when British forces occupied New York.

to send me accounts of disasters that had occurred off the Port of New York, western Long Island, and nearby New Jersey. Eventually a card file of nearly 2,000 such disasters was assembled—more than can be fitted into a book.

Information on those disasters, and their results, comes primarily from people: Sandy Hook pilots, ship captains, tugboatmen, Coast Guardsmen, firemen of the New York Fire Department's Marine Division, divers, fishermen, and a few remaining veterans of the old Life Saving Service that preceded the Coast Guard.

Old newspaper files, microfilm, diaries, letters, documents, Life Saving Service reports, and bound volumes of the New York Maritime Register kept at the Maritime Association of the Port of New York have been consulted. A voluminous publication called *American Maritime Cases*, used by Admiralty lawyers, was a great help; as were special libraries. A tall pile of early *Harper's* and *Scribner's* magazines, forgotten for generations in a family attic, has proved a treasure trove.

The New York area has had a much more eventful maritime history than Long Island's eastern end. But relatively few New Yorkers were born there, so it is rare to find a parent or grandparent who can hark back to the time when Manhattan Island could be reached only by water, and marine disasters were frequent. They knew little of the sea trade to which America's greatest port and greatest asset owes its existence; of the tragedies and brave deeds that have taken place in New York Harbor, the North River (Hudson), East River, the nearby Atlantic Ocean, and Long Island Sound; or how safety laws, inventions, and organizations that now protect lives and property afloat have resulted from major catastrophes.

I am happy to have found some men in the New York area who could furnish a background for their waterfront; and to know that, in the South Street Seaport project, city dwellers will have a growing awareness of their heritage.

Men, old and young, with vast saltwater experience in and around the port, have been generous with their time and knowledge. I have learned much, made new friends, and enjoyed it. I am deeply grateful. What I have learned is set down for young or old New Yorkers—to take the place, perhaps, of the grandfathers' tales they may have missed.

Jeannette Edwards Rattray

East Hampton, Long Island,
New York

CONTENTS

ILLUSTRATIONS

Illustrations

PERILS OF
THE PORT OF
NEW YORK

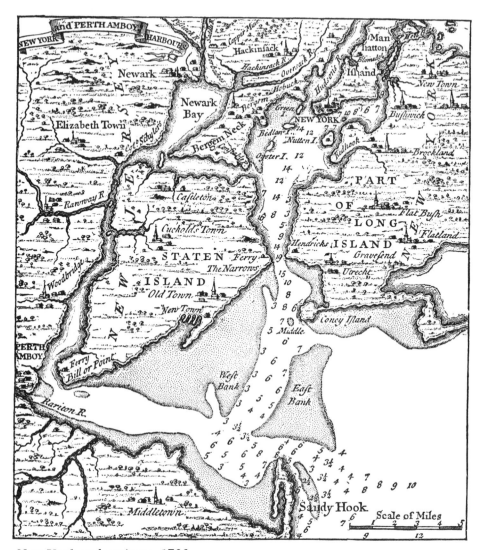

New York and environs, 1733

1

DISASTERS:
17TH CENTURY

NEWS of the first recorded marine disaster at the Port
of New York and vicinity took a long time to get back to the ship's home port
of Amsterdam. The disaster occurred in late January or early February, 1614,
when Adriaen Block's ship, the Tiger (Tijger in Holland Dutch), caught
fire. She was anchored in the Hudson River off what is now Dey Street in
lower Manhattan, loaded with furs and making ready to sail back home.

The Tiger burned fast. Block and his men managed to pick up a few
spare sails, some rope, and some shipwright tools, as they escaped in the
ship's boat.

But for that accident, which destroyed his ship to the waterline, Block
might never have made the discoveries that, when he finally reported in
Amsterdam, led to Dutch settlement in what was to be called, for fifty years,
Nieuw Amsterdam.

Adriaen Block was a master mariner and a highly successful trader.
He had left Amsterdam in October, 1613, on his fourth fur-trading voyage
to the mouth of the Hudson River. He commanded two ships, which crossed
the Atlantic together. He sent one ship, the Fortune, up the Hudson to build a
trading post and barter with the Indians.

After the Tiger burned, Block and his crew were alone with the Indians
and no ship. Luckily for them the Indians proved friendly. They helped the
traders build four rough huts, where the Hollanders lived the rest of the
winter (a hard one—the Hudson was blocked with ice), and helped them

cut down oak and hickory trees to build a small new ship. The huts made the first European settlement on Manhattan Island.

The new vessel, which Block named the Onrust (Restless), was finished late in the spring of 1614. The Restless was 44½ feet long with an 11½-foot beam, and of 16 tons displacement. Block considered her too small for the sail back to Holland, but not too small for coastal exploration. He took his little Restless, the first seagoing vessel ever built on Manhattan Island, through the dangerous passage in the East River which he named "Hellegat" (Hell Gate). He sailed up the New England coast as far as Marblehead, Mass. He discovered the Housatonic and Connecticut rivers and mapped the shoreline. He named Block Island, at the ocean entrance to Long Island Sound, after himself. He sailed all the way around Long Island, discovering that it really was an island, and reentered New York Harbor from the ocean side.

Meanwhile his partner on the Fortune had scouted as far as Cape Cod. Block boarded the Fortune and returned on her to Holland. He put the other captain on the Restless, directing him to continue explorations south of the mouth of the Hudson.

In 1890 the Holland Society placed a plaque on the old Federal Office Building at 45 Broadway to commemorate the first construction of a ship by Europeans in this country. In 1916 some of the prow, keel, and frame timbers of the Tiger were unearthed during subway excavations at the intersection of Dey and Greenwich streets. The waterfront had been filled in, so that the timbers lay nineteen or twenty feet below the surface of the street. The parts protruding into the subway excavation were sawed off. Tests have positively identified the fragments. They are preserved in the marine gallery of the Museum of the City of New York.

A model of the Onrust, or Restless, was presented in 1967 to the Port of New York Authority by the Port of Amsterdam for eventual display in the new World Trade Center.

THE BRAVE PENELOPE

The first recorded wreck on Sandy Hook, N.J., was that of a Dutch vessel in 1620. Among the passengers was a Dutch bride of eighteen, born Penelope Van Princis in Amsterdam. Her husband's name is not known. The ship's crew and the other passengers made their way to Nieuw Amsterdam, but Penelope's husband had been injured in the wreck, so she stayed with him in the woods.

They were discovered by a party of Indians, who killed the husband and left Penelope for dead. She had a fractured skull, her left shoulder had been hacked, and she was slashed terribly about the body.

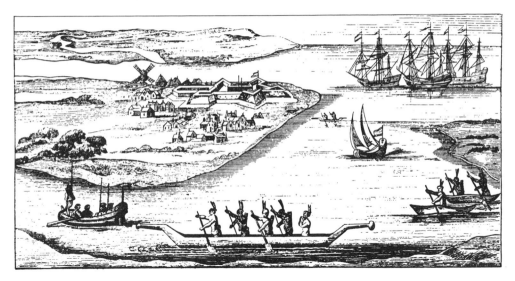

An early, and largely imaginary, view of New Amsterdam

But she survived. She crawled into the hollow of a tree, so the family legend says, and existed there for seven days on no other food but tree fungus and a little rainwater. On the seventh day she saw a deer passing by with an arrow sticking in it. Shortly afterward, two Indians appeared.

The younger was about to kill her, but was prevented by the older Indian. He carried Penelope to his wigwam and dressed her wounds. When she was well enough he took her to Nieuw Amsterdam and made a "present" of her to her countrymen—receiving valuable presents in return.

In 1624 Penelope married Richard Stout. She is said to have lived to the age of 110, at which time her offspring numbered 502. The Stouts settled in Middletown, N.J., in 1648, where they were among the founders of the Baptist Church. One of their descendants became State Senator Richard Stout of Monmouth County.

CAST AWAY UPON LONG ISLAND

The following, set down in his *Journal* on March 30, 1636, by John Winthrop, founder of the Massachusetts Bay Colony (which included Connecticut), may refer to Hell Gate or may not. But since it speaks of the "Dutch plantation," and the people were bound for Virginia, they must have been making for that dangerous passage, or have been in it.

"Mr. Wither [a clergyman] in a vessel of 50 tons, going to Virginia, was cast away upon Long Island, with a W.N.W. wind. The company (being about 30) were, most of them, very profane persons, and in their voyage did much to reproach our colony, vowing they would hang, drown or, etc., before they would come hither again. Seven were drowned on landing; some got in a small boat to the Dutch plantation, two were killed by the Indians, who took all such goods as they left on shore. Those who escaped, went towards Virginia in a Dutch bark, and were never heard of after, but were thought to be wrecked, by some Dutch pails, etc. which were found by the Indians thereabout."

In Volume II of the Winthrop Journal are two more entries regarding wrecks of vessels making for, or in, Hell Gate.

In 1640 a pinnace, the Make Shift, so-called because it was built of the wreck of a greater vessel at the Isle of Sable, and by that means the men saved, was "on a voyage to the Southward and cast away upon a ledge of rocks near Long Island, all goods lost but the men saved. . . . There is no winter but some vessels have been cast away in that voyage."

A pinnace was either a ship's boat, long and narrow and built to row fast, or a decked craft designed to sail and row, often fitted with a two-masted shallop rig.

John Winthrop records on October 3, 1643, that three ministers were being sent to Virginia from Connecticut: Mr. Tompson, Mr. Knolles, and Mr. James. Later he notes their departure from New Haven on October 7. The journey to Virginia took eleven weeks. "As they passed Hellgate between Long Island and the Dutch, their pinnace was bilged upon the rocks, so as she was near foundered before they could run on the next shore. The Dutch governor gave them slender entertainment, but Isaac Allerton of New Haven, being there . . . procured them a very good pinnace."

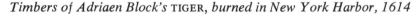

Timbers of Adriaen Block's TIGER, *burned in New York Harbor, 1614*

Model of the RESTLESS, *built to replace the* TIGER

THE PRINS MAURITS

A Dutch ship, the Prins Maurits, was wrecked on Fire Island, then called South Beach, on March 9, 1657. She was named for Maurice of Nassau, Prince of Orange (1567–1625), the famous general who rescued the United Netherlands from Spanish domination and became head of the state.

The Prins Maurits was bound for what is now New York, but on April 13, 1657, Vice-Director J. Alrich reported her wreck from Fort Amsterdam (N.Y.) to the "Commissioners of the Colonie of the Delaware." On May 7, 1657, he wrote a first-hand account of it to the Burgomasters of Amsterdam from Fort Amstel (now New Castle, Del.):

"I embarked on the 21st December of last year, in the ship Prins Maurits, with one hundred and thirteen souls, including Colonists, free mechanics, soldiers and attendants, together with sixteen matrosses, in all 129 souls, and proceeded with them on the proposed voyage, and after some storm and other obstacles reached, on the 8th of March, the vicinity of the

Manhattes, and was in daily expectation of arriving there."

(The word "matrosses" will puzzle most readers. A matross was a gunner's assistant, or mate. Its first recorded use in English was in 1639; it was not used after 1750. It is from the Dutch matroos and the French matelot, meaning sailor.)

Continuing the quote: "The ship grounded at 11 P.M. on March 8th. Accordingly on the 9th of March, in severe, bitter and freezing weather, with drifting ice, after great trouble, through dangerous breakers in a very leaky boat, with considerable water in it, we succeeded in reaching the shore on a broken spit or foreland, in which neither bush nor grass grew, nor was any trace of firewood to be found.

"On the third day we, for the first time, saw and spoke some Indians, who informed us that it was the foreland of Long Island and that the place was called Secoutagh." (Now West Islip; once the Indian village of Secatogue.)

"Meanwhile, the ship getting nearer the shore, we, from time to time, unloaded and saved all the dry articles. Having met and experienced this misfortune, I sent an Indian, with advice thereof, to General Stuyvesant, who immediately sent us a small sloop and came, himself, on the second day after, to us at the above-mentioned place, which lies about twenty leagues north of the Manhattes. On the other, or land, side of said place, a small opening or inlet to a river has been discovered, which a small sloop can enter; but most of the goods were brought over land to the other side to be loaded on the river."

THE HALCYON

A few pages from an old log were copied in June, 1949, for the *Long Island Forum*. A search through the correspondence of the magazine, twenty years later, did not reveal the source.

The log entry described the adventure of a seventeen-year-old boatswain in 1695 on the "unseaworthy ship Halcyon bound back from the West Indies and seeking the most likely shelter from a hurricane that had raged for more than two days." From the description it is thought the wreck occurred at Jones Inlet. The ship sounds like a pirate, but in the 17th century privateering was perfectly respectable if directed against vessels of an enemy country; England and France were warring in 1695.

"We carried no cargo," the young boatswain wrote, "except what we had took from three small French vessels that had chanced to cross our way and this was little enough for the thirty-nine men that had shipped on her five months before in hopes of making a nice return from the voyage."

They had been running ahead of the storm, bound for New York, but failed to clear the Long Island coast. "Captain Rose decided to seek shelter inside the outer beach. . . . Intending to run through a likely looking inlet between two sandy points, we came in with our foresail, the mainyard being lowered down a-port-last. I being in the bow and looking earnestly ahead, of a sudden I saw the sea breaking up against a low bar seeming to be almost from point to point.

"Upon such sad discovery of death before us, and where our graves were like to be if sudden means were not used, our helmsman brought the ship to . . . and hoisted up our mainyard and set our mainsail. Finding this would not do without more sail, I run up the shrouds to heave out the main-topsail. Then I saw high dunes on the weather bow, as the sea pressed us towards the shore insomuch that we were forced to let our yards and sails down, to cut away our mainmast and hove yards and sail overaboard, and put overaboard our anchor.

"We finding the sea heaving us still to the shore, we put over another anchor, and, finding the wind and sea still pressing us to the shore and but little more drift, we cut overaboard our foremast and put over another anchor, which was the last we had to trust to. Then we found the ship to ride fast.

"But riding against the overgrown sea in such a manner, the ship's bow did begin to open, so we cut away the bowsprit for, the foremast being gone, the bowsprit, for want of the forestay, lay so heavy on the bows and falling into the sea caused the bows to give way. With the bowsprit cut away, this secured our bows and prevented our sinking there just outside the bar.

"Having nothing left now but a mizzen-mast, we lay like a great lighter in the sea. We hove the lead overboard and found the ground to be so foul with other sunken ships and wreckage so that our cables were in danger of being cut. The fall of the foremast had broke the upper deck down on the gun-deck and our two boats (being one in the other placed on the deck) to pieces.

"So thus we waited all that night and at daybreak, it proving less wind, we worked to fit up the long-boat. When done it was agreed on to launch the boat overboard for we could not hoist her out for want of mast and tackles.

"And thus we abandoned ship and made through the inlet to the bay that lay between the beach and the mainland."

2

LIGHTHOUSES
AND
LIGHTSHIPS

U<small>NTIL</small> 1737 there was not one aid to navigation at the entrance to New York Harbor from the sea. In 1764 the Sandy Hook, N.J., lighthouse was built. It is the oldest one in the United States still in active operation. The original wooden lighthouse was replaced in 1769 by the present white brick and stone tower. At first it was called the New York Lighthouse, because a group of merchants of the New York—Raritan Bay area had held a lottery to raise funds for its erection. Maintenance costs were defrayed by a tax of twenty-two pence per ton assessed on ships entering the harbor area.

At the beginning of the Revolution, when the British fleet lay off New York, American seamen dismantled the lighthouse to avoid enemy use. Later it was restored by the British, only to have Captain John Conover of the Continental Army, in 1776, make a successful foray with field guns mounted on boats, which shot away the lighthouse apparatus. Captain Conover lost several men in the process.

During that war a number of loyalist troops were raised in New Jersey. Since they were outnumbered and surrounded by Continental forces, they retreated to Sandy Hook, using the lighthouse and keeper's cottage as their headquarters. It was then called Lighthouse Fort and Refuge Tower. The Tories stayed bottled up on the Hook through the whole war, finally surrendering when the war was over. Men who died there during those years were buried close by. Every once in a while another of their graves is discovered.

After the war, in 1790, New York and New Jersey disputed ownership of the lighthouse, because the latter state owned the four acres of land it stood on. This was settled by ceding the tower and the land to the United States. Congress took over control of all lighthouses along the coast. Before that, states with seaports had supported their own.

KEEPERS OF THE LIGHT

For 100 years keepers of the light saved lives in shipwrecks. A keeper would launch a dory even in a gale. The boats were not self-bailing and there were no life jackets, so many keepers lost their lives in desperate attempts at rescue.

In 1819 a lighthouse keeper was paid up to $350 a year. He had to be over eighteen years old; to know how to read and write; and to be competent for his duties, which were considerable. By March, 1874, a light keeper's pay averaged $600 a year, determined by the importance of the light and the responsibility put on the keeper. He and his family had to live in barren, isolated, and exposed parts of the coast. The lamps had to be kept clean and

Sandy Hook Lighthouse, Fort Hancock, N.J.

filled and free of ice and snow; with the wicks trimmed. They were lighted punctually at sunset, every day. The foghorn had to be sounded when needed. The light keeper was instructed to keep a daily journal of events, and careful accounts.

For fueling the light, the best sperm whale oil was used, to begin with. According to an article by Charles Nordhoff in *Harper's New Monthly Magazine* for March, 1874: "Our Lighthouse Board now uses the best quality of lard-oil, made on purpose for the establishment. Kerosene and other mineral oils have been used in the British Provinces and in Europe to some extent, but there are certain obvious risks attending them which prevent their use with us.

"There are at this time half a dozen electric lights in Europe, but their number is not increasing. They have proved extremely expensive in the maintenance. . . . It is said that this light, which is no doubt more powerful than any other in clear weather, does not penetrate fog so well as the oil light."

The Navesink, N.J., Light, four miles south of Sandy Hook, was the first to use electricity in this country. Sandy Hook Light used gas in 1903.

The 1874 *Harper's* article said of the keepers: "Experience has shown our Lighthouse Board that the best light-keepers are old soldiers and sailors, and it is its desire, we have been told, that the maimed of those who served in the war for the Union should, where they are physically and mentally competent, receive these places . . . for the petty though important place of light-keeper has too often been made a political prize, and thus the service, which requires permanence, has been injured."

The service was directed by the Treasury Department until 1852; then lighthouses were placed under the Lighthouse Board. Light keepers gained Civil Service status in 1896. In 1903 the Department of Commerce took over control of the lighthouse service. On July 1, 1939, it was transferred to the United States Coast Guard.

Of the keepers it has been said: "The light keeper stands his vigils for all humanity, asking no questions as to the nationality or purpose of him whom he directs to safety."

The lights must *never* fail.

MANNED AND UNMANNED

Within living memory there were literally dozens of lighthouses along the north and south shores of Long Island, around Manhattan Island, and in nearby New Jersey. Today most have been discontinued or sold; many have become private residences. Automation is proceeding rapidly, and channel buoys have multiplied.

10

In addition to Ambrose, there are two other light stations in the New York area with resident personnel. One is Execution Rocks, built in 1850 and rebuilt in 1868, on the approach to the East River from Long Island Sound; it warns mariners of dangerous rocks off Sands Point. The other is West Bank (Range Front) in New York Harbor.

The lighthouse at Sands Point, off Manhasset, Long Island, was replaced by an automatic steel tower in 1922; it had been in operation since 1809. . . . Throg's Neck Light at Fort Schuyler has been replaced by an automatic beacon. . . . Stepping Stones Light, off Great Neck, Long Island, built in 1877, is no longer manned. . . . Neither is Staten Island Light at Richmond, Staten Island.

Robbins Reef Light, out in the Upper Bay from Bayonne, N.J., built in 1839 to guard a reef that had caused many ship fatalities, was replaced in 1965 by an automatic signal. It stands a mile from land. The light keeper used to row his children to school on Staten Island.

The twin light towers at Navesink, N.J., built in 1828, have been unwatched since 1949; one light there was discontinued in 1898.

The "Little Red Lighthouse" on the northern tip of Manhattan Island, overlooking the Hudson at Jeffrey's Hook and hidden by the George Washington Bridge, is the only lighthouse ever built on Manhattan Island, as far as can be discovered. It was at first only a red post with two lanterns, to warn boatmen of treacherous rocks. The lighthouse became superfluous after the brilliantly lighted bridge was built. It is now preserved by the city as part of a park, and can be reached from 168th Street.

The Coast Guard now has some 300 light and sound navigation aids between Sandy Hook and the George Washington Bridge, on the Hudson side, and up the East River to the Whitestone Bridge.

THE CHANNELS

In 1609 Henry Hudson complained of a "very shoal'd barre" at the entrance to what is now New York Harbor. Not much was done about that for some 300 years.

Ocean voyages to and from New York end and begin at the bar off Sandy Hook. That is twenty-five miles from the foot of Manhattan Island, if one follows the course around the elbow made inside the Hook by sand, silt, and the battle of current against tide. This course is the Main Ship Channel. For years it was the chief highway into and out of the port.

In 1907 the United States government began to dig a channel 2,000 feet wide and 40 feet deep (since then, deepened by 5 more feet) to cut across the elbow and save over three miles between the city and the sea. This was named Ambrose Channel, after the physician-engineer Dr. John Wolfe

Ambrose. He had battled Congress for eighteen years to get an appropriation for this work, but died long before it came to pass. The old East Channel, which could be used only by pilots very familiar with changing depths and conditions, thus became the Ambrose.

Until 1907 there were two other entrances: Swash, which cut off part of the elbow; and Gedney, which had been deepened to 30 feet in the late 1880's.

LIGHTSHIPS OFF THE PORT

Travelers returning from Europe by ship used to feel almost home when they sighted one of the lightships off the Port of New York. But the four lightships that once lay off the port are no more. Fire Island, Sandy Hook, Scotland, and Ambrose lightships have passed into maritime history.

In February, 1822, New York merchants convened to obtain a floating light off the harbor, with the result that Sandy Hook Lightship, first vessel ever placed in the open sea to guide ships to a port in the United States, was stationed off the Port of New York from 1823.

When the twin lights at Navesink, N.J., on the highlands south of Sandy Hook, were completed in 1828, the Sandy Hook Lightship was removed to another station. A lightship of the name was on duty nearest New York Harbor until 1908, when its name was changed to Ambrose and its position was shifted.

In 1868 Scotland Lightship, sister vessel of the Sandy Hook Lightship, was first placed three miles off the Sandy Hook shore on Outer Middle Ground, part of a great shoal off the Hook. It was named after the British steamship Scotland, bound for New York from Liverpool, which wrecked on that spot on December 1, 1866, after a collision with an American sailing vessel off Fire Island. The Scotland, badly damaged, tried to reach Sandy Hook, where the captain hoped to beach her inside the bay. He failed to make it. The lightship was placed over the wreck, but later was moved much farther out to sea.

Scotland Lightship, moored about four and a half miles westward of Ambrose Channel, was rammed by a schooner on January 30, 1909. The lightship survived and remained on that station until June, 1964, when a new Ambrose Lightship took a new station to serve both its own and the Scotland's duty. Scotland was replaced by a huge automated buoy.

When the second Ambrose Lightship went off duty permanently in 1967 it had been stationed twenty-two miles from New York, anchored in seventy-eight feet of water. She was a 128-foot vessel, with a light fifty-six feet above the sea, visible for thirteen miles.

MORE COLLISIONS

The lightships off New York rode out storms. But they seemed to be sitting ducks as they rocked at anchor on the waves, targets for onslaughts by passing vessels—especially in fog. Collisions involving fog generally happen in the early morning hours when fog is thickest and probably human energy is at lowest ebb. Two accidents to Coast Guard vessels on Ambrose Station occurred at 4:04 A.M. and 4:20 A.M., respectively.

On March 28, 1950, at 4:04 A.M. in a heavy fog with visibility of less than 150 feet, the lightship's hull was punctured by the Santa Monica of the Grace Line. None of the fifteen Coast Guardsmen abroad was injured. The lightship was towed to Marine Basin Shipyard in Gravesend Bay the next day for repairs. The Santa Monica was undamaged.

The Ambrose was undergoing her annual maintenance and repair job at St. George Coast Guard Base on Staten Island at 4:20 A.M. on June 24, 1960, when Relief Lightship W.A.L. 505, taking her place, was hit by the United States cargo vessel Green Bay, in a dense fog. The Green Bay, of the States Marine Lines, 460 feet long and 6,300 tons, was outward bound from Port Newark, N.J., for India and the Middle East, with 8,100 tons of general cargo aboard. After she cleared the Narrows, visibility had decreased to zero. The lightship, with a twelve-foot hole in her side following the collision, sank at once. The crew of nine Coast Guardsmen was rescued by the Green Bay, which suffered some damage to her stern.

A joint Marine Board of Investigation, in its report made June 5, 1961, placed blame for the collision on certain personnel of both vessels.

The Coast Guard buoy tender Firebush marked the wreck site at once with a lighted gong wreck-buoy. The lightship lay in 193 feet of water. Then the wreck got lost. A *New York Times* story on November 14, 1961, said: "The precise location of the wreck is uncertain."

It was not until October 19, 1962, that a U.S. Coast Guard and Geodetic Survey vessel found the hulk, which had drifted some distance away from the original charted position. Then the wrecked Relief was destroyed by explosive charges, to assure that it would constitute no menace to navigation.

AMBROSE LIGHT STATION

Ambrose was the last lightship to go. She weighed anchor for the final time on August 23, 1967. Her predecessor (1909–1964) is now a museum piece, tied up at a New York dock and open to the public along with other historic vessels as part of the South Street Seaport project, where other days and other ways of seafaring are memorialized.

Ambrose Lightship and its successor, Ambrose Light Station

The solitary sentinel at the entrance to Ambrose Channel, off the nation's busiest seaport, is Ambrose Light Station. It is a four-deck structure on four legs, rising 141 feet above the water, some eight miles off Rockaway, Long Island, and the same distance from Sandy Hook, N.J. It is red and white; not beautiful. Someone said it looked like a warehouse on stilts.

Four Coast Guardsmen at a time are stationed on this luxurious but lonely tower within sight of the great city. They tend its six-million-candlepower light, 136 feet above mean low water. A seventy-foot square roof over the top deck serves as a helicopter airport. The men maintain the foghorn and radio beacon. They radio weather reports daily to the Rockway Coast Guard Station and keep records of water temperatures. Six men are assigned to the station. Each is on duty for two weeks, then has a week's liberty ashore. The duty is monotonous but is not considered dangerous.

So far, the tower has escaped any of the collisions that plagued its predecessors, the lightships, from time to time. Coast Guard authorities say the risk of storm damage is almost negligible. The companies that built the tower certified that it would withstand winds in excess of 125 knots, and waves sixty-five feet high.

THE TEXAS TOWER

Much has been learned about construction of towers since the tragic end of the U.S. Air Force's Texas Tower No. 4 on January 15, 1961, when twenty-eight men perished with it in an icy northeast storm. That tower lies on the bottom of the sea in 180 feet of water, eighty miles southeast of New York City and sixty-five miles east of Barnegat, N.J.

The structure, built at a cost of $21 million in 1957 to provide missile and aircraft warning for the protection of the Port of New York, was actually obsolete, due to the speed of modern technology, within two months after it went into service. It was the southernmost of five such towers planned for the Atlantic coast. Only three had been built.

The Texas Towers (Nos. 1 and 5 were never built) were so named because they resembled offshore oil rigs. No. 4 had a triangular platform for helicopter landings, 200 feet on a side. It stood on three 300-foot steel legs, which were planted in mud and fine silt twenty feet below the ocean floor. Its double-deck platform cleared the water by sixty-seven feet. There was room for seventy men, with a gymnasium and a recreation room.

The 6,000-ton radar tower had from the beginning a bad reputation as a "wobbler." A leg was damaged and replaced during construction. Storms in 1958 and 1959 did some damage. Then Hurricane Donna in September, 1960, with waves sixty to sixty-five feet high, really did it.

William Smythe of Montauk, Long Island, a professional diver with thirty-three years experience (he had worked for thirteen months raising the Normandie, and seventeen months underwater in the Corinth Canal in Greece) made an inspection and took underwater pictures after the hurricane.

One morning, late that November, he and his wife called on me. We had a fine visit. He was a tall, powerful man of sixty-one years, with a ruddy face and cheerful smile. We talked about diving. "I wanted a change, after farming and railroading," he said. "I like diving. You know, there aren't many of us pros."

He talked freely about the Texas Tower. "It may have to be abandoned," he said. "We certainly hoped no storm would come up, those five nights we spent taking underwater pictures to show the extent of the damage. I figure repairs would cost $10 million. We can't let the men know, of course."

He had reported to the authorities that the tower was unsafe. Publicly they pooh-poohed the report. But the Air Force evacuated most of its men on November 17, leaving a skeleton crew of fourteen airmen aboard, together with an equal number of repairmen.

The veteran diver went back on board November 30. He knew the danger, but he was needed to assist with the repairs. He telephoned his wife everyday, to allay her anxiety. He had been there for forty-five days when the final storm struck on January 15, 1961. He had expected to leave the tower on January 17, and retire.

The last contact with shore was on Saturday, January 14, when the supply boat came out. On Sunday the sea ran high, with gale winds. The tower had two lifeboats, but launching them in such a rough sea was impossible; the boats could not be held in a proper position. The Coast Guard offered to take everybody off with helicopters, but was refused. In any case, the flight deck was covered with sand, gravel, and cement, which was to be poured into the hollow legs of the tower to steady it.

At 3 P.M. the northeast wind was blowing fifty knots, with gusts of seventy-five. No helicopter could land in such a wind, though by that time the repair materials on the flight deck had been thrown overboard. No rescue ship could tie up alongside.

Yet Captain Gordon T. Phelan, USAF, commanding officer on the tower, was still confident they could ride out the storm. He was also reluctant to abandon all that expensive equipment. Finally, however, he decided to evacuate by daylight on Monday, January 16.

At 7 P.M. on Sunday radio and radar contact with the tower was broken off. The end came about 7:33.

On April 2, 1962, the special Senate Preparedness Sub-Committee laid the catastrophe to "multiple errors." They blamed the "unconscionable neglect" of the designing firm; the building contractor; the Navy's Bureau of Yards and Docks, which had supervised construction and repair; and the Air Force. The Navy, they said, had ignored warnings. And there were deviations from the original design. One of the key designers said he was surprised it had stood up so long. He had considered it unsafe for weeks. One of the builders said that with braces broken the tower was at only 55 percent strength prior to January 15.

Less than two weeks before the Texas Tower tragedy, plans had been announced to replace all East Coast Lightships with similar towers. The Coast Guard towers that have replaced the lightships, however, are built close inshore—not far out at sea like the one that, in hindsight, seems to have been doomed almost from the first.

It has been pointed out that the public need not lose all faith in the platforms because of this disaster. The wreck of January 15, 1961, and subsequent investigations taught a terrible lesson.

The East Hampton, Long Island, *Star*—hometown paper of Diver Smythe—commented editorially: ". . . We need not damn other Texas Towers because of the failure of one. Read the bloody history of England's attempts to build a lighthouse on Eddystone Rock. Many lives were lost before success. But those lives saved many more."

3

EXECUTION TO
HELL GATE

EXECUTION Rocks, at New York's back door by water, must be passed by every vessel entering the East River from Long Island Sound. These rocks have been the scene of innumerable shipwrecks. Past Execution, coming in from the Sound, is Hell Gate with its whirlpools and rocks. The currents are still dangerous but the rocks less so, since blasting in the mid-19th century.

The first European on record as making that passage, through Hell Gate and past Execution, was Adriaen Block, in 1614.

Legend has it that the name Execution came from a very unpleasant practice. According to one story, in early Colonial times a murderer would be manacled with chains to staples driven into a rock at low tide. As the tide rose, he would be engulfed. . . . Another version is that American revolutionaries were once chained by the British below the high-tide mark and left to drown.

A lighthouse was built on that outcropping of rock, off Great Neck, Long Island, in 1850.

Ten miles past Execution is Hell Gate. Pirates are said to have lurked on Big Mill Rock in the East River, then to have swarmed aboard ships struggling through Hell Gate, attacking the crews and making off with the cargo.

Pot Rock, a pyramid in mid-channel at Hell Gate surrounded by deep potholes in which the water boiled and roared in whirlpools, was perhaps the most notorious of the rocks near Hell Gate until it was removed in 1866 by U.S. Army engineers. That was where the British pay-ship, HMS Hussar, came to grief in 1780.

The pay-ship had been anchored off the southern tip of Manhattan Island since September 13. Besides her crew, she had on board some fifty American prisoners from prison camps in England, destined for exchange with the American Army. There was also a large Marine guard, which gave rise to waterfront opinion that the Hussar had something on board more necessary to the British Army than the American prisoners.

By the fall of 1780, pay for the British troops was long overdue. Desertions were becoming common. It was not a good time for a pay-ship to be in New York Harbor. The forces occupying the city were jittery. In July, 1780, a French fleet had put in at Newport, R.I. The British still had a preponderance of sea power, but by November land attack in New York seemed imminent, and it was imperative that the Hussar proceed to another rendezvous. So she was ordered out—to an anchorage off the Connecticut coast, or perhaps to join Admiral Marriot Arbuthnot's fleet in Gardiner's Bay, off the eastern end of Long Island.

Captain Charles Pole was faced with a problem. The most direct route was up the East River and into the narrow neck of Long Island Sound, then along the coast. A large British squadron would be a buffer between him and the French. But the prospect of taking a sailing ship up the East River in 1780 was far from pleasant. The HMS Hussar was a beautiful, shining new, three-masted frigate of twenty-eight guns, with a precious cargo. At Hell Gate a vicious riptide boils through the river between the Long Island shore and the twin islands, Great and Little Barn, later to be called Randall's (now Welfare) and Ward's islands.

The alternate route to Connecticut or Gardiner's Bay would be the long

Hell Gate, 1775

way around—back through the Narrows, then along the whole south shore of Long Island to Montauk Point. That is a lee shore with no good harbor for a vessel of any size on its entire length. The outside route would be time-consuming and would expose the Hussar to possible attack by sea.

So Captain Pole decided to take her up the East River. He engaged a local river pilot, a Negro slave belonging to the Hunt family of the Bronx. Told of the proposed route, the pilot listened quietly, then advised against it. But the captain ordered him to the wheel.

The ship, 114 feet long with a 40-foot beam, set sail from Beekman's Wharf, nosed around the tip of Manhattan, and proceeded up the East River toward Crown Point. With a man on the chains swinging a lead, they passed treacherous ledges named Great and Little Mill Rock. Another obstruction, Pot Rock, lay broadside to the current, protruding 130 feet into the channel, with its black mass only eight feet below the surface at low water. This was the final obstacle before reaching the relatively quiet waters of Long Island Sound.

The strong river current suddenly swept the Hussar off her course and pulled her toward the deadly ship trap, Pot Rock. She fetched up, broadside on.

The river poured in through a great hole in her wooden side. The ship began to list. The captain tried to land her on Stony Island, on the south shore of the Bronx—not a real island, but a tip of land almost surrounded by water at high tide. She never made it. Off Stony Island (now Port Morris in the Bronx and opposite Hallett's Point on Long Island—what is now called Astoria) the Hussar went down in sixteen fathoms of water on November 3, 1780.

As she settled, the boats swung out, all packed to the gunwales. All but one of her crew were saved. It was believed at the time that the American prisoners, chained below decks, perished.

The frigate rested on the bottom, but the tops of her masts showed above water in the channel above Pot Cove. Someone had run the free end of the ship's hawser ashore. This was made fast to a big tree on the river bank. The protruding masts marked the ship's position all through the following winter, then disappeared into the muddy water.

The British declared there was no treasure aboard the Hussar when she sank. But their salvage attempts began almost at once. So did everybody else's. But that is another story.

A BOLD MAN

Captain Elihu S. Bunker of Nantucket was known as a bold man. On March 21, 1815, he took his wood-burning steamboat Fulton (134 feet

Captain Elihu S. Bunker's FULTON, *first steamboat through Hell Gate, 1815; drawing by Samuel Ward Stanton*

long, 36-foot beam, 327 tons, sloop-rigged, with one mast) with thirty passengers aboard, bound from New York to New Haven, Conn., through Hell Gate. That was the first steam vessel ever to attempt it.

Then on October 15, 1816, Captain Bunker did something that had been thought impossible. He took his new, strongly built passenger steamer, the 150-foot Connecticut, through the Gate against the full force of the tide, making a "novel and interesting experiment." The ship fought the racing, boiling current with everything she had. It took three tries—and "moments of breathless anxiety"—but she made it. "Mechanical science has achieved a victory over elemental force," the newspapers reported.

HURL GATE

In December, 1833, the sloop Irene, Captain J. H. Cook of Greenport, Long Island, master, struck the rocks at "Hurl Gate," so the newspapers reported. She went to pieces, floated off in a gale at high tide, and drifted down river to the eastern bank.

In early Victorian times it was considered improper—or perhaps unlucky—to spell out d——l or h——l. Some conservative editors were still avoiding the naughty words on December 8, 1864, when the schooner William Penn of Port Jefferson, Long Island, bound from New Haven to

New York, overturned at the same place. Captain Wesley Stevens of Southampton, Long Island, was drowned.

DIMINISHING THE DANGERS

When he visited New York in 1842, Charles Dickens reported that he saw from shipboard "Hell Gate, Frying Pan, Hog's Back, and other notorious localities."

In 1845, New York merchants appealed to Congress to clear the channel. The Suffolk *Democrat* published the following on November 10, 1848: "The U.S. schooner Petrel, Captain Porter, has been engaged in making soundings at Hell Gate for a month past, and completed the work on Saturday last. Soundings have also been made by him on the rocks in New York Harbor known as Diamond Reef and Princess Reef, one having but twelve feet of water and the other thirteen. During the time the schooner Petrel was at the Gate, upwards of fifty vessels have gone ashore there. Seven were ashore in a single day.

"One-half the disasters came from Pot Rock, which has eight feet of water upon it. The top of this rock is not larger than a barrel's head.

"Captain Southard, pilot at the Gate, says he will contract to blast the rock thirty feet below low water for $6,000. Frying Pan Rocks are thin-edged rocks of twenty-four inches at top, with deep water around; they can be blasted. So with Ways Reef, inside of Pot Rock. There is also a rock called Distillery Rock, near the ferry, a very dangerous one. The removal of Pot Rock alone for $6,000 would be a saving of many lives and much property."

Captain Southard's reasonable offer does not seem to have been taken up. But between 1852 and 1918 the Federal government spent over $6.5 million on the East River project, mostly blasts at Hell Gate.

In 1866 Brigadier General John Newton began nineteen years of such operations, culminating with the blasting of Flood Rock, south of 92nd Street, toward the Queens shore, on October 10, 1885. A great crowd assembled for that long-awaited event.

The rocks at Hell Gate had been accessible to workmen for only a few minutes a day—at slack water—until a new device for mining and blasting from the inside was devised. This was first used in 1874 on Hallett's Reef (Hallett's Cove was the early name for Astoria, Long Island). At Flood Rock four miles of tunneling was done inside the rock. When the day came, the explosion was heard forty miles away at West Point. Nine acres of solid rock were demolished. The channel width was doubled from 600 to 1,200 feet and the depth increased to 26 feet.

The channel is now 35 feet deep at mean low water. But it is still narrow, twisting, and treacherous where the two tides meet. The East River is a battleground for tides from the Sound and from Sandy Hook, which conflict from 42nd Street to the Triborough Bridge. The greatest disturbance is between the northern tip of Welfare Island and the southern side of Ward's Island; there is a four-and-a-half-foot difference in tide level.

WRECK MASTER BROWN

Wreck Master W. E. Brown of Astoria, Long Island, is often mentioned in contemporary newspaper reports as getting stranded vessels off the rocks in the early 1870's. On August 30, 1871, he rescued the E. P. Church, a fishing schooner ashore at Ketch Point on the east side of Blackwell's (now Welfare) Island. On January 15, 1872, the schooner Jacob Lorillard, loaded with iron and bound from Bridgeport, Conn., to New York, filled at Fort Point, Hell Gate, and was hauled off by Wreck Master Brown. On May 26 of the same year the Lorillard was again in trouble, sunk in the East River by a steam tug. She was raised on June 7 by Brown.

On July 20, 1872, the schooner Diadem of Sayville, Long Island, bound from Newburgh, N.Y., to Fall River, Mass., with a cargo of coal, was run into in Hell Gate by the steamer Galatea. The Diadem sank in five minutes, in twelve fathoms of water off Ward's Island Bluff, directly in the track of vessels passing through the Gate. Shortly afterward, the wreck of the Diadem was struck by the schooner Flagg of Greenwich, Conn., which capsized. Her crew was rescued by Wreck Master W. E. Brown.

The sloop George B. Bloomer, bound from Hartford, Conn., with a cargo of brownstone for building the high-stooped houses that then lined city streets, went ashore on Negro Head on August 24, 1872. She filled and rolled over. She was put on the Astoria beach by Wreck Master Brown. The schooner Justice, bound from New York to Narragansett Pier, collided with the yacht Emily at Hell Gate on September 21, 1872. Three months later Wreck Master Brown was still trying to get the Justice off the rocks. He aided the schooner Alpha in August, 1873. She was loaded with lumber from St. John, New Brunswick, when she beached and filled on the Gridiron. He helped the schooner C. J. Erickson, at the same place.

Tyler Gibson, a Hell Gate ferryman and fisherman, lived on Mill Rock at the north end of the Gate, off 92nd Street, in the 1870's and 1880's. He could be called a one-man Coast Guard, for he saved many people from drowning.

TRAFFIC HAZARDS

Commodore Jim Fisk's famous 373-foot-long Providence, a Fall River steamer launched in 1866, had a series of mishaps beginning on August 3,

1871, when she collided in Long Island Sound with two schooners—the William McCobb of Bucksport, Maine, bound from Jacksonville, Fla., for New Haven, and an unknown vessel. On December 8 of the same year, the Providence grounded on a reef off Delancey Street, New York City. She was hauled off. On October 15, 1872, she was going through Hell Gate on her way to Fall River when she collided with a drilling machine and was badly injured. The passengers were transferred to the steamboat Stonington.

A little later the Providence went aground after a week of fog. That night Captain Brayton of the Providence turned to his pilot and said: "There's your damned old boat. You get her off. I'm going to sleep." He banged the pilothouse door and turned in. Captain George Chase was master of the Providence on December 10, 1907, when she crashed into the crowded East River ferryboat Baltic in a thick fog. One Brooklyn-bound passenger was drowned when the liner's steel prow almost tore away the women's cabin of the ferry. Captain Chase was reported to have handled his ship admirably.

The steamboat Bristol of the Fall River Line went ashore on the Gridiron at 4 A.M. on November 1, 1871. The Bristol, 373 feet long, carrying 842 passengers, had been built in New York in 1867 by the famous shipbuilder William H. Webb. She got off that time; but the Bristol burned at her dock in Newport, R.I., in 1889.

On May 2, 1872, the schooner William R. Knapp of New York was rammed by the steamer City of Hartford between Hell Gate and Astoria. The whole of her stern was carried away and she sank immediately. The cook drowned.

The steamer Hope, bound from Blackwell's Island to Hart's Island on May 13, 1873, was run down at Hell Gate by the steamer Americus. The Hope was cut in two and four men were lost. She lay off the Gridiron for years.

On September 7, 1873, the steam tug Vixen was run into by the steamship Granite State and cut in half. Captain Perkins of the Vixen was drowned. The engineer was picked up, badly hurt.

The schooner Fanny Fern, so-called after the nom de plume of a popular New York newspaper columnist of the period, was sunk at Hell Gate in December, 1874. She was raised and taken to Hallett's Cove. Later she was being towed through Hell Gate alongside the tug D. S. Stetson when she slewed onto Middle Ground, knocking a hole in her bottom. The tug cast off its towlines and refused to render assistance. The Fanny Fern sank in twenty minutes.

On February 3, 1880, the British brig Guisborough, bound from New London for New York foundered on Crab Meadow. Three men were lost.

The sloop Hannah Ann, 45 tons burden, of Huntington Harbor, Long

Island, with a cargo of eighteen cords of hickory wood, went on the rocks at Hell Gate on October 21, 1882. She was owned and sailed by Captain Oliver Hall and Ezra Sammis. A newspaper reported: "On account of the sea caused by passing steamers she was thumped about on the rocks so badly as to cause her total wreck. The cargo, sails and rigging were all that was saved."

On October 21, 1882, the City of Worcester, a new iron steamboat of the Norwich and Worcester Line, bound to New London, was on her way up the East River in a dense fog, at night, when she "struck on a reef that makes out from the New York shore called the 'Governor's Table' where she remained about three hours in a very perilous position, after which she was assisted to a vacant dock in a leaking condition."

The Fall River Line paddle steamer Pilgrim hit an uncharted rock off Blackwell's (now Welfare) Island in 1884 and cut a 125-foot gash in her bottom. She made the dock unaided, being the first American steamship to be double-hulled, with transverse bulkheads.

After the great blasting of October 10, 1885, which deepened the channel, accidents diminished appreciably.

The Plymouth of the Fall River Line had some bad luck in December, 1899, when she grounded on the rocks at Riker's Island in a fog, at very low tide. Captain George Chase had his 600 passengers taken off. The vessel was a partial loss. On March 19, 1903, the outbound Plymouth, then under Captain Elijah Davis, was struck in a fog by the westbound freighter City of Taunton. Captain Davis reversed after he sighted the bow light of the other steamer, but his steering gear fouled. Four stewards, a watchman, and one passenger were lost. The crippled steamer was steered by hand to New London. In November, 1913, the Plymouth struck an uncharted rock at Hell Gate and gashed her bottom. She was later rebuilt.

In November, 1908, the 271-foot-long Metropolitan Line Steamer H. M. Whitney, Captain Theodore Hone, master, had to choose between sinking two barges in Hell Gate or striking hard on a menacing rock. The captain chose the rock. The Whitney foundered on the rocks at Sunken Meadow (on the Ward's Island side, just west of the Gate). She was raised months later.

Mrs. Emily Barto, a New York artist, told about a Hell Gate accident to the four-masted freighting schooner Emily Baxter, of which her father, Captain Wilbur Newton, was owner and master. This happened on November 26, 1910. "Papa said that in passing a government dredge in Hell Gate, on his way home, as the keeper of the dredge had omitted to put out a lantern and it was dark, the Emily Baxter ran into the chains. In three minutes she was upside down. Captain and crew were sitting on her keel.

"My father was a devout Methodist. He had been trying for years to

The steamer OREGON *on the rocks at Hell Gate, 1846*

convert an old man who had been originally a fine mariner, but the moment he went ashore, he became seriously inebriated. As they sat perched precariously, my father took advantage of the situation. He said: 'Well, Jim, now is the time to pray.' Jim replied hotly: 'Hell, Captain, *Now is the time to swim!*' "

Captain Thomas Rowland was inbound from Providence, R.I., in August, 1928, with the Chester W. Chapin of the Fall River Line, when she sank the fifty-year-old tug Volunteer in Hell Gate. The tug lost one of her crew. The Chapin was mired on a sandbar but was later hauled off. The collision was due to confusion when a third ship appeared out of the Harlem River. Captain Rowland had sounded a distress signal prior to the collision.

THE FLUSHING

On September 7, 1963, the 83-foot tugboat Flushing of the Red Star Towing and Transportation Company capsized and sank in thirty seconds in 125 feet of water at Hell Gate. She was bound from Stamford, Conn., to Jersey City.

The Captain, Charles L. Scouten, and three deckhands were lost. Six crewmen were saved. Coast Guard, police, fire, and civilian craft came to the rescue. Sam Klausner of Forest Hills, Long Island, and his thirteen-year-old son, Calvin, hauled the engineer onto their cabin cruiser from the barge,

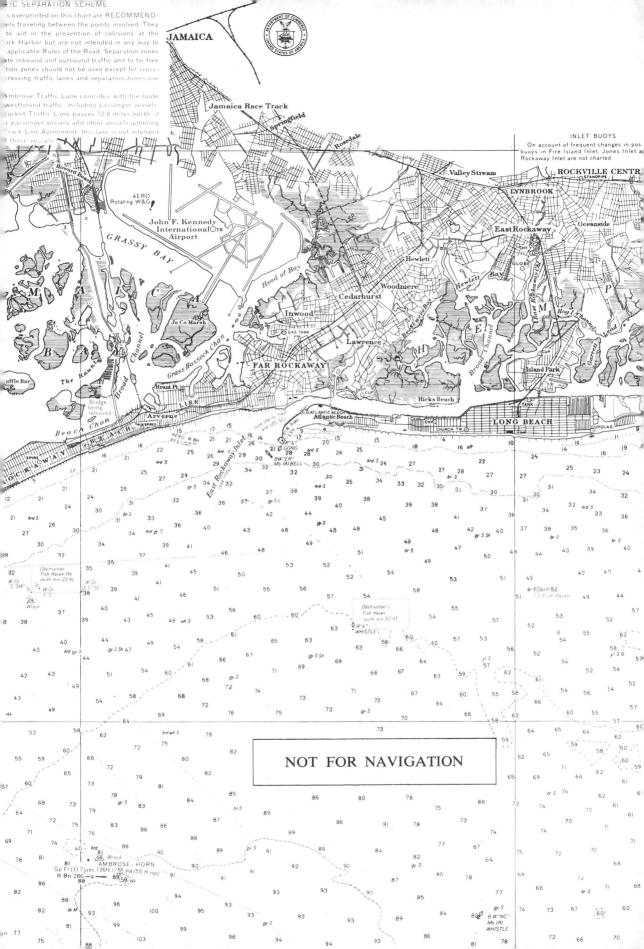

NOT FOR NAVIGATION

which drifted ashore later at Riker's Island. When the Flushing capsized, the cook, Louis Johnson, was in the galley preparing corned beef and cabbage. He could not swim, so he always kept a life preserver handy. He had drifted half a mile when a helicopter picked him up.

Captain Joe Sweeney, now retired, was with Red Star for forty-seven years, forty-four of them in the pilothouse. He had been mate on the Flushing at one time and he knew her crew. He discussed the sinking:

"The Flushing was towing the Thresher, a flat coal barge 145 feet long, 2,200 ton capacity, but empty. She was coming in from the Sound, between Triborough and Hell Gate Bridge, at 10 A.M., bucking the tide, when an eddy suddenly pulled the barge ahead of the tug. The tug was swung around. She keeled over on her port side.

"I believe if the lines on that barge had been twelve feet out, she never would have capsized. If your rope is long enough and the tug's engine is stopped, just let her drift. There'd be enough slack between so the barge would drift alongside. Or, if they'd had the old manila rope. That's safer. It would have parted, the bits would have pulled out. But they had nylon lines, too tough to break."

The bodies of Captain Scouten and deckhand Johan Foldik were recovered in the river near Hell Gate. A Merritt-Chapman & Scott Corporation diver made unsuccessful attempts to secure lines to the sunken tug and to find the bodies of the other two men. After three tries the salvage company gave up, and Red Star abandoned the tug.

Then Captain Edward Sanchez of New Bedford, Mass., thought he could raise her. He gambled on it, using six men and $10,000. And he won. He sent down a skin diver. (Captain Sweeney thinks this was the first time a skin diver was ever used on a salvage job. "But," he says, "a regular diver like from Merritt & Chapman with an air line was no good here on account of the tide is so strong.") The skin diver found the bodies.

On one tide, Captain Sanchez had slings under the Flushing. Then he got permission from the government to tie up traffic at Hell Gate for thirty minutes. At the next tide he raised the funnel out of water. He put the tug in at the sewerage disposal plant dock nearby on Ward's Island. He had been so sure he would do the job that he had notified the newspapers, radio, and television stations he would bring her up. That happened on the day President John F. Kennedy was shot. There was no publicity about the raising of the Flushing. But the $100,000 tugboat was his.

Captain Sanchez had the main engine running the next day. He put the Flushing in shape. He still owns her. "He's the kind of a man, when he's doing a job, he doesn't stop for anything," Captain Sweeney said.

4

THE NEW YORK– SANDY HOOK PILOT

THERE were pilots when the Dutch ruled Nieuw Amsterdam, but the first official notice of the necessity for a pilot followed a great storm on March 9, 1694. The Assembly of the Colony of New York made an "Act for Settlyng Pilotage for All Vessels That Shall Come Within Sandy Hook."

On April 14, 1784, the legislature of New York State passed new laws to regulate the licensing of pilots. A legal paper dated 1801, which has been preserved, is an indenture of one John Kelso, sixteen, who was to be taught the "Art, Trade and Mystery" of a pilot . . . for five years, at the sum of $7 per month." During that time he was to obey his master; he pledged himself not to "commit matrimony," gamble, or drink. His master was to teach him to pilot vessels to and from the city of New York "by Sandy Hooke."

Today's pilot undergoes training longer than that given a lawyer or a doctor: It takes fifteen years to make a fully licensed branch pilot. The New York–Sandy Hook Pilots' Association has a long and proud history. In the great city where change is the order of the day, there is no group quite like it.

Coming in from Europe, the liner slows down at the mouth of New York Harbor. The New York–Sandy Hook pilot is coming aboard. As soon as he steps foot on the deck, a small red and white flag snaps in the breeze just forward and above the bridge. That flag means the pilot has the conn.

His word is law. He gives the orders, guiding the great ship through the Hook and the Narrows and the intricate traffic to a position in the stream off the ship's pier. At that point a docking pilot comes aboard. He gives orders to the tugs that push and pull the liner into her berth. Outgoing, the docking pilot will move her back into open water.

Channels can change even in a few weeks; but the pilot would know them all, even if every buoy and danger mark were removed.

FROM FATHER TO SON

This "art, trade and mystery" has always been very much a family affair. Many of today's Sandy Hook pilots are second and third generation in the profession, with uncles and brothers and cousins who are also pilots. Many of their forebears have lost their lives in line of duty. Regardless of that, a pilot can think of nothing better for his sons. He is intensely proud of his vocation.

Charles Edward Russell, then a young New York newspaperman, went out to a pilot boat on an assignment in 1887. He made friends with pilots and was invited to go along several times on long cruises. Pilots owned and manned some thirty schooners then, and they scattered over a 600-mile radius looking for customers. He wrote *From Sandy Hook to 62°*, published in 1929. It is now a rare book, but just as thrilling and entertaining as it was in his time. He calls the pilots "red-blooded and two-fisted men . . . astride of a job full of sudden twists and crises, prepared for these whatever they might be, but still keeping in the background something rather surprisingly gentle and contemplative. There was to be remarked among my pilot friends a singular native courtesy, unstudied, uncalculating, honest; a kind of instinctive sincerity of goodwill that persisted, but not to the point of compromising with the line of professional dignity. This, after a time, I thought must be another triumph of tradition as much as of training and of the instincts of the race . . . pilots have certain things they must not do: they must not be familiar on duty and they must not be vulgar. . . ."

A pilot can retire at sixty. It is mandatory now at seventy. The majority keep on working as long as they can.

Captain George Seeth retired after serving as a pilot more than fifty years. He keeps busy enough still, writing and speaking on nautical subjects. He is second-generation in the Pilots' Association. His father went to sea on a Danish four-master at fourteen and arrived in New York in 1871. Nine years later he got his pilot's license. He served until 1918.

Captain Seeth says: "My father's uncle built the first steam whaler. He built one of the first twin-screw ships in Scotland. That ship celebrated its century of service in Lake Windermere, not long ago, and is the oldest ship in British registry. My grandfather was captain of a Scotch sealer. She was

The New York pilot boat, 1880's

stuck in the ice in the Arctic above Norway all one winter. Out of 360 men, one-tenth were still alive in the spring, when they were rescued by a Danish vessel. My grandfather married the daughter of the captain of the ship that rescued them.

"My family were all adventurers."

Captain Seeth has two brothers, Julius and Fred, both retired pilots. Julius Seeth guided the first Queen Elizabeth in, on her maiden voyage on March 6, 1940. Captain George Seeth's son, George Jr., is a pilot. His grandson, another George, is in training. Douglas Seeth, a nephew, is a pilot, and also one of the leading yachtsmen on Long Island Sound.

Asked how piloting came to be such a family affair, Captain Seeth said: "Well, it's a private enterprise. A pilot has the privilege of sponsoring one boy at a time, as candidate for apprentice. If he has a likely looking son, he would naturally name him."

Captain William C. Hall of Garden City, Long Island, has been a pilot since 1949. He says: "I am the last of the Halls in the business."

His father and grandfather were pilots. His great-grandfather was a ship news reporter for the old New York *Tribune* and the Associated Press. His great-great-grandfather was captain of a sailing ship that carried molasses in

31

barrels from New Orleans to New York, when hearty breakfasts of pancakes and sausage required great quantities of molasses. "There's plenty of salt-water in my blood," he says.

"My grandfather, another William C. Hall, was apprenticed in 1862. Once he was blown offshore, gone for two weeks, given up for lost. He died of a heart attack on board ship in Quarantine, in 1908. But he got the ship in. My father, Warren A. Hall, became a pilot that year."

The captain's great-uncle, John R. Hall, was also a pilot. John R. Hall's only son, John L., followed the same profession.

Captain Edmund W. Florimont, now retired after forty-one years as a pilot, remembers Captain John R. Hall very well. "Always wore a stiff shirt," he says, "never wore an overcoat no matter what the weather was. A severe man, but we respected him. I was an apprentice then." Captain Florimont was sponsored by his pilot uncle, Captain Walter Earle.

Captain John L. Hall, now deceased, told a few years ago how as a little boy he used to be sent by his mother to the pilots' office, then at Beekman and South streets, to get his father's pay. The father might be at sea for weeks at a time. Those were the days when each boat competed with all the others, except when taking its turn on station off Sandy Hook. The old gentle-man said his dad sometimes took him along, on school vacations, for a cruise. On one of these pilot boat trips he was 450 miles from New York.

The pilots' office in John L. Hall's boyhood was on the second floor, over a saloon. The clerk would pin the money in an inner pocket so the youngster wouldn't lose it on the way home. Each company, the captain said, had a closet in which to keep its oilskins, and there was a large bin in which coal for their stove was kept. In the middle of the room was a table where the waiting pilots played cards or dominoes.

Until fifteen or twenty years ago, there was a pilots' clubroom at the headquarters, then at 6 State Street, New York City. That has been discontinued. "They don't have to hang around waiting for a job anymore," Captain William W. Sherwood, then New York Pilots' Association president, said. "We have better information on expected arrivals, and radio communication to the pilot boats. We just get the pilots on the phone when they're first, second, and third in turn. No need for card games."

Headquarters now is at 1 Bay Street, Staten Island, N.Y., the old Coast Guard base.

RIGOROUS TRAINING

Piloting is not a safe or a soft life. Only men who love the hard, bitter life of the sea could face the prospect of those long years of training and dis-cipline. But a boy born and bred to ship-handling has a great advantage to start with. There is always a waiting list of applicants. The lucky youth nominated for pilot training begins as "spare boy." He scrubs decks, keeps the boats cleaned and manned. In former days he rowed the yawl—today replaced by the power launch—and everlastingly cleaned out spittoons.

He always addresses the pilot as "Mr." or "Sir," and hopes to be up there himself someday. He used to apply as a candidate at fourteen and would be lucky if he got his full license at thirty. Today, trainees must have at least two years of college, and have completed their military service. But they still begin by doing menial chores.

An apprentice never talks back. He knows that when the pilot gives an order, he means it. Many lives, in heavy weather, might depend on a single word. The discipline is much like that on an old-time man-o'-war. This is "an ancient guild in modern dress." Training is tough. Examinations are much more difficult today than they were a generation ago. But there are seldom any dropouts.

From "spare boy" the trainee moves up to "youngest man," and works his way to bo'sun or "oldest man." For seven years he works six days on, three days off, and is paid the minimum Federal hourly wage. After that he becomes a deputy pilot, a limited branch pilot, then finally emerges, full-fledged. At that stage he makes a good living.

"It's a great life," Captain Seeth says. "I took all the bad things out to sea, and they couldn't come back with me."

A pilot is on call twenty-four hours a day, 365 days in the year, taking his turn in rotation.

FROM SAIL TO STEAM TO DIESEL

The transit from sail to steam made great changes. The work done by some thirty small schooners up to 1897 is now done more effectively by three diesel-powered pilot boats, the New York, New Jersey, and Sandy Hook.

A new New York, with "Pilot No. 1" painted in large letters on her bow, arrived in New York from Wisconsin on May 24, 1972, and went on station off Ambrose on July 1. The $2.5 million boat is the first newly constructed vessel of her type to make her debut in New York in seventy-five years; she is third of that name. She received the traditional harbor welcome, complete with surface and aerial escorts and a fireboat salute. The New York is 182 feet long, with a 34-foot beam and antirolling tanks for stability in rough weather.

Fishing vessels were converted to steam, at first, for use as pilot boats. Steam was used from 1897 to 1940.

Before 1895 (to eliminate sail completely took a couple of years), individuals or small companies owned the sturdy pilot schooners of 60 to 75

Pilot yawl, 1906, transferring off-duty pilots from pilot boat NEW YORK *to the* NEW JERSEY

tons burden, around 75 feet long, each with a large number prominently displayed on her canvas. These would race to the side of an incoming ship. The first pilot to reach the deck got the business.

Sometimes a dozen pilot boats at a time would take part in what amounted to a perpetual schooner race. They would cruise as far south as Bermuda, as far north as the Grand Banks, in search of New York-bound vessels. The schooners rode deep for their size, drawing twelve to fourteen feet, but there were plenty of casualties.

Steamers were the prizes. A pilot's pay is based on the amount of water the piloted vessel draws. Although some modern steamers of average size draw less water than did the big sailing ships—such as the clippers— the steamers made easier work. Bringing in a sailing vessel was a long-drawn-out job. The pilot could take care of many more steamers in a day.

Due to the terrific competition, the New York Harbor pilots became perhaps the finest group of sailors ever produced in America.

INTERNATIONAL SAIL

The first international yacht race, the start of the America's Cup races, was won by a pilot boat.

During the first half of the 19th century, the New York pilot boat was the fastest ship that sailed. It combined what was considered great speed with what was certainly great stability. It was as seaworthy as many a battleship. A peculiar style of schooner rig and keen, strong lines started a new kind of marine architecture.

In 1849 a Sandy Hook pilot, Captain Richard Brown, decided to have a pilot boat built that would beat anything else afloat. He went to a New York yacht builder, George Steers. The resulting schooner, the Mary Taylor, beat with the greatest of ease everything that came her way.

About that time a New York merchant received a letter from a London correspondent suggesting that one of the famous American pilot boats might be sent over for the projected Crystal Palace Exposition in 1851, the first of the world's fairs.

The New York Yacht Club was enthusiastic about the idea. A new boat on the lines of the Mary Taylor but slightly larger—88 feet long—was built by Steers and named the America. She was taken across the Atlantic by Captain Brown, wearing the Mary Taylor's sails. Her racing sails were bent on over there. On August 22, 1851, she won the Royal Yacht Squadron regatta at Cowes. She sailed in so far ahead that the London *Times* reported an inquiry:

> "Is the America first?"
> The answer, "Yes."
> "What's second?"
> The reply, "Nothing."

The pilot boat won the cup. Queen Victoria, who visited the yacht, sent Captain Brown a gold pocket compass with a personal note.

PILOT BOAT DISASTERS

The pilots could generally prevent disasters to other vessels, but not always to their own. In spite of their speed and seaworthiness, the sailing pilot boats were in constant danger of being run down by steamships in the latter part of the 19th century. It has been said that every pilot boat retired since the coming of steam had been run down and sunk at least once.

Fifty-six pilot boats were totally lost between 1838 and 1895. Others were wrecked, sunk in collisions, or otherwise hurt. Almost 100 pilots met violent deaths in that time.

All aboard perished on the Franklin, driven ashore in a gale in 1838. A summer storm in 1839 took the Gratitude and the John McKeon, lost with all hands. The San Jacinto in 1842, the Fly in 1843, the Mary Ellen in 1845, the Commerce and the Yankee in 1852, the Thomas H. Smith and the Washington in 1857—all went down with no survivors. In 1863 the William J. Romer struck a submerged wreck near New York and sank. One pilot was lost. Romer Shoal was named for that catastrophe. The George Steers went down in 1865. In 1869 the A. T. Stewart was rammed by the steamer Scotia, while she was serving at Sandy Hook as station boat.

The Caprice was damaged in February, 1870, in a collision with a steamer. She was repaired and survived five disasters, but the sixth was fatal. In 1876 she was struck in the Narrows by the SS New Orleans, sunk, and was raised. In 1878 she was caught by a hurricane off Barnegat, dismantled, and abandoned. Back on duty in January, 1881, she lost three men in a snow-storm off Long Island. She was caught in the blizzard of 1888, but survived that. In January, 1890, she was returning to her station from Brooklyn and went on a shoal—the West Bank in the lower bay. After that, she was junked.

The Abraham Leggett was becalmed in 1879 in the lee of the SS Naples. The steamship rolled over on the Leggett and crushed her.

Maritime accidents do not always occur when visibility is poor, although they are more likely to happen in fog or snow. "It was a clear, cold day in December, 1883," wrote Paul Van Wicklen in the magazine *Via Port of New York*, "when the pilot boat Columbia sighted the steamer Alaska. There was a gale and the sea was ugly, shooting spray into the freezing air. The Alaska seemed to stop on the schooner's approach, but seconds after apprentices had placed their yawl in position to deliver the pilot, the big ship unexpectedly forged ahead. A wave sluiced off the steamer's bow to capsize the yawl. When the bow of the Alaska rose again in a pitching motion, it came down with a lethal blow, splintering the Columbia like a matchbox. All hands went down—four pilots, four sailors, and a cook."

During the blizzard of March 11–12, 1888, "the colossus of storms," not a vessel entered or left the Port of New York.

The Charles H. Marshall (New York Pilot Boat No. 3) gave a complete and continuous record of weather along the coast for two days. Then she was thrown on her beam-ends, ice-covered, in the wind and rain and huge seas, twelve miles east-southeast from Sandy Hook Lightship. She righted herself and was driven 100 miles before the storm, but finally came in safely. Thirteen vessels were blown ashore along the New Jersey coast near Sandy Hook, sunk or damaged; twenty in New York Harbor and along the New York coast; nine off New England. Six vessels were identified, abandoned at sea. Seven nameless derelicts were sighted after the storm. Nine pilot boats were lost, and seventeen pilots.

The Pilots, painting by Gari Melchers, "showing strong, self-reliant qualities of those who are called upon to assume full control of ships and human freight."

The Phantom, described as "a beautiful schooner, fast, seaworthy and weatherly," which had rescued passengers and crew of the Cunarder Oregon when she went down off Center Moriches, Long Island, in 1886, went out in the blizzard with eight aboard. She was never heard from again.

The Enchantress, with nine men, was last seen off Barnegat on March 12. The William H. Starbuck was hove to, near Barnegat, when the Japanese, a fruit steamer from the Mediterranean, crashed into her, breaking the bowsprit. The two vessels rebounded. The next wave smashed them together again. The overhanging stern of the steamer struck the pilot boat's main rigging, sweeping off the mainmast. One pilot, two sailors, and the cook were lost. A lone pilot stepped a new mast on her. She went to sea again a week later.

The Hope became a mass of splintered wood on the point of Sandy Hook, but her nine men were saved. The Edward F. Williams, the W. W. Story, the Edmund Blunt, and the Centennial went ashore and were lost at Sandy Hook. The Edmund Driggs was lost at Bay Ridge, Brooklyn. The Ezra Nye was hammered to pieces near the southern end of the Manhattan Beach railroad pier.

The Edward Cooper, which was to founder at sea on Christmas Day, 1892, went ashore at Sandy Hook in the Horseshoe, wedged in ice, in the great blizzard.

The storm started on a Sunday night. According to *From Sandy Hook to 62°*, the "stout old America, one of the best vessels that ever went afloat . . . came into port, safe and defiant, on Thursday afternoon. John Shooks, a keen-eyed youth, son of an old-time pilot, had just advanced out of the first stages of his apprenticeship and been made boatkeeper. It was his first trip in that capacity. The America was cruising off Fire Island when the gale came down, with a sudden fierce testing of the young man's worth. He put the schooner under a storm-trysail and the last reef in the foresail and stuck it out where he was. Everything was covered with thick ice, but he came through without a single mishap, and by this showing of skill and grit proved that he had earned his new place."

That "stout old America" was not the winner of the first international cup race in 1851. It was designed after that winner, by the same man, George Steers, and named after her; but all the pilot boats had a number. She was America 21. The young boatkeeper had taken Captain Seeth's father, just before the blizzard set in, out to a freighter—which he brought in safely. The term "boatkeeper" corresponds to captain of the pilot boat, when the full-fledged pilot is not aboard.

John Henry Shooks was the uncle of a New York–East Hampton man, Edward J. Shean. Mr. Shean says: "His father and my grandfather was Captain John Shooks, a pilot. One of my great-grandfathers, Captain J. J. Canvin, had a pilot son and two pilot grandsons. I could have been sponsored for the Pilots' Association," he says, "but my father was a New York banker. I chose Wall Street."

Captain J. J. Canvin was over seventy-five when he was drowned in January, 1890, bringing in a brigantine, the Edward Cushing, from Port au Spain, Trinidad. According to a newspaper account at the time, the Cushing was off the Highlands when Captain Canvin was taken aboard from the pilot boat Charles H. Marshall. He reached the barkentine with great difficulty. A fierce gale was blowing and a heavy sea running; it was intensely cold. The vessel had to beat against a northwest wind for port. The pilot worked the vessel all night, gaining only a few miles. Early next morning the gale struck the Cushing broadside, sending her over almost on her beam end. The pilot was thrown from his feet. Before he could recover himself, he slipped along the ice-covered deck into the ocean. The paper said: "For the past forty-five years he had been guiding ships safely into this port. His son is a commissioned Sandy Hook pilot, and two of his daughters are married to pilots. . . . There are only two or three previous cases on record where a pilot has lost his life after boarding an incoming vessel."

LATER PILOT BOAT DISASTERS

On August 17, 1901, the pilot boat James Gordon Bennett was cut in two by the Alene of the Hamburg–American Line, which was bound from New York to the West Indies. The accident happened off Scotland Lightship. Three pilots and a steward were lost, two pilots were saved.

One night in February, 1906, a yawl from the New York was caught under the stern of that big pilot boat. It was in the midst of a southeast storm. A giant sea came heaving in and the yawl tried to cut it too close. The New York lifted to the rise of a big comber, then sat down upon the yawl. A New York *Herald* story said: "There wasn't a piece big as a stove-lid left of her." Captain George Seeth, who was an apprentice at the time, says he is sure that both of the boys at the oars were picked up.

On December 15, 1906, the pilot boat Hermit was rammed, cut in two, and sunk by the SS Monterey, inbound from Havana, off Sandy Hook Lightship. The Monterey was about to take the pilot aboard. All ten men on board were saved, but New Jersey pilot Frank Neilson died of injuries incurred in the sinking.

On May 13, 1912, the Ambrose Snow was rammed and sunk by the Clyde liner Delaware in the Lower Bay, New York. All were saved.

The 157-foot steam pilot boat New Jersey was sunk in the fog on July 10, 1914, in a collision with the fruit ship Manchoneal near Ambrose Lightship. There was no loss of life.

Captain Seeth recalls a fatal accident on December 14, 1919. A pilot had just boarded the Japanese steamship Taiyo Maru. As the pilot's yawl left the side of the ship, the captain started her ahead. The ship was so light that the propeller was half out of the water. A heavy snow squall blew the ship down on the yawl, and the wash from the propeller turned the yawl upside down. Joe Baeszler, an apprentice, came up under the yawl. The other boy, George Beebe, Jr., was drowned.

On January 26, 1933, a yawl went to the SS Black Gull to take off pilot Hugh McIntyre in the midst of one of the worst storms on record. The yawl, the pilot, and two apprentices were lost. Both pilot boats searched all night for the missing yawl. Early the next morning a bakery wagon driver saw a small boat with three men in it overturn in the heavy surf off Long Branch, N.J. The yawl and its crew had stayed afloat for over seven hours. They might have made shore if one of the oars had not broken while they were trying to land.

The pilot boat Sandy Hook, 361 tons, built as the yacht Privateer, was steaming off slowly in a dense fog about 6 A.M. on April 27, 1939, looking for ships to board, when she was struck by the Norwegian motorship Oslofjord. She notified the pilot boat New York of her trouble, and the New

York went off to help her. Some of the pilots and most of the crew went aboard the Oslofjord. The Sandy Hook made for shallow water, but sank about a mile north of Ambrose Lightship, seven miles off Sandy Hook, in eighty feet of water. The New York reached her just before she sank and took off Jack Sullivan, one of the pilots, as well as the captain, mates, and engineers.

RESCUE OPERATIONS

Although their primary purpose is preventing rather than curing disasters, New York–Sandy Hook pilots have been ready and able to render heroic assistance in catastrophes. They are "handy by," as the Long Islanders put it.

On December 18, 1908, the British steamship Daghestan collided with the SS Catalone a quarter mile southeast of the Gedney Channel buoys. The pilot boat New York took off twenty-eight of the Daghestan crew. A little later the pilot put the captain and a few of his men back aboard. They stood by all day, but the captain refused to let the New York tow the Daghestan to shallower water. Just before she sank, the pilot boat took off the captain, put a buoy on the wreck, and notified the wreckers and Coast Guard. Next morning the crew was put on board the Catalone, which was still standing by. At that time the Daghestan was lying under eighteen feet of water. She was later blown up by the Coast Guard.

The Fort Victoria of the Furness Line, on the Bermuda run, was rammed by a Clyde Line steamer on December 18, 1929, and sank at the entrance to New York Harbor. The pilot boats New York and Sandy Hook rescued her 400 passengers and crew as she was going down.

On September 8, 1934, when the Morro Castle burned off Asbury Park, N.J., with a loss of 125 lives, the pilot boat New York not only picked up survivors at the scene but actually acted as a rudder for the burning vessel while she was being towed to safety. (The New York was off-station, but another pilot boat is always left on-station in an emergency.)

The general public takes the pilots' operations for granted and knows very little about them. As Charles Edward Russell said: "Piloting is one of the few honest businesses left in the world that get no aid from the publicity man. They want none of this hero business."

PILOTING A SUB

Captain George Seeth recalls an experience that he now thinks amusing, but that probably did not seem so at the time. He was bringing a U.S. submarine into the Port of New York in 1945. "This sub," he says, "had

Taking on the pilot

quite a history. She rescued the fliers after those bombing raids on Japan.
Went into a Japanese harbor so close they could watch a horse race ashore.
This day she arrived outside New York Harbor it was blowing a gale o' wind,
southeast, heavy sea running. At first the submarine captain thought it would
be impossible for a pilot to board her, so he started toward the channel to
try to get in by himself. When he saw those heavy seas breaking at the channel entrance, he realized that if he touched, the sub would be turned over
and lost. He turned around and went offshore again.

"Aboard the pilot boat, we discussed the possibility of boarding that
sub. Finally a young pilot came to me. He said: 'You haven't entered into
this at all. I think I know what that means. Would you go aboard there?'

"I answered: 'That's up to the man on the turn.'

"He was a heavy man—200 pounds to my 135. I knew it would be
impossible for him to board it. I had the next turn. He wanted me to change.

"So I got in the yawl with two rowing. They pulled toward the sub. I
hailed her and said, 'Go astern, very slowly.' I got into the bow of the yawl,
and after a heavy sea had passed, we hit abaft the stern of the sub. I jumped
into the air, hands up. The sailors grabbed my wrists and lifted me aboard.
I ran to the island [in the center of the sub]. There were iron steps on the
side leading to the conning tower. I was wet to the knees by the heavy sea. I
forgot that there was an iron rail three feet above the deck, around the top
of the island. I hit it. Split my nose open, bled like anything; the ship's
doctor patched me up.

"We turned around and went in. Docked at Pier 6, Staten Island, alongside another sub. And my job for the day was finished.

"My wife's father had never been aboard a submarine. Next day I asked if I could bring him and two friends aboard. We were invited to the mess room. There was a cake, with a Purple Heart in the center. The captain told my father-in-law he didn't think he or anybody else would have taken the chance of getting aboard, outside, last night. He said I had been wounded in the line of duty."

CLOSE CALLS

An old-timer says: "Piloting is easier than it used to be. But there are still hardships enough. Heart trouble is our occupational hazard."

Captain W. A. Mitchell, former president of the New Jersey Pilots' Association, says that one of the pilot's riskiest chores is that high climb up the ladder to the bridge of a ship, at the mouth of the harbor. "It's five stories straight up the side of a ship, and sometimes there's another four stories up to the bridge. When the captain says, 'Good morning,' you have hardly the strength to reply."

The Jacob's ladder is still generally of rope, although sometimes it is a chain. It must be flexible.

Captain E. W. Florimont, who found that climbing the ladder up the side of a ship was taxing his heart and retired rather early (he served forty-one years), calls piloting "the most wonderful job in the world."

Asked if he remembered any close calls, he said: "Oh, of course I had a couple of collisions, but nothing to worry about. Except once in 1948 or thereabouts, when I was taking out the Queen Mary. It was clear in the harbor. When we approached the fairway buoy, a blanket of fog shut down. The Mary had two radar stations, which were manned. By the time we were close to the buoy it was so thick you couldn't see the bow from the stern. The lookouts on the bow saw a blue light flashing ahead. We reversed engines. Stopped. A searchlight showed an aircraft carrier, inbound, enchored adjacent to the fairway buoy, only forty or fifty feet from us. The only remedy was to put full power on our rudder. We managed to avoid contact. I could have dropped my hat on the carrier. Our radar never showed it. They are improved today."

THEN AND NOW

It is interesting to study pictures of the New York Harbor pilots of seventy or eighty years ago and compare them with the pilots of today. The present-day pilot looks in better physical trim, but he has the same air of authority and complete dependability. It is a pleasure in this era of doubt

Going up the side, 1950

and uncertainty to meet someone who looks like the right man in the right place.

The pilot in the 1880's did not look in the least like a seafaring man. According to the photographs he was bearded, rather fearsome, meticulously dressed in frock coat, high silk hat ("beaver"), and gloves—like the Wall Street tycoon of his day. Across his ample front was a watch chain nearly as heavy as a ship's anchor chain. By the 1890's, when he left the pier in New York for the station boat, the tall silk hat had been replaced by a black derby.

Once aboard the station boat, the pilot took off his store clothes and put on something old and comfortable that he had brought along in his handbag; something suitable for lying around waiting and playing pinochle. A perpetual game went on in the cabin.

When the pilot's number was called, he put the good clothes back on again in the twinkling of an eye, picked up his handbag and the New York newspapers he was taking to the ship's captain, and boarded the yawl that would take him to the incoming ship. One wonders how he managed to climb that swaying rope ladder in a high wind with a heavy swell, wearing a stiff hat; and what happened to the store clothes when he was doused up to the shoulders by an icy sea as the ship rolled.

One of the older pilots says: "Oh, that wasn't too hard. If you jam a derby hat well down on your head it's like an iron helmet; it stays there."

Today the Sandy Hook pilot on duty wears business clothes with a soft felt hat, or a cap—the same outfit that a passenger on the ship would wear. A young Navy officer returned from a tour of duty in the Far East says the pilots in Japan are still very formal in their attire. He recalls seeing one Japanese pilot maneuvering a tug and three tows, shouting orders down a long tube to the engine room, with a smokestack belching black cinders all over him—he was dressed in the stiffest of starched whites.

CARRIED AWAY

In an old scrapbook kept in the Pilots' Association headquarters is an obituary of Captain John R. Hall, retired Sandy Hook pilot whose father was a ship news reporter. Captain Hall died January 19, 1933, after piloting for fifty years. He had been reported missing several times. The blizzard of 1888, the paper said, caught his pilot boat, the Thomas S. Negus, outside the harbor—but it survived. Two years later, in a storm nearly as bad, Captain Hall was unable to transfer from the liner he was piloting at the end of the channel. He was carried to Bremen on the outboard ship Aller of the Hamburg–American Line. His son, Captain John L. Hall, used to tease his father about this until 1929, when he was carried off in the same way by the Reliance of the same line.

It was the rule that if a pilot, due to the stress of the weather or any other cause that is no fault of his, is unable to be taken off an outbound vessel, he shall be compensated at the rate of $100 a week and have his transportation and expenses paid until he is returned to New York. Today the company gives him an airline ticket back home if he is "carried away."

ON STATION

In the days of sail there was no permanent station boat. Now at least one pilot boat rocks endlessly twenty miles seaward from the Battery, on station year in and year out in all kinds of weather.

Captain William C. Hall recalls: "In my experience I remember the pilot boat leaving its station just once, and that was for only four hours, back

44

on November 24, 1950, in a southeast storm. Some gusts that day were as high as 110 miles an hour. Ferry service from New Jersey and Staten Island was suspended. The Hudson–Manhattan tubes were out. The Jersey meadows and La Guardia Airport were flooded. The storm cut a narrow swath, ending up in Quebec I think.

"I was on the pilot boat New Jersey. In this 1950 blow, three pilots were injured—two by falls, one by flying glass. It was impossible to stand up, let alone board a ship. We led one ship of the American Export Line in, finally put a pilot aboard her in Gravesend Bay. Lucky to have no collisions or other disasters."

ONCE UPON A TIME

For the first 150 years of New York Harbor pilots, it was every man for himself. A ship's captain could take pilotage or leave it. He would often take pride in sailing his own ship right up to the dock; and each pilot boat was on its own. It took a great disaster to bring matters to a head, to systematize and regulate the highly individual and competitive business of pilotage then carried on by numerous sailing vessels.

Two American packets carrying immigrants, mostly Irish, from Liverpool to New York—the ship Bristol and the bark Mexico—went ashore on Long Island on November 21, 1836, and January 2, 1837, respectively. Both disasters were due to the lack of a pilot. Nearly 200 lives were lost.

That was a stormy winter. On each occasion the vessel hove to off Sandy Hook, then flew the flag and sounded the gun for a pilot, but in vain. Contrary to their usual disregard for adverse weather, pilots working on those particular days had apparently taken refuge well back in Sandy Hook Bay. During the following nights each ship was driven aground—the Bristol on Far Rockaway Shoals, the Mexico ten miles eastward on Hempstead Beach.

Then in 1854 there was another dire disaster involving great loss of life when the captain of an incoming transatlantic ship refused pilot services. After that, any vessel entering New York Harbor from a foreign port was obliged to use a pilot.

POLITICS

From about 1820 to 1850 New York City's business and public services were permeated with politics. Even piloting, according to Charles Edward Russell's *From Sandy Hook to 62°*, passed "into a state of chaos and slop." He says that political heelers who didn't know a ship's keel from a staysail were solemnly licensed as pilots. They hired apprentices to get ships in and out, while they took their ease at the public-houses.

The shipping interests complained. Then came the Bristol and Mexico disasters. It was a scandal. New Jersey took the first step, appointing a Pilot Commission as the sole licensing power, to keep the politician at a distance. Stiff examinations were established. The first authorized pilot under the new dispensation was Theophilus Beebe, who owned and operated a fishing smack out of Fulton Market. There have been Beebes in piloting ever since.

New York went its way, unbridled, until 1845. Then insurance underwriters and the shipping interests took the matter into their own hands. They created an unofficial Pilot Commission, requiring a pilot to be an expert shipmaster who knew every bit of the area. Finally in 1853 New York State passed the proper legislation.

An extra pilotage fee was charged if a pilot's services were accepted fifteen miles or more outside of Sandy Hook. This was when the pilots began cruising far out to sea. The pilot boat would hoist its signal, a large plain blue flag at the mainmast, on a pole that enabled it to swing free and be seen. The incoming vessel would respond by hoisting her own pilot signal forward, meaning she had no pilot and wanted one. Whoever reached her first got the job.

THE PILOT'S RADIUS

Today the pilot goes aboard the incoming ship, or gets off the outward-bound one, at the bar off the point of Sandy Hook, some twenty miles below the Battery. He is taken from the station boat to the incoming ship by the boarding launch, which has replaced the rowing yawl.

Until 1907, when United States Army engineers made a new channel on the site of the old East Channel, wider and deeper than the old Main Ship Channel, and renamed it the Ambrose, New York City was three miles farther from the sea than it is now. A depth of 35 feet was made in 1907. Today a vessel drawing up to 45 feet can go through that six-mile-long passage. But even now, in spite of dredging, the Hudson River and ocean tides together drift sand onto bars that shift and obstruct. It takes someone intimately acquainted with changing depths and weather conditions to know when channels can be used safely.

The boundary for inland waters for New York Harbor is a line drawn from the Rockaway Point Coast Guard station to the Ambrose Channel Light Tower, thence to the abandoned Navesink Lighthouse (South Tower). On the North River, very few ships are taken above Pier 97, although a full New York–Sandy Hook pilot's license is good for the North River (Hudson) as far as Yonkers and up to Welfare Island in the East River.

46

THE PILOT'S AUTHORITY

The pilot's authority after he boards a ship is a complex legal question. Captain William W. Sherwood, a former Pilots' Association president, explains that under Admiralty law a pilot is adviser to the ship's master. "He gives up the conn to you, but is still master of the ship and responsible. He can countermand your order. The Coast Guard, too, have a right to examine any marine casualty, and they have, upon occasion, held pilots responsible for negligence."

The pilot's word is law, up to the point where the captain orders him into a situation where he doesn't care to go. Then legally the responsibility for consequences sheds from the pilot's shoulders and rests on the captain. Few captains have the temerity to exercise this authority.

The pilot knows all the harbor ranges, landmarks, and habits of local shipping. He can navigate in and out without a glance at the chart, and he can steer a safe course through the harbor on the most meager visual information. There are times when the compass is of little use to him, as when going through a bridge, or in the vicinity of dangers or aids to navigation, and so forth. He must know his position at all times.

An example is an experience recalled by the veteran pilot Captain George Seeth: "The Majestic was sailing at midnight. We left the dock in the North River when it was still ebb tide. As we came down past Quarantine on Staten Island, I called the captain's attention to how brilliant the New York City lights were.

"Off Fort Wadsworth a few hundred yards later (that's on the lower end of Staten Island), we ran into a fog that was just as though somebody had put a bag over your head. Julius [Captain Seeth's pilot brother] had the Bremen sailing at 2 A.M. I had the wireless warn him of the fog.

"It was really bad. First we had a ship on our starboard bow. We swung left to clear her. Then one on the other bow. We zigzagged, just managing to clear that. Finally I heard what I thought was the last bell on my port side. I backed full speed, to counteract the effect of the tide running out, and dropped anchor. We turned the ship around head to the tide by using the propellers.

"The captain said, 'Well, where are we now?'

"I went to the chart and put an X on it.

"He said, 'My God, man, how can you say the anchor is there?'

"I went to the stern of the ship and watched. Within an hour I saw a little red flash—one of the buoys at the upper end of the channel. The mate was in the wheelhouse. I called him on the telephone from the stern to find out how she was heading. I knew the buoy was dead astern.

"When the flood tide made at daybreak, I hove up the anchor and went to sea.

"The captain couldn't figure out how anyone could determine, after all the changes of the ship's heading and the tide, where it would be at that point.

"Captains are used to being at sea; they never navigate at close quarters. A pilot has an almost automatic sense of timing, which can only be attained by years of experience."

On one day, during World War II, there were some 400 ships in New York Harbor requiring pilot services—as many as might be expected in a week, in peacetime. There were not enough pilots to go around. Some licensed pilots were brought in from other ports to help out. After a week's trial the outsiders gave up. Local knowledge is imperative.

The term "branch pilot" was explained in a *New Yorker* article by William Wertenbaker. The term dates from the 16th century. Trinity House, the corporation chartered in 1514 by King Henry VIII to promote shipping, awarded a certificate known as a "branch" to pilots who passed its examination. "When a pilot has received his branch," says Mr. Wertenbaker, "he is able to take any ship—the largest liners, aircraft carriers, huge, sluggish tankers—to and from any part of New York Harbor."

THE COAST PILOT

A coast pilot and a New York–Sandy Hook pilot are in two different categories. Captain William F. Smith is a coast pilot. He holds a license from Boston to Norfolk and for the Cape Cod and Ches–Del canals. He has also taken vessels from Boston to Florida during his forty-six years at sea. During World War II he was on active duty with the Navy, taking convoys between New York, Boston, and Norfolk.

He says the coastal men call the Sandy Hook men "fence pilots—that go from one buoy to the next." But, he admits, they know their area in depth.

THE PILOTS' ASSOCIATION TODAY

The full name is the United New York–Sandy Hook Pilots' Benevolent Association. It is generally called just the Sandy Hook Pilots. Actually there are two associations working together—the New York Pilots' Association and the New Jersey Pilots' Association. The current head of the New York group is Captain Harry Breitenfeld; Captain Lester T. Earl heads the New Jersey pilots. The two groups have separate membership rolls but otherwise work cooperatively, sharing facilities, equipment, revenue, and expenses.

By 1895 it had become evident that thirty schooners scattered over a 600-mile radius were impractical. Two steam pilot boats, with an auxiliary schooner, could do the job from bar to pier. The two associations thus consolidated and rivalry was ended. The association bought the schooners at the owners' own figures. More educational requirements were instituted for pilots, as well as retirement pensions.

Coastwise vessels are not obliged to use a pilot, but often do. Nor is the Navy obliged to do so, but it generally does for its capital ships—battle-ships, carriers, and cruisers—and sometimes for destroyers and submarines. It is up to the officer in charge of the ship.

All proceeds of the New York–Sandy Hook Pilots' Association are turned in together and divided once a month, share and share alike. A pilot has no set time off. But as one says: "We manage mostly to get home a night or two a week, when there are lots of names on the list ahead of us. If you are on the list and don't answer when your name is called, you are fined three days' pay. You get holidays when you ask for them. But your whole pay stops when you are absent. We make our own rules, mostly. We own and operate the boats and are beholden to no one."

5

STRANDED

FROM Coney Island to Montauk Point, along the south shore of Long Island, there is not a vestige of a harbor that can be entered by a vessel of any size. If, in sailing-ship days, a ship was brought near the coast through faulty judgment on the part of the navigator, or because he was unfamiliar with the coast, and there was a strong wind bearing on shore, the ship's doom was usually sealed. A sandbar parallels the beach a quarter of half-mile distant, for nearly the whole length of the south shore. Vessels were often grounded on this, and were pounded to pieces by being alternately lifted up and thrust down by each successive wave.

That stretch of shore which includes Rockaway, Jones Beach, and Fire Island has often been called a ship trap. The sandbars shift. There is a long, sloping beach that creates a vicious undertow when seas are heavy. Wrecks, however, have almost gone the way of the Life Savers' Lyle gun and the breeches buoy. Modern communication, better built ships, and the passing of sail have drawn the teeth of the ship trap. Almost.

The island's north shore, bounded by Long Island Sound, has some harbors. And normally the Sound is not as rough as the Atlantic Ocean—although it can kick up, and it has rocks.

HURRICANES

Not so long ago old salts along the coast hardly needed to be told by radio what the weather was going to be. A man would step out of his back door before daylight, sniff the wind, look at the vane on the barn, come in and take a look at the barometer. Then he knew . . . or he was pretty sure he did. Even the most scientific modern weathermen still have not figured out all the vagaries of a hurricane.

Morton's "New England Memorial" describes a 1635 hurricane as a great storm that "blew down houses and uncovered divers others, divers vessels were lost at sea; it caused the sea to swell in some places so that it arose to twenty feet right up and down, and made many Indians climb into trees for their safety."

Long Island was not settled then by Europeans. Hollanders of Nieuw Amsterdam acquired land that year at Flatlands, later called South Brooklyn, and formed a colony there in 1636. The first English settlements on the island were at Gardiner's Island in 1639 and at Southold and Southampton in 1640.

It was in 1636 that John Winthrop of the Massachusetts Bay Colony wrote in his *Journal* about a clergyman, traveling to Virginia with a party of thirty, being "cast away upon Long Island with a WNW wind."

A devastating storm in 1690 destroyed many whaleboats at Fire Island and opened an inlet, then known as the Great Gut, between Great South Bay and the ocean. A hurricane in 1723 did much damage to shipping.

The "Christmas storm" of December 24, 1811, a northwest blizzard, drove seventy vessels onto Long Island's north shore. Four sloops went aground at Oyster Bay; one at Oak Neck Beach; others at Cow Bay, Little Neck Bay, Flushing Bay; and many to the eastward.

The sloop Sally Ann of North Hempstead, Long Island, Captain Mott, master, went on a shoal at Newtown, Long Island, in that storm. Captain Mott swam ashore and found an eighteen-foot ladder, which he used to get his nineteen passengers off safely.

The linestorm—any storm coming around the autumnal equinox, in the second half of September—has often caused shipwrecks. The hurricane of September 23, 1815, was a topic for years. The wind shifted, as it often does in such storms. It began with a tremendous southeast gale in early morning; then blew from the south, sending up a great tide; after three hours it turned southwest, with heavy rain.

The United States government began to issue hurricane warnings in 1873. Today, radar-reconnaissance crews of the U.S. Air Force and Navy, and the Coast Guard weather patrol, provide hurricane warnings and lessen the danger.

The great blizzard of March 11 and 12, 1888, and the hurricane of September 21, 1938, are outstanding examples of storms that have inflicted great losses of life and property in the New York–Long Island area. The center of the 1938 storm missed New York City as it cut across Long Island and swept up through New England. Newspapers of the time reported 300 small boats sunk off Nassau County on Long Island, and even more off Suffolk. The south shore bore the brunt of it, but some 200 small craft were sunk or driven ashore in Manhasset Bay on the north shore. Sloops were found on front lawns and in swimming pools. A motor boat went through the window of a grocery store in Port Washington, Long Island.

The barometer fell to 28.72; there were hundred-mile winds on Long Island (a wind of seventy-five miles per hour is considered of hurricane force). The gale backed around from northeast to southwest in the middle of the storm. Three Suffolk County Coast Guard stations were demolished —Shinnecock, Moriches, and Potunk. There was considerable loss of life.

That 1938 hurricane began a series of bad storms for the area. Others followed in 1944, 1950, and 1954. Some inlets through Barrier Beach on the south side of Long Island were opened. Others were closed.

THE TRIAL

One of the most gruesome recorded accounts of a shipwreck is the description by one Thomas Eustace of his experiences when the ship Trial, Captain Trask, master, went on the rocks on Long Island's north shore. The north shore, washed by the waters of often-turbulent Long Island Sound, is rocky, very different from the flat, shifting, sandy beaches on the south side. It does have some deep, safe harbors.

A small book published in London in 1820, *Shipwreck Off Long Island, Near New York: The Adventures of Thomas Eustace* describes that wreck, which occurred on January 18, 1809. Eustace, a former British tar, told his tale to an unnamed clergyman who had befriended him upon his return to England.

The book's frontispiece shows a legless man holding out his hat with one hand, a copy of the book in the other. There is a drawing of the wrecked ship and Eustace's rescuers. He is saying: "Here we hung from Friday night till Saturday afternoon, clinging to the ropes and rigging, when a ship hove in sight!"

Verses from a long, harrowing Isaac Watts hymn are quoted. They begin:

> Would you behold the works of God,
> His wonders in the world abroad,
> Come with us mariners and trace
> The unknown regions of the seas.

By the time Eustace had returned to England his memory for place names had grown hazy; but as far as one can make out from his book and from an article in the *Times* of London for March 16, 1820, the Trial was an American merchant vessel. She loaded at Northport, Long Island, with spars for shipbuilding, and sailed for Charleston, S.C. Returning to Northport they laid to, ready for sailing the next morning. "But nevermore was that ship to sail! That night most of our crew were doomed to end their voyages in a watery grave!"

At nine o'clock at night a tremendous storm came up. The ship parted her cables. "Having no anchor to stay her course, the vessel drove for nine miles upon a ledge of rocks, stretching into the sea from Long Island. After several very heavy seas had broken over her, she bilged, filled with water, and upset!"

Eustace and most of his comrades got outside the ship. They hung by their hands on her sides, grasping ropes and rigging. There they remained, at the mercy of the billows, on a night "when the cold was so intense that cattle on land were frozen to death in their stalls! So that ever since they have in those parts remembered the days by calling them 'Cold Friday and Cold Saturday.' "

Some of the sailors became exhausted and fell, to rise no more. Two or three were frozen to death with their hands still clenched in the rigging. The three who survived were ready to give up all for lost when, at "3 or 4 in the afternoon, a ship hove in sight, and most providentially, she came by!"

The survivors' frozen hands were pulled away from the ropes. They were taken to "Long Island, near New York." After about a week they were conveyed by a small packet back to Northport, where for seven weeks friendly Long Islanders tried to save Eustace's limbs. Finally a consultation of fourteen surgeons was held. Not one of them had ever performed an amputation before. Eustace chose one doctor, who spent an hour and a quarter hewing off one leg. A Colonel Knowlton who was present "swore that if I survived this cruel hacking he would himself pay the expense of having an experienced surgeon to take off my other limb, sooner than I should again be butchered alive!!!"

That promise was kept, five weeks later. The skillful surgeon performed the second operation in only fifteen minutes. The other two sailors underwent similar surgery. Later, Eustace lost eight fingers in the same way. He received very kind treatment, he said, in a hospital supported "by a penny per week, stopped out of the wages of all American seamen." Later he recuperated at the home of one Captain Brown. The captain, when Eustace was able to work, made him his bookkeeper and in return gave him board and lodging and sufficient wages to buy clothes.

Eustace returned to his native village of Chinnor in Oxfordshire, married, and had two children. He became deputy manager of the Workhouse at Amersham in Bucks for a time, and later lived in Woodrow, near Amersham.

THE NESTOR

The old-line packet ship Nestor, Captain Place, master, bound from Liverpool to New York with a cargo of lead, coal, and salt, went ashore at three o'clock of a December morning in 1824 off Hempstead, Long Island, about twenty-eight miles from Sandy Hook. "She bilged, and is probably totally lost," a record of the time stated. "Goods between decks were saved. . . . At 5 A.M. the sea made a clear breach over her; people were trying to save rigging. . . ."

THE PRESIDENT

On the night of December 4, 1831, the Charleston Line packet President, Captain Wilson, master, went on Romer Shoals in a violent northwest wind. A pilot was on board. The tempest increased. Next morning the packet pulled two anchors, drifted, then struck hard. Her spars and rigging were all ice. At 4 A.M. water burst into her bottom, and within half an hour the cabin was filled. All twenty passengers were on deck, nearly frozen. The mainmast, mizzen, and foremasts were cut away, coming down with a great crash.

At 10 A.M. the jolly boat was made ready. Seven persons, including the captain, got safely to land. The captain hurried for help as the weather worsened. At 2 P.M. a sail was seen bearing down from Staten Island for the wreck. At 3 P.M. it anchored three-quarters of a mile away, as near as it could get, among the breakers and shoals. The longboat was launched, and at 5 P.M. the schooner Major Howard of Staten Island had the passengers aboard. The steamboat Bellona met the Howard and took them on at 8 P.M., landing them at Roosevelt Street Wharf, New York.

THE BRISTOL AND THE MEXICO

Two awful disasters fresh in the mind of Nathaniel S. Prime in 1845 when he wrote his history were the loss of the American bark Bristol, carrying 100 passengers and 16 officers and men, on Rockaway Shoals on November 21, 1836; and of the American bark Mexico, with 112 passengers and a crew of 12, which came ashore on January 2, 1837, at Point Lookout, Hempstead Beach, only about ten miles from where the Bristol had been wrecked. Two hundred lives were lost from these two vessels, wrecked only seven weeks apart. Most of those who perished were steerage passengers, immigrants coming from England and Ireland by way of Liverpool.

These two disasters, followed by more bad winters with numerous shipwrecks, were powerful factors in the creation in 1848 of the United States

Life Saving Service; in 1915 it became the Coast Guard. The early Life Saving stations were manned by volunteer crews, who fired cannon to summon help when a ship in distress was sighted.

An almost contemporary account of the tragic strandings of the Bristol and the Mexico is given in *Historical Collections of the State of New York*, by John W. Barber and Henry Howe, published in 1842.

A tall white marble monument was erected in 1840 to the 200 victims; it stands in Rockville Cemetery, which was established in 1791 near the old Sand Hole Meeting House between Lynbrook and Rockville Centre.

The Bristol was on the return trip of her maiden voyage when she left Liverpool on October 16, 1836. She made a fair passage across the Atlantic. On Saturday night, November 20, she arrived off Sandy Hook. On making the light at Atlantic Highlands, Captain McKown had hove to and hoisted a signal for a pilot. About 1 A.M. a wind came up. The captain brought the ship to the wind and stood offshore under easy sail. No pilot showed up. Just before 4 A.M. on Sunday, the ship went aground on the shoals at Far Rockaway.

It was dark, with a thick fog. The Bristol struck so lightly on the shoals

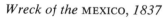

Wreck of the MEXICO, *1837*

that there was little apprehension on board. But soon the very high sea began to break over her decks. The captain advised the passengers that it would be safest to stay below. The gale increased.

After the Bristol had been on the shoals for about an hour, one tremendous wave carried away boats, bulwarks, and everything else movable. Hatches had been well secured, but the waves' force tore them open. In minutes the bark filled. Steerage passengers were below, and all but a few of those who happened to be standing near the hatchways were drowned instantly. And silently. Survivors said they never heard a sound.

At 11 P.M. the tide ebbed. Boats came out from the shore twice, rescuing thirty-two. The third time, the small boats were swamped.

One passenger was taken off the bowsprit. The captain and others were on the mizzenmast. When that fell they lashed themselves to the taffrail, where for four hours icy seas broke over them.

One of those who perished was Arthur Donnelly of New York, who twice yielded his place in a lifeboat to others. He took to the foremast, but this soon went by the board. His wife and children were taken ashore.

Eighty-four were drowned. The vessel was a total loss. By the next morning only her stern-post remained visible.

The 300-ton American bark Mexico, Captain Charles Winslow commanding, left Liverpool, which was then the great embarkation point for emigrants, on October 26, 1836. Most of her 112 passengers were traveling steerage. Her crew of 12 was smaller than that of the Bristol, her passenger list larger. She was a much older ship than the Bristol and had fewer conveniences.

The whole voyage across the ocean was stormy. The cold was intense in the unheated quarters below decks. High waves prevented kindling of fires to cook any food (in those days emigrants had to furnish their own food). Because the ship was delayed in the heavy weather, the passengers' small stores were used up before the end of the sixty-seven-day journey. Even supplies for the crew were almost gone. For the last eleven days the captain had a daily ration of one biscuit and a half-pint of water issued to the passengers. The crew and miserably seasick passengers were nearly starved and quite exhausted by the time the Highlands of New Jersey were sighted on New Year's Eve. On January 1, 1837, the ship proceeded to Sandy Hook. Distress signals for a pilot were sent up.

It was Sunday. No pilot came to relieve the vessel. A snowstorm came on, with a high wind, blotting out all sight of land from the ship and any possibility of discerning its position. All that night the ship remained near the Hook. Again on the following day rockets were sent up for a pilot to bring the Mexico into New York Harbor. Because of the rough sea and lack of pilot regulations (corrected after the tragedy, largely through the efforts of State Senator John Alsop King of Jamaica, Long Island), no pilot would venture forth.

The gale increased. The vessel was blown toward land. After hours of imminent foundering, the bark struck at 5 A.M., January 2, on Long Beach, then an island (called Hempstead Beach) and now a great playground for New York City.

Whole families were found frozen to the rigging when Captain Raynor Rock Smith, a fisherman and Wreck Master, crossed on the ice to Long Beach with a few other hardy volunteers and managed to launch a boat on January 3 and approach the Mexico. They found a few still alive, clinging to the bowsprit, including the captain, four passengers, and three crew members. Night came on. Mountainous waves prevented another rescue attempt. That night the vessel broke up. One hundred and sixteen perished.

Seventy-seven bodies were recovered from the Mexico. They were brought to the barn at Lott's Tavern on Hicks Neck, south of what is now Baldwin. Peter T. Hewlett purchased a plot in the old Sand Hole Church cemetery, which became known as the Mariners' Lot. Oliver S. Denton furnished lumber for the coffins. The sexton of the church who dug the graves had to use an axe since the frost was five feet deep.

Sixty-two bodies of those lost on the Bristol were placed with those from the Mexico. Local residents subscribed to a fund for the monument to those who had risked their lives to begin a new life in America—and lost. The monument was made at Sing Sing, N.Y., and brought to East Rockaway by sloop.

Today the tall monument over the barren stretch of the huge common grave looks rather forlorn and forgotten.

THE SHEFFIELD

On Saturday, November 11, 1843, the Liverpool packet Sheffield with 130 passengers and crew aboard was entering New York Harbor in a southeasterly gale at 1 P.M. with a pilot. The ship, headed for Staten Island Light, struck on Romer Shoal.

Passengers, mostly immigrants in the steerage, stampeded. Captain Charles W. Popham took charge. He had a flag upside down, a distress signal, run up on the yardarm. Rockets and flares were sent up at dark when no sign of aid had appeared.

High seas pounded the packet. Rain poured down. The cabin began to take water, driving people up on deck. The Sheffield's three masts were chopped down and pushed overboard to lighten her. Tea and bread were served. Prayers were said. The Bible account of St. Paul's shipwreck and deliverance was read. The water rose higher. Everyone expected to die.

The vessel heeled over on her starboard side and seemed to be settling.

The captain, a good man, was asked to launch his lifeboats, but he dared not give the word. With a heavy sea still running, it was impossible to get 130 people into three small boats.

Captain B. Earl, keeper of Staten Island Light, had seen the Sheffield strike late that afternoon. The Coast Wrecking Company, later to become a great salvage organization, had its headquarters on Staten Island. The lighthouse keeper sent a message to Captain Oliver Vanderbilt (brother of Cornelius). He fired up the boiler of his little steamer, Wave. Then towing an empty lighter, he coasted for two hours in the dark around the shoal, bucking the heavy seas. He found rigging and masts adrift. "Good God! They have all perished," he said. He was ready to turn back, when Captain Popham lit a blue flare. The small steamer crossed the shoal.

The passengers sang "Praise God from Whom All Blessings Flow" as they were taken aboard the rescue vessel and the lighter at 1 A.M. on Sunday. Six hours later they were on dry land in New York.

According to the narrator of *The Stranding of the Sheffield*, published in 1844, the voyage, begun on October 5, had been one of "continued affliction" from the weather. All on board, however, had the highest praise for the captain. He was presented with a Bible by the grateful passengers.

It was probably the same Sheffield, sailing from Hull, England, instead of Liverpool and under another master, which was in trouble again on February 12, 1845, in a great storm with gales and ice.

The *Journal of Commerce* reported on February 15 that she had bilged, with about ten feet of water in her hold, on Gilgo Bar, Long Island, about thirty-two miles from New York. "The vessel is lying hard on the beach, and the probability is, that she will be a total loss, with a considerable part of her cargo," the paper said. Passengers and crew were landed safely.

She was insured at Lloyd's for $18,000, with $2,000 insurance on her freight, seventy-five tons of which was linseed oil. The captain, John E. Gillespie, was half-owner of the ship.

CAPTAIN DAVIS' JOURNAL

A journal kept by Captain Daniel Davis of Mt. Sinai, Long Island, has notes on shipwrecks from 1847 to 1923. The captain is very short on dates, but his feeling for a vessel is touching. Time and again he would say something like this: "Sloop General Green died at Far Rockaway Inlet"—no date. Or, "Sloop Annie E. Leete died at Flushing under the Ministry of Capt. Stummey, 1905"; Schooner John Brooks died a natural death at Mariner's Harbor, S.I."

To Captain Davis, a ship was something human. What he meant by a

The RUSLAND, *stranded 1877*

vessel's natural death was, presumably, that she just wore out, like an old person. She did not meet her death by accident. Thus a ship driven by a howling gale onto a dangerous shore died an unnatural death. It would be natural for a well-built ship to stand up under the buffetings of fate, as a person should. But sometimes it was more than her frame would bear.

THE JOHN MINTURN

The bark John Minturn, Captain Starke, master, was wrecked on the New Jersey coast on February 14, 1856, in a terrible storm. Sixty lives were lost. A New York pilot, Thomas Freeborne, was on board. He froze to death, together with fourteen of the Minturn's crew. For some reason, ascribed at the time to politics, there was no help from the Wreck Master on shore. Pilot Freeborne gave his coat to the captain's wife, who was on board with her children. A monument was erected in Greenwood Cemetery, Brooklyn, as a testimonial to Thomas Freeborne's self-sacrifice.

THE RHINEHARD

The bark Rhinehard, inbound from Bremen, Germany, with 300 on board, anchored 500 yards off shore near Rockaway on November 16, 1866.

A bottle was thrown overboard that night with a message asking for a pilot. It stated that the vessel had anchored during a gale and that the masts had been cut away to prevent the anchor from dragging. The bottle reached shore next morning. All rigging had been carried away and furniture was floating around her when the stranded vessel was discovered.

All hands were saved.

THE W. A. HOLCOMB

The bark W. A. Holcomb of Bath, Maine, bound from Iloilo in the Philippines to New York with a cargo of sugar, went ashore at Long Beach, Long Island, on October 24, 1880. All seventeen on board were saved, including the captain's wife and child. The vessel was a total wreck; by October 26 the sea was making a clean breach over her.

She had stranded in a gale of wind at 2 A.M., three-quarters of a mile off the Long Island coast, a half mile east of U.S. Life Saving Station No. 32 (Long Beach East). The Life Saving men sent up a signal rocket. No answer, until 5 A.M. Then the Life Savers returned to the beach. The Short Beach crew, Station No. 30, tried with a new and larger boat. It was no use. Then the crew of No. 33 (Long Beach West) arrived. Finally at 8 A.M. the vessel was reached safely and all were taken off.

THE AJACE

The Italian bark Ajace of Genoa, 566 tons, Federico Morice, master, bound for New York from Antwerp, Belgium, in ballast (scrap iron and empty kerosene barrels) went to pieces on Rockaway Shoals on March 4, 1881, with a loss of thirteen lives.

The worst gale of the season had begun on March 3 along the New York and New Jersey coasts. The sea was terrific. Rain fell in torrents; fog was dense. By 7:30 A.M. on March 4, surfmen judged the wind was blowing 50 miles an hour. By 11 A.M., when the fog lifted, wreckage was strewn all along the beaches. At Coney Island, piers were torn away. One side of a hotel, bath houses, and a marine railway were wrecked. Large vessels were carried high upon the meadows from Raritan Bay.

At 9 A.M. during the height of the gale, the Rockaway Beach Life Savers sighted a bark standing directly toward the station, under close-reefed topsails, about two miles away. Suddenly the ship was hauled around to the southward and westward. She went pitching along the outer edge of Rockaway Shoals on her lee. The flood tide was then setting in. The bark sagged rapidly to leeward. She struck bottom on the point of the shoals. Her topmasts fell.

60

The Life Savers sprang for the surfboat. They could not launch it through the breakers in front of the station, so they hauled the boat half a mile to Jamaica Bay, hoping to get through the inlet. This was also impossible, for the sea was a mass of foam. They sat at their oars. Fog closed in again. They could not see the vessel. The Rockaway men hoped she had worked her way off.

The sole survivor of the fourteen on board the Italian bark was a seaman, Pietro Sala, rescued half-drowned after clinging to the ship's cabin, which had been torn from the hull and was drifting. He told a terrible story.

The shock of striking the shoal on the starboard side had demolished the Ajace's steering gear. Waves at once burst over her and began tearing her to pieces. Her crew gathered at the stern in utter despair. The captain could not restrain them.

One man held up a picture of the Madonna. They prayed to her. Suddenly the ship's carpenter drew a knife and cut his throat. Then three others slashed their necks savagely. Their bodies were washed overboard. The others gradually became exhausted. One by one they were snatched by the waves.

When the fog began to roll back, between 10 and 11 A.M., the poop deck, cabin house, and one mast were floating off Manhattan Beach, about two and a half miles from where the Ajace had struck. Captain Charles Bebensee of the Coney Island station, looking through his marine-glass, made out wreckage with a man clinging to it, feebly waving a cap. The life-saving crew gave everything they had, in the struggle to reach the seaman. It took an hour and a half to reach him where he drifted, a mile and a half out. The crowd on the beach cheered wildly as the rescue was effected.

LIFESAVING MEDAL AT SIXTEEN

The 603-ton bark Martha P. Tucker, built in 1874 at Bath, Maine, bound from Port Tampa, Fla., to Carteret, N.J., with a cargo of phosphate rock, was driven ashore about a mile west of Point Lookout Life Saving Station, south of Freeport, Long Island, on August 29, 1893. She was nineteen days out from Tampa when she was lost.

She had weathered an extraordinary gale on August 24 off Georgia. When the second storm struck after midnight of August 28, Captain George Mitchell supposed he was off Barnegat, N.J. It was blowing hard from the southward. At 3 A.M., fearing he was getting too near the New Jersey coast, he hauled off to the eastward.

The ocean shores of New Jersey and Long Island, extending southward and eastward, make two sides of a triangle, which has its apex at the mouth of the Hudson River (New York Harbor). On the western side lies Staten

Island, and across a narrow channel still further west is the port of Carteret, where the Tucker was bound.

The bark was driven much further to the leeward than had been estimated. Suddenly, early on August 29, a furious squall swept over her. The foretopsail sheets parted and the sail was torn from the bolt ropes. The sailors were scarcely aloft to bend on a new topsail when a momentary clearing showed their position. The captain ordered the men down from the yards, ordered the helm up, and beached the vessel head on. The tide was almost at flood, so the bark fetched up with her bow only about 200 yards from shore.

White-topped waves tumbled in, flooding the decks fore and aft. Seamen and officers climbed into the rigging. The rock-laden vessel weakened with the pounding of the seas. The mizzenmast, where the crew had taken refuge, swayed—a warning that it would fall before long. So all hands except one sailor, Andrew Anderson, left the shrouds and struggled forward to the bowsprit and jibboom, which were less exposed to the waves. Anderson was the only person lost.

This happened just three days before the Life Saving station at Point Lookout was to reopen. All Long Island stations were inactive in those days during the months of May, June, July, and August. Only the keeper remained on duty during the summer.

Keeper Andrew Rhodes had allowed his sixteen-year-old daughter, Jennie, to invite three young ladies from Freeport to spend the night at the station. When the wreck was discovered, about 6 A.M., Keeper Rhodes telephoned nearby stations for help and also called a watchman at the nearby Point Lookout Hotel. Four men assembled, by 8 A.M., and Riley Raynor, the boy who had first spied the vessel, helped them try to run the apparatus cart out of the boat room. It was too heavy. Just then the girls arrived. They helped push and drag the unwieldy gear as near as possible to the wreck. Finally the Lyle gun was laid on a rude platform, fired with five ounces of powder and a No. 9 line. The shot landed the line directly over the jibboom where the sailors were clinging. They seized it.

The young women who had helped haul the apparatus heartily joined in the work of pulling the breeches buoy to and from the wreck. When the third sailor had been landed, four men who had seen the stranded vessel appeared on the beach and relieved the girls, who went to the station to prepare dry garments and hot food for the survivors.

While these rescue operations were going on, a message came from the Long Beach station reporting a schooner ashore half a mile west of that place, with seven men in the rigging. It was the C. Henry Kirk, bound from New York to Virginia, riding in ballast. She had been driven well up on the beach at high water. The crew was landed safely, but that vessel and the Martha P. Tucker were a total loss.

Sixteen-year-old Jennie Rhodes received a gold lifesaving medal from the Life Saving Benevolent Association for her part in saving the eleven men from the Martha P. Tucker. The medal is now in the East Rockaway Old Grist Mill Museum.

THE JOHN E. MOORE

The John E. Moore, a steamboat, had taken 150 men on a fishing excursion on Thanksgiving Day, 1897, when the vessel ran aground in a fog on Romer Shoal. She began to fill. The passengers panicked, fighting to get into the lifeboats.

Captain Hennessey on the pilot boat Walter Adams came along. He and Captain Morrell of the Moore tried to calm the excursionists. The Walter Adams took them off. Last to leave the steamer were Captain Morrell and the mate, who played "She May Have Seen Better Days" on his accordion as the last of the rescued were taken off the John E. Moore.

The Moore was hauled off, repaired, and returned to its previous service of transferring immigrants from incoming steamers to Ellis Island.

THE ARLINGTON

The three-masted schooner Arlington of Boston left New York on August 17, 1909, with 800 tons of pea coal. She stranded in a heavy easterly gale off Long Beach, Long Island. Only the vessel's mast and the bowsprit, with the crew of nine hanging onto it for dear life, were above water when the Long Beach Life Saving crew shoved off through the surf to their rescue. They brought only eight ashore. The ninth man, the mate, had gone off on a floating hatch, with ropes tied in the hoisting rings to hold him erect. He drifted for two days, then was washed up on the beach at Asbury

The schooner ARLINGTON, *Long Beach, 1909*

Park, N.J., drowned. The U.S. Revenue Service cutter Seminole, sent out to find him, had failed because of the high seas and driving rain.

The mizzenmast and foresails of the Arlington remained hoisted for several days after the stranding. Then she went to pieces. One of the surfmen at the Life Saving station used some of the Arlington's deck planking for sills on his house at Rockville Centre.

The captain said afterward that he had been misled by the lights of the Hotel Nassau, which he took to be those of some great liner. Believing himself far from shore, he took no soundings before they stranded.

FIRST-HAND WRECK STORY

The American screw steamer Princess Anne of the Old Dominion Line left Norfolk, Va., for New York on Tuesday night, February 3, 1920, with a general cargo valued at $1,103,431. Captain Frank Seay carried a crew of seventy-four and thirty-two passengers when his ship became a total loss on Rockaway Shoals.

The Princess Anne encountered bad weather all the way up from Norfolk. By Thursday night a heavy snowstorm was raging, with a northeast gale. Pilots and steamship captains agreed afterward that it was the worst storm around New York in twenty years. Long Island Sound steamboat lines stopped all movement of their vessels from terminals. Six steamers were jammed in the ice off Larchmont, N.Y. On the south shore of Long Island, wreckage was strewn for miles. On land all roads were blocked.

Captain Seay of the Princess Anne had missed two buoys at the east entrance to Ambrose Channel, where he should have altered his course to port.

Captain George Seeth, retired New York–Sandy Hook pilot, remembers the Princess Anne well. "She was about five miles east and north from her estimated position," he says. "A pilot boat chased her, flashed a searchlight and blew his whistle; but the captain, who was a regular trader (Old Dominion Line ships were regular—you could set your clock by them) thought he knew. Paid no attention to the pilot boat's flashing and blowing. . . . As a coastal ship, he didn't have to take a pilot. But we could have put her on her course from Scotland lightship.

"The Princess Anne was loaded with cases of shoes. One case would contain just left shoes, another only right—so the crew wouldn't broach the cargo and steal."

At 2:30 A.M. on February 6, the Princess Anne was grounded on West Bar, three-quarters of a mile southwest of Rockaway Point.

Louis P. Pearsall of Oceanside, Long Island, raised around the water and a powerful oarsman, had been taken on as surfman in the U.S. Coast

Guard (illegally) before he was sixteen. He was only sixteen and a half when the Princess Anne came ashore. He says: "On the night of February 5–6 the Long Island coast was being whipped by a northeast gale with snow, sleet, and rain. A treacherous surf was boiling on the beaches. Bungalows on the ocean front at the Rockaways were being swept off their spiles and broken up by the waves.

"I was called at 2 A.M., February 6, for tower watch at the Rockaway Point Coast Guard station. About 3 A.M. came a lull in the snow and sleet. I spied from the tower window a row of white lights to the west of the station, in the vicinity of the Shoals, off Rockaway Point. I called Captain William Tooker. No distress signals had been set off by the vessel. Captain Tooker told me to call Bob Carman, an old-time surfman at the station. Bob gave a look and said, 'Whatever that vessel is, it's piling up on the shoals.'

"I was sent on the west patrol. Captain Tooker directed me to burn a Coston signal light when I arrived at the key post house. That meant the vessel had been seen, and assistance would be on the way.

"It looked impossible to reach Rockaway Point by land or sea that day. The Arverne station crew was summoned to help. My father, Arthur W. Pearsall, was in the Arverne crew, with Captain Joseph Meade. While those men were tramping the six miles to Rockaway Point, Captain Tooker had his men making ready to launch the self-righting, self-bailing power lifeboat down the ways on the bay side. The crew chopped away the ice from the ways. A big steel police patrol boat from New York Harbor tried to clear a path through the ice for the lifeboat, but it made no impression. Then Captain Meade and Captain Tooker abandoned the power boat. They decided to take the service boat, powered by oars and men, on the boat wagon to the beach. They borrowed Army mules from nearby Fort Tilden to draw it.

"The snow and ice were from four to six feet deep. In some places the lead mules sank in the snow up to their ears and had a hard time getting out again. Finally the mules balked. The crews, and a few newspapermen on the scene, hauled the boat by hand the rest of the way—two miles. We arrived close to the end of the Point late in the day.

"Captain Meade picked a boat crew from the two crews assembled. I had served under him at Arverne; I was very proud when he chose me as one of the picked crew.

"Surfmen held the boat, bow out, pushing it into the water. Captain Meade kept watching that boiling surf. Then he roared, 'Give Way Together!' We started, with him at the steering oar. But we were rebuffed, and back on the beach again. Only his good management kept us from being upset broadside to the surf. We made two more tries, equally unsuccessful.

"At 9 P.M. attempts to get near the steamship were abandoned. It was snowing heavily. The steamer was hard aground by the ebb tide, well off-

The PRINCESS ANNE, *Far Rockaway, 1920*

shore, so using the breeches buoy was out of the question. She was headed north and south, with a slight list to starboard. By that time her wireless was cut off. She lay in thirteen feet of water.

"Captain Meade said that the Princess Anne, aside from having no lights, little water, and little food, was in no immediate danger because the wind had changed from northeast to northwest. Her No. 3 hold was full of water from the pounding, but the bulkheads were holding and the sea was going down. Sandy Hook could be summoned with its power lifeboat if the vessel showed signs of breaking up.

"Captain Meade left me to stay on watch, at a Rockaway beach bungalow, in case the stranded vessel showed a distress signal. At 5 A.M. the lifeboat was again hauled to the edge of the surf. We took to our oars and were soon past the danger point. The surf had calmed somewhat. A New York City police launch took us in tow. We made several trips, taking off passengers. The Coast Guard cutter Manhattan was anchored close by. The Princess Anne's crew stayed aboard."

A *New York Times* story of Tuesday, February 10, 1920, tells of trouble with the crew. They refused to go without their luggage, which the Coast Guard boats could not manage. The surfboat was loaded down to its self-bailing deck as it was.

Captain Frank Seay, who had been injured on the way north (a broken leg), had been taken ashore on Saturday. On Sunday night at 10:30, when the ship's plates began to snap with a noise like machine-gun fire, the crew panicked. The first officer had to draw his pistol to quiet them. The plates kept snapping until midnight. Then there was a two-foot break across the vessel, just forward of the engine room. The entire ship was flooded below the main deck.

At daybreak the ship's flag was displayed, upside down, for immediate assistance. The Rockaway Point crew went out. The crewmen were still

66

balky. A wireless was sent to the New York police patrol. It was after 9 A.M. on Monday when Captain George Carman, with a power sloop, finally got them off.

That day the Princess Anne broke in two amidships. The forward cargo mast and the stern rudder head remained above water for many years after the superstructure had been destroyed by the seas on Rockaway Shoals.

THE JOSEPH CONRAD

Alan Villiers, Australian-born author, British Navy commander in World War II, and master sailor, bought the full-rigged, 100-foot ship Georg Stage in 1934 in Copenhagen, where she had been built in 1882. She had been used to train eighty Danish cadets annually on cruises about the Baltic and the North Sea. The new owner rechristened her the Joseph Conrad. She sailed from Copenhagen on September 3 on her first deep-water voyage. Thirty-two were aboard, eight of whom were cadets.

On January 2, 1935, having sailed 6,766 miles, she was in New York Harbor when her anchor chain snapped during a squall. She drifted across the harbor and smashed on the rocks at Bay Ridge, Brooklyn. She was badly holed. Merritt-Chapman & Scott refloated her. After a spell in dry dock she came out in good shape for her longest voyage: She sailed January 31 on her way around the world.

On October 16, 1936, she was back in New York. She had been at sea for 555 days, covering 57,800 miles. On August 4, 1947, she passed through the Narrows, astern of the tug Christine Moran. The next day she was berthed at Mystic, Conn., alongside the whaler Charles W. Morgan, as part of the Marine Historical Association. She is used as a base for Sea Scouts and Girl Mariners taking courses in maritime subjects.

IT STILL HAPPENS

Once upon a time a vessel going on a sandbar in a storm was almost certainly doomed. That is no longer true, and strandings seldom occur. Most maritime disasters nowadays are caused by collision or fire. But wind and weather can still make trouble for big, powerful ships.

The 634-foot-long British "baby supertanker" Chelwood Beacon ran aground on the morning of January 23, 1966, at the lower entrance to New York Harbor—two miles east of Sandy Hook Lighthouse—in a sleet storm with an eighteen-knot wind. Her captain, Peter Jones, reported that the ship was in danger of breaking up in waves from fifteen to twenty-five feet high. There was a crack in the hull, the rudder post was unusable, and he was afraid the vessel might break in two.

She carried 30,000 tons of crude oil from Punta Cardon, Venezuela, and was headed for Perth Amboy, N.J., at the entrance to Arthur Kill. With a draft of just under thirty-four feet when fully loaded, it was essential for her to remain in the deep-water Sandy Hook Channel and Raritan Bay Channel to her destination. But somehow, with the poor visibility, she had strayed into water only twenty-four feet deep—onto a treacherous shoal known to mariners as False Hook.

The Coast Guard closed Sandy Hook Channel temporarily because of the stranded ship. (The channel's main use is for tankers headed for Perth Amboy and other oil ports on the Arthur Kill.)

While a Coast Guard cutter constantly circled the stricken tanker in a wide arc to break the crashing of the waves, two boats of the New York–Sandy Hook Harbor Pilots' Association maneuvered close enough to the tanker to take off the first thirty-nine crew members shortly after 7 P.M. on January 23. They scrambled down rope ladders and leaped to the boats below.

Captain Jones, Harbor Pilot C. J. Keating, and eleven other men remained on board until 8 A.M. January 24, when the tanker's master decided that the risk of losing lives was too great to warrant keeping anyone on board. The Coast Guard cutter Yeaton arrived at the Battery the next day with the last thirteen survivors, who had served twenty-three straight hours of emergency duty.

Three salvage vessels, a Merritt-Chapman & Scott salvage craft and two Moran Towing and Transportation Company tugs—with a combined horsepower totaling 8,700—failed to move the Chelwood Beacon on February 17. She was hauled off eventually, but it was a tough job.

THE MARY A. WHALEN

The 167-foot coastal tanker Mary A. Whalen, diesel powered, launched in 1938, went aground at 10 P.M. on December 23, 1968, at the breakwater off Rockaway Point in Queens, Long Island. She was going from Bayonne, N.J., to Island Park, between Long Beach and Oceanside in Nassau County, with a cargo of 150,000 gallons of oil and a crew of seven. There was a high wind, and ice. Oil began to seep out. She sat there for two days.

On December 25, Coast Guard helicopter HH-52 got a small line from the tug Cathleen Moran onto the tanker. Then the crewmen were able to haul a ten-inch hawser from the tug. But when the tugs tried to pull the tanker off the sandbar, the towlines snapped. However, they promised—and did—get her off on December 26, so the crew, still on board, "had a real good Christmas."

6

THEY BLEW UP,
OR WERE
DEVOURED

On Saturday, May 15, 1824, the steamboat Aetna
of the Citizens' Line, 125 tons burden, built in Philadelphia in 1816, was on
her way from Washington, N.J., with passengers from Philadelphia. She was
under the command of Captain Thomas Robinson.

At 7 P.M. the Aetna came abreast of Gibbet Island (now Ellis Island),
within sight of the city, when her boiler flue collapsed. There was a tremendous explosion. Of the thirty-seven on board, thirteen were killed instantly
—some in the cabin. Some jumped overboard; others were scalded and died
later of their injuries. Only a few escaped unscathed. Two boats from the
Quarantine Station came to the Aetna's aid, as well as a passing steamboat,
the United States, which towed the wrecked vessel to a New York pier.

Newspapers of the time reported that this disaster "caused more gloom
in New York than the late lamented Albion." (The Albion packet had
sailed from New York on April 1, 1822, and was lost on April 22 off Ireland, with all hands.)

The Aetna catastrophe was one of six fatal accidents due to boiler
explosions that occurred in New York in 1824 and 1825. In the early days of
steam this was a common occurrence. More steam boilers blew up than
ran, in spite of the fact that they carried a pressure of not much over thirty
pounds. According to modern engineering officers, "Considering that early
steamships used saltwater, in square-shaped boilers with no safety devices,

it's a wonder they didn't all blow up."

The use of saltwater, even in those far-off days, seems almost incredible. Yet in his *Steamboat Days* (1925), Fred Erving Dayton says of transatlantic steamers of the Collins Line, built 1849–1850: "Using saltwater, scale in tubes became troublesome and the unequal expansion of the front and back tubes caused them to leak, with heavy expense for cleaning and repair. . . ." Howard I. Chapelle of the Smithsonian Institution says: "Yes, the early oceangoing steamers used saltwater in their boilers, and they had to stop, drain boilers, and chip scale out of them . . . they also blew up very handsomely."

FULTON THE FIRST

Fulton Street and the old Fulton Fish Market in New York, Fulton Street in Brooklyn, and many vessels have been named after Robert Fulton, whose fame rests on the fact that his Clermont ("Fulton's Folly"), which traveled from New York to Albany in 1807, was the first practical steamboat to be floated in America.

The first United States naval steamship was originally named the Demologes. The 2,475-ton ship was launched at New York on October 29, 1814, but was not ready for sea until late in February, 1815. That was after the death of Robert Fulton and the end of the War of 1812. The frigate was immediately renamed Fulton the First.

The public had flocked to the launching of the "queer looking craft," but her captain and crew were unenthusiastic. There were no skilled mechanics to handle her engines properly. Until June 4, 1829, she was kept at the Brooklyn Navy Yard to receive and train sailors. On that day she blew up and became a complete wreck.

The Fulton was moored 200 yards from shore. After the explosion, fragments of the frigate floated down on the shoals in front of Manhattan. People rowed around in hundreds of small boats, picking up the bits.

This catastrophe, which killed thirty-three, including three women, with an estimated twenty-nine wounded, was not due to a faulty boiler. It was caused either by carelessness or revenge on the part of a gunner's mate, who died. It seems that there were barrels of gunpowder on board, used to fire the morning and evening gun. A story circulated at the time was that the gunner had been flogged that morning and had "thus made an end to his own and everybody else's miseries."

Fulton and other pioneers in steam of his time, notably Colonel John Stevens of Hoboken, N.J., endured first apathy, then ridicule. "A crackpot invention" was the opinion of many. But Fulton persisted stubbornly and with his future father-in-law, Robert B. Livingston, obtained a monopoly for

FULTON THE FIRST, *launched 1814, blown up in 1829*

inland and coastal waters, which included the Hudson River and Long
Island Sound. They soon had a busy fleet. Colonel Stevens' inventor son,
Robert L. Stevens, had to take their Phoenix, launched shortly after the
Clermont, from New York to Philadelphia on the open sea. A little "steam
kettle" it was called by the unbelievers. Fulton's steamboats had paddle
wheels; the Stevens vessel was a screw propeller.

The Fulton steamboats on the Hudson soon aroused jealousy. They
were rammed by other craft, as often as the latter could get away with it.
That danger was in addition to the frequent boiler trouble. Soon some of the
riverboats were built with boilers hung outside, over the water, so that passengers would not be injured if an explosion occurred.

In 1826 the "safety barge" was invented, to please passengers who
feared a boiler explosion. These barges were built to look like steamboats, but
without power. They were fitted out luxuriously for that time and were
capacious. An early one on the Hudson could accommodate 180 persons in
the dining cabin (which was also the gentlemen's sleeping quarters; the
ladies' staterooms were above). The safety barge was towed by a powerful
steamboat, and the two vessels were connected by timbers six feet long. Advertisements pointed out that on the safety barge there would be no danger

71

whatever: no noise of machinery, no vibrations of the boat, no heat from engines, nothing unpleasant. But the passage was slow.

Pine wood was the usual fuel for early steamboats. Fearsome flames leaped from the tall stacks. At first there was a prejudice against coal, although it was much less bulky than wood. Coal did not come into common use on steamboats until about 1845.

Samuel E. Newton of Cedarhurst, Long Island, born in 1886 of a seafaring family, related a few years ago what happened to a relative of his, Captain David Havens, in the 1840's. Captain Havens owned a tugboat. He was towing a ship through Hell Gate when the tug's boiler blew up, to the height of the masts of the ship being towed alongside. The captain and his pilothouse went up sixty feet. He lived four hours. The pilothouse and wheel lay up on the rocks at Hell Gate for several years.

By 1838 the Federal government had become concerned about steamboat fatalities. Legislation was passed establishing inspectors of hulls and boilers at the chief American ports. However, these inspections proved very casual and superficial. It was not until August 30, 1852, that pilots and engineers had to be licensed.

The accidents continued.

RACING RIVERBOATS

There was great rivalry among the Hudson River captains. Owners cut fares to promote trade, and advertised speed. There was much betting. Only a few of the cautious realized the danger from overstrained boilers.

The Day Line steamer Reindeer, 790 tons, on the New York–Albany run, had outraced the Henry Clay on July 1, 1851, making the trip in seven hours, forty-four minutes, with six landings. Then on September 3, 1852, the Reindeer exploded and burned at Saugerties. Six persons were killed outright, and twenty-five later died of injuries.

The side-wheel steamer Henry Clay, largest merchantman of her time, built in 1845, which had lost the race with the Reindeer the year before, met a tragic end some five weeks before the Reindeer disaster.

On July 28, 1852, the Henry Clay, on its way to New York from Albany, was racing with the Armenia. All day long Captain Tallman of the Henry Clay had kept his vessel neck and neck with his rival. As they reached the lower river the Henry Clay forged ahead. Suddenly fire was discovered— the excessive heat of the boilers or the stacks had ignited the woodwork. The captain headed the Henry Clay for shore at Riverdale (a part of the Bronx) and ran her hard aground. But the passengers were mostly huddled in the stern, where the water was deep. Imprisoned there by the flames amidships, they panicked and fought for life preservers. Sixty died, including many prominent New Yorkers. Seven men were indicted for manslaughter in connection with that disaster. The subsequent widespread indignation sparked legislation in 1852 for a more stringent inspection and rules for steam vessels.

On October 29, 1863, the brand-new luxury side-wheel steamer St. John, of the People's Line, on the night run from New York to Albany, had a boiler explosion in which fifteen persons died. But she continued on the Hudson for fifteen years after that, until she was finally destroyed by fire at her winter quarters at the foot of Canal Street in New York City. The St. John was called a "floating palace." She was 420 feet long, of 51-foot beam, the largest steamboat in the world at the time except the Great Eastern.

On December 5, 1863, the Isaac Newton, Captain W. H. Peck, master, bound up-river, exploded and burned to the water's edge opposite Fort Lee, N.J. Nine died; seventeen were scalded. She was a fine ship—405 feet long with 48-foot beam, 1,540 tons, splendidly furnished.

THE WESTFIELD DISASTER

The most appalling and spectacular explosion of a vessel in the New York area occurred at 1:30 P.M. on Sunday, July 30, 1871, at the foot of Whitehall Street in Manhattan. One hundred and four lives were lost; scores of injured were hospitalized.

The Staten Island ferry Westfield lay in her slip ready to start. The captain was at his post. The engineer was on his way to the engine room. Crewmen were standing ready to unhook the chains and cast off. "Over four hundred souls were on board," *Harper's Weekly* reported on August 12, 1871, "lured by the delightful weather from their crowded homes to breathe the pure sea air and enjoy the grass and shade of the uncontaminated country.

"Suddenly there came a terrible crash, and in an instant the steamer was a wreck. The huge boiler had exploded. Those who witnessed the disaster say that there was first a dull, crunching sound somewhat like that made by the fall of a large building, followed immediately by the sharp hiss of escaping steam.

"The main deck was forced upward for a considerable distance; the beam and planks were torn into fragments. . . . The pilothouse was hurled into the air to a great height, and, falling back upon the hurricane deck, was shattered to pieces. . . . The heavy smokestack was also blown high in the air, and fell into the general wreck. Escaping steam filled the boat and many were scalded who would otherwise have escaped unhurt. . . ."

Two Battery boatmen, Mike Quigley and Pat Collins, were heroes in that disaster. They hauled in over seventy-five people from the water and from the vessel.

The cause of the explosion was not immediately ascertained. The United States inspector of boilers had examined the Westfield's boiler only two months before, pronouncing it safe. The engineer was considered capable and trustworthy. A fragment of the boiler picked up on deck was thought to be of unsound iron. The Treasury Department ordered an investigation with a "jury of businessmen and practical mechanics who will render a verdict and place the blame were it belongs."

The explosion was eventually laid to "low water and boiler not in fit condition to run." Jacob Vanderbilt and Henry Robinson were indicted and, on September 16, 1871, pleaded not guilty. Evidently an insurance settlement was made. There is no record of further legal development.

TIMES HAVE CHANGED

The Steamboat Inspection Service was honeycombed with politics from its inception in 1838 until drastic reforms were made in 1903. Gradually boiler and engine construction improved. Wood as fuel for ships was succeeded by coal. Steam was succeeded by turbine and diesel; now, to a limited extent, atomic power is being used. Engines seldom blow up of their own accord anymore. But the incidence of explosions aboard ships carrying oil or other inflammables, due to collision or fire, is very great and very hazardous in a crowded port such as New York.

SALLY AND THE SEA SERPENT

There is something about the sea that gives rise to fancies and superstitions, even among the most intelligent or the most earthbound. There are very few people who do not harbor some small private superstition, and the vastness of an ocean seems to make a tall story grow taller. One of the stories that crops up perennially is about the sea serpent.

An authority on underwater exploration was quoted not long ago as saying: "In the depths of the sea, there may still be gigantic creatures of which we have no knowledge; and, with this possibility, remote though it may be, in the background, it is unwise to deny the existence of sea serpents."

A drawing of a sea serpent attacking a vessel off the coast of Long Island in 1819 was published in Paris that year. The caption, translated, reads: "View of the American schooner ["goelette" was the French word] the Sally, at the moment when she is being attacked by a SEA SERPENT off the coast of Long Island (United States) the 17th of December, 1819."

Whatever became of Sally? Her chances look pretty slim in the French

SALLY *and the Sea Serpent, 1819*

drawing, with the horrid monster rearing up, its jaws open wide enough to swallow the schooner, fangs bared, its body much longer than the little boat.

The following is a true story of a schooner named Sally, wrecked off Long Island. The dates do not correspond, but it is just possible that the two stories are connected.

On September 18, 1810, the schooner Sally, Captain Ebenezer White, master, bound from New London, Conn., for Barbados with a cargo of horses, was found on her beam ends, no one on board, west of Southampton, Long Island, by the sloop Orpha, from St. Bartholemew's for Nantucket. The Sally's captain, mate, and one seaman were lost. Four of the crew had been saved from the wreck by the sloop Lady Washington, bound from New London for Norfolk. No further details of that wreck were available.

Sea serpents were reported fairly often in the 19th century. One such monster aroused New England two years before the alleged peril of the Sally. Its story is told in a small, well-worn, leather-covered book printed in New York in 1819. The book is titled *A Dictionary of the Most Uncommon Wonders of the Works of Art and Nature; particularly of those which are most remarkable in America.* It was compiled by James Hardie, A.M. There is a long chapter on the sea serpent.

Perils of the Port of New York

In a preface the author says: "The existence of the Sea Serpent has been doubted by some. Its repeated appearance is now, however, so established by the concurring testimony of hundreds of respectable witnesses as to put even scepticism itself at defiance." An 1817 appearance of a sea serpent is described.

On August 18, 1817, the Linnaean Society of Boston formed a committee to collect evidence after a monster had been seen in and near Gloucester Harbor. It was reportedly seen there from August 10 to 23; then headed south on August 28; and in Long Island Sound from October 3 to 5.

It was described as like an enormous snake, black or dark brown, about three feet in diameter, and tapering somewhat at both ends. The length was reported as from 70 to 120 feet. It undulated as it moved, and its head was reported snakelike, with a long tongue. One person saw a bright eye.

Boats were fitted out from Cape Ann with harpoons, and whalers hunted the animal. One crew from Boston searched for two or three days without luck, and finally brought in a great "horse mackerel"—today's tuna. They tried to pass it off as a sea serpent, and charged admission.

Again in 1819 a sea serpent was reported off Nahant, Mass. Perhaps

The steamer PETREL *exploding in North River, 1858*

Ferry WESTFIELD *after explosion, 1871*

that was the one that attacked the Sally. In 1826 another was said to be off Nantucket. Others were sighted in the Atlantic in 1827 and 1833, and ten more were reported between 1848 and 1877. On July 28, 1860, the New York *Illustrated News* carried a drawing of a bark at sea, with an enormous serpent—longer than the vessel—alongside. The caption read: "Another appearance of the sea serpent. Its attack on the bark British Banner. From a sketch furnished by the captain of the bark, Mr. W. Thomas."

A few years ago a group of young Coast Guardsmen at the headquarters of the Third District, U.S. Coast Guard, on Governor's Island, N.Y., were asked: "Can you think of any pet superstitions of Coast Guardsmen today?" They could, and did. But on the subject of sea serpents one young man said, "Flying saucers took the place of sea serpents, for our generation."

Speaking of scoffers at superstitions, Hendrik Van Loon said, in his *Ships*: "Try spending a few nights in an open boat under a starry sky!"

7

TUGS, TOWS, AND SALVAGE VESSELS

SHE struck a rock in Hell Gate; hole in bottom; hauled off. Tugs towed her to pier." Or: "Disabled; arrived in New York in tow of tugs; cargo got off." Such notes, when New York newspapers ran more shipping news, would give the name of the ship and the time and place of the casualty. But generally the hard-working, indispensable tugs that refloated vessels (or tried their best to do so) and the wrecking company that salvaged cargoes remained anonymous—unless they themselves got into trouble.

The early tugs were side-wheelers, steam-powered wooden vessels until the 1930's when steel-hulled diesels came into use.

The first commercial tug in New York Harbor was the 146-ton Staten Island ferryboat, the steamer Nautilus, built in 1817. On January 26, 1818, she was tied up after her regular ferry run. She saw the sailing ship Corsair, inbound from Charleston, S.C., in difficulty a mile below the Narrows. The Nautilus got up steam, went out and offered her help, and towed the Corsair into Quarantine dock.

The opening of the Erie Canal in 1825 gave great impetus to the towing industry. The steamer Henry Eckford, 153 tons, was built that year to tow grain barges from the West through the canal and down the Hudson. (She exploded in New York on April 27, 1841, with one man lost.)

Captain Curtis Peck began operating towboats in the East River and Long Island Sound in the early 1820's.

In 1828 the Rufus W. King began its long career as the first regular tugboat in New York Harbor. The King would transport passengers from the Battery to ships anchored in the Lower Bay before departure for Europe. Ship reporters for the newspapers went out on her. She sometimes towed sailing ships out to Sandy Hook Lightship.

By the 1880's steam tugs were used regularly to bring in sailing ships from Sandy Hook. Nowadays a team of tugs will always nose a great ship in and out of her berth. (Well, not always. The long tugboat workers' strike which began on Feb. 1, 1970, caused captains of great liners to dock their own ships unaided, "with a dazzling display of seamanship," so the newspapers commented.)

A New York *Herald Tribune* writer said in 1963: "Call them tugs or tows, there are 430 of them chuffing around New York Harbor at present, docking and undocking liners and freighters, or towing bunker barges full of oil, scows full of anything from slag to garbage, or dumpers full of mud. Roughly eighty of them are the property of railroad companies, and lug behind them as many as sixty railroad cars on special carfloats. Some 5,000 men work on the tugs.

"Nearly all the tugs in New York that aren't railroad-owned are in the possession of large commercial companies; only about a dozen are left that are the property of individuals or of very small companies—a holdover from the 1800's when nearly all tugs were owner-operated, and competition for incoming boats' patronage was clamorous or even violent."

In the last ten years the number of tugs in the harbor has dropped sharply. Two hundred would be a likely figure today. There are fewer passenger sailings; bigger general cargo ships and tankers have also cut into the market for tug services.

The Moran and McAllister fleets are now the largest. In November, 1850, Michael Moran, a seventeen-year-old boy only a month in this country from Ireland, got his first job—on the Erie Canal. By 1855, on his twenty-second birthday, he had saved up enough to buy a canal boat. Soon he owned another. In 1860 he joined his younger brother, Richard, in New York, and the Moran Towing and Transportation business was born. Nowadays the prolific Moran family has names enough for all its tugs.

McAllister Brothers, Inc., was started in 1864 by Captain James McAllister, with a single sail-driven lighter. Some time ago McAllister bought out the Russell Towing Company and Dalzell. Today the company operates on all coasts of this country and on the Great Lakes.

Fifty or sixty years ago there were some twenty tug companies operating in and around the Port of New York. Now there are only two major companies docking and undocking ships—Moran and McAllister. Pushing and pulling an enormous liner, stopping and starting at her bow and stern, is a risky job. A tugboat crewman must put in at least three years of duty before he can sit for the Coast Guard examination and get his captain's license; he must have some twenty-five years of harbor experience before he is ready to dock a big passenger liner.

The Red Star Towing and Transportation Company was started in 1897 by tugboat captain Sam Sanders. His grandson, Robert Sanders, is now its president. The company, which has a dozen tugboats and a fleet of Sound and Harbor coal barges and sand scows, does general towing. Its services include docking and undocking merchant, passenger, Army, and Navy ships.

M. & J. Tracy is another New York Harbor towing company. It has a small fleet of tugs and a large fleet of coal barges and some oceangoing coal carriers.

THE DOCKING PILOT

Captain Joseph Sweeney, retired Red Star tugboat captain, explains that the docking, or riding, pilot who takes over when the Sandy Hook pilot has brought a ship within a mile or so downstream of its pier is also a tugboat captain. "Red Star," he says, "has two captains that work out of the office. The company also has a couple of captains who dock ships with the tugs Newport and Norwalk. These are what we call 'day boats'; overtime is paid when the tug is out after eight hours. They carry a captain and a licensed deck mate, so when the tug captain goes aboard a ship, the licensed mate takes over the tug.

"The men working out of the office get a regular captain's wage, plus what they call 'pilot money' for docking the ships. They are on call to go to work at any time, day or night. They make good money.

"Moran Towing and McAllister Brothers Towing Company have about eight men who make even more. This money is pooled in each company. The oldest captain in the pool gets what they call a full share, then, according to length of service in the company, a man gets a three-quarters, half, or quarter share. It is possible for the man with the quarter share to dock more ships than the older men.

"The docking pilot today tells on a shortwave radio what he wants each tug to do. We answer him with the tug whistle or walkie-talkie radio."

Captain Sweeney has described the system of signals given by the docking pilot and the tug's reply. Years ago, they used only a small mouth whistle.

"The docking, or riding, pilot who eases a vessel into or out of her

Tug M. MORAN *on a rescue mission*

berth takes complete charge on the bridge, just as the Sandy Hook pilot does when she is out in the stream. He knows local conditions, and the insurance companies want him there. However, the captain of the ship remains responsible at all times. He can override the pilot at any time he thinks it necessary."

SALVAGE

On January 30, 1870, the ferry Union, running from Manhattan to Hoboken, N.J., was given a deep gash on her port side below the waterline by an oceangoing tug. The Union had been crunching through ice floes on a routine trip, heavily loaded with passengers, horses, and wagons. The ferry reeled and began to capsize.

Captain Thomas A. Scott, who had taken on the job of salvaging the wrecked Scotland in 1869, was on the deck of his wrecking tug Reliance, only 200 yards away, when the Union was struck. He scrambled to the pilot-house and ran the Reliance's nose along the ferry rail. He jumped to the Union's deck and ordered her terrified passengers to the starboard side. The ferry slowly righted herself.

Working furiously, Captain Scott stuffed the gaping hole with blankets and clothing. Waiting for more to be gathered up, he forced his own body into the hole. Ice, smashing into the hull, pinned his right arm to the planking and ripped it open from shoulder to wrist.

An hour later the Union was safe in her slip, her passengers ashore. Captain Scott was half-conscious, in shock from loss of blood and immersion in icy water. It was a month before he could go back to work. He received a check for $100 for his clothing and broken ribs.

Two years later F. Hopkinson Smith, New England artist and writer who was also a lighthouse builder, won the contract to build a lighthouse on a reef west of Fisher's Island on Long Island Sound. He hired Scott, who had established the T. A. Scott Company in New London, as construction foreman.

"Race Rock Lighthouse was a project for the brave," a *New York Times* writer said in 1960 when the Merritt-Chapman & Scott Corporation celebrated its 100th anniversary.

Captain Israel J. Merritt, who had been in salvage since 1835, organized the Coast Wrecking Company in 1860. He had received a gold medal from the Life Saving Benevolent Association in 1856 for the midwinter rescue of an entire ship's crew on Barnegat Shoals. Three years later he was awarded $500 in gold for saving the sixty-five-man crew of the Black Warrior off Rockaway, N.Y.

William E. Chapman went into the lighterage business as the Chapman Derrick and Wrecking Company of Brooklyn in 1881, after some twenty years of routine chores around New York Harbor. His salvage tugs often "crossed the bow" of Merritt tugs. On January 25, 1896, the two companies went to court after an altercation about the American liner St. Paul. She was a famous ocean greyhound that had gone ashore in a fog at Long Branch, N.J. (Racing, it was said, with the Cunarder Campania.)

The insurance people decided the salvage job should be shared between the two contenders. They floated the St. Paul on February 4. In 1897 the two businesses consolidated as the Merritt-Chapman Derrick & Wrecking Company. (The 13,000-ton St. Paul, and her sister ship the St. Louis, were the only American major passenger ships built between the Civil War and World War I.)

On April 25, 1918, the St. Paul, which had brought the two wrecking companies together, was in trouble again. She was being berthed at Piers 60 and 61, North River, when she suddenly heeled to port and settled on her side in fifty-four feet of water. Three lives were lost. She was floated clear by Merritt-Chapman on September 11.

In 1922 Merritt-Chapman and T. A. Scott merged as the Merritt-Chapman & Scott Corporation. In 1968 Merritt-Chapman & Scott's Derrick and Inland Salvage Division was sold to Raymond International of New York.

THE RESOLUTE AND THE JACOB BELL

The Resolute, a side-wheeler, was one of the first screw-propelled tugboats. One morning in 1850 she was moored at the foot of Wall Street. All hands were seated at breakfast, in the cabin abaft the boiler—when it blew up. All were killed.

The Jacob Bell was another early tugboat, kept busy with all kinds of work. She was still new when she was hired for $150 to take a party to Hart's Island for a prizefight. The owners, Dackerty & Sons, had made their money in the slave trade; otherwise they were very straitlaced. They did not approve of the prizefight trip.

A day or two after that charter, the Jacob Bell was taking a New York Methodist Church group up the Hudson for a camp meeting at Sing Sing. The church people and the owners, who were on board, took the captain to task. There was a great row, with pistol shots. Just off the Palisades, above Fort Lee, the pilot left his wheel for a moment to see what was going on. The captain, in a rage, came up and took the wheel. He ran the Jacob Bell aground, smashing the engine and crushing her bottom. She was a complete wreck.

THE COAL BARGES

Someone has said, "The bottom of Long Island Sound from Execution to New London is paved with coal"—from the coal schooners and barges that have gone down there.

When coal first took the place of wood for domestic and business use, it was carried from the mid-Atlantic mine ports to industrial New England on sailing craft. *The Great Coal Schooners of New England: 1870–1909*, written by Lieutenant W. J. Lewis Parker, USCG, published in 1948, tells that story.

By 1908, tow barges had generally superseded the schooners in the coal-carrying trade. By the 1920's coal was going by steamer or rail, and fuel oil was fast taking its place.

The *Vineyard Gazette* of Martha's Vineyard, Mass., ran a long article in 1963 headed "Tugboats, Barges Were Once Great Coal Carriers of Coast." It told how, in 1908, a great battle over the tow barges was being fought in Congress. Oscar S. Straus, then Secretary of Commerce and Labor, told the legislature that the tow barges were "the most dangerous form of navigation along our seaboard."

Each tug pulled four to six barges through Long Island Sound, totaling 3,000 tons of coal apiece, dropping them along the way to Boston or to Portland, Maine. Returning, the tugs picked up long strings of empty barges. Until 1908 there was no limit to the number of barges strung out behind a tug. There was no legal limit to the length of towing hawsers. Sometimes a tug and tow would stretch out for two-thirds of a nautical mile.

A *Harper's Monthly* magazine article in 1909 described the traffic and some of its dangers: "With a tow stretching half a mile or more and a snap-the-whip effect on the last in line, it is no easy matter making the sharp turns necessary in threading one's way across troubled waters. . . . No wonder they are gray, these quiet, alert men who handle so dexterously their tugs and heavy charges strung out precariously astern. . . ."

By 1908, so the *Vineyard Gazette* said, there were between 400 and 450 seagoing barges of 100 gross tons. (Presumably the writer meant along the northeast coast.) "They carried some 1,200 men—an average of three to a barge. . . . Necessarily, tugs of the most powerful description were built to tow these barges. . . . The W. E. Luckenbach was a good example of these high-seas tugs. She was 154 feet long, measured 454 gross tons, and had engines of 1,100 horsepower. . . ."

Coal barges, at that, were safer in some ways than the present-day barges that carry oil. On December 28, 1968, the Esso 31, a 2,400-ton barge, caught fire off Quarantine Station in Rosebank, Staten Island, as it lay alongside a tanker unloading crude oil. It burned for an hour. The tug Dalzellera nosed it away to the main channel. Other tugs, the Coast Guard, and city fireboats aided. Captain David Cloughsey of the barge was burned. Esso Uruguay, carrying 50,000 tons of crude oil from Venezuela, moved away.

TUGS IN TROUBLE

Five out of a tow of six boats that left New York on Janaury 20, 1881, for South Amboy, N.J., went down off Sandy Hook two days later. One in the tow reached Raritan Bay. Two men were missing from the towboat Heath and two each from the Gardner and the G. Brothers.

The speedy Moran tug F. W. Vosburgh was in trouble in 1895. She was much in demand to carry reporters to scenes of New York Harbor disasters, and could outstrip competitors racing to the outer harbor for business. She was 100 feet long, built in Nova Scotia. Dick Moran, at the age of nineteen, became her captain in 1888. There was a great row with the Harbor Pilots' Association because a licensed pilot was supposed to be twenty-one. The youth proved his qualifications. He died in 1894.

The Vosburgh was bound from New York for Sandy Hook on March 12, 1895, when she struck Romer Shoals in a thick northeast snowstorm. Her captain, Frank Butler, and the six-man crew were rescued by men from the Sandy Hook Life Saving station.

The Red Star tug Devon, Captain Russell Holland, master, collided in Hell Gate channel on August 30, 1960, with the tanker Craig Reinauer. The tug had been going to the aid of a small tank vessel, the Helen Miller, which was in a dangerous position. The Devon's steering gear failed, leaving her drifting in the tide. Captain Holland made a sharp starboard turn, backing across the path of the Craig Reinauer. The ebb tide carried him into the tanker. The Devon sank near Hallett's Point and lay on her side off the beach. She was raised and is running today.

The Russell No. 18, a 75-foot diesel tug, turned turtle in the new Elizabeth Port channel on September 18, 1962, after pulling a freighter away from its berth. Captain Frank Fargo and two crew members drowned. The tug was raised the next day. The U.S. Coast Guard oceangoing tug Tamaroa, 205 feet long, the only one in the Third Coast Guard District, was in drydock with her shaft out for her annual overhaul on March 14, 1963, when she developed a 55 to 60 percent list to port. She slid down halfway under water, sinking aft, her bow remaining on the dock. Her bottom was holed. Repairs were estimated at $1 million. Forty crewmen escaped. A young boatswain was court-martialed, charged with opening valves of the floating drydock.

The 108-foot tug Patricia Moran went down in less than three minutes after a collision with the 225-foot tanker Morania Marlin on January 12, 1966, in Kill Van Kull, between Staten Island and Bayonne, N.J. The tug listed and heeled over after the impact. The tanker, in turn, was struck by a 200-foot barge being towed by the 105-foot tug Diana L. Moran. The tanker suffered bow damage. Four men were lost and six saved from the Patricia Moran.

At the Coast Guard investigation there were conflicting testimonies. Captain Camille Terreault, master of the tanker, said it was not his craft but the barge that sank the Patricia after running over her stern, while the Marlin and the Patricia were still stuck together. Another witness said the barge struck the tanker but never came in contact with the Patricia.

George Hermann, consultant and troubleshooter for the Red Star Line, recalls the sinking of the Red Star tug Ocean Queen on March 12, 1969. The 94-foot tug, towing the barge Bouchard No. 110 with 20,000 barrels of petroleum, was going up the East River. The 572-foot tanker Four Lakes, of Texas City Refining Company, was going south. It was 3:30 on a sun-shiny afternoon when the Four Lakes rammed the Ocean Queen, just below Hell Gate off East 90th Street.

Captain Joseph Meier, forty-nine, who was steering the Ocean Queen at the time of the collision, went into the water and was never seen again. Four men were rescued. The barge did not sink.

The cook, Richard Hessen, survived his second sinking in Hell Gate. He had been on the Red Star tug Flushing on September 7, 1963, when she sank in almost the same spot, drowning four. Another survivor of the Flushing disaster, Robert Robinson, nearby on the tug Newport on March 12, 1969, looked at the expanse of water spreading around Ward's Island and said: "Here's where the entire Atlantic Ocean is trying to go up and the entire Long Island Sound is trying to go down."

ERRANDS OF MERCY

Two tugs, chartered to take provisions to the steamer Cavour, stranded at Long Beach, Long Island, foundered on February 2, 1902, about eleven miles east of Sandy Hook Lightship, in a northwest gale and an ugly sea. The E. S. Atwood, Captain Richard Wray, and the John E. Berwind, Captain Kerns, each had a crew of seven men. They were rescued by the German steamer Barcelona from Hamburg.

The Cavour was a Lamport & Holt Line steamer of Liverpool, 410 feet long, 3,151 tons. She was headed for New York from Buenos Aires with a cargo of coffee, raw hides, wool, and tallow. She had grounded in a snowstorm on January 31. By February 2, provisions were running low. The captain said he had lost his bearings; had mistaken the Life Savers' warning lights for the lights off Sandy Hook. He had three passengers and a crew of forty on board. The Life Savers had gone off to her, but got a cool reception.

The Cavour was floated on February 6.

The British tramp steamship Drumelzier, 340 feet long, 3,625 gross tons, Captain William Nicholson, master, was outward bound for Swansea, Le Havre, and Dunkirk on Christmas Day, 1904, carrying a cargo of steel and copper, when she went aground on the bar two and a half miles east of Jones Beach, Long Island.

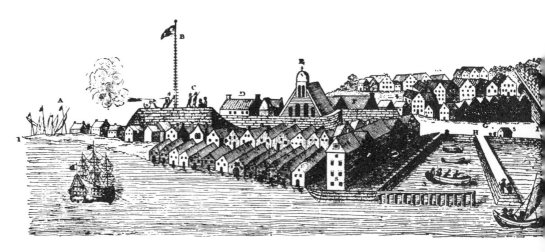

According to Charles Dunn and Graham Snediker, divers, in *Fishing Long Island Waters* magazine, the Drumelzier had the "dubious distinction of being the first outward-bound vessel ever to come ashore there. . . . Instead of following his regular course, Captain Nicholson managed to navigate an almost circular course, practically guaranteed to carry him and his ship across Long Island, if steaming on land had been possible."

The Drumelzier was scheduled to leave Atlantic Docks, Brooklyn, on Monday, December 26. The thirty-two crew members had high hopes of intensive celebrating ashore before she sailed, but Captain Nicholson had other ideas. He wanted the whole crew on board during the holiday—he was afraid they would take on too large a cargo of liquid Christmas cheer and fail to report on time for the scheduled departure. So . . . he sailed a day ahead. This did not set well with the crew.

At 9 A.M. on December 25, when the Drumelzier dropped her lines, it promised to be a bad day on the ocean. The men were disgruntled. The captain was angry. A Christmas spirit did not prevail, but very likely other spirits were aboard. That evening, proceeding at twelve knots in a heavy snowfall with fog, the Drumelzier piled headlong onto a bar—only eight hours after leaving her Brooklyn berth.

By the next morning the storm was worse. The wind had shifted to southeast. Spray was breaking over the mastheads of the freighter. The deck was covered with ice. The bridge and lifeboats were carried away. The rudder was gone. The boilers were crashing against the bulkheads. Water rose several feet deep in the engine room. The vessel's hull showed a deep crack. The keel, flattened, had pushed up the smokestack.

Life Saving crews got to the Drumelzier early on December 26. They offered to take the crew ashore, but the men declined their aid. By that afternoon aid was impossible. Although two Merritt-Chapman salvage tugs

New York in 1673

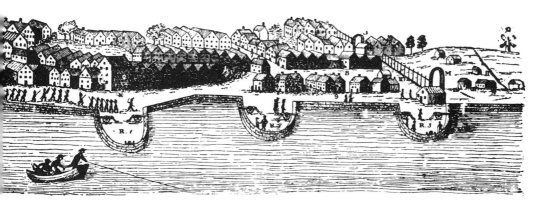

were standing by, they could do nothing. The wind and cold increased. The revenue cutter Mohawk came from New York but could get no nearer than half a mile from the disabled ship.

On the evening of December 28 it looked as if the ship would break up before dawn, losing all hands. Conditions were so bad that the crew could not even venture on deck. Rivets were yanked out of hull plates by the convulsions of the dying Drumelzier, and shot from bulkhead to bulkhead like bullets. A small tug had been sent by the New York *American* with newsmen and lifesaving apparatus. It could not get near.

The tug went back to Sandy Hook. The Treasury Department ordered the Sandy Hook Life Saving crew to attempt to reach the wreck. At 2:45 A.M. on December 29 the new, powerful Catherine Moran, Captain Robert Deaken in charge, took aboard the newsmen, pulled in at Sandy Hook station, and made fast to the lifeboat for the forty-five mile pull through the heaving sea.

At 8 A.M. the Catherine Moran lay outside the bar, within sight of the Drumelzier. The five-ton lifeboat had a mile to go, but it was completely sheathed in ice. Once chopped clear, it managed to cross the bar, half the time out of sight in the waves. The Life Savers got a rope to the Drumelzier. They had taken sixteen crew members off by 11:30 A.M. The rest of the ship's company, as well as a parrot, two cats, and a goat, stayed on board. At 1 P.M. the captain knew his time had come. He signaled to the crews of Oak Island and Fire Island stations to come out and save the remainder of the crew and officers. The wrecking tug I. J. Merritt hauled the fifteen men, plus the pets, through the surf. The ship, owned in Liverpool, England, was only nine years old when she met her end.

The Drumelzier broke up. She has since worked well inshore of where she struck. She lies south of Fire Island Inlet, making a favorite spot for fishermen, who have renamed it the "Quadrant Wreck" because it is possible for a boat to tie up to the rudder quadrant. Skin divers say it does not offer much excitement to them, but it is good for novices.

The Drumelzier's crew, which included Norwegians, British, Germans, an Irishman, and a Barbados Negro, all far from happy when they left Brooklyn, said afterward: "Everybody knows it's bad luck to start a voyage on Christmas Day."

8

THE LAST PIRATES

ODDLY enough, at one time New York Harbor had a grim reminder of the wages of sin at its front door—for 100 years called Gibbet Island—and another at its back entrance, still called Execution Rocks.

At New York's front door, entering the port from Europe or the south, is Ellis Island. Sixteen million hopeful immigrants entered the United States through Ellis Island from 1892 to November 12, 1954, when it ceased operations.

An early name for Ellis Island was Oyster Island. At another time it was called Bucking or Buckins Island. After a pirate named Anderson was hanged there in 1765, it went by the name of Gibbet Island. No one seems to know how many other hangings took place there in the years between, but it was still called Gibbet Island when two pirates were hanged there in 1831, and another in 1860.

THE BRIG VINEYARD

Big-time piracy was on the wane in 1830 when the burning of the brig Vineyard made headlines in the New York papers.

George Coggeshall in his *Voyages*, published in 1852, said that he was in the West Indies in 1823 when the islands, particularly around Cuba and the Isle of Pines, swarmed with pirates, who lurked in bays and creeks near Cape Antonio. When an unarmed vessel passed near they would sally out and capture it, often killing every soul on board. Captain Coggeshall intimated that the inhabitants of Cuba were not unfriendly toward the pirates.

But in November, 1830 (he wrote), two of these desperate men, Americans, had been chased out of Cuba and were in New Orleans, where they had thus far evaded punishment. There they signed on with Captain William Thornby of the brig Vineyard, bound for Philadelphia. They were Charles Gibbs, seaman, of Rhode Island, and a young Delaware Negro, Thomas J. Walmsley, who became the cook and steward.

The Vineyard cleared from New Orleans on November 9, 1830, for Philadelphia with a cargo of cotton, sugar, and molasses, plus $54,000 in Mexican specie, consigned to Stephen Girard of Philadelphia. On board, besides Captain Thornby and the two miscreants, were the mate, William Roberts; seamen Aaron Church (a Block Island Indian), James Talbot, John Brownrigg, and Henry Atwell; and Robert Dawes, cabin boy.

The brig had been five days at sea and was off Hatteras when the steward, Walmsley, discovered there was a good deal of cash on board. He told some of the crew. Then Gibbs, with Church, Atwell, and Dawes, made plans to kill the captain and mate and divide the money.

On the night of November 23 the captain was on the quarterdeck. The cabin boy, Dawes, was steering. The cook came up on deck. Obeying a prearranged call from Dawes to trim the binnacle light, Walmsley knocked the captain down from behind with a pump brake, and killed him by repeated blows. Seaman Gibbs then went forward. He and the cook threw the captain's body overboard.

Meanwhile, Mate Roberts heard the commotion. He ran up the companionway. Church and Atwell attacked him but failed to kill him. Roberts retreated to the cabin. In the struggle between him and Church, Atwell, and the cabin boy, Roberts was severely hurt. He was still alive and begging for mercy when the conspirators threw him overboard.

Talbot and Brownrigg, who had not been in the conspiracy, took to the rigging as they witnessed the murders. They hung there, white with terror. They were called down by the others and were offered their lives and a share in the booty if they kept silent. They accepted the terms.

Gibbs was made navigator. The day after the murder the money and other valuables were brought on deck and divided. Gibbs steered for Long Island. In sight of land the pirates scuttled and fired the Vineyard, then took to the boats.

Gibbs, Walmsley, Brownrigg, and Dawes, with $31,000, put off in the longboat. Church, Talbot, and Atwell, with the balance of the money, were in the jolly boat. They had a long row before they attempted to land.

The sea was rough. The wind blew a gale. In attempting to cross Rockaway Bar the jolly boat upset. Its crew and their share of the money went to the bottom. (A "jolly boat" is a small boat so-called from the Danish "jol"—it came to be called "yolly boat" and finally "yawl.")

For some undisclosed reason the occupants of the longboat threw overboard all but $5,000 of the specie, perhaps because it might have weighed them down and they would have drowned in the surf like the others. At any rate, the four of them reached shore off Pelican Beach, which was then a part of Barren Island but is now Coney Island. They immediately buried the remaining $5,000 in the sand.

They soon met one Nicholas S. Williams of Gravesend and told him a pitiful tale of shipwreck. He directed them to the northwest shore of Barren Island where John Johnson, his wife, and brother lived. The Johnsons took in the shipwrecked mariners for the night.

Brownrigg and the Johnson brothers had to occupy chairs in the living room. As soon as the others were asleep, Brownrigg revealed the whole crime. The next morning the pirates asked Johnson to take them to a hotel at Sheepshead Bay where they could get a boat for New York. This was done. The Johnsons returned quickly to Barren Island. They found the spot described by Brownrigg and removed the money to another hiding place.

Meanwhile, Gibbs and his party were bargaining with Samuel Leonard, Sheepshead Bay hotel keeper, to take them to the city. Suddenly Brownrigg declared he would go no further with them. He denounced Gibbs, Walmsley, and Dawes as pirates and murderers. He told the whole story. Before he finished talking, Walmsley fled to the woods. The innkeeper's servants seized and bound Gibbs and Dawes. Walmsley was soon captured. Justice Van Dyke was called. He issued warrants for the arrest of the three men, who were soon jailed in Flatbush.

Squire Van Dyke, guided by Brownrigg, went to the spot where the $5,000 was supposed to be buried. It had vanished. So the Squire arrested Brownrigg, and he joined the others in Flatbush jail. Later the four were taken to Bridewell prison in New York.

Brownrigg had already turned state's evidence. So did Dawes. Gibbs and Walmsley were tried, convicted, and hanged on April 23, 1831, on Gibbet Island. Before he died, Gibbs confessed to having killed over 100 officers, seamen, and passengers, including women.

But that was not the end. What had become of the $5,000? Officers of the law and agents of insurance companies made a thorough search. The money was still missing. John Johnson and his wife planned to get the money without the aid of brother William. In the dead of night they stole out and unearthed it. They hid it in two parcels, farther away from the house.

Brother William's rage when he discovered the money was gone was fearful. In revenge he told the insurance people in New York. They sued John, but could not prove his guilt.

John Johnson was not destined to enjoy his ill-gotten wealth. One par-

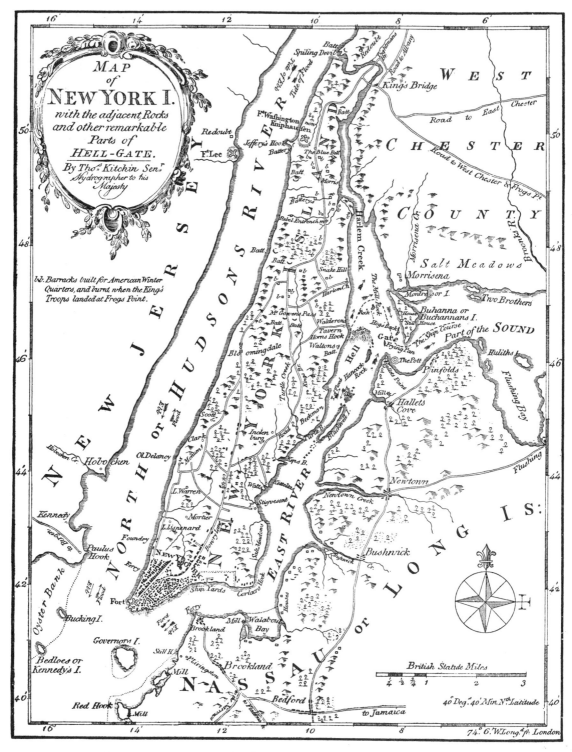

A British map of New York Island

cel, $3,400, was found. The other $1,600 was lost. It had been buried too near the water, and the tide had washed away the landmarks Johnson had placed to designate the spot. Eleven years later a great storm swept over Dooley's Bay (or Cove—at the northwestern end of Barren Island, also called Dead Horse Bay; it was separated from the mainland by Dead Horse Inlet). The storm laid bare the treasure, scattering dollars all over the beach. Two or three families living in the vicinity reaped a harvest. They told of their find. Crowds of excited people combed the sand for months thereafter looking for money, but found none.

Gibbs had been a thoroughgoing rascal and made no bones about it. Captain Coggeshall, author of *Voyages*, had known and liked the murdered Captain Thornby. He told how a U.S. Navy captain had talked with Gibbs while the latter was in the New York prison awaiting execution. Gibbs told the Navy captain it was very easy to make a pirate in just a few weeks, "even of a pious young man." He explained how he had turned two such young men into first-rate pirates. He had a boat's crew killed in their presence. Then he and his accomplices put ropes around the young men's necks, blindfolded them, and told them they were to be hanged. "Will you join us, if we spare your lives?" the young men were asked.

They joined.

THE E. A. JOHNSON

The last pirate ever hanged in New York—and probably in the United States—was Albert Hicks of Rhode Island, who met his end on Gibbet Island on Friday, July 13, 1860.

His hanging was a spectacular affair witnessed, according to contemporary newspaper accounts, by some 12,000 persons. They took in two shows at once on that day. The Great Eastern was in New York Harbor. The largest steamship in the world, 693 feet long, 120 feet wide, "unsinkable," with five stacks and six masts—a sight to behold. Throngs of visitors came from far and near and cheerfully paid $1 apiece to go on board. An old diary kept in East Hampton, Long Island, tells of people there making the 100-mile journey to see the wonderful ship.

The New York papers devoted column after column on March 22, 23, and 24, 1860, to a "Mysterious Tragedy!" An oyster sloop, the E. A. Johnson, had been found abandoned at 6:30 A.M. on March 21 between Sandy Hook and Coney Island, under circumstances which left no doubt that murder was involved.

The sloop was first discovered by the crew of the schooner Telegraph, Captain Listare, and later by the steam tug Ceres, Captain Downs. The Johnson's sails were down, hanging over the rail. The bowsprit, evidently carried away in a collision, was floating in the water alongside. Large quantities of blood all over the deck was the first thing the two captains noticed on boarding the vessel.

"In three places there were pods of gore," the New York *Herald* said, "showing that some bloody substance had been dragged along the deck and thrown overboard. The cabin's appearance was horrible. The floor, ceiling, and furniture were covered or spotted with blood."

The Ceres towed the Johnson to Fulton Market Slip and tied her up. The police, coroner, and doctors were on board by noon. The pier was crowded with fishermen and market dealers and the curious public.

The coroner examined the cabin. He declared it had been the scene of a sanguinary struggle. It had been ransacked. Clothing, bedding, and papers were strewn everywhere, but no trace of the captain's papers or money was found. On a slate were lines. Evidently the captain had been thinking what to say in a letter home: "I now take my pen in hand to let you know I am well, & I hope you are the same. I left Egg Harbor . . ." There it broke off.

Newspapers of the 1860's reveled in gore. The Suffolk *Weekly Times* of Greenport, Long Island, devoted five and a half columns to the E. A. Johnson story, copied from the New York *Herald* of March 22 and 23.

A coffeepot covered with blood and human hair was found in a corner near the stove. A broom seemed to have been used to sweep blood from the floor, but instead of disappearing, the blood collected in the grooves between the boards. A hammer, marked with blood, was found in the companionway. The ladder leading to the deck was bloody. Blood was on the lockers. There were four fresh and distinct marks as if a knife blade or sharp hatchet had been used on the beams and ceiling. One of these marks was bloodstained too.

In the pocket of a pair of breeches, twenty-nine cents was found wrapped in a bit of bloodstained paper. The torn-off handle of a carpetbag, or valise, was found. Stove, cooking utensils, the berths in the cabins—all were stained. Futile attempts had been made to wash the floor near the stove and the woodpile.

On deck, a trail led to the spot on the rail where the print of a bloody hand and a knife indentation seemed evidence that a victim's hand had been cut off before he was thrown overboard.

Amidships on the starboard side, a second victim had apparently been murdered. Further forward, near the main hatch, was a third pool of blood; a fourth was around the foremast and forecastle hatchway.

A small boat had evidently been lowered and taken away from the vessel's stern.

It was soon discovered that the oyster boat had left Catherine Market Slip, New York, on March 15 for Keyport, N.J. On board were the captain,

George Burr of Islip, Long Island; Nicholas Clock, mate; and two young brothers, Smith and Oliver Watts, hands, both of Islip, where E. A. Johnson was half-owner of the sloop.

The vessel had reached Keyport safely and left for Deep Creek, Va., where they were to load Chesapeake Bay oysters. Captain Burr was said to have had over $1,000 in his possession when they left Keyport. This was for the purchase of his cargo.

Captain Nickerson of the schooner John B. Mather of Dennis, Mass., said that at 3:30 or 4 A.M. on March 21, off West Bank (in the lower bay of New York), he collided with the sloop E. A. Johnson. The sloop was standing north, as if running for New York. He was sailing almost due south. He saw only one man on board the sloop at the time. That man was steering. No words were exchanged after the collision. The Mather was damaged so badly that Captain Nickerson had to put her back to New York for repairs.

On his arrival in the East River he recognized the sloop tied up at Fulton Slip as his acquaintance of the early morning. He recalled that at the time of the collision a boat had swung from her stern.

He said that in his twenty-five years' sea experience he never saw a more bungling piece of work than that performed by the Johnson's steersman. After the crash there were no calls for assistance from the sloop. Just a dead silence, except for a few words spoken by Captain Nickerson (contemporary newspaper stories do not reveal his comment).

Captain Burr, thirty-four years old, left a wife and five young children. He and the Watts brothers were highly regarded in their Long Island community. No one knew anything about the mate, Nicholas Clock, who had been engaged just before the Johnson sailed.

On March 23, police reported that a man answering to the description of the mate had come ashore on Staten Island on the morning of March 21 in a small boat, which he said belonged to a vessel sunk in a collision with a schooner a few hours before. He said the sloop's captain had been killed by the collision and that he was the only one on board who had time to escape in the yawl. Later that day the yawl was seen by some fishermen, adrift in the lower bay.

There was great excitement in the city, and talk of a lynching. It was concluded that the carnage was all the work of one man, who had first killed the two boys, then gone below to the cabin and killed the captain in his berth. The theory was that the collision was intentional, to sink the sloop and thus hide traces of the crime.

Movements of the mate, the so-called Nicholas Clock, were traced without too much trouble. He had arrived at Vanderbilt Landing, Staten Island, just too late to catch the first boat for New York City, and had to wait over for the 7 A.M. boat. While waiting he talked with the dockkeeper, Abram

Egbert, and inquired where he could get something to eat.

With good appetite he consumed in a nearby saloon two hot gins, two eggs, and an oyster stew. Then he called for another egg. He chatted with Peter Van Pelt, the saloonkeeper, and when he paid fifty cents for his meal, he told the man to keep the change. Instead of change, he said, he would accept a cigar.

The boy who waited on him, Augustus Gisler, was offered a $10 gold piece as a tip. The boy thought he was joking and refused it. Later the boy reported that the man had "told the boss not to cheat himself, as he had plenty of money and could pay for everything he bought." The man carried a clothes bag, apparently well filled.

He talked with deckhands on the ferry Southfield, and showed them his bagful of money. He said he was the owner of a sloop named the William Tell. He told details of a collision and a loss. He asked one of the deckhands to count the money—about $300. He claimed he was in a great hurry to charter a towboat and save his sloop.

On March 24 the New York *Tribune* reported that the supposed murderer had been arrested. He had been recognized by a Captain Baker, who had an oyster business in the Spring Street Market, as having been on board the sloop E. A. Johnson.

Then Selah Howell, the other half-owner of the vessel, identified the mate. He had taken supper with the captain and "Clock" the night before they sailed. At New York lodgings that "Clock" had rented under another alias, "William Johnson," police found Captain Burr's silver watch. Edward Watts, brother of the dead boys, identified the daguerreotype of a young lady in Islip as the property of his brother, Smith Watts. This was found in Smith Watts' coat, crammed into the clothes bag. Police caught up with the mate in Rhode Island. There he admitted that his real name was Albert Hicks.

Hicks was charged with murder. He readily admitted the crime, but said he was not alone in it. He said that on the night of March 20–21 there were actually five people on board the sloop—Captain Burr, the two Watts brothers, himself, and the devil.

Between 9 and 10 P.M., he said, one of the Watts brothers was in the bow when the devil told him to get ready. "I seized a heavy instrument," he said, "and accompanied by the devil, crept into the bow."

He described in detail the killing of the three men. The captain, a powerful man, fought desperately, but he finally dispatched him, Hicks said. After leaving the bodies on deck about an hour, he threw them overboard.

Then he made another confession. In February, 1844, he said, he had been on board the ship Saladin. The vessel had grounded near Halifax, Nova Scotia, and the authorities came on board. They found the captain, mate, and two sailors missing. The crew told them that the officers had died at sea, and

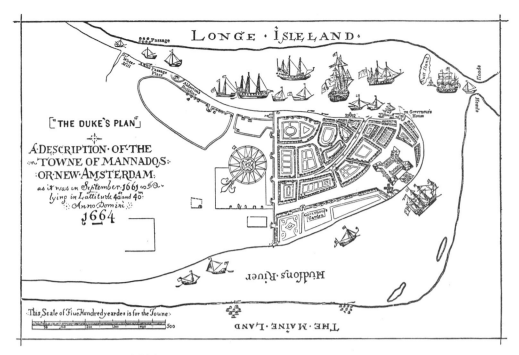

An English map of 1664

the two sailors had fallen overboard. Several of the crew were executed for these crimes.

Hicks now said the Nova Scotians had hanged the wrong men. The devil was aboard on that trip, too. It was really he and the devil who had killed the men on the Saladin.

The New York jury found Hicks guilty in seven minutes. He was declared a pirate and the hanging was set for Friday, July 13, 1860, on Gibbet (now Ellis) Island.

Hicks got himself all dressed up for the execution. At Canal Street he was put on the steamboat Red Jacket. There were 1,500 persons on board, so the stories say—all going to the hanging.

But the Great Eastern was in the harbor. Federal Marshal Rynders asked Hicks if he minded a postponement of two hours while they sailed over to see the wonderful "unsinkable" British ship. Hicks replied that they could arrange as many postponements as they wished.

Finally no less than 12,000 people had arrived to witness the execution, swarming all over the harbor in every kind of craft. Hicks was duly hanged.

And that ended the age of real piracy, as far as the Port of New York was concerned. Bomb threats and plane hijackings, which amount to the same thing, are not so named.

9

LIFESAVING:
NEW YORK AREA,
FROM 1848

THE United States Coast Guard celebrates its anniversaries from 1790, when Alexander Hamilton, as Secretary of the Treasury, organized the Revenue Cutter Service. This merged with the Life Saving Service in 1915 to form the Coast Guard.

However, up to 1847 the United States government had made no provision for aid from shore to shipwrecked mariners. In that year Congress authorized an appropriation of $10,000 to build lifeboat stations along the New Jersey shore and to provide apparatus "for better preservation of life and property from shipwrecks on the coast." Actually, the first appropriation, of $5,000, went to Boston.

The first government-operated lifesaving station, a small building now preserved as a Coast Guard museum, was built in 1848 at Sandy Hook, N.J.

The Massachusetts Humane Society, active since 1785, had built many small relief stations along that coast, before the government took hold. In 1849 a group of prominent New York merchants, shipowners, and underwriters, who had been deeply concerned about recent marine disasters off the Long Island coast, decided to do something about it.

The *Suffolk Democrat* of Huntington, Long Island, announced on December 14, 1849: "The Life Saving Benevolent Association of New York, of which Walter R." (Restored) "Jones of Cold Spring is President and John

D. Jones of the same place is Secretary, have made provisions for the erection of ten buildings on the shore of Long Island, intended as relief houses for seamen ship-wrecked on our shores. Mr. Daniel Smith, of Huntington, is now erecting these houses. They are to be located as follows: At Eaton's Neck and Fisher's Island on the north side, and at Amagansett, Bridgehampton, Quogue, Bellport, Moriches, Fire Island, Near Rockaway, and Barren Island on the south side. Each building is to be provided with one of Francis's life boats, a mortar for throwing rockets with lines attached, from the shore to the wreck, also one of Shepherd's box stoves, fuel, provisions, cooking utensils, etc."

That was the beginning, for New York State, of lifesaving operations from shore.

The government appropriated very moderate amounts for lifeboat stations each year, but until 1854 the stations were manned only by volunteers. In that year Congress authorized funds for new stations and for paid keepers (at $200 a year) and two superintendents of stations for Long Island and New Jersey. Gradually, the association's lifeboat stations, and others operated privately or locally, were absorbed as part of the government system.

Walter Restored Jones, first head of the Life Saving Benevolent Association of New York, which had promoted the first Long Island lifesaving stations, was also the first president of the Atlantic Mutual Insurance Company. His association, as well as the company, is still very much in business. It has not missed a meeting since 1849. Among its activities are aid to unemployed seamen, especially if they have participated in rescues at sea; special recognition of members of the New York City Police Department for lifesaving along the waterfront; and giving medals to individuals for marine rescues. It has provided a scholarship fund for the New York Merchant

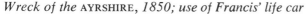

Wreck of the AYRSHIRE, *1850; use of Francis' life car*

Marine Academy, and has given modern training equipment.

The Life Saving Benevolent Association of New York kept records and made reports from 1850 to 1865. The first official United States Life Saving Service report was not published until 1876.

In a report of the Life Saving Benevolent Association of New York for 1851 is an item: "Eaton's Neck Station, August 25th, 1850—Life boat used by B. Downing. Took off John Clark from wreck of schooner Jane. He would certainly have drowned in a very short time if he had not been relieved."

That was the first rescue in which equipment from a U.S. Life Saving station was used on Long Island.

At a meeting of the association held October 30, 1850, it was resolved to give Benjamin Downing of Eaton's Neck, Long Island, $50 and a like sum to his son, Benjamin Franklin Downing, sixteen years old, and in addition to each a medal "in the form adopted by the Association . . . the cost not to exceed, together, the sum of fifty dollars."

Benjamin Downing, the sixty-six-year-old keeper of the lighthouse at Eaton's Neck and volunteer lifesaver, was lame and had only one arm. In order to rescue two men clinging to the bottom of a small capsized schooner out at sea, he had a lifeboat drawn to the shore with the help of two yoke of oxen. Because of the raging storm, none of the six men present would help man the boat. Downing and his son handled it themselves, succeeding in landing John Clark, owner of the schooner. The other man had started to swim ashore and was drowned.

The boat used was designed by Joseph Francis, inventor of lifesaving equipment. It was 25 feet long, made of galvanized iron, and equipped to be rowed by six men. The lame old man and his young son had performed a truly wonderful feat.

THEY KNEW THE COAST

Up to 1871 lifesaving crews were still volunteer. Only a keeper was paid. The work of saving ships and men imperiled by the sea was a humanitarian duty, like that of the volunteer firemen in villages today. It was also a source of pride, an opportunity to show a special knowledge and skill. Often a local man who knew the surf and the sandbars could work a stranded vessel off into deep water before the professional salvage companies could get there—something the unions would frown upon today.

All along the Atlantic seaboard the average man was a combination fisherman-farmer. Many had sailed away on whaling voyages or on merchant vessels, returning home with experience that entitled them to take the lead in rescue operations, or in the whalechase off their native beaches.

Long Island's south shore, with its shifting sandbars and its silting-up inlets, was as familiar to these coastal villagers as their own back yards. The same was true of nearby New Jersey. Both shores were strewn with wreckage in sailing-ship days. Newspapers from the 1840's to the turn of the century were constantly reporting schooners, sloops, and fishing smacks in trouble; fairly often it would be a larger vessel—a brig, brigantine, bark, full-rigged ship, or steamship.

In the years before all lifesavers became paid government employees, the cry of "Ship Ashore!" would bring able-bodied, experienced surfmen to the beach on the run. A fishing dory or the twenty-eight-foot whaleboat would be ever ready on the shore.

In winter, which was whaling season—and also wreck season—small boys would often get up early and spend an hour or so before school time watching the sea from a sand dune. If the boy sighted a whale he would raise his coat on a pole or an oar, from the beach bank. Then the "weft," a familiar signal (an old American flag was used, within living memory, in an eastern Long Island town) would be flown from the scuttle of a house near the beach. The first to sight a whale would get a half-share of the proceeds.

The news traveled fast. There would be a stampede for the whaleboats. Then, if the boat-header or captain would accept him, a man could ensure a place at an oar by throwing his coat on a thwart. If what the watcher saw offshore turned out to be a vessel in trouble, news would go around the village with lightning speed. Lifesaving was a very local and very personal affair a century or so ago.

The women would gather on the beach, waiting to see if they could offer shelter and food and warm clothing to survivors. Many a shipwrecked mariner was succored in village homes. Some stayed on the rest of their lives.

PAID PERSONNEL

By 1871 the system of having only a keeper with pay was not working out very well. Stations and equipment were deteriorating.

The New York *Herald* published a scathing article on "Our Life Saving Service" on February 14, 1871, following a calamity off New Jersey on January 23 and 26, when fourteen lives were lost from the bark Kate Smith and the schooner Alfred Hall. The *Herald* asserted that "mariners entering the Port of New York had been led to believe the service was efficiently provided with boats suitable to save life, and all the additional appliances which experience has suggested. . . ." But "those in maritime circles and the public were inquiring into the avowed effectiveness of the Life Saving Service of the United States as it is now being carried on. . . . Mayhap the widespread publicity of the *Herald*'s reporter's investigations in this matter will be of such exceeding interest . . . that a more systematic remedy will be entered upon by the government to check the terrible fatalities of our dangerous coast and the present service so overhauled as to cause some little reliance to be placed upon it in the future. . . ."

Keepers of the station houses, the *Herald* said, should live at or near the stations. At Long Beach, N.J., it cited, the keeper of No. 14 lived 100 miles away. The keeper at No. 15 lived six or seven miles away. "They might as well be in Washington or San Francisco." The New Jersey coast was not being patrolled, the paper charged; crews were never drilled; efficiency was lowered by involvement in politics.

The article praised two faithful and efficient officers: Henry E. Huntting, superintendent of District No. 3 on Long Island; and Henry W. Sawyer, superintendent of District No. 4 in New Jersey. "But they only visit the station houses once in three months. They would be better judges if they patrolled a beach during a northeast storm, as did the *Herald* reporter."

"Some beaches are uninhabited," the *Herald* went on, "so that few could supply much assistance with a wreck. Notice to the mainland is a necessity. Of the coast population, nearly all are surf boatmen, skillful, daring, and accustomed to the breakers. If a shipwreck should occur and an alarm be given on shore, men will not be wanting. Means for timely notice should be provided. Every station should have a large mounted field piece that could be loaded, run to the top of a sand hill and fired. Any lesser noise would be of little avail during a storm. Mortars, for this service, would be of no better use than a boy's pop-gun."

Whether or not the adverse publicity stirred up the government to appoint Sumner I. Kimball as head of the Revenue–Marine Bureau in 1871, it was he who really created the Life Saving Service. He dismissed the incompetent political appointees. He reorganized the service so that a boathouse crew consisted of the keeper (with boatswain's rank) and six surfmen, all paid, experienced men who drilled and walked beach patrols. In 1878 he was made General Superintendent of Life Saving Stations, in which office he remained until that was merged with the Revenue Cutter Service as the United States Coast Guard in 1915.

Between 1871 and 1915 the service was still very much a local affair. When the first printed report of the Life Saving Service appeared in 1876, it listed thirty-six lifeboat stations in District No. 3, which then included the coasts of Rhode Island and Long Island. Stations were also established at lighthouses, and the keepers (who were apt to be Civil War veterans resident in the neighborhood) took charge of boats and apparatus as part of their official duties. Keepers of Life Saving stations and lighthouses bore early-settler names.

The list of the first keepers at stations in District No. 3 follows:

RHODE ISLAND:

Point Judith	Joseph N. Griffin
Narragansett Pier	Benjamin Macomber
Block Island (northeast side)	William P. Card
Block Island (southwest point)	Samuel Allen

LONG ISLAND:

Montauk Point	Jonathan Miller
Ditch Plain, Montauk	Samuel Stratton
Hither Plain, Montauk	George Osborn
Napeague	Elijah M. Bennett
Amagansett	Charles J. Mulford
Georgica (East Hampton)	James M. Strong
Bridgehampton	Baldwin Cook
Southampton	Charles White
Shinnecock	Lewis K. Squires
Tyana	Edward H. Ryder
Quogue	Mahlon Phillips
Tanner's Point	Franklin C. Jessup
Moriches	William Smith
Fargo River	Sidney Penney
Smith's Point	Joseph H. Bell
Bellport	George W. Robinson
Blue Point	Charles W. Wicks
Lone Hill	James Baker
Point O' Woods	George W. Rogers
Fire Island	Leander Thurber
Oak Island (east)	Henry Oakley
Oak Island (west)	Prior Wicks
Jones Beach (east end)	Augustus C. Wicks
Jones Beach (west end)	Townsend Verity
Meadow Island	Leander Lozee
Long Beach (east end)	Quincy L. Raynor
Long Beach (west end)	Henry F. Johnson
Hog Island	Joseph Langdon
Rockaway Beach (east end)	Daniel Mott
Rockaway Beach (west end)	Isaac Skidmore
Sheepshead Bay (east end of Coney Island)	Cornelius Van Nostrand
Eaton's Neck	Darius Ruland

Henry E. Huntting, Bridgehampton, N.Y., Superintendent
Nicholas Ball, New Shoreham (Block Island), R.I., Assistant Superintendent

District No. 4, coast of New Jersey, had forty lifeboat stations; John G. W. Havens of Bricksburg, N.J., was Superintendent.

The 1876 Life Saving Service report gives John C. Patterson as keeper of Station No. 1, at Sandy Hook, N.J., which is about as far south as marine disasters reported in this book will go.

The Brooklyn *Daily Eagle* wrote about Long Island Life Saving stations on August 18, 1895, and gave a list of their keepers. The article states that "the crews are made up from able-bodied and experienced surf men residing near the stations where they are employed. They must be under forty-five years of age at the time of enlistment. They must be able to read and write and have a knowledge of the four rules of arithmetic . . . and possess a thorough knowledge of surf boats. . . ."

In 1895 the Third District Superintendent was Arthur Dominy of Bay Shore.

Lifesavers were off during the summer months, in the early days; only the keeper remained on duty year-round. The crew men could go home, tend their gardens, do some fishing. But in the early 1890's there were some bad wrecks in summer, so by 1898 the men were off only two months, and on for ten.

The "seventh man" in a lifesaving crew dates back to before 1900. The lifesavers had complained to Washington in the 1880's that a six-man crew was not enough. The regulation rowing lifeboat, with six oarsmen and the keeper giving orders, left no one ashore to help draw up the boat on the beach as they landed, which was often with great difficulty. With the "seventh man" a station would have six surfmen during the fall months; then seven from December 1 to April 30, the season when most catastrophes could be expected.

It took time to rid the service completely of politics. A packet of old, browned letters is preserved in the family of a Long Island Life Saving station keeper of 1879 and the early 1880's. It includes a letter dated August 30, 1880, from the Superintendent of the Third District. He directed the keeper (both the superintendent and the keeper were retired whaling captains, and good friends) to: "See that half of your crew are Republicans and half are Democrats as per arrangement made last August by the General Superintendent of the Life Saving Service."

The keeper in question had not made up his crew according to these directions. He had used his best judgment, knowing the men. Some correspondence ensued. The keeper stuck to his guns. He was reappointed in 1881, and his recommendation for the head man at a nearby station was honored.

This same packet of letters shows that it was not until 1903, when a reply from Washington stated that the method for Life Saving appointments had been changed. Now the best qualified man, regardless of his political affiliations, would be chosen.

By 1881, a keeper's pay had gone up to $700 a year, which was considered a "lucrative position," and one much sought after.

EARLY RESCUE BOATS AND EQUIPMENT

Another invention often credited to Joseph Francis of 10 Broadway, New York City, whose lifeboat was used at the first Long Island Life Saving stations, was the Francis Corrugated Metallic Life Car. That was first tried out on Long Island in 1849 by Walter Restored Jones, president of the Life Saving Benevolent Association of New York. (Francis's corrugated metallic lifeboat used in 1850 at Eaton's Neck and at other stations was unpopular with the crews and fell into disuse after a few years.)

Only a few months later, on January 12, 1850, the life car tried out in 1849 saved the lives of 201 persons from the foundering immigrant ship Ayrshire, bringing them through a surf in which no boat could have lived. The Ayrshire, on her way to New York, was off Squam Beach, N.J., when she went aground in a howling snowstorm.

The volunteer rescuers saw that the ship showed signs of breaking up quickly. They dragged the carronade to the beach. A shot, with line attached, was rammed down the barrel. The mortar exploded and the shotline arched toward the stricken vessel, falling directly across her deck. The crew grabbed the line and bent it to the Ayrshire. Aided by this line, a strong hawser was hauled through the surf and made fast to the vessel.

The oddly shaped, all-enclosed metal life car was then attached to the hawser and pulled through the breaking surf to the ship. It could carry two to four persons on each trip. The life car went back and forth until darkness closed in. One hundred and twenty passengers were safe on shore. Then one passenger, afraid of staying on board overnight, panicked and jumped on the outside of the car. He was swept off and lost. At dawn the following day the rest of the passengers and crew were taken off.

John Maxem, keeper of the Squam Life Saving Station, was awarded the Life Saving Benevolent Association medal for his part in the rescue.

The life car was made a part of every station's equipment. Up to that time the breeches buoy and lifeboats were the only rescue apparatus. In a heavy sea the breeches buoy passenger was liable to be drowned on his way in. However, that was used oftener and longer than the less easily maneuvered life car.

A problem arose with regard to this life car. For many years a violent dispute raged between Captain Douglas Ottinger and Joseph Francis as to which was the legitimate inventor of the metallic life car. There were lawsuits. The matter came up on the floor of Congress. It seems never to have been resolved. Both men probably played a part in its development. The life car is now a museum piece, along with the horse-drawn beach wagon, the breeches buoy, and the Lyle gun, although these were in use until after World War I.

The invention of the line-throwing gun has been credited to Lieutenant David A. Lyle of the U.S. Army Ordinance Department. He certainly did develop a very effective appliance, but it was not the first of its type. An Englishman, Captain Manby, had developed a line-throwing device much earlier.

The Coston light, a pyrotechnic, was adopted by the Life Saving Service in 1873 for use by the beach patrol at night and in thick weather to give notice upon discovery of a wreck or a vessel in distress that they are seen and help is at hand; and to warn vessels running dangerously near the shore.

Since wooden ships have been replaced by steel, wrecks are apt to take place farther offshore. Both the Coston light and the shore patrols have been discontinued. Many of the lookout and signal towers at coastal stations have gone, along with many of the stations; but towers are still in use at Fire Island and at Manasquam Inlet, N.J.

The greatest change in lifesaving procedure is in the type of boat used in that service. Fast motorboats now go out of protected harbors or inlets, instead of rowing boats launched through the surf off the open beach. Helicopters have been, and will be, more and more important in coastal search and rescue work. However it is the high-speed motor rescue boat and the new and powerful 44-foot steel motor lifeboats that have actually replaced the old beach apparatus. Helicopters still have some limitations in night searches. And an old-time Life Saver says of them: "In east and no'theast gales, I wonder!"

The New York *Herald* for February 14, 1871, which urged the government to "remove the barnacles" from the Life Saving Service, was particularly critical of the various types of lifeboat used at that time.

William D. Wilkinson, former Marine Curator at the Museum of the City of New York and now Associate Director of the Mariners' Museum in Newport News, Va., is considered a knowledgeable expert on the history of Coast Guard small craft. He says: "There has always been considerable confusion about the coastal lifeboats and the surfboats of the old U.S. Life Saving Service . . . the words are often used interchangeably, but the two are distinctly different types.

"In the sense of function both were, of course, 'lifeboats.' However, with regard to inherent form and design, each was a unique type of craft. Generally the lifeboat was much larger, more heavily constructed, and usually was not only self-bailing but self-righting. Normally it was kept either afloat at a sheltered mooring or launched from a slipway. Lifeboats were almost always fitted with sails—although these were not always used—and had to be pulled by large crews. The lifeboat hull form used in the United States was directly related to the lifeboat type as evolved in England.

"The surfboat generally was a much smaller craft, of very light construction. It was developed for launching from the beach directly into the surf. It could be pulled by a small crew and rarely carried sail. Early types were neither self-bailing nor self-righting. Later models had self-bailing. As developed, the surfboat was more uniquely an American type, with its form probably influenced by the local fishing craft with which the Life Saving crews were most familiar—such as the whaleboat, seine boat, and dory."

A Life Saving Service publication called *Along the Coast* spoke in 1909 of the boats then used in that service. The article bore out Mr. Wilkinson's statements. It said: "There are several varieties, all developments of the boat found in use among the shore fishermen or surfmen of the Long Island and New Jersey coasts for crossing the surf on the outlying sandbars in their daily fishing when the first boathouses or stations were placed there."

Three were mentioned: the Beebe, the Higgins & Gifford, and the Beebe–McLellan surfboat, "all built of white cedar with white-oak frames, with dimensions of 25 to 27 feet in length, 6½ to 7 feet beam, 2 feet, 3 to 6 inches depth amidships, and 1 foot 7 inches to 2 feet 1 inch sheer or gunwale. They were flat-bottomed, with little or no keel; draw six or seven inches of water; are light, propelled with six oars, without sails, and are expected to carry besides their crews, from ten to twelve persons, although as many as fifteen have been landed at a time in a bad sea. . . . The Beebe–McLellan boat has the self-bailing quality incorporated. This feature has been added within the past two years, but few of them are so light as to be readily transported along the shore. . . . Even at those stations where the most approved self-bailing and self-righting boats are furnished, the surfboats are generally preferred by the lifesaving crews for short distances and when the number of imperiled people is not large. . . ."

The original Beebe surfboat was built in Greenport, Long Island, by F. C. Beebe for the Bridgehampton, Long Island, Life Saving Station. Lieutenant C. H. McLellan was to hold a test of surfboats at Bridgehampton. The keeper went to Greenport and ordered a boat from Beebe. It outclassed all others. It was shown in exhibitions at Chicago and in Paris. Nearly 400 of these were built. Then, in conjunction with Lieutenant McLellan, Beebe built more than 150 self-bailing boats.

Mechanized lifeboats were introduced in the Life Saving Service in 1899. They had become quite general by 1909, when the 32-foot Elizabeth, fitted out by C. H. McLellan, by then a captain in the Life Saving Service,

Long Beach Life Saving Station crew; they rescued crew of ARLINGTON, *1909*

was brought out from Bayonne, N.J., for use in Fire Island Inlet.

It has become unnecessary to train Coast Guardsmen in launching a rowing boat through the surf. Only a few fishermen still have that skill. It was a fine thing, though, to watch on a rough day the split-second timing, the men waiting "until a slatch made," then: "Shove 'er in!" all together, at the signal from the man in charge. He scrambled aboard over the stern, the last man in.

A "slatch," according to Webster's dictionary, is an obsolete nautical term. But it is still commonly used on the south shore of eastern Long Island, where nothing changes as rapidly as on the island's west end. It means a brief lull in a succession of heavy breakers.

A race between lifesaving boats off the Australian coast was shown on television a few years ago. The participants were volunteers, who work through the heavy surf usual on those shores. The skill of those young Australians would have pleased the Long Island surfmen of a generation or two ago. Almost none of the old Life Savers, who preceded the Coast Guard, are living now. In their time, men had to go out from the Life Saving stations all along the coast, through the surf in rowing boats, whereas today's rescue operations are performed by motor craft going out from protected harbors.

108

UNDER KIMBALL, 1871-1915

During the years of relative peace when Sumner I. Kimball was Chief Superintendent, the Life Saving Service flourished and built up a proud tradition. The men were content with their months of communal life and with their pay, meager enough by modern standards.

They lived well, keeping the stations "neat as a pin," taking turns doing their own cooking, proud of their bread baking and pie making. They fitted into their jobs "like a duck's foot in a mud puddle," as the old saying goes. They rose to emergencies, performing spectacular feats of seamanship, calmly, all in the day's work.

Anyone who has dipped into the official Life Saving Service reports from 1876 to 1915 knows that life was just one emergency after another at the coastal stations in those years. Now and then some especially spectacular disaster or rescue got into the newspapers. One example is a story published in the Brooklyn *Daily Eagle* in 1908. It was headed: "The Most Heroic Rescue on the Long Island Coast This Winter." The story concerned the stranding of the British iron tramp steamer Roda, 100 yards offshore from Jones Beach, halfway between Jones Inlet and Fire Island. Her bones lie there today. She was carrying a cargo of copper ore from Huelva, Spain, on February 13, 1908, when she struck, hard on, at 6 P.M.

The ship's captain, W. J. Beaven, was not seriously alarmed. It was foggy. Sea was moderate. He would need tugs to get off. He ordered his foghorn to sound the danger signal, in a continuing series of blasts.

Surfman Jacob J. Baldwin of the Jones Beach Life Saving Station was walking his beach patrol. He heard the horn and rushed back to the station, calling, "Ship ashore! On the outer bar."

Keeper Stephen Austin promptly ordered the self-bailing, oar-propelled surfboat down to the shore. He stood at the steering oar while she headed out toward the blackness where the foghorn sounded. They hailed the ship's skipper, offering to take all hands ashore. The British captain refused. He asked them to notify his New York agents and have tugs sent to pull him off. The fog was blowing away and the seas were building up.

By seven o'clock the next morning it was really heavy weather. Austin and his crew went back to the Roda and again asked the ship's company to come ashore. Again they refused. All day the wind increased and the surf rose. By midnight a terrific gale struck all along the coast. The beach patrol reported that the Roda was sending up distress signals.

At 1:30 A.M. Keeper Austin called out his crew and fifteen volunteers from a salvage company who were temporarily quartered at the station, assigned to salvage or refloat some vessel that had come ashore earlier. Once more the men dragged the heavy self-bailing surfboat down to the boiling sea's edge and then, waist-deep in spent waves, shoved off.

By the time they reached the ship it looked as if she might break up at any time. The keeper's report states: "Pulled to ship. Captain called out that all was ready to go as he feared his masts was going. Landed 12 men.

"2nd trip. Storm fast increasing. Landed 8 men.

"3rd trip. All clear from shore, by heavy seas forced back on shore. Started again and by a hard fight reached ship. The captain, first mate, and chief engineer refused to leave. I told him how his chances stood and assured him I would land them safe but he refused to get in surf boat. Landed and returned to station about 4:30 A.M. and made them [the previously rescued crewmen] comfortable as possible."

Keeper Austin knew that there must be another trip. Three men were still on the ship, which was now pounding to pieces on the bar. At 11 A.M. on February 15, the Roda was almost invisible from the beach because of flying spray. At that moment Captain Beaven capitulated. He signaled shore that he must leave his ship.

Lifeboat at wreck of PRINCESS ANNE, *Rockaway, 1920*

Again the Life Savers and the wreckers turned out, aided by the rescued British sailors, to drag the lifeboat through the sand and wade into the surf for another launching. The six-foot Austin was again at the steering oar. By the time they reached the Roda, seas were breaking all over her. The three officers jumped into the heaving boat and were landed safely after a wild dash through the surf. This was the Life Savers' seventh trip to the Roda.

Austin was later able to sit down and write after Item 55 of his wreck report the word: "None." The item referred to the number of lives lost. His report and a copy of a letter of commendation written by Captain Beaven of the Roda were published in the 1908 report of the Life Saving Service. The letter began: "We the undersigned members of the crew of the British S/S Roda now stranded on Jones Beach Long Island beg to express our appreciation of the gallant conduct of the Boat's Crew employed in rescuing us from the above named vessel on the morning of 15th February 1908 in very heavy weather and under exceptional circumstances. We must say that your conduct on this occasion is worthy of the greatest praise, and the manner in which the rescue was carried out, worthy of American Seamen. . . ."

FIDELITY, DEVOTION, AND COURAGE

The Life Saving Service had only been merged with the Revenue Cutter Service as the United States Coast Guard for five years when the American coastal steamer Princess Anne stranded at 2:30 A.M. on February 6, 1920, on Rockaway Shoals. The whole story of that disaster is told in Chapter V; but the comments of a New York *Sun and Herald* reporter, on February 15, 1920, are worth quoting.

He wrote of the fidelity, devotion, and courage of the Coast Guardsmen: "Take the two Rockaway stations for shining examples . . . for generations they have been manned by men bearing the names of Pearsall and Henry and Abrams, Van Nostrand and Verity, Snedeker and Phipps: Hewlett, Rhinehart, Carman, Tooker, and Meade. You will find the same names on the rosters of Point Lookout and Long Beach and Lone Hill and Fire Island. . . . These are men working at the trade that their fathers followed all their lives and whose grandsires were the keepers of stations, for the service does not know the term captain.

"Some of the men at the Rockaway stations were born on the job. . . . Rows of tiny cottages containing the womankind of the life savers surrounded both stations. Sometimes the babies came into the world with a regular doctor alongside, sometimes not. . . .

"The public knows little of their work . . . for they have never worked for credit and their pride runs very high."

THE COAST GUARD TODAY

In sailing-ship days, disasters generally occurred during winter storms. Now, with the proliferation of pleasure-boating, a fine summer weekend can be the most dangerous time. A young Coast Guardsman at the Rockaway, Long Island, station said: "The busiest stations in the United States are here, Short Beach, and Sandy Hook. And our biggest headache is from the pleasure boats—the Sunday sailors."

That was shortly before the new Coast Guard station at Fort Totten, on the northernmost tip of Queens County, Long Island, was commissioned. Pleasure-boat disasters were the chief reason for opening this station, which is under the control of Coast Guard Group New York. The Coast Guard set down 1971 as the worst year for pleasure-boating deaths in United States history.

To the average civilian, what is now covered by Coast Guard District No. 3, the Eastern Area, is confusing. It includes not only the area around the Port of New York but other parts of New York State; a bit of Vermont; parts of Connecticut; Rhode Island, Massachusetts, New Jersey, Pennsylvania, and Delaware. The rescue coordination center dispatches ships and planes in answer to 10,000 distress calls a year.

Group New York has its headquarters on Governor's Island, which from 1794 to 1966 was an Army base. The old Coast Guard base at St. George, Staten Island, is now used as a Coast Guard Reserve Training Center, and headquarters for the New York–New Jersey Pilots' Association is nearby. Until 1967 Staten Island was the base for the weather cutters and buoy tenders; in that year these activities were also centralized on Governor's Island.

Lifeboat stations (search and rescue units) in the Greater New York area and south to Sandy Hook, N.J., which are still manned, are at Eaton's Neck, Montauk (Star Island), Moriches, Shinnecock, Fire Island, Short Beach, Atlantic Beach, Rockaway, and Fort Totten, on Long Island; and Sandy Hook in nearby New Jersey.

Duties of the Coast Guard are manifold and diverse. The service gives ten classifications: Ocean Stations, Law Enforcement, Search and Rescue, Merchant Marine Safety, Reserve Training, Port Security, Aids to Navigation, Military Readiness, Ice Breaking, and Oceanography. A peacetime Coast Guard is called a "seagoing handyman for almost every department of the government."

To supplement the Coast Guard's efforts to protect the seagoing public, organizations such as the United States Power Squadron and Coast Guard Auxiliary have been formed to teach safe boating practices. There are records, complete with foghorns, whistles, and other waterfront sound effects.

There is a Federal law against reckless or negligent operation of a motorboat. Classes, however, cannot teach common sense. The law appears to have little effect on speeding, lack of life preservers, poor seamanship, and disregard of weather reports on the part of landlubbers turned boatmen for a holiday.

Coast Guard personnel, during and since World War II, have ceased to represent the old coastal families, familiar with the shoreline. Descendants of the old surfmen are scattered and generally otherwise occupied. The service now attracts men from everywhere. They are better educated and better trained than the old-timers were, even though they may have no seafaring tradition behind them. Enlisted men are sent to boot camp for basic training; then they may go on to one of many schools maintained by the service. Officers are trained at the Coast Guard Academy in New London, Conn.

Between the two World Wars, in both of which the Coast Guard served with great distinction, the old Revenue Cutter duty of detecting smugglers was revived. The Coast Guard had the thankless job of trying to enforce the unpopular Eighteenth (Prohibition) Amendment from January 17, 1920, to December 5, 1933. The coasts of Long Island and nearby New Jersey were very active during this period.

In 1939 the Lighthouse Service was combined with the Coast Guard.

This is a proud service. A Coast Guard spokesman says: "The United States of America is unique among nations in developing a military service basically humanitarian; supporting the dignity, importance, and worth of the individual human being."

10

FIRES AND
FIREBOATS

No New Yorker could be unaware of the fire engines clanging through the streets day and night, answering an average of some 700 calls a day, at latest count. But the quieter branch of the New York City Fire Department—the Marine Division—is much less known.

That division has eleven diesel and diesel-electric fireboats and a tender on station in the Port District, on the Manhattan, Staten Island, and Brooklyn waterfronts. Large capacity, high-speed pumps on each boat can deliver thousands of gallons of water a minute into massive deck-mounted monitors and towers, or through the hundreds of feet of hose carried on each boat. The concentrated stream of water from the forward monitor can smash down a concrete wall or rip a huge steel pier door off its hinges. Oil fires in the harbor are dealt with by massive applications of foam.

Largest of the fireboats is Firefighter, 134 feet long, built in 1938 and still going strong. She can come in with the strength of twenty land fire companies, throwing 20,000 gallons of water a minute at pressures up to 300 pounds per square inch. The force could topple over a building.

The trend today, however, is to smaller and faster craft. The latest boat is shallow-draft, named James F. Hackett, in service in the Jamaica Bay area. She can send 2,500 gallons per minute.

The only time the average citizen is aware of the Marine Division, except in a catastrophe, is when a maiden ship arrives at the Port of New York. It is traditional for her to be welcomed by one or more fireboats, with plumes of high-flung spray. Other harbor craft sound sirens. Police boats and harbor tugs join the welcoming committee; police, Coast Guard, and private helicopters circle overhead.

Marine disasters within the port area are frequent—and but for the Fire Department's Marine Division, could have been infinitely worse. It seems unbelievable that firemen on duty could be attacked, even shot at, in recent years as representatives of the "Establishment." And it is incredible that it has become necessary to keep protective covers on all apparatus to prevent sabotage.

FIRE AT SEA

In the days of wooden sailing ships, which seldom carried enough life-boats, fire at sea was a terrible risk. A whale-oil lamp would upset on a brig. That was the end of the vessel. An overturned kerosene lamp or an over-heated wood-burning cookstove could set a ship alight like a torch. In early steamboat days faulty boilers frequently exploded, starting a fire. In modern times, collision and inflammable cargo are the most frequent causes of ship fires.

It always takes a catastrophe to effect safeguards. New marine safety regulations were made for the United States Merchant Marine after the night of September 8, 1934, when the Ward Line's luxury liner Morro Castle caught fire off Asbury Park, N.J. One hundred and twenty-five of her 549 passengers and crew perished.

Frank Rushbrook, an English career fireman, wrote in his book *Fire Aboard: The Problems of Prevention and Control in Ships and Port Installations*, published in London in 1961: "Every passenger liner, every cargo vessel and every oil tanker built before the Second World War represents a floating fire risk of awful severity. Lessons learned at dreadful cost during that war have been taken seriously by most ship-owners and ship-builders (prompted by compelling legislation) in the last decade, a revolution in marine architecture which is by no means complete." He goes on to quote from Shakespeare's *King Henry VI*:

> A little fire is quickly trodden out,
> Which being suffered, rivers cannot quench.

Frank Rushbrook suggests basic legislation to protect ships from fire. He describes equipment aboard ship; fireproofing in design and construction; training of personnel; firefighting at sea or in port; and prevention in docks and harbors. That author believes all passenger vessels of 15,000 tons and upwards should carry at least three trained firemen in every watch, in addition to more highly trained officers than at present.

The HENRY CLAY, *Hudson River liner, burned off Riverdale, N.Y., 1852*

FIRE IN PORT

New York Fire Department men say that fire risks on shipboard are even greater in harbor than at sea. Discipline is relaxed; there is smoking, and a careless match may start a blaze. Some merchandise, particularly cotton, is often on fire before it is loaded.

As a rule, it is possible to berth the average ship alongside a wharf in American Atlantic ports. This makes dealing with a cargo cheap and easy and is convenient for passengers. But it also increases fire risks. Sheds on wooden piles, with wooden superstructures, really make horizontal flues through which flames can rush with lightning speed; and there is the risk that fire will spread to adjacent buildings.

The first fire protection ever provided for New York City's waterfront from the water side was something called a "floating engine." It was built in 1800. A crew of twenty volunteer firemen rowed it from its berth at Roosevelt (Peck) Slip and manned the "coffee-mill" pump in relays. It was not a success, and was dismantled in 1818.

New York City had to depend on volunteer firemen until 1865. That year, the Metropolitan Board of Fire Commissioners took over and established a paid force. Soon afterward they felt a need for some vessel to fight fire on and along the river fronts. A steam salvage tug, the John Fuller, was hired in 1866 on a call basis from John C. Baxter & Son, ship chandlers, of 308 West Street. The John Fuller was equipped with fire pumps, hose, and

116

salvage gear. It could throw thirteen streams of water. It was advertised as a "wrecking and fire steamer."

New York's first full-time fireboat, city-owned and built in 1875 for the purpose, was the wooden-hulled William F. Havemeyer. She was berthed at the foot of Pike Street on the East River. Engine Company No. 43 was organized to man her, with two officers, two engineers, a pilot, and five firemen. In 1883 a second fireboat, the Zophar Mills, went into service. She was iron-hulled, 120 feet long, with a fire pump capacity of 6,000 gallons per minute. The Mills served for fifty-two years.

THE GREAT REPUBLIC

New York City had no paid fire department and no fireboat on December 27, 1853, when three noble ships were destroyed on the East River waterfront by a fire that started from overheated ovens in a bakery a block away. The flames were fanned by a northwest wind. The area from Wall Street to City Hall was threatened before the fire was quenched, four days later.

Most famous of the three ships was the largest and fastest of all clippers, the side-wheeler Great Republic, 325 feet long, of 53-foot beam, 38-foot depth, 4,555 tons burden. She had four masts, four decks, and carried a crew of 100 men and 30 boys. The famous shipbuilder Donald McKay built her in Boston, where she was christened with great fanfare on October 4, 1853. Longfellow's admiration for the shipbuilding genius was put into poetry:

> Build me straight, O worthy master!
> Staunch and strong, a goodly vessel,
> That shall laugh at all disaster
> And with wave and whirlwind wrestle!

Longfellow omitted the greatest threat of all—fire.

Donald McKay's brother, Lauchlan, was to command the ship on her maiden voyage to Liverpool. The Great Republic was in New York, almost loaded, at her Front Street pier, with two tugboats engaged to nose her out from her berth. The two brothers sat aboard her at midnight, drinking to a successful voyage. At 12:30 A.M. the cry of "Fire! Fire!" rang out.

The Great Republic was ignited by a spark lodged in her tightly furled main topgallant sail. Flames ran along her cordage to the main royal and skysails. The top of the 130-foot mast could not be reached by water from a hand engine. The brothers offered $1,000 to any man who would go aloft and cut off the fire, and the mainmasts above the masthead. There were no takers. At 5 A.M. the tallest mast came down.

117

Tied up south of the Great Republic on that night of December 27, 1853, were the clipper ship Joseph Walker, the clipper White Squall, and the ships Whirlwind and Red Rover. All caught fire.

The Joseph Walker, 1,326 tons, built in New York in 1850, was almost ready to sail for Liverpool. She burned on the spot. The White Squall, also three years old, had arrived the week before from San Francisco. She burned to the water's edge, then drifted toward the Brooklyn Navy Yard. The Whirlwind and the Red Rover were towed aflame into the open river and were saved.

Tugs had tried to tow the Great Republic out into the stream; but the tide was low, and the great ship's heavy keel rested on the bottom. She was scuttled. When the tide rose again the two upper decks were still above the waterline. The wreck smoked for two days. The hull could not be saved. Water-soaked corn and wheat in the hold swelled and broke knees and beams of the lower deck. The remains were sold.

It took a year to rebuild the Great Republic. She sailed on her first voyage February 21, 1855, arriving at London sixteen days later. Rebuilt, she registered only 3,357 tons and had only three decks, but she still had four masts, was still the largest ship in the world, and one of the fastest afloat.

She carried 1,600 troops to the Crimean War. She made a passage of ninety-two days from New York around Cape Horn to San Francisco in 1857, then carried Union troops in the Civil War. In 1867 she was put on the Pacific Mail run to Japan and China. In 1869 she was sold to a British merchant and foundered, three years later, in a hurricane off Bermuda.

THE EMPIRE STATE

The Fall River Line steamer Empire State, Captain Brayton, master, had a series of disasters after being launched in 1848. A visiting British author wrote in 1853 that "Cleopatra might envy the splendor of this floating palace."

In April of that year the Empire State caught fire in Long Island Sound. The 240 passengers were taken off safely. Later that year she collided with an unlighted schooner while making a fast turn to avoid hitting another schooner that was lighted. The Empire State was disabled and taken in tow.

In July, 1856, her boiler blew up off Point Judith, with three fatalities. On March 18, 1858, she was westbound with seventy-eight passengers in a heavy fog, thought to be on course for Sands Point Light, when she struck a rock and sank. The passengers and some freight were taken aboard the Cornelius Vanderbilt. Ten days later the Empire State was raised. She served until the end of the Civil War.

Clipper JOHN J. BOYD *burning at pier, North River, 1860*

STANDARD OIL YARD

There was no such thing as a tanker in the 1860's and 1870's when the Standard Oil Company had a yard at Hunter's Point on Long Island. Ships from all over the world, more often than not wooden and under sail, came there to take on barrels of oil. Fires were frequent.

Two vessels burned there in one day—October 25, 1868: the brig Lord Hartington, 170 tons, bound for Cork; and the 467-ton steamer Kings County. And 1872 was a bad year. In one day—July 30—four vessels were destroyed. The Norwegian ship Elpis, 517 tons, bound for the Baltic, lay in the yard loaded with 4,200 barrels of oil when she was lost in a fire that started from a burning canal boat alongside. The American brig Roslyn, 382 tons, bound for Trieste; the British bark Edward, 575 tons, of Halifax, Nova Scotia; and the brig Max were also total losses. On August 5, 1873, the Australian brig Oscar, 402 tons, loading oil for Queenstown, New Zealand, was set afire and wrecked by a burning barge nearby.

SEAWANHAKA

The 612-ton, 230-foot long, side paddle-wheel steamer Seawanhaka, which plied between Peck Slip in New York City and Glen Cove and Sea

Cliff, Long Island, burned to her keel on June 28, 1880, in the East River off Ward's Island.

She had left her uptown landing at East 33rd Street about 4:30 P.M. with some 300 passengers aboard, mostly home-bound commuters. Shortly before 5 P.M., at the entrance to Hell Gate, there was an unexplained explosion in the engine room. The wooden partition between engine room and fire room ignited. The engineer was badly burned. Captain Charles D. Smith was in a terrible predicament. There he was, in narrow, tricky Hell Gate with its rocks and tides. He had the Hartford liner Granite State to starboard, and to port, just ahead, were four schooners and a tug. So he drove her right ashore on Sunken Meadows, between Ward's and Randall's islands, quartering, so that she lay along as well as up on the beach. The wind blew across her, leaving one side quite clear of fire, so it was possible for passengers to jump off.

Captain Smith was alone in the pilothouse while flames were running up the wheelpost and licking his hands. He knew he had to hold on, and he did. He was frightfully burned. The Secretary of the Treasury awarded him a gold medal for heroic action on June 25, 1881. Sadly, he died on the very day the medal arrived to commemorate his gallantry. His crew had behaved splendidly too.

A Hell Gate pilot who inspected the trend of the keel after the accident said: "No man ever beached a ship in better shape than that."

Among the Seawanhaka passengers commuting that day from the city to homes on Long Island's north shore were such notables as Charles A. Dana, editor of the New York *Sun*; William R. Grace, merchant prince, who was soon to be elected mayor of New York City; J. W. Harper of Harper & Bros., publishers; and S. L. M. Barlow, a large stockholder in the company that owned the Seawanhaka. Charles Edgar Appleby, a prominent Long Islander, went over the side. He was observed to be "treading water, very calm."

Most of the passengers kept their heads, saved their own lives, and tried to save others. Some panicked, in spite of the captain's shouted instructions to crowd forward ahead of the flames. The death toll was given by newspapers of the time as from twenty-four to fifty.

THE NUTMEG STATE

Another Sound steamer, the Nutmeg State, a propeller on the run from Bridgeport, Conn., to New York, grounded on October 14, 1899, off Sands Point, two miles east of Execution Rock. She caught fire and burned, a total loss. Thirteen persons were lost, ten of them crew members. Captain F. H. Beebe of the City of Lawrence rescued 30 passengers.

Long Island Sound steamer SEAWANHAKA *burning, 1880*

The fire was discovered at 5:30 A.M. Captain Charles M. Brooks blew the whistle for assistance, then tied it down. Mate Patrick Coffey and three of the crew were in a port cabin near the flames. They tried to get out through the dead-eye. It was too small.

A man put out in a rowboat from shore, tried to enlarge the opening so they could crawl through. The hands of Coffey and his men could be seen clutching—but the fire reached them before the woodwork could be broken away.

THE HOBOKEN PIER FIRE OF 1900

It is estimated that nearly 400 lives were lost on Saturday, June 30, 1900, at the Hoboken, N.J., piers of the North German Lloyd Line in New York Harbor.

At 4 P.M. hundreds of curious visitors had come to inspect the four latest additions to the German line, the ocean liners Kaiser Wilhelm der Grosse, the Saale, the Main, and the Bremen. Fire broke out amongst merchandise on Pier 3, next to where the liner Saale was moored. In less than fifteen minutes the flames swept from pier to pier, fed by cotton, turpentine, and oil lying unprotected on the docks. A strong breeze from the south carried the fire rapidly over a quarter of a mile.

At that time the New York Fire Department, including its fireboats, had no jurisdiction in the state of New Jersey. It was unable to give aid to vessels in distress until they were in the open stream and neutral waters. Then it did heroic work.

Sightseers on the Kaiser Wilhelm der Grosse heard hundreds of barrels of pitch exploding from the heat like gunfire. They made a wild rush for the gangways. Panic was averted by the ship's officers, who announced that the vessel would proceed immediately into midstream. A stern hawser was already glowing from the heat. With decks ablaze, woodwork crackling, and clouds of steam roaring through her exhaust pipes, the ship made a terrifying spectacle as she slowly made her way to safety. The "K.W.D.G.," built in 1897, a twin-screw ship of 14,350 tons and four funnels, was damaged but not seriously. Tugs went to her aid. The guests were transferred. The fire just spoiled her looks.

In World War I she was sunk off Africa, on August 26, 1914.

The other three German vessels involved in the Hoboken fire of June 30, 1900, not having steam up, could not escape. They were lost.

The Saale, expected to sail shortly for Bremen with a cargo of copper, cotton, and general merchandise, cast loose and drifted slowly into the stream, a menace to shipping and a funeral pyre to those on board. Some were imprisoned below decks. Hundreds jumped overboard, and some were picked up by passing boats. Fireboats surrounded the smoking hull. The hose played on one naked arm while a man's voice screamed for help, saying that forty men and women were with him. A desperate effort was made to haul the man through the porthole, but it was too small. A stewardess was heard calling from a cabin port on the main deck, where the fire was eating its way through a paneled door. A tug gave her a hose length and she fought the flame—but lost.

The Saale finally grounded off Ellis Island. Captain Mirow of the Saale was found dead in his cabin.

The Main, which had arrived in New York a few days before, was 1,000 feet away from the outbreak, but caught fire almost at once. Her decks were swept bare as if hit by a tornado. There was no time to cast off. The fire ate through the hawsers.

Only 16 out of 150 on board escaped. They were all coal-passers or engineers. They closed the door to the coal bunker and stayed there for nearly eight hours—until 11:30 P.M., when the Main was grappled by a fireboat. Its crew heard voices, located the imprisoned men, and hauled them one by one through a coal port. All but one recovered.

The Bremen, crowded with visitors, drifted away from the burning docks and became a torch to all shipping and wharves with which she came in contact. Carried to the New York shore, she imperiled all docks from West 33rd Street to the Battery. One lighter passed her, caught fire, and drifted alongside the Baltimore & Ohio railroad wharf, which promptly in its turn took fire.

Tugs and fireboats finally got the Bremen under control. The fireboat New Yorker took twenty-eight people off her, through red-hot portholes. But seventy-four lives were lost. She was beached in shallow water off Weehawken.

The great Hoboken pier blaze of June 30, 1900, destroyed many smaller

The SAALE, *one of three German liners destroyed by fire at Hoboken, 1900*

craft—coal barges, lighters, and canal boats, as well as the ocean liners.

On the New Jersey side, the fire fighters saved from serious injury the Scandinavian–American docks that adjoined the North German Lloyd; also the Hamburg–American, Holland America, and Wilson Line sheds and their vessels.

The fire was under control in six hours. But according to the book *Fires and Firefighters* by John Kenlon, chief of the New York Fire Department, 1911–1931, and first chief of the Marine Division; "Nobody who saw it ever forgot the Hudson on that summer twilight, four great liners vomiting flame and smoke, surrounded by puffing tugs and busy fireboats, while perhaps two dozen smaller craft floated hither and thither in the most congested waterway in the world, aflame from stem to stern."

RESULT OF CATASTROPHE

Since April 11, 1902, the New York Fire Department has been specifically responsible for firefighting in the entire Port of New York area, on both the New York and New Jersey sides. The city of Newark has just one fireboat, which never comes into the harbor. At the time of the Hoboken pier fire, a New York Fire Department fireboat was refueled on the Jersey side, and New Jersey actually sent New York City a bill for it.

The 1902 law says that the Greater New York City Charter grants jurisdiction over harbor fires: Authority to protect any vessel in the Port of New York or in or upon any dock, wharf, pier, warehouse, building, or other structures bordering upon or adjacent thereto, shall be vested in the Fire Department of the City of New York. That includes all waters of the North and East rivers and the "harbor embraced therein or adjacent to or opposite to the shores of New York."

CRIMINAL NEGLIGENCE: THE GENERAL SLOCUM

On Tompkins Square, just off East 10th Street in New York City, is a small stone monument that reads, in part: "They were the earth's purest children, young and fair." Oddly enough, this is in a very mixed neighborhood, which became known in the 1960's for "hippie" disorders. The monument was put up in memory of the children who perished in New York City's most frightful marine disaster, the burning of the excursion steamer General Slocum in the East River near Hell Gate at 10:11 A.M. on June 15, 1904.

Within sight and sound of shore, 1,021 persons (some accounts give a larger total—no one will ever know exactly), mostly children, bound on a Sunday School picnic with their mothers, were burned to death or drowned. Scores of others were maimed or disfigured for life. There were 407 survivors. In a matter of minutes after the first alarm, the old wooden side-wheel steamer was a shapeless mass of debris. Nothing could stop the flames.

In 1904 that section of the lower East Side, from Houston to 14th Streets, was a closely knit community known as Little Germany. Almost everybody belonged to St. Mark's Evangelical Lutheran Church on East 6th Street. The excursion was the annual Sunday School outing of that church. The picnic was to be at Locust Grove, just beyond Throg's Neck in the Bronx.

Only about fifty of the excursionists were men. Most of the fathers were at work in the city while their families went on holiday. The pastor, the Reverend George F. Haas, was with the party. His wife and daughter drowned. He nearly died. Of the approximately 1,500 on board, only 23 were crew.

After June 15 the German–American community scattered, to Yorkville in Manhattan and Queens on Long Island. There were suicides and mental breakdowns. Most of the survivors and the bereft families tried to forget. The Tompkins Square neighborhood is now populated by a few elderly Lithuanians, Puerto Ricans, and drifters. The monument to the children is somewhat battered and largely forgotten. St. Mark's Church became a synagogue long ago.

Out in Queens, a Lutheran congregation still remembers the General Slocum. Nine hundred and fifty-eight bodies that were recovered were buried there in a mass funeral. An annual memorial service is held on the Sunday nearest June 15.

The General Slocum, 280 feet long with a 70-foot beam and 13-foot draft, built in 1878, had been chartered for this important event in the lives of hard-working people who lived crowded into a few city blocks. The day dawned fine and warm. The picnic party assembled at the Third Street pier at 8:20 A.M. Flags were flying, a band was playing German and East Side airs, children were laughing. Two ministers were on hand to welcome the mothers and Sunday School teachers. Two policemen went along to see that nobody fell overboard. As the General Slocum pulled away from the pier at nine o'clock, passengers sang the great hymn that Martin Luther and his followers had sung as they entered the Diet of Worms to stand trial for heresy: "Ein Feste Burg Ist Unser Gott" (A Mighty Fortress Is Our God).

All was joy and gladness for one short hour. About ten o'clock they entered Hell Gate. Chowder was being prepared in the galley for lunch. As the Astoria ferry Haarlem passed, its crew waved to the children playing on three decks.

When the Slocum was off Casino Beach, the Long Island point closest to the Bronx, Superintendent Grafling of the Gas Works there noticed a wisp of smoke. He reached for his field glasses. By the time he found the range, flames were shooting up from the ship. He had heard band music coming over the water only a moment before. Now he heard shrieks of terror.

A dredge captain at Astoria blew four blasts on his whistle. Other boats began to toot warnings.

On board the Slocum, the first warning was sounded when the vessel was abreast of 130th Street, about 300 feet from the Bronx shore. Mothers hurried their children toward the stern, but a brisk head-on breeze and the vessel's momentum as it shot toward Long Island Sound on the flood tide fanned the flames sternward.

Passengers started to panic. Some jumped overboard, clothing ablaze. Others fought for the life preservers, which came to pieces in their hands. The fire hose was rotten and it burst. Lifeboats were fastened so securely to their davits that they could not be launched. The crew, raw deckhands, had never been drilled. They tried only to save themselves.

Captain William Van Schaick, sixty-one, was a mariner with forty years experience, and the only captain the General Slocum ever had. He was respected, but seemed to be accident-prone. The Slocum is said to have had the longest list of minor accidents, prior to the 1904 holocaust, of any steamboat in the New York district.

Captain Van Schaick had the wheel, off 90th Street; but at 138th Street

he turned it over to Pilot Edward Van Wart and ordered beaching at North Brother Island, nosing right into a northeast wind. Afterward, it was said that a worse place to beach a vessel would be hard to find. If the captain had ordered sharp left rudder the ship would have beached within a minute or two, the fire would not have spread so fast, and there would have been a good chance of taking most of the passengers off.

Instead, the ship at full speed took the long way around. It crashed against the rocky northeast shore of the island, not opposite 145th Street, the nearest mainland, but almost out of sight around the bend. The water there is deep. The island slopes off at a pitch of about forty-five degrees. Observers wondered why the captain did not beach her on the Bronx shore. He never did explain that satisfactorily.

Just after the Slocum struck, Captain Van Schaick, followed by his two pilots, Edward Van Wart and Edward Weaver, jumped onto the deck of the tug Jack Wade. The captain did not even wet his feet. Most of the deckhands swam to safety. Only one crewman drowned. George Conklin, chief engineer, stuck to his post and lost his life. Everett Brandow, second engineer, was finally alone at the throttle, and lived to be the lone member of the crew cited for heroism.

From Casino Beach, Superintendent Grafling watched the starboard rail on the upper deck collapse and send a mass of debris and people into the water. This, he said afterward, completed the panic. As the ship hit the rocks, the hurricane deck gave way and the upper works crashed down, hurling some of those still aboard into the water or onto the blazing hull. The vessel lodged finally at Hunt's Point, burned to the waterline.

Few of the passengers could swim. Women and children were not taught that, ordinarily, in 1904. Most of them stayed on board too long, in any case.

Some heroic rescues were made. At least one of the Slocum's crew, besides the two engineers, behaved as a mariner should. William R. Trembly swam ashore again and again with drowning women. Jack Wade, owner and master of a little tug named for himself, happened to be at the North Brother pier and was able to ease up on the Slocum just as she struck. He rescued about 150 and was well scorched himself. The tugs Theo and Walter Tracy also did noble work.

The city tug Massasoit was at North Brother and was nearest behind the Slocum when she struck. But the Massasoit drew too much water to get close. Her mate, Albert Rappaport, jumped into the water, swam to the steamer, grabbed two babies, and swam back. The Massasoit's captain was putting his boats over as fast as he could. The Franklin Edson, a small steamer that drew less water, went up to the side of the burning vessel where people were jumping from the decks, and dragged them on board.

Thomas Cooney, a reserve policeman, saved eleven persons, then drowned as he went after his twelfth.

James Gaffney, engineer on North Brother Island, played a hose on the burning ship but gave that up to form a human chain of doctors and nurses, pulling a score to safety and recovering fifty bodies. Nellie O'Donnell, an assistant matron at one of the hospitals, who had never before swum a stroke in her life, jumped into the water and rescued ten before she fell exhausted. Mary McCann, a convalescent patient, rescued twenty and then collapsed.

It all happened so fast. By the time the fireboat Abram S. Hewitt responded to the call, which came at 10:12 A.M., and left her Brooklyn berth, picked up New York Fire Department Chief Edward F. Croker at the foot of East 67th Street, and arrived on the scene, its men were able to make many rescues but their principal job that day was the recovery of bodies. (Edward F. Croker, twenty-eight years in the New York Fire Department, was its commissioner from 1899 to 1911; a very able man.)

The GENERAL SLOCUM *on fire in East River; 1,021 lives lost*

Bodies were collected and medical aid given at the foot of East 138th Street. By 3:30 P.M. the Potter's Field boat Fidelity began to transfer the dead to the Bellevue pier at East 26th Street where the pitiful victims could be identified.

Captain Van Schaick and Pilots Van Wart and Weaver were arrested, as were all of the crew the police could round up. Aside from minor burns, the captain was unhurt.

When hard-boiled reporters for the New York City papers arrived on the scene to cover the holocaust, some of them broke down and wept. Others had to turn away, physically sick.

President Theodore Roosevelt ordered an investigation. The Department of Justice indicted Captain Van Schaick, the managing directors of the steamship company, and the manager and three employees of the Nonpareil Cork Works where the Slocum's life preservers had been made. It was claimed in court that the Cork Works had put iron bars into the life preservers to give them the legally prescribed weight. There was no law that covered this vicious act.

The Slocum's fire prevention and lifesaving equipment had been inspected and passed just a short time before the catastrophe. Two local inspectors and a supervising inspector were dismissed from the service. A careful reinspection of 268 vessels showed an alarming incidence of defects.

The investigation revealed the probable start of the fire in a cabin where lamps and oil, gasoline, brass polish, and other inflammables were kept. Some thought a cook stove might have exploded and started a fire in oily ropes and rags nearby. The sheet of flame, seconds later, suggested loose material and brittle paint on old wood.

When the case came to trial the only one convicted was Captain Van Schaick. He was charged with manslaughter and failing to train his crew in fire drill. In January, 1906, he was sentenced to ten years at hard labor in Sing Sing for criminal negligence.

In 1908 the sentence was commuted, after a petition signed by 1,000 persons connected with the shipping industry had been carried to President Roosevelt. The President took cognizance of the captain's advanced age and considered the vessel's operators to be the real offenders. New York papers called the General Slocum disaster the result of "a combination of official carelessness and monstrous callous cupidity on the part of the manufacturers of lifesaving equipment."

As the laws stood at that time, no financial relief could be obtained from the Slocum's owners for the bereaved or for the injured survivors, beyond the value of the vessel. No personal liability was chargeable to vessels used in rivers and inland waters, nor could the families sue the government. The wreck was raised and sold for $1,800. She was turned into a barge, but sank and was finally abandoned a few years later off New Jersey. However, as always following a catastrophe, inspections were tightened up and equipment was improved.

A newspaper story following the disaster told how Captain Samuel H. Berg of 55 Stanton Street, New York City, had saved the lives of fifty passengers from the Slocum. He was a powerful swimmer and a professional lifesaver. The United States Volunteer Life Saving Corps of New York gave him a gold medal for this feat.

The New York papers that month carried pitiful advertisements for missing persons known to have gone on the Slocum, such as: "Would you kindly let me know if you have seen a boy of the following description . . ." with a picture of the boy.

THE SURVIVORS REMEMBER

Directly after the disaster, the Organization of the General Slocum Survivors was formed. Members met once a month, except in summer, at Mozart Hall, 328 East 86th Street, Manhattan. Once a year, usually on the second Sunday in June, they have gone all these years with their families to Middle Village in Queens, Long Island. Trinity Lutheran Church is situated in the cemetery where the General Slocum monument stands in the center of many graves. On the monument is the burning ship, faced in bronze.

The survivors' group used to stand for the service in the cemetery plot; but since 1958, due to weather and the advancing age of the members, it has been held within the church. The Reverend Paul H. Wasmund, chaplain, whose father conducted the service until he retired in 1948, said in 1968: "I doubt if there are over twenty members today."

In 1963 the late Miss Anna Sackmann, then secretary of the group, said: "Today there are thirty members, twelve of whom are actual survivors of the General Slocum fire. William Weigele of the Bronx, now president, is not; he is just an interested friend. I was on the excursion, aged fourteen. We were a family party of eleven. Two of us came back."

Her mother, a sister, a brother, an aunt, and five cousins were lost. Another brother, the late Charles R. Sackmann, was president of the survivors' group for ten years. "He was playing in the street, the day before the picnic," Miss Sackmann said, "and was hit on the head with a stone. So he was in the hospital and couldn't go."

THE BLACK SEA

The tanker Black Sea exploded at Pier 5, Bayonne, N.J., on February 23, 1927. Burning gasoline poured through a hole in the tanker's side, endangering other ships and piers. The fireboat John Purroy Mitchel made fast to the burning vessel while the fireboat William L. Strong poured streams over surrounding waters to prevent the fire's spread. The Mitchel caught fire. Its crew were forced below before they could cut the lines. But the two fireboats smothered the blaze.

The Black Sea's captain and three men were fatally burned before the arrival of the fireboats.

THE PANUCO

On August 18, 1941, the American freighter Panuco, docked at Pier 27 at the foot of Baltic Street, Brooklyn, caught fire. The crew delayed turning in an alarm. They tried to control the fire themselves. The ship, its cargo of sisal, and the pier were all burning when the box was pulled. A thousand barrels of oil on the pier went off like fireworks, exploding every few minutes. The Panuco was towed into shallow water and beached. Thirty-four lives were lost, and the ship was destroyed.

THE JOHN ERICSSON

On March 7, 1947, the U.S. Maritime Commission's John Ericsson, the former Swedish–American liner Kungsholm, burned on the north side of

Pier 90, North River, Manhattan. The 600-foot, twin motorship of 20,000 tons became a total loss. She was to have sailed for Europe the following day with 512 passengers.

The Queen Elizabeth, moored on the south side of the same pier, was threatened. The pier was crowded with many of the Elizabeth's 2,231 passengers, plus visitors, baggage men, and others at the time the fire was discovered—2:24 P.M. The traffic congestion impeded the movements of fire apparatus. The Elizabeth was scheduled to depart for England at 4:30.

The fire, which started amidships on the Ericsson, was apparently caused by a short circuit in the electrical wiring. An investigation brought out the fact that some crew members had tried for twenty minutes to put out the fire before turning in an alarm. Shore apparatus and two fireboats fought the fast-spreading blaze, aided by a fleet of railroad and other tugs with their monitor nozzles. At 5:45 P.M. Chief Frank Murphy declared the fire out.

The John Ericsson had been taken over by the U.S. Government six days after Pearl Harbor and converted into a troop carrier. In 1947 she was being operated by the United States Lines. Only half of her crew of 414 were aboard at the fire's outbreak. Eighty longshoremen were loading cargo.

On March 12 the Maritime Commission announced that the expense of refitting the nineteen-year-old vessel would not be justified, due to her age and hard usage during the war. The loss was tentatively set at $1,500,000.

TWO DISASTERS IN ONE DAY

Fireboats and helicopters fought the blaze, on July 19, 1952, when the Poling Bros. No. 18 tanker exploded and burned in the East River off 73rd Street. Three crewmen were rescued; one was lost. The burning ship drifted toward Queensboro Bridge.

On that same day the Black Gull, a Norwegian freighter with a cargo of zinc, tin, and castor oil, was set afire by naphthalene and subsequently abandoned sixty-five miles southeast of Montauk Point. The Merritt-Chapman & Scott vessel Curb left Staten Island to go to her assistance, on a message from the Coast Guard cutter Yeaton which was standing by. The Black Gull's lifeboats had burned.

The freighter was towed through rough seas to New York. She arrived in the lower bay on July 21, still smoldering. The New York City fireboats poured in streams and put out the fire, but the Black Gull sank in twenty-three feet of water. She was refloated on July 29 and some of her cargo salvaged. Then she was scrapped.

She carried a crew of forty-two and nine passengers. The liners Gripsholm and Excalibur joined Coast Guard craft in the search for survivors. Eventually forty-four survivors, eight hurt, were landed in New York.

STAR OF THE SEA

She was said to be the last four-masted schooner licensed for sea duty, when she sank in twenty-eight feet of water in Hempstead Harbor, Long Island, on Sept. 4, 1955. The following February, her ninety-five-foot masts sticking out of the water were judged a menace to navigation. The Army Corps of Engineers was given permission to raise the hull, beach and burn her.

The schooner had been used as a training ship for the Cadet Midshipmen's Training Corps, teenagers, at 26th Street and East River, since 1953. She was fore-and-aft rigged, 175 feet long, of 791 gross tons. She was built in 1917 at Bath, Maine, for the coastal trade in lumber, coal, and fish scrap. As the Annie C. Ross she used to come into the Promised Land fish factory dock at Amagansett, Long Island.

In 1941 she was laid up in Newtown Creek, Queens. While in retirement she had a fire that burned out her after house. In 1953 the boys of the training corps reconditioned her. A ship-rigging concern offered to renew her standing rigging. She was a handsome vessel, widely known and admired.

THE NEBRASKA AND THE EMPRESS BAY

Eight fireboats and a tender, besides land units, U.S. Coast Guard, and Police Department craft, were involved on June 25, 1958, when a collision and fire placed crowded New York Harbor in double jeopardy. The crash occurred at 12:24 A.M.

The 438-foot motorship Nebraska of Gothenberg, Sweden, a freighter of the Swedish Trans-Atlantic Steamship Co., bound from New Haven, Conn., to Port Newark, N.J., and the U.S. tanker Empress Bay, 189-foot steel motor vessel of the Tanker Petroleum Corporation, going from the Standard Oil Co. of New Jersey terminal in New Jersey to Mt. Vernon, N.Y., collided and caught fire opposite Pier 29, Manhattan, and directly beneath Manhattan Bridge. The Empress Bay exploded, damaging the bridge. Two men were killed on the Empress Bay and thirty-five were hurt.

She carried a cargo of 280,000 gallons of high-test gasoline. The bow of the Nebraska struck her amidships on her port side, releasing great quantities of oil. The Nebraska was entirely coated, from her waterline to the boat deck. The river was covered with great patches of gasoline. The whole East River in the vicinity of Piers 29 and 31 seemed on fire, as the fuel spread directly astern of the two vessels. The bow of the Nebraska remained embedded in the Empress Bay for an hour and a half while the Nebraska maneuvered her engines to keep the vessel in the river, away from the piers.

Heat radiation from the dispersing of inflammable cargo under the

The NEBRASKA *and* EMPRESS BAY, *after collision in East River, 1958*

Manhattan Bridge started a second fire on the BMT subway ties, blocking the right-of-way between Manhattan and Brooklyn. The bridge fire was confined to the tracks, ties, and roadbed of the BMT.

The two ships, wrapped in flame, had to be held in the channel and secured against the running tide. The Coast Guard and Police Department helped prevent further traffic on the river, and searched for survivors.

Captain Eugene E. Kenny of the fireboat William J. Gaynor, who has since retired with the rank of Battalion Chief, went to the aid of the burning vessels. He says: "That was the biggest operation I was ever in. Luckily, our station was only 500 yards from the collision. We were at the Nebraska in five minutes. The Gaynor had to pass through patches of burning oil, trying to rescue trapped crew members. All were removed from forward; the Nebraska's main deck was forty feet above the waterline; ours was thirty feet. They had a drop of ten feet onto the pilothouse of our little boat. It was like jumping onto a postage stamp. They clung onto us like flies. More crew were in the port fantail, and we got them. We rescued thirty-seven in all, two of them women; many with their clothes on fire.

"But in the second operation the Gaynor was struck by the revolving blade of the Nebraska's port propeller, causing a rip in our hull below the waterline. We had to withdraw to prevent sinking. Two firemen were injured."

Meanwhile, the tug Valmorac arrived on the scene and recovered several survivors from the water. The tug Dalzellera also removed four men from the burning Nebraska, and later pulled the two vessels apart. In all, thirty-one were injured on the Nebraska, but none were killed.

On the tender Smoke III, Acting Chief Roald L. Olsen saw an injured man in the burning water. He dove overboard and held the drowning man afloat until the Smoke could come alongside. He received awards for his lifesaving feat. Candido Santiago, a schoolboy on Broome Street, saw a man in the water, swam to him, and, aided by a policeman, held the man up until a passing tug pulled them on board. The boy received a bronze medal and $50 from the Life Saving Benevolent Association.

When the fire on the Nebraska had been brought under control, she was towed from the East to the North River and berthed. She was moved on August 20 to Liberty (formerly Bedloe's) Island, and partly raised. Her damage was assessed at nearly half a million dollars.

The day after the collision, the Empress Bay could be seen with her stern under water and only part of her bow visible. She had sunk immediately after being separated from the Nebraska. When the tug Dalzellera was pulling on the Empress Bay, trying to get her into shallower water, the motor vessel George Whitlock II, eastbound, tried to go between the tug and the Empress Bay, so that the tug had to drop the towline and the Whitlock collided with the stem of the Empress Bay. The Empress Bay became a total loss.

The East River was closed to traffic until August 20 due to seepage of the high-test fuel oil. Motorists using the bridges were warned against smoking. Civilian tugs aided the regular services in maintaining patrols.

The U.S. Coast Guard Marine Board of Investigation decided that the collision was the result of negligence on the part of the pilots of both vessels. The pilot aboard the Nebraska erred in navigating at an excessive speed and in ordering a left rudder upon initiating a two-whistle signal for which no assent had been received from the Empress Bay. The pilot of the tank ship was at fault because he used a cross signal in answering a two-blast signal with one, instead of the danger signal followed by one blast, which would have clearly indicated his intentions. This was contrary to the rules of the road.

However, the subsequent action of the Nebraska's pilot "merits approbation," the report said; "his skill and tenacity while facing the hazard of the gasoline-laden tanker and his own vessel, both almost completely involved in flame, prevented a serious waterfront conflagration in the Port of New York. A similar devotion to duty displayed by the master and men on watch on the bridge and in the engine room was in the finest tradition of those following the sea."

Commendations were given to officers and crew of the tug Dalzellera, to Captain Kenny and his men of the fireboat Gaynor, and to the captain of the tug Valmorac.

THE CONSTELLATION

The U.S. Navy's super-aircraft carrier Constellation (C.V. 64), which has been under fire in Vietnam, suffered two major accidents shortly after her christening at the Naval Shipyard in Brooklyn. On December 19, 1960, when she was only 85 percent completed, a disastrous and stubborn fire killed fifty civilian workers and injured 267 others, including forty firemen and some yard employees.

The fire at the Navy Yard broke out at 10:30 A.M. Leaking oil on the hangar deck ignited. Only eighty-five of the ship's personnel were present at the time, but there were over 3,200 workers. If construction had been completed and the crew all on board, it was thought afterward that the fire would have been extinguished in less than a minute.

The Constellation, 1,050 feet long, 252 feet wide at the flight deck, 22 stories high at its tallest point, was damaged severely. The fire meant a delay of seven months in completion and a loss estimated at $47 million.

When the fire broke out, hundreds of the workers were cut off by the flames. Edward F. Cavanagh, Jr., then New York Fire Commissioner, said this was the biggest search-and-rescue operation that had ever confronted a fire department. Four marine companies took part. The Navy and police also helped to fight the stubborn blaze.

The tug Carol Moran came alongside, with several other tugs of the Moran fleet. Captain Lars O. Thorsen and the crew of the Carol put up ropes and a ladder, effecting the escape of 250 naval shipyard employees. The men on the tug were given a commendation and a check by the Life Saving Benevolent Association of New York.

The JOHN J. HARVEY, *fighting fire on* RIO JACHAL, *Manhattan, 1962*

The Constellation was in trouble again on November 6, 1961, during her sea trials, about sixty miles southeast of New York, when a fire killed four men and injured nine.

THE TEXACO MASSACHUSETTS AND THE ALVA CAPE

One of the most prolonged and hazardous firefighting operations in the history of the New York Fire Department started with a collision of two tankers, the Texaco Massachusetts and the Alva Cape, in a narrow, dogleg passage in Kill Van Kull, between Bayonne, N.J., and Staten Island, about 200 yards from the Bayonne Bridge. It happened at 2:12 P.M. of a fine, clear day—June 16, 1966.

The collision was followed by fire on five vessels. Of the 110 men on board the tankers and their tugs, 33 were listed as dead. Sixty were hospitalized. Two weeks later, explosions on one of the damaged ships killed four men and injured others.

The American tanker Texaco Massachusetts, 16,500 tons and 604 feet long, having discharged her gasoline cargo, was leaving Newark Bay in ballast on her way to Port Arthur, Texas. The tug Latin American was alongside her. The British motor tanker Alva Cape, 11,000 tons and 547 feet long, carrying 140,000 barrels of naphtha picked up in Karachi, Pakistan, was bound for Bayway, N.J. Both ships had experienced pilots aboard. The Alva Cape was about to turn right into Newark Bay, accompanied by two tugs, the Esso Massachusetts and the Esso Vermont, when the two tankers collided bow-on. There was a grinding crunch. The Alva Cape's starboard side was gashed from waterline to deck. Naphtha began gushing into the water and onto the tug Latin American. The five vessels soon sat in a lake of naphtha.

From there on, the Texaco Massachusetts–Alva Cape affair was a Moran story, as well as a story of a tanker collision and terrible fire.

Admiral Edmund J. Moran, Chairman of the Board of the tug company, sat through the entire afternoon of the disaster in the room where the company's tug dispatchers work, so he could hear the actual voice reports by radio telephone from the seven Moran tugs that went to the scene.

Fortunately, the Julia C. Moran was at the Moran shipyard at Richmond, Staten Island, with her engine going when the first word of trouble came over the radio from Moran headquarters at 17 Battery Place, New York. The Moran dispatcher, who had been alerted by the Coast Guard, spoke through his desk mike, asking all tugs in the area of the Kills to see if they could help, adding that "it looks as if there has been a tanker crash." This was before the fire.

Just three and a half minutes after the crash, the tug Latin American burst into flame. That fire was not caused by the collision itself. The naphtha ignited when the Latin American started to get under way again, with a naphtha-soaked engine room.

The Julia C. Moran, Captain George Sahlberg in command, left the shipyard less than a minute after the crash and was first to arrive at the scene. Her captain could see the two tankers dead in the water, locked into each other's sides by the collision. The tug was only 400 yards away when an explosion and fire occurred on the Alva Cape. The Julia Moran kept on going. She pulled twenty-three survivors out of the fiery waters. They were Chinese seamen, violently sick from shock and fright.

Captain Richard F. Pinder of the Texaco Massachusetts saw that the men on the Latin American were being choked by naphtha fumes. He shouted, "Let go the tug!" The engines were racing, the tug white-hot, survivors testified. There was a series of explosions. Captain Pinder ordered his men to jump. He himself died of a heart attack a few minutes later, trying to swim from his burning ship.

Captain Graham Cecil Lewis of the Alva Cape was listed as missing after the fire. There were no survivors from the Esso Vermont.

Fireboats and tugs did heroic work. The New York City fireboat Governor Alfred E. Smith and a Coast Guard cutter tried to put out the blazing cargo on the Alva Cape. The Texaco Massachusetts, with her tanks empty but not yet cleaned, was full of gases; she presented a terrible risk. If flames from her had reached the great gasoline tanks at Bayonne, just across the channel, half the New Jersey port area might have been laid waste. High-pressure hoses and chemical-foam compound from the fireboats finally took care of that.

At 2:50 P.M. tugboat captain John Cray of the Harriet Moran arrived on the scene. He found the Alva Cape completely enveloped in flame; also the tugs Esso Vermont and Texaco Latin American. Portions of the Texaco Massachusetts were on fire.

Tugboatmen from the Helen L. Tracy raised a boarding ladder and hauled up the Massachusetts' anchor so she could be towed. Captain Cray undertook to pull the burning tankers apart. Maneuvering his tug through the blazing water, he made a towing hawser fast to the anchor chain, so that his tug and others (all seven Moran tugs were involved in that operation) could pull together. Captain Ollie Ericksen of the Susan B. Moran climbed up into the Massachusetts' wheelhouse and steered her as she was towed.

They finally got her to Bay Ridge, Brooklyn. Captain Cray said this was the most serious rescue operation he had ever been in.

Twelve days after the collision, at 3:49 P.M. on June 28, the Alva Cape was again racked by fire and explosions. The naphtha cargo was being removed to Gravesend Bay. Merritt-Chapman & Scott had nearly completed the pumping-out job when four explosions occurred in quick succession. The weather had been very hot for two days. Fire Commissioner Robert O. Lowery had ordered, on June 27, that the cargo departments of the Alva Cape be inerted through the introduction of carbon dioxide into the tanks. On June 28 he ordered the firemen off the tanker because of an impending electrical storm.

The heat probably contributed to the blasts, but Fire Chief John O'Hagan laid the explosion and fire to the mixing of naphtha and oxygen in the pumping out operation. The Coast Guard later concluded that if the safety requirements of the Fire Department had been complied with, in all likelihood the second disaster could have been prevented. Experienced seafaring men who watched the operation on the Alva Cape were of the opinion that she was not being handled right; that her steel cable scraped and caused sparks.

There were four known dead that day. One tug, the Susan Moran, took ten men off the blazing tanker. Louis Rubine, Jr., in command of the fireboat Alfred E. Smith, was blown off and injured. Twelve firemen were injured and a fireboat severely damaged.

On June 30, 1966, it was reported that Federal authorities had ordered owners of the ruined Alva Cape to take the ship out to sea 110 miles southeast of Ambrose Channel, where the water is a mile deep, and sink her. She was judged a serious menace in the harbor. Authorities in New York said no such order had ever been given here in their memory. The ship still had from 10,000 to 15,000 barrels of naphtha in her unruptured tanks. It was thought she might be creating more and more gases all the time.

The owners asked the Moran Towing and Transportation Company to do the job. They agreed, but only with the provision that the United States Navy would go along and sink the hulk with gunfire or a torpedo. The Navy refused.

The owners thought it would be possible to scuttle the ship at sea without resort to demolition. However, on July 2 the burnt Alva Cape was towed out of New York Harbor by the Kerry Moran and the Nancy Moran. She still had over a million gallons of highly volatile naphtha in her tanks. Ambrose Channel was closed for two hours, the time it took to get the Alva Cape through the Lower Bay and out to sea. At the request of the owners, the vessel was sunk on July 3, in 1,200 fathoms of water, by gunfire—fifty-seven rounds of five-inch shells from the U.S. Coast Guard cutter Spencer, 110 miles southeast of New York Harbor. She burned furiously as she went down, her naphtha having been ignited by the gunfire.

As always, there were long, drawn-out repercussions. The Port of New York Authority complained that since 1953 there had been twenty-six accidents in the vicinity of the June 16, 1966, collision; and that it had repeatedly asked the Federal government to widen the channel (it was only 2,000 feet wide at the point of the catastrophe).

On August 11, 1966, the docking pilot of the empty American tanker Texaco Massachusetts and the other docking pilot on the British Alva Cape were charged with negligence. On April 27, 1968, the former's license was suspended for six months. The case of the latter was still pending. On October 25, 1967, the Federal Transportation Safety Board had attributed the crash to failure of persons in charge of navigation to exercise "due caution."

The harbor tug Julia C. Moran became the first East Coast tug to receive the "Gallant Ship" plaque, created in 1928, the highest Federal award to a merchant vessel for outstanding action in a marine disaster. On November 14, 1967, crewmen of the New York City fireboat Governor Alfred E. Smith were honored by the Maritime Administration for their outstanding performance at the scene of the collision.

Captain George Sahlberg, now retired, who had commanded the Julia C. Moran on that fateful day, was presented with the Merchant Marine Distinguished Service medal. Other tug captains and crewmen received citations. In December, 1966, Captain Sahlberg received the Valor Medal of the American Bureau of Shipping. Mayor John Lindsay of New York presented him with the Times Square Good Citizen Award for this same rescue work. Captain Sahlberg, forty-five years on shipboard and a retiring

Traditional fireboat salute to a maiden vessel, New York Harbor

sort of man, was the city's guest of honor over a long weekend and appeared on television. He blinked under the glaring television lights and said, "It's brighter here than when the Alva Cape blew up."

THE HANSEATIC

A tricky, five-alarm fire nearly destroyed the Hamburg–American liner Hanseatic on September 7, 1966, as she lay at her berth at Pier 84, Hudson River and 44th Street. The Hanseatic, 673 feet long and 30,030 tons, largest ship of the West German merchant marine, was expected to leave in about four hours for Cherbourg, Southampton, and Cuxhaven, when the fire broke out at 7:30 A.M. Luckily, the crew of 500 were aboard; and only three of the 425 passengers had arrived. All were evacuated safely.

The fire started in the engine room and spread fast. It was thought that diesel oil, from a ruptured fuel line or a faulty gasket, had leaked and reached the ship's hot engines.

Fifteen minutes after the fire started, the Hanseatic's sprinkler system had a power failure. This put two out of three fire pumps out of action. Superheated vents kept threatening to turn the vessel into an inferno amidships. Chief of Department John T. O'Hagan described the companionways used by the firemen as "hot and ripe." The tremendous heat warped the steel bulkheads and made it difficult to open engine-room doors. Fire ran beneath the deck plates from the first engine room to the second; these flames were hard to reach. In an area of cherry-red steel, firemen feared that if they put water on the tanks holding 100 tons of heavy fuel oil, the sudden cooling might rupture them.

Also, it was low tide, and the ship with her holds full of water might settle to the bottom of the slip. Fireboat captains, remembering how the Normandie had capsized in 1942, used water very judiciously on the Hanseatic.

The Navy tug Naugatuck raced to the pier from the Brooklyn Navy Yard, with chemical foam; fireboats and land apparatus brought up more. The ship's crew advised a second access to the engine room area, opening the way for using the foam concentrate.

Chief of Department O'Hagan says that the main problem was to confine the fire on the upper decks. It had shot upward through ducts and spread outward, topside. The ship's plans were useful in the firefighting. Three fireboats were on the scene, together with 250 firemen, 100 policemen, engine and ladder companies. Flames raged for six hours, out of control. Finally, at 4 P.M., the fire was extinguished.

On November 25, 1966, the Hamburg maritime court ruled that the commander could not be blamed, but that the first engineer was late in informing the bridge of the blaze. The Hamburg–American Line praised the New York fire fighters.

ON CHRISTMAS EVE

It is unusual for a fire to appear to be the aftermath of a party on shipboard, although this is often enough the case on land. A rollicking Christmas Eve party aboard the 381-foot Norwegian tramp steamer Dianet, swinging at anchor off West 89th Street in the Hudson River, appeared to have been the cause of a blaze discovered at 4 A.M. on December 25, 1967. Three crew members died; eighteen persons, including three women, were hospitalized.

The Dianet had arrived in New York on December 17 from Buenaventura, Colombia. She had on board a cargo of 8,020 tons of sugar destined for Yonkers. Since no Yonkers berth was available at the time, she was allowed by the Coast Guard to anchor in an area reserved for naval vessels.

The Dianet was five years old. She carried a crew of twenty-nine and the captain, but two men were on shore leave. The captain, I. J. Avlijavlebo, was on board, asleep. He was notified of the fire at 4:15 A.M. The first report to the Fire Department came from a motorist driving along the Henry Hudson Parkway. He noticed the flames at 4:22 and called headquarters.

Three fireboats—the John J. Harvey, John A. McKeon, and Governor Alfred E. Smith—tied up alongside the fiercely burning ship. They pulled out twenty-four men and prevented the fire from reaching the cargo of sugar. One crew member was hauled through a below-decks porthole which, a fireman said, "couldn't have been much more than twelve inches wide." Three firemen were injured.

The fire had apparently started some time after midnight in the lounge on the main deck, or in the crew's quarters below. The men said the Christmas Eve party had ended about 10:30. Two or three hundred empty beer cans were found in the waste bins on deck.

At dawn the Dianet was a ghost ship, blackened and covered with ice, her superstructure 80 percent wrecked. One hundred and fifty firemen had fought the flames and brought them under control by 7 A.M.

The captain and six crew members stayed on board to help fight the fire. Afterward, three Moran Towing Company tugs took the Dianet to Pier 6 in Hoboken for repairs and assessment of damages.

FIREBOATS IN TROUBLE

On January 24, 1892, the Zophar Mills collided with the fireboat New Yorker, hitting her head-on near the waterline on the port side, during a heavy fog. The New Yorker's crew managed to keep her pumped out until she could be berthed in a shipyard. On February 13, 1899, the David A. Boody, second Brooklyn fireboat, was returning from a fire when she was rammed by ice and sunk in the East River at the foot of Corlears Street. The crew had tried desperately to pump her out, but to no avail. She was raised, reconditioned, and served until 1914. Brooklyn's first fireboat, the Seth Low, on duty until 1916, sank at her dock a year later.

On December 3, 1956, the Fire Fighter was nearly lost to the City of New York. The Luckenbach pier in Brooklyn was on fire. The Fire Fighter was battling the flames when primacord, a detonating fuse containing the high explosive PETN, caused a devastating explosion that rocked the fireboat, injured several of her crew, killed many people on the pier, and damaged buildings in the area. It cost $1 million to put the Fire Fighter back into shape again.

Ten men of New York's marine fleet have died in line of duty since the first fireboat was put into service.

MARINE SERVICE ORGANIZED

New York was the first American city to organize its fireboats into a marine unit. Once upon a time New York waters had three separate fireboat units. The city's first steam fireboat—and first in the United States—was the John Fuller in 1866. Then in 1885 Brooklyn built the Seth Low, which looked like a tug, and in 1892 the 105-foot David A. Boody. Long Island City used the services of a salvage tug, the Protector, on a rental basis. It had pumps and hose, as well as salvage and wrecking gear, and performed effectively (1893–1898) at several serious fires in oil-refining plants along the shores of Newtown Creek. But in 1898, when the Greater City was formed, Brooklyn and Long Island City Fire Departments were consolidated with New York's.

Edward F. Croker, twenty-nine years in the Fire Department and its commissioner from 1899 to 1911, set up the Marine Battalion on June 16, 1905. Four years later the Battalion became the Marine Division.

Chief Croker was a fireboat enthusiast. He inspected the fleet on Sunday mornings and often directed rescue operations from the deck of a fireboat. He was on the fireboat New Yorker, which saved twenty-eight persons from the burning, drifting German liner Bremen in the holocaust of June 30, 1900, at Hoboken. At the General Slocum fire of June 15, 1904, which took 1,021 lives, the first company to respond was Engine 51, the fireboat Zophar Mills, then moored at 97th Street and East River. Edward Croker immediately cleared the Abram S. Hewitt to take him aboard. He stayed on the scene all day, directing search-and-rescue operations. He was a nephew of Tammany leader Richard Croker. He used to say that his name, Croker, was the greatest handicap in his career.

FIRE DEPARTMENT LIBRARY

The New York Fire Department has a library, considered best of its kind in the country. Until April, 1971, it was located in Long Island City, quite a jaunt from midtown Manhattan but well worth the trip. It is now in the new Fire Department Headquarters Building at 110 Church Street, New York City.

For many years, until February, 1972, when illness forced his retirement, Clarence E. Meek, once a fireman himself, then made assistant chief, presided over the library's 11,000 catalogued items relating to fires. He is intensely proud of this pioneer in fire department libraries, which includes a collection of several thousand books and documents, rare items of firemanic literature given to the library by Deputy Chief James G. O'Hanlon.

Librarian Clarence E. Meek was for years associate editor of *WNYF* (With New York Firemen), the department's magazine. He received many citations for his work with the library and the magazine, and for assembling historic fire equipment pieces for the New York Fire Department Museum in Manhattan.

Since early 1972 the librarian has been Acting Lieutenant Paul Stolz. The library has a tremendous amount of material on fires, firemen, fire apparatus, and fireboats.

11

COLLISION

THE skipper of a ship out in the open sea can keep an easy mind, in ordinary weather. But approaching a busy port, with narrowing seaways, he has to cope with rocks and shoals and tides, and other vessels—with heavy traffic and little room to maneuver. Collisions, even today with all the communication and navigation aids, account for a heavy percentage of maritime disasters. Fog, always a danger at sea, becomes doubly dangerous in confined waters. And some mariners consider snow even worse than fog.

In *Rise of New York Port*, Robert Greenhalgh Albion says: "In almost every seaport the fog is heavier just outside rather than inside the harbor. At Robbins Reef, in the Upper Bay at New York, the total (based on the average hours per year for a quarter century or so in which fog signals were operated at various stations) was 438 hours; and at Hell Gate, 192." These figures are from fog statistics of the U.S. Lighthouse Service.

"True ocean fogs," report the Army engineers, "seldom reach the inner part of New York Harbor, although troublesome light fogs more frequently settle over the water during the morning hours. Off the Hook, conditions are worse, and in the old days often led to grounding on the bar."

The heaviest score of fog at any port south of Maine was at New York's Ambrose Lightship—876 hours.

Some years ago when schooners were plentiful, the master of a large coastwise steamer trading to the southward of New York said that rarely a year went by when one of his company's steamers did not sink a schooner. He complained that the schooners' foghorns were hard to hear; that the sailing vessels often ran without lights, to economize on oil.

In *The Great Coal Schooners of New England, 1870–1909*, Lieutenant W. J. Lewis Parker, USCG, wrote that the fault was just as often on the side of the steamer officers who insisted on racing through fog to keep on schedule, and were constantly misjudging the speed of sailing vessels whose bows they tried to cross.

THE SCOTLAND

The British steamship Scotland of the National Steam Navigation Co., Ltd., built in 1865 for the Liverpool–New York run, was inbound for New York on December 1, 1866. Whether or not that day was foggy, does not appear. When about ten miles off Fire Island, the Scotland collided with the Kate Dyer, a sailing ship of 1,278 tons, built in 1855, bound from Callao to New York with a cargo of cotton.

The Dyer sank.

The Scotland, badly damaged, made a run for Sandy Hook. The captain hoped to beach her inside Sandy Hook Bay, but she sank on Outer Middle Ground, part of the great shoal off the Hook. There she went to pieces in a gale.

New Jersey boatmen gathered up great quantities of cheese and beeswax that floated off from the Scotland. Captain Thomas A. Scott of New London blew out the Scotland's side with explosives and completed salvage of the cargo, landing it on the old Sandy Hook dock.

Temporarily, a light was placed over the remains, for the wreck became a great danger to navigation. Shipping interests petitioned the United States government to establish a lightship there. This was done in 1868. The new lightship was named after the wrecked Scotland. Later, its location was changed to a spot much farther out at sea.

THE CHRISTIANE

The 285-ton Danish bark Christiane, coming into New York from Rio de Janeiro, Captain Cornelius Isbrandtsen, master, was rammed by the steamer North America and sunk six miles east of Sandy Hook, N.J., on December 27, 1866. The captain and eleven crewmen on board the bark were lost; also Harbor Pilot Joseph Fredell.

The North America, outward bound, rescued four members of the Christiane's crew, and kept going. It was months before news of the disaster reached New York or the home port in Denmark.

A hundred years later, the pilot boat New York took Jakob Isbrandtsen, great-grandson of the Christiane's master and head of the Isbrandtsen shipping interests, and Captain William W. Sherwood, president of the New York Pilots' Association, to the spot where the Christiane had gone down. Mr. Isbrandtsen cast a wreath from the stern of the pilot boat.

CAPTAIN GEDNEY'S NEW CHANNEL

The Home, a steamship 198 feet long, built in 1837 in New York for the New York–Charleston route, struck a buoy on "Captain Gedney's new channel" at Romer Shoal, New York Harbor, on October 9, 1867. She was fast there for four hours, then floated and did not appear damaged. She left New York in a gale. North of Hatteras she began to leak. She went to pieces off Oglethorpe Light, two nights out of New York. All hands—eighty —were drowned.

The channel was actually not so very new in 1867. Up to 1837 the old Main Ship Channel over the bar had a minimum depth of 21 feet at low water; high tide gave it 4 or 5 inches more. In 1837 Lieutenant R. T. Gedney, USN, discovered an outer extension in the alternative channel which bears his name—with a minimum of 23 feet at low tide.

QUICKSTEP BUOY

The American bark Quickstep was run down by an outward-bound British steamer and sunk, in lower New York Harbor, date unknown. The wreck was removed and a bell buoy placed on the spot to mark the shoal. "Quickstep Buoy" is near West Bank.

SUNKEN BARGES A MENACE

Late in December, 1905, the coastwise steamer City of Atlanta of the Savannah Line, outbound, crashed into a submerged scow in Swash Channel, south of Romer Shoals, and had to put back to her North River pier. She had struck on her starboard bilge and heeled far over to port. The steamer carried passengers and United States cavalrymen bound for Fort Oglethorpe, Ga.

It turned out that the barge was one of two that had been sunk on December 27 in Swash Channel by the schooner Bessie Whiting. The barges had been in tow of the tugboat John Fleming.

Later that same day, the incoming Clyde Line steamer Comanche struck a submerged wreck in Swash Channel and listed, but little damage was found. The barges had been buoyed after sinking. It was believed that they had shifted position toward the center of the channel.

In 1906 the SS Etruria collided with a barge on her way out of the

Staten Island ferry NORTHFIELD *after collision, 1901*

harbor. A towing tug had cast two barges, neither of which had motive power or means of signaling. They were adrift in mid-Hudson River opposite New York City in a fog, while the tug was delivering a third boat. The tug was held in fault for the collision. The liner could not make out the barges until it was too late.

On December 31, 1968, the U.S. Army Corps of Engineers outlined a plan to rid New York Harbor of hulls and dangerous floating debris. The removal of 149 deteriorated piers and 1,972 derelict vessels would cost $28,848,000, they said. Studies showed it would take eight years to eliminate the sources of drift and dispose of the material.

THE FINANCE SINKS

The White Star Line freighter Georgic, over 10,000 tons, on the Liverpool to New York run, collided in fog at 7:40 A.M. on November 26, 1908, in New York Harbor, one mile east of Sandy Hook Point, with the Panama Railroad Company steamer Finance.

The Finance, with eighty-five passengers, was on its way to Colón, Panama, carrying mail and general merchandise. She sank in five minutes, going stern-first to the bottom. Many leapt into the sea. The captain used a revolver to stop crewmen pulling away in the first yawl, and made them return. Twenty-five women and children took their places. Three passengers and one officer were lost. All might have been saved if they had stayed aboard, for the Finance sank in shallow water. The Georgic was unhurt.

HOLLAND TUNNEL HAMPERED

The Holland Tunnel was under construction on June 1, 1926, when the Washington Irving of the Hudson River Day Line (largest excursion steamer ever built, 3,104 tons, with 6,000 passenger capacity) sank right over the tunnel.

The Irving had left her pier at Desbrosses Street that morning in a heavy fog. Very shortly afterward the barge Seaboard Oil No. 415, in tow of the steam tug Thomas E. Moran, collided with the day liner. Captain Deming of the Irving managed to land passengers and crew at Pier 9, Jersey City; but two lives were lost when the Irving settled to the bottom with only her hurricane deck above water.

Work on the tunnel was stopped until the vessel could be removed.

RESCUE IN AMBROSE CHANNEL

The British cargo and passenger ship Fort Victoria, once on the Liverpool–Boston run, was bound from New York to Bermuda on December 18, 1929. She was sunk in Ambrose Channel at the entrance to New York Harbor, with 400 passengers aboard, when she was rammed by the Clyde liner Algonquin. The pilot boats New York and Sandy Hook rescued passengers and crew of the Fort Victoria as she was sinking. "They behaved well," *The New York Times* reported on December 19.

THE SINKING OF THE LEXINGTON

At 6:35 P.M. on January 2, 1935, the Colonial Line steamer Lexington was bound from New York to Providence, R.I., with 125 passengers on board. Many of them were Harvard and Brown University students returning from the Christmas holidays. The Lexington had left her pier at 6:05 and was heading up the East River. She was between the Brooklyn and Manhattan bridges when she was split in two by the tramp Arrow Line freighter Jane Christensen of San Francisco. She sank in twenty minutes.

Some passengers were at dinner. Young people were dancing. There was a great crash. One survivor who had been in his cabin said, "I saw a big black hulk drift past the porthole." The ship's musicians played on calmly for five minutes, as if nothing had happened. There was another great crash, and dancers were thrown to the floor.

Still there was no panic. The freighter had hit forward, on the starboard side. Part of the saloon was stove in, but the boilers did not explode. The doomed ship was quickly surrounded by tugboats. The Pennsylvania Railroad tug Elmira rescued many, as the steamer's officers kept passengers moving. Captain William O. Pendleton remained calm. Some survivors were in the water three-quarters of an hour before they were picked up. Baggage from the Lexington was floating around them.

Seven crewmen were lost, according to Coast Guard figures.

Half of the Lexington floated to the foot of Grand Street, a quarter-mile from where she was rammed. The other half sank off Market Street.

The Lexington, 246 feet long, 2,249 tons, of 46-foot beam, was built in 1890. She made the twelve-hour run to Providence every night.

The Jane Christensen, formerly the Westbow, was owned by the Christensen Steamship Co., a subsidiary of the Arrow Line. Built in 1918, she was 409 feet long, of 3,500 tons, 54.2-foot beam. She was carrying lumber. The captain, John A. Wickman, said the collision was caused by a cross-current. The pilot on the bridge of the Lexington, Captain Harris Angell, said the freighter had swerved and crashed into the Sound steamer. Police gave the cause as a misunderstanding of signals.

The Lexington had suffered two earlier collisions. On March 17, 1919, the tug Jameson was sunk in the East River by the inbound Sound steamer. It was seven o'clock of a foggy morning. The tug sank at once; its crew was rescued.

On October 6, 1919, the steamer was rammed at Hell Gate by the U.S. submarine 0-7. The submarine headed across the liner's bow and holed it. The master of the Lexington at that time was Captain Gray. One newspaper account said that three men on the submarine were pitched overboard and that seven lives in all were lost. Another paper stated that no one was hurt.

THE MOHAWK

The 387-foot, 5,896-ton liner Mohawk of the Newport News S.B. & D.D. Co., outbound from New York, collided off Sea Girt, N.J., on January 25, 1935, with the Norwegian freighter Talisman. The Mohawk, a great hole torn in her side, listed and sank in less than an hour. Captain Joseph E. Wood had tried to beach her, but the engine room flooded. It was difficult to get out the lifeboats since the davits were thick with ice.

The Algonquin of the same line as the Mohawk, and the Limon of United Fruit Line, came on the scene. The Algonquin picked up four of the

Mohawk's boats with ninety-seven person. The Limon picked up two other boats with only a few survivors.

Forty-five were drowned, fifteen of them passengers.

THE EASTWIND COLLISION

Heroic action by two engine-room crewmen of the U.S. Coast Guard icebreaker Eastwind is credited with saving the vessel from sinking, or blowing up, when she collided in a fog with the 504-foot Gulf Oil tanker Gulfstream, sixty miles southeast of Barnegat, N.J., on January 19, 1949. The following is from official files.

The icebreaker took fire and burned for seven hours. Thirteen Coast Guardsmen were killed and twenty-one injured. The Eastwind was towed to Brooklyn on January 22 and repaired.

Three minutes after the crash, lights went out. There was no power to work the water pumps. The gasoline-powered pump was knocked out in the collision. One of the vessel's three engine rooms was flooded, and another partially so; neither could be used. Lieutenant Commander Charles E. Leising, engineer officer of the icebreaker, testified that two enlisted men, Ronald R. Wehner, twenty-three, and Louis D. Wilson, twenty-four, had gone down to the aft engine room, only one of them wearing an oxygen mask, to turn on a generator, which subsequently restored light to the ship and power for the auxiliary pumps. "But for these two men, I don't think the ship could have been saved," he said. Leising himself received a Coast Guard commendation medal for firefighting.

Another hero of the Eastwind disaster was Engineman 3d Class Robert Conners. He died in a futile attempt to rescue a shipmate, Fireman Apprentice John V. Zerr, who was trapped by fire below the main deck.

Captain John A. Glynn, USCG, commander of the Eastwind, was court-martialed but completely absolved of negligence. Charges were brought against his watch officer and navigator, Lieutenant Roland Estey. And Captain Henry G. Coyle, skipper of the tanker, was judged slow in reaching his wheelhouse after being notified that his ship was heading into a fogbank. The Gulfstream's chief officer, Lawrence Welsh, was found by the board to have failed to reduce speed as the tanker entered the fogbank. But judgment on all three was light because of mitigating circumstances on both sides.

Although the Eastwind's radar clearly indicated an approaching object at 1,300 yards, Estey was unable to see the ship. He thought the radar was displaying a false target, and disregarded it. The Gulfstream, which was not equipped with radar, was going at top speed when she entered the fogbank. Chief Officer Welsh notified his captain of the lack of visibility so that the senior officer could give the order to reduce speed. Just as Captain Coyle came into the wheelhouse, the bow of the Gulfstream sliced into the one-and-five-eights inch-thick steel plating on the starboard side of the ice-breaker.

IN THE MUD OFF BAY RIDGE

A collision recalled with some amusement—by parties not involved—took place in clear weather at 12:33 P.M. on June 27, 1950, in Bay Ridge Channel. The Excalibur of the American Export Line, 416 feet long and 9,350 tons, commanded by Captain S. N. Groves, collided with the 5,146-ton motor vessel Colombia, a Danish freighter 452 feet long, carrying a few passengers. The Excalibur was off for a Mediterranean cruise with 114 passengers and a cargo of medical supplies. The freighter was inbound. Both ships were damaged in the collision.

It was brought out in court that the Excalibur's captain, who lived in Bay Ridge, had swung over to the Brooklyn side of the channel in order to wave at his wife as he went by. He should have been to starboard, the usual course. By this maneuver the Excalibur had indicated that she was favoring the port side; so the inbound Colombia gave two short blasts, indicating a starboard-to-starboard passage. The Excalibur did not accept that but gave one short blast indicating a port-to-port passage. Then, as Captain Christian Mikklesen of the Colombia testified later, he had rudder failure.

Both vessels blew. Captain Mikklesen gave an order to turn sharp left, so the newspapers said, without the knowledge of his Sandy Hook pilot. "No time," he said.

The bow of the Colombia struck the Excalibur just forward of her passenger quarters. The Excalibur was still going full speed, her master in charge.

The Excalibur was beached on Gowanus Flats, her bow on the mud off Bay Ridge, with a fifteen-foot hole in her port side. A fire started in her paint storeroom. The Colombia's prow was smashed. Damage to the two ships amounted to $1.25 million.

No lives were lost. The Excalibur was blamed for the crash.

THE FAIRISLE

At 1:10 A.M. on the fog-shrouded night of July 23, 1956, the 486-foot American freighter Fairisle, inbound from Florida with a 5,000-ton cargo, collided with an outbound Panamanian tanker, the San José II, about three and a half miles south of Ambrose Lightship. The Fairisle suffered a gaping hole in her port side at midship. Both ships were damaged. No lives were lost, but two men were injured. Seven passengers and forty-six crewmen

Freighter FAIRISLE *after collision, July 23, 1956*

were on the Fairisle. The Coast Guard picked up thirty-nine in lifeboats.

Two days later, her engine room awash and four holds open to the sea, the Fairisle was being towed to Gravesend Bay when she settled on her starboard side in thirty feet of water, about a mile offshore of Brooklyn. Merritt-Chapman & Scott's Derrick Division started salvage work in September. On December 24 the Fairisle was refloated. Five days later a fifty-mile-per-hour gale struck Gravesend Bay. The vessel was towed to Pier 11, Staten Island, where salvage was finally completed. The Fairisle was bought by Seatraders, Inc., of New York.

Captain Kean of the Fairisle was found guilty of negligence and speed.

THE SANTA ROSA AND THE VALCHEM

The Santa Rosa, a new Grace Line cruise ship with 512 passengers aboard, inbound for New York, knifed into the American tanker Valchem at 3 A.M. on March 26, 1959, twenty-two miles east of Atlantic City, N.J., between the Hudson and the Delaware rivers, in a patchy fog. The impact drove a hole halfway into the tanker in the stern section. Two boilers were demolished, and ventilators were scooped off by the Santa Rosa's bow.

"Four men died, forty-four were injured, and about $1,890,000 went down the drain in property damage," Captain Donald F. Miley said in an article published in March, 1963, in *United States Naval Institute Proceedings*. The article was titled "Left-Handed Ship-handling."

Fires broke out on both ships, but the liner was able to tow the tanker to Brooklyn.

George Horne, veteran ship editor of *The New York Times*, writing in 1964 recalled the Santa Rosa–Valchem collision and that of the American Export liner Constitution with the Norwegian tanker Jalanta, off the entrance to New York Harbor on March 1, 1959. The latter occurred five miles south of Ambrose Lightship, in a fog. No one was hurt.

Mr. Horne said: "All four ships were in fog-radar situations and later testimony given at official inquiries showed that all four had made minor course alterations on the basis of radar pictures. And all four turned to port, or left, when danger appeared on the scopes." He went on to quote the Safety Convention that deals with this point. . . .

Retired New York–Sandy Hook pilot George Seeth says: "Radar doesn't solve all your problems.

"In confined areas and approaches, where there is danger of collision, too many objects appear on the radar screen at the same time, including land. . . . And a great difficulty is—men who are not properly trained to interpret radar pictures."

JIM STEERS

The Steers Sand & Gravel Company of Northport, Long Island, sustained two tragic losses in 1958 and 1962. Their diesel tug Jim Steers, two years old, foundered on January 19, 1958, in an icy gale and rain, between Kings Point and City Island, near Stepping Stones Light. She was last seen at Throg's Neck. All three men on her—Captain Albert Reichert, his son, and a crewman—were lost. The tug was found five weeks later. They had been bound for Connecticut. Albert Reichert, captain of the Steers, had twenty-two years experience in towing and merchant marine.

On January 21 the master of the tug Champlain, towing an oil barge, Hygrade 18, toward New York, said he thought the barge had hit something west of Stepping Stones that night. The barge was dented on the port bow.

On January 1, 1962, the Gwendoline Steers, a 150-ton tug owned by the same company, was lost in a gale and a blinding, freezing snowstorm. The cause has remained a mystery. Her captain, Robert Dickman, and a crew of eight, were taking her from the Bronx to Northport. She was seen entering Huntington Bay; then turned and headed back out into the Sound. She was last heard from some two miles northwest of Eaton's Neck. One man was found frozen in a lifeboat. The other eight went down with the tug, which was not found until the next summer.

THE SHALOM AND THE STOLT DAGALI

The Norwegian tanker Stolt Dagali was cut in two by the Zim liner Shalom shortly after 2 A.M. on November 26, 1964, off the New Jersey coast, about twenty-one miles south of Ambrose Light. The liner passed right through the tanker. The crash occurred in heavy fog, although both ships were equipped with radar. The stern of the Stolt Dagali sank; her forward three-quarters wallowed helplessly in a rough sea. By dusk she had drifted seventeen miles north of the collision scene. The impact drove a forty-foot gash in the starboard bow of the Shalom and blunted her prow, but she was able to return to New York under her own power.

Planes, helicopters, and cutters rushed to the scene. Tugs stood by. The Shalom herself picked up two survivors of the Stolt Dagali. Nineteen were lost from the tanker; twenty-four were rescued.

The Israeli ship had sailed at midnight on a West Indies cruise, with 616 passengers and a crew of 450. At 2:10 A.M. when the accident occurred, the vacationers were just settling down after farewell parties. The 25,338-ton luxury liner, which had arrived in New York on her maiden voyage only the previous spring, was commanded by Captain Avner Freudenberg. He had been at sea, man and boy, for thirty-one years. Master of the 19,150-ton Norwegian tanker was Captain Kristian Bendiksen, with thirty years of experience at sea.

This was the first cruise the new Shalom had ever made. Before the accident she was reported way off the normal course of cruise ships leaving New York for the Caribbean, and actually in the course usually reserved for inbound cargo ships on coastal courses. She was going very fast.

Frank Braynard, writer on steamships and former ship reporter, who was public relations head for Moran Towing for thirty years, says: "I was in the engine room of the Shalom a few weeks after the crash. A most enthusiastic young Israeli engineer was proudly showing me around. I saw a large light-up sign whose working attracted me. I asked him what it meant.

"He said: 'Oh, that sign lights up when the bridge orders full speed astern while we are going full speed ahead . . . it happened only a little while ago. . . .' Then he suddenly put his hand over his mouth. The sign read WRONG MANEUVER, meaning that if the particular order just issued from the bridge is carried out, the engine turbines would be stripped. It is an example of modern-style preventive engine-room control."

Of the Stolt Dagali, Mr. Braynard says: "I saw colored photos taken by skin divers inside the sunken stern of the tanker. One showed a woman passenger, her life belt on, drowned. Her head was against the ceiling, her feet dangling. The story was that she had gone back into her cabin to get something. Her life jacket was red.

"I went out aboard a Moran tug called to assist two other Moran tugs bringing in the forward section of the tanker. We left at 8 P.M. and found the escorting convoy and the smashed forward hulk at about eleven. As we came up to take our position 100 feet behind the bow on the starboard side, our rubber bumper tug nose edged slowly against the wet steel of the tanker's bow.

"There was the most unearthly, frightening whinelike sound you ever heard—just like a high, shrill, injured voice. The soul of the tanker remnant was greeting the rescue tug. Our place was to hold the broken bow from turning to the right. Torn shreds of steel hung in the ocean from the ripped-off stern and acted like a perpetual right-turn rudder. We got in, and anchored off a little way from under the Narrows bridge, in Gravesend Bay. When the convoy master ordered the man aboard the bow to let go her anchor, you should have heard that sound. One long, scratchy scream of a hiss, as the anchor chain rushed out after the anchor and disappeared into the black water.

"The bow section was filled with valuable oil, of course, and it was most important to bring it in."

The New York Times commented editorially on November 27, 1964: "The collision of the Israeli liner Shalom and the Norwegian tanker Stolt Dagali off the Jersey coast is a reminder of how far modern technology remains from conquering all the dangers of the sea. . . . When visibility is zero or nearly so, the commander of a ship must rely on his foghorn to give warning of his presence and on the foghorns of other vessels to warn him that they are near. Even more important, the skipper of a large modern vessel counts on his radar as a substitute for normal vision. Fog, after all, can play strange tricks with sound waves, too many for mariners to depend on their ears alone for safety. Radar is far better but it, too, can be an untrustworthy guide. Indeed, in crucial situations it may prove useless because the image of a nearby ship can be lost in the confusion of radar echoes bouncing off choppy seas. Even when radar works perfectly, there is still the question of whether those it serves are paying adequate attention, interpreting the information available to them correctly and exercising good judgment

Smashed section of American tanker VALCHEM *after collision with* SANTA ROSA, *1959*

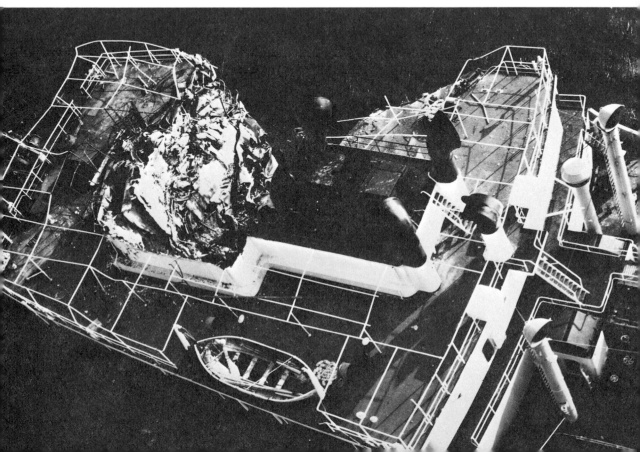

in making decisions. In the last analysis, even the best of modern technology can be made worthless by human failure. . . ."

A lengthy legal tangle followed the Shalom–Dagali crash. A story current at the time among divers and fishing captains is that when divers went down to look at the Stolt Dagali's engine telegraph to see what position it was in, they found that someone had already been there and had either changed or removed it. That story was denied by both sides.

12

BREAKING
THE ICE

Crossing from Long Island to Westchester County on the Throg's Neck Bridge, it is possible on a clear day to see Execution Rocks Lighthouse. This light once had a woman as assistant keeper. She was Lucy Edwards Sherman, wife of Charles Sherman, the lighthouse keeper. On January 3, 1874, she was appointed assistant keeper, at $400 a year, in spite of a ruling made in the 1850's that "neither women nor servants" could be lighthouse keepers. In her case, it was necessary.

The western end of Long Island Sound was often frozen over, so Charles Sherman and his other assistant—a man—had to walk across the ice to New Rochelle, N.Y., to bring back mail and necessary supplies. Sometimes they could not return for days.

The winter of 1875 was severe. That end of the Sound was solidly frozen over in February. Mrs. Sherman had sent for her cousin, Louisa Edwards of Wainscott, Long Island, to come spend the winter. She could keep her company and teach the children.

Louisa's daughter, Mrs. Amy Osborn Bassford, tells this: "Mother, like any properly reared girl of her time, worked all that winter on her wedding outfit. She was to marry John Osborn in June. Among other things she made a patchwork quilt, on which she put the last stitches on her wedding morning. She gave me the quilt.

"One evening, so she told me, the other assistant lighthouse keeper came back from a trip across the ice to the mainland a little the worse for

Execution Light, from a watercolor by Cyril A. Lewis

wear. He sat by the fire watching Cousin Lucy and Mother at their sewing. Finally he muttered: 'Can't understand it. Can't understand it. She cuts 'em to pieces and then sews 'em together again.' "

In February of that bad winter of 1875, the big Sound steamers generally managed to fight their way through a narrow lane, except for ten days when there was no communication by water through Hell Gate to Sands Point. Four Sound boats were locked in the ice.

The forty-year-old schooner Oakwood, bound with coal from Perth Amboy, N.J., to Narragansett, R.I., was frozen in for two weeks at Whitestone on the East River. Captain Walter R. Hazard of the Sound steamer City of Lowell, who had once commanded the Oakwood, tried to go to her aid. A sudden fissure in the ice opened up, causing the prow of the City of Lowell to cut into the starboard side of the schooner. The crew jumped off onto the ice. The Oakwood sank.

The brand-new, 1,900-ton steamer Cornwall of the Great Western Steamship Line, from Bristol, England, was entering the East River on February 14, 1875, with 450 passengers, when she was forced by the ice toward Governor's Island. She struck bottom off Castle William. She was later hauled off.

March of 1875 was no better. The brig Rapide, bound from New York to London, was anchored off Robbins Reef when she was cut into by ice. She was towed to Red Hook, and filled. She was finally raised by the Coast Wrecking Company.

The Port of New York still had ice on April 14, 1875, when the German bark Aeolus from Antwerp was caught by ice floes off the Battery and carried down the bay, where she collided with the British brig Annie Wharton and lost her mizzentopmast.

OLD-FASHIONED WINTERS

Coast Guardsmen at Governor's Island say those "old-fashioned winters" and the idea that the Gulf Stream has changed its course, thereby changing our climate, are a myth. "The weather is no different," they say. "A ship can avoid trouble today because technology for mariners has improved so much, and information service on the weather. And we keep the ship lanes open."

There was a great freeze in the war winter of 1779–1880, when the British were occupying New York. The Narrows and Upper Bay were frozen solid. In one day eighty wagons of provisions for British troops on Staten Island were sent across the harbor on sledges.

"The year without a summer" was 1816–1817. Every one of the twelve months had frost, but it did not turn really cold until February, 1817. On February 4 a steam ferry that had been running for two years was wedged in a field of ice between Peck Slip, Manhattan, and the New York Steamboat Wharf. The East River was so full of ice a few days later that a solid bridge of ice had formed. Thousands crossed the river on it, "including some females," the Long Island *Star* reported. The bridge broke up when the tide changed. Cold set in again on February 19. The harbor was closed by ice at the Narrows and at Hell Gate. For two weeks horse-drawn sleighs could travel from Long Island to Governor's Island. There were thirty-six straight days of sleighing at Flatlands, in Brooklyn.

Generally, the strong tidal currents kept the Narrows open. But in February, 1818, no vessels could get in or out of New York for six days, and floating ice from the Hudson was a great menace.

In December, 1831, a great ice floe from the Hudson drifted down into the East River. It cut a brig from stem to stern that was loading at the end of a dock. She sank so quickly that the stevedores barely escaped with their lives.

The winter of 1835–1836 was also severe. An old diary kept in East Hampton, Long Island, tells how on February 5, 1836, men walked the three and a half miles from Gardiner's Island to the mainland across the ice, just as they were to do nearly 100 years later. (On February 9, 1934, people walked across ordinarily turbulent Gardiner's Bay to the island; and in New York City a then record low temperature—fifteen below zero—was registered.) On February 17, 1836, a horse and sleigh were driven across Gardiner's Bay; and the next day, a heavily loaded sleigh and sledge.

In January, 1856, the Columbus, one of five Vanderbilt steam ferryboats operating between New York and Staten Island, had its hull crushed by ice, just off the Battery. Passengers walked off on the ice to Governor's Island. The only fatality was a horse, drowned in its harness.

For most of the winter of 1856–1857, Long Island Sound was entirely closed to navigation. No arrivals passed through Hell Gate from January 17 to February 24, 1857.

THE WINTERS OF 1917 AND 1918

The winters of both 1917 and 1918 are remembered as rugged. Eighteen ships were frozen in the ice at one time in February, 1917, off the Bushwick Terminal piers in Brooklyn. Gravesend Bay was closed to navigation from Fort Hamilton to Sea Gate. Recruits at Fort Slocum on David's Island crossed to the mainland on the ice.

THE MAINE

New York had no icebreakers on February 4, 1920, when the liner Maine of the Providence and Stonington Steamship Company became a total loss on Execution Rocks. Half a dozen other steamers, as well as fishing smacks and tugs, were ice-blockaded in that vicinity for days.

The Maine was a steel single-screw ship, 310 feet long and 2,395 tons. She was considered fast and beautiful when she was launched in 1892. On the night of February 4, 1920, she was bound east when she met floating ice and a blinding snowstorm at the entrance to Long Island Sound. A gale was blowing and there was a full-moon tide. She turned about for New York and struck, stern first, on Execution Rocks at high water. She was doomed in half an hour. When the tide fell, it carried the Maine down onto jagged rocks, puncturing her hull and pushing engines and boilers through the deck.

Fortunately she was carrying only a few passengars. The fourteen horses on the freight deck were frightened when the water came in. The Maine hung there on the rocks for three days and three nights. Drinking water ran out; they used melted snow. Food ran low. Finally help got through the ice to the Maine and to the freighter Pequonnock, which lay helplessly imprisoned nearby.

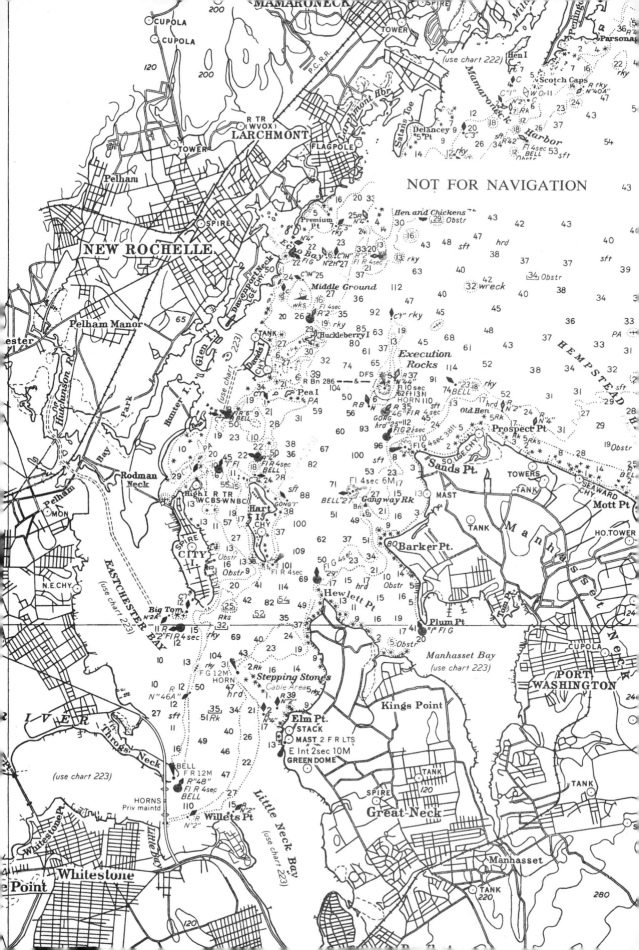

Some of the Maine's crew had to stay on board until March 3, when the wreck was turned over to the underwriters.

COAST GUARD ICEBREAKERS

The Coast Guard's first icebreaker was a crude affair, a seagoing tug acquired after World War I. She was rebuilt, renamed the Kickapoo, and sent up to Maine where it gets really cold.

After the uncommonly cold winter of 1933–1934, the Coast Guard received calls for assistance from up and down the Atlantic coast. President Franklin D. Roosevelt issued a directive that the Coast Guard should aid in keeping waterways open within the reasonable demands of commerce, and that the Navy should assist. Today ice-breaking is one of the Coast Guard's major responsibilities. It is now the only service with ice-breaking vessels.

Icebreakers vary in size from the 310-foot USCG Glacier to the 230-foot Storis. The average icebreaker is in the 269-foot class, such as the Westwind and Eastwind, which were stationed in New York until 1966. These are massively reinforced in the bow, which is undercut to ride up on a sheet of ice, come down, and break it. They are beamy and equipped with a water-pumping system in their hulls that can set up a rocking motion or add extra weight to the bow to help break through especially thick ice. The 269-footers are of 6,515 tons displacement. They have a maximum cruising range of 28,000 miles and can attain a speed of sixteen knots. They are distributed in major United States ports and move around as needed.

Coast Guardsmen at the Third District, USCG headquarters, say: "We can use, for most ice conditions here, our 110-footers with ice-breaking bows. The Hudson River is kept open most winters with these cutters that look like tugs, aided by an 180-foot buoy tender. We keep one of the smaller all-purpose vessels in Great South Bay, Long Island, when necessary.

"Half a dozen cutters are assigned, in hard winters, to keep a track through the Hudson all the way to Albany. If the river were blocked by ice for four or five days, shoreside supplies of fuel would be exhausted. The fuel barges have to get through."

13

FERRIES AND
BRIDGES

Until 1883 when the Brooklyn Bridge was completed, the only way to reach Manhattan Island was by water. In the days before bridges and tunnels, automobiles and helicopters, ferryboats converged upon Manhattan from all points of the compass. Ferrying was by oars and sail for nearly 200 years after the first colonists came.

The earliest regular ferry between Long Island and what was then Nieuw Amsterdam ran from the foot of the present Fulton Street in Brooklyn to the foot of Peck Slip in Manhattan. This was inaugurated by Cornelis Dircksen in 1642. He had a small inn and a farm near Peck Slip, also a piece of land with a house and garden on Long Island, near what was later Fulton Ferry. When Dircksen was not rowing people across, he kept busy with his farm and garden. A passenger could summon him by blowing a conch shell hung on a tree. Dircksen sold out in 1652 to one Cornelis de Potter, who leased the ferry to others.

Beginning as a private enterprise, ferrying eventually came under control of the Corporation of the City of New York, and the ferry companies leased from the city. A great dispute raged for years between New York and Brooklyn over shore rights and ferry franchises. The old ferry house in Brooklyn was burned down in 1748 in the course of a controversy. Not all the Brooklyn ferries ran from one locality. Nathaniel S. Prime's *History of Long Island* (1845) says there had been three in constant operation from Williamsburg since shortly after 1800.

Not only the East River and the North River (Hudson) and Staten Island had ferries to Manhattan (Staten Island had one from 1712); Long Island Sound had many vessels that sailed regularly between Long Island's north shore and the city, avoiding Brooklyn and the land route thereto. That was disliked by travelers because of the robber-infested Howard's Woods, between Jamaica and Brooklyn. The Whitestone Bridge to the Bronx follows a route on which the old horse ferry, built about 1776, used to carry cattle, horses, and wagons.

Whatever route he chose, the early traveler took his life in his hands. Before steam ferries were invented, rowboats or flat scows were used in waters around New York; or sloops or piraguas, all of which were at the mercy of wind and the tides that run furiously in both the East and North rivers. The piragua was a flat-bottomed boat with a foremast raked forward and the mainmast raked aft; undecked, except sometimes at the ends. These were "remarkably unseaworthy, often overturning during gales, drowning passengers and losing or ruining cargo."

Horses, carriages, and cattle on the hoof, which butchers bought for the New York market, were a great nuisance. Calm weather was preferable for transporting livestock; otherwise is was very unsafe. Disasters reported in New York papers in the 18th and early 19th centuries give some idea of ferryboat perils and discomfort.

In 1741 the ferry Thomas Jones of Oyster Bay, Long Island, upset in Long Island Sound. Four men, three women, and six horses were drowned.

On January 15, 1784, a New Jersey ferryboat got into floating ice and was damaged so badly that it sank. The eight passengers were thrown into the water. They climbed onto a cake of ice carried by the North River eddy around into the East River. All the slips there were so choked with ice that it was difficult for a small boat to go to the relief of the marooned men. Finally a boatload of soldiers did manage to rescue all but one, a Negro who had frozen to death.

Again in 1784, the *Independent Journal* reported that a ferry from Brooklyn to New York had suddenly overset. One of the horses on board had shifted, which startled the others so that they all moved to one side. The boat filled. The three passengers and two ferrymen saved themselves by swimming until they were picked up, exhausted, by boats from shore.

On December 17, 1795, a Brooklyn ferryboat turned over while crossing the East River: "One man and seven fat oxen drowned."

On April 2, 1798, about noon, "the large ferryboat which plies between the ferry stairs at Fly Market, New York, and Brooklyn across the East River, unhappily sank in a gust of wind. Eight men were in the boat, five of them boatmen and three passengers. All were drowned but one boatman."

In May, 1801, a passenger on the ferry from Fly Market related his experiences. There was little wind, he said, when they started, but it was expected to blow very fresh. The passengers asked the boatmen to brail up the sails (to haul them up with a rope, preparatory to furling). The men refused; they were intoxicated. The passengers talked of taking charge themselves, but the first gust that came along upset the boat.

One woman and five men drowned immediately. The other six aboard were saved after spending an hour and a half in the water. "But," the story concluded, "one, being spent, could not lay hold fast; he let go and was drowned. Three horses and a chair on board." (A chair was a two-wheeled carriage with leather springs.)

THE STEAM FERRYBOATS

When steam ferries first came in they were just about as dangerous as the little sailing ferries that turned over at a breath of wind. Boiler trouble occurred with alarming frequency, and the boats would blow up.

The first steam ferry to New York was the Juliana, which John Stevens put on the Hoboken–New York run in 1811. In August, 1812, the Jersey Association, with which Robert Fulton was connected, began to use steam on the Paulus Hook Ferry from Jersey City.

During the War of 1812, sixteen-year-old Cornelius Vanderbilt ran a ferry service between Staten Island and the Battery, New York. Thus he first earned his title of "Commodore" as the ferryboat captain.

On January 24, 1814, Robert Fulton and William Cutting were given authority to establish a steam ferry between Beekman's Slip, New York, and the old ferry slip in Brooklyn. The Nassau went into commission on that run on May 10 of that year. "A noble boat," the newspapers termed it. In one day it carried 549 passengers, one wagon, two chairs with horses, and one saddle horse. One evening that summer the Nassau took a shipload on a pleasure excursion up the Hudson. There was music and dancing, "a refinement, a luxury of pleasure unknown to the Old World," the press reported.

Extra rowboats were kept on hand by the ferry company, however, since the new steamboats had a way of blowing up at the slightest provocation.

In 1814, the same year that the New York–Brooklyn steam ferry was inaugurated, Moses Rogers of New York invented a contraption called the team-boat, or horse-boat, which ran from Catharine Ferry, New York, to Brooklyn. This had a waterwheel in its center, powered by eight horses. The team-boat, it was claimed, would be safer in winter; the steamboats were not only "troublesome but expensive."

THE GENERAL JACKSON

On August 23, 1836, the seven-year-old steam ferryboat General Jackson, 174 tons burden, was crossing the East River from Long Island to the foot of Walnut Street, New York, at 4:30 A.M. She was three-quarters of the way across when the steamboat Boston, passing down the river, struck her near the bow. The General Jackson sank in less than three minutes.

Eight or ten persons leaped from the ferryboat's deck onto the deck of the Boston. The rest were swept off as the Jackson went down. The Boston lowered her boats immediately, but of the twenty-five passengers on the ferry, six were missing; fourteen horses and wagons also went to the bottom.

The newspapers reported that the Boston had swerved to avoid hitting a small boat in her way and was carried by the strong tide into the ferry.

THEY WANTED A BRIDGE

By 1850 there were municipal ferries running from seventeen different slips around Manhattan Island. The bustling ferryboats snarled up river traffic.

A ferry ride in those days must have been a shattering experience. A newspaper of that time described the Brooklyn ferry as a "Noah's ark—a confusion of dead and live stock; hucksters . . . milkmen and their pails; hay-carts, wagons, drays, men, women, children, pigs, sheep, ducks, pigeons, geese, hens, clean and unclean things, all . . . huddled together." It was not until 1864 that ferryboats and tugs, their pilots and engineers, had to be licensed. Even then, the licensing was a very slipshod business.

In 1866 the East River froze solid. The Hudson was blocked too. No boats could get across. There was a great uproar that winter for a bridge across the East River.

John A. Roebling was appointed in 1867 as engineer for the proposed Brooklyn Bridge. Two years later, while engaged in determining the location of the Brooklyn tower, a ferryboat entering the slip thrust the timbers on which the great engineer stood, in such a way as to catch and crush his foot. He died of lockjaw sixteen days later.

He was killed by the ferry which his bridge and later ones would eventually put out of business. His son, Washington A. Roebling, finished the bridge, which opened with great fanfare on May 24, 1883.

THE JAMES FISK, JR.

Ferries were still very big business in 1869 when the James Fisk, Jr., and the Jay Gould were built to carry passengers from the Erie Railroad depot in Jersey City to West 23rd Street in New York. These two financiers, James Fisk and Jay Gould, had gained control of the Erie. They made William Marcy ("Boss") Tweed a director. Tweed arranged for favorable legislation in Albany. Another associate was Daniel Drew.

Fisk had a taste for the nautical. He and Drew became partners in a Long Island Sound steamboat line. Fisk, then president of the Narragansett Steamship Company, liked to wear an admiral's uniform on board his ships. He would make a dramatic arrival by tugboat when all were assembled, so the story goes, with his "female favorite of the hour also in naval attire, with gilt buttons, epaulettes, etc."

From his ferry Fisk ran a free line of omnibuses on the New York side. The buses ran past the Grand Opera House, which he had bought, to the old Fifth Avenue Hotel, which he had built.

Jay Gould was forced out of the Erie in 1872 for fraudulent stock sales, but he went right on to gain control of 10,000 miles of American railway. On January 6, 1872, Fisk was shot and killed in New York City by E. S. ("Ned") Stokes, who with Fisk's former mistress, Josie Mansfield, was blackmailing him.

Fisk's ferryboats and steamships outlived him.

On February 23, 1878, the James Fisk, Jr., was crossing in ballast from Pavonia, N.J., when, off West 13th Street, North River, she collided with the Staten Island–New York ferryboat Castleton, which was also crossing without passengers. Each boat lost one man, and each was partially wrecked. The Fisk, at least, survived to become the Passaic and later the Broadway.

THE WESTFIELD AND THE NORTHFIELD

The worst ferryboat disaster in the New York area occurred on July 30, 1871, when 104 lives were lost from the Westfield. That story is told in Chapter 6.

On June 14, 1901, the New York–Staten Island ferry Northfield was rammed and sunk just after leaving her slip. Of the 995 passengers aboard, only five lost their lives. She was hit by the Jersey Central ferryboat Maunch Chunk, inbound for Whitehall Street.

THE LAST EAST RIVER FERRY

When Long Islanders from the eastern end—over 100 miles away—wanted to visit New York, up to the time the Long Island Rail Road went all the way out to Montauk in 1895, they could make the trip by water from Sag Harbor, up the Sound. The Long Island Rail Road owned a fleet of boats that plied between Sag Harbor, Greenport, and New York. Rails had

Ship Ashore, old print

come to Greenport, on Long Island's north fork, in 1844.

After 1895, well within living memory, passengers who came all the way from the end of the island took the train to its terminal at Long Island City, then boarded a ferry across the East River to a pier on East 34th Street. After more than three hours on the railroad, then the ferry ride, then another half-hour or so on the cross-town trolley (in pre-taxi times), many east-enders would stay at the old Herald Square Hotel at Sixth Avenue and 34th Street. It was all red plush and lace curtains, considered quite grand by country children visiting the city.

The main terminal for the Long Island Rail Road—and for the several smaller local railroads that preceded the united L.I.R.R.—was at Hunter's Point, Long Island City. From 1854 to 1925, ferries ran across the East River from there. The ferry to East 34th Street continued almost fifteen years after the Pennsylvania Station was completed on September 8, 1910, and the first trains ran through the tunnel linking Long Island to Manhattan.

THE MANDALAY

Ferryboats built in the 1900's had become more substantial and boilers more reliable. Accidents were fewer. But fog remains a hazard, always.

168

The former railroad ferryboat Express had been turned into an excursion steamer and renamed the Mandalay by the time she met her end in 1938. She had been built in 1889 with a broad bow, to carry Pullman passengers bound from Boston to Washington, in the middle of the night, from the Harlem railroad yard down the East River to the Pennsylvania Railroad terminal at Jersey City.

After the Titanic disaster in 1912, the United States Government required every vessel to carry a life preserver for each passenger. That may have been a contributing factor to the decision of the railroad ferry operators to discontinued their passenger service. They ran for a few years, carrying freight only. Then when the Hell Gate Bridge opened about 1917, the operation ended entirely and the old Express became the Mandalay.

On May 28, 1938, Captain Philip R. Curran had 350 picnickers on board the Mandalay, coming from Atlantic Highlands, N.J. At 6 P.M. he was drifting in New York Harbor, in a heavy fog, when the Bermuda-bound liner Acadia, with 115 passengers on board, collided with the Mandalay. The Acadia's steel prow cut into the old wooden vessel's side like a knife.

The excursionists were helped across to safety, then the Acadia backed away. At 6:15 P.M. the keel of the Mandalay was in the mud at the bottom of the harbor.

NEW YORK'S BEST BUY FOR A NICKEL

The Staten Island–Manhattan ferry is the only one in operation now, not counting the city's institutional ferries. One of these huge boats that ply from the Battery to St. George, Staten Island, around 300 feet long and broad to match, solid as a bridge, can carry more passengers on each trip than the Queen Elizabeth I ever did. Of course, the opening of the Verrazzano–Narrows Bridge cut down somewhat the flow of commuters taking the water route. The Staten Island–Brooklyn ferry, which had run for seventy-five years, went out of business on November 25, 1964.

With a multiplicity of bridges in all directions, some people have feared that the days of the ferry might be numbered, to the distress and inconvenience of thousands who commute by water from Staten Island. At latest tally the ferry carried some 67,000 commuters a day.

The New York City Department of Marine and Aviation has assured ferry riders that there is no thought of discontinuing the operation. And, almost unbelievably, the five-cent passenger fare is still in effect, in spite of a Citizens Budget Committee complaint in 1968 that "in addition to a pack of Life Savers, the only thing a nickel can buy in New York today is a ferry ride. But Life Savers don't cost fifty cents a pack to make—a ferry ride does."

Perils of the Port of New York

Following Mayor John Lindsay's recommendation of increased fares to aid the city's ailing economy, Charles G. Leedham, the city's Commissioner of Marine and Aviation, announced on March 14, 1971, substantial raises on rates for passenger cars, buses, trailer trucks, and motorcycles. But the traditional five-cent passenger ride remained the same. That was originally mandated in the 1898 City Charter creating Greater New York, and was guaranteed in perpetuity, according to popular belief, when Staten Island became part of the city that year.

On May 30, 1972, it was announced that instead of paying five cents each way, beginning that fall, travelers on the Staten Island ferry would pay ten cents for a round trip. This was to speed morning rush-hour service; fares would be collected only at the Whitehall Terminal in Manhattan. Prior to this ruling, tourists had to get off on the Staten Island side and pay five cents to get back on.

Although ferry passengers are mostly commuters, there are people who take that relaxing ride across New York Harbor for pure pleasure. Returning from Staten Island at dusk, the light-spangled concrete canyons of Manhattan beckon beautifully. And there are young couples who find it "the last nickel date in New York, maybe in the United States . . . if you want a place to talk all night, this is the place." Edna St. Vincent Millay once wrote a tribute to a ferry in "Recuerdo" (Spanish for Remembrance).

> We were very tired, we were very merry
> We had gone back and forth all night on the ferry.

14

FINDERS, KEEPERS

ONCE upon a time, in a less affluent society, any-
thing cast up by the sea, whether it was a stranded ship or a whale, would
afford a welcome addition to the income of shore-front village families. From
the end of August to the first of May, men who lived along the Long Island
shores, where sailing ships often came to grief, would keep a sharp eye on the
beach. This was open season for wrecks. In stormy weather, if her man was
off fishing or whaling, the wife would mount a short ladder in the garret and
open the scuttle (a square hole in the roof just big enough for head and
shoulders to lean out; every old house in the east end villages had one). She
would apply her eye to the long spyglass and see what was going on offshore
or on the beach.

Most Long Islanders, a century or so ago, lived off the produce of their
inherited acres, and of the sea. The same was true of nearby New Jersey. A
Long Island whaling captain, born in 1830, used to say that when he was a
boy a family could get along nicely for a year on $100, cash money.

It was exciting, then, when something extra rolled in from the ocean.
More often than not it would be lumber, carried by coastwise vessels. This
always came in handy. A mast could make a village flagpole. Sometimes a
ship would carry coconuts, peanuts, or exotic fruit. Trees and shrubs were
thrown overboard, a century ago, to lighten a French ship. These, or their
descendants, still flourish. Ships ashore in the Port of New York–Long Island
area have left behind furniture, small boats, cattle, tea, Siamese cats, a
monkey, a bedraggled parrot or two. Spanish gold pieces, perhaps from
pirate ships, have been picked up from the sand within living memory.

A winter beach-walker during the Prohibition Era might very well discover a burlap-wrapped case of whiskey, or even champagne, bobbing in the surf. He would probably risk life and limb to salvage it.

While the rewards may not be tangible today, a brisk walk along the winter beach can be far more rewarding than the same walk in summertime. The sea and the sky and the sand are all yours.

Charlton Ogburn, Jr., who studied the sand and the seaweed and the shells along the Atlantic seaboard for his book, *The Winter Beach*, said: "Whatever the hardships and perils of the past, it is certain that never before has man been so hounded by distractions. Perhaps the appeal of the winter beach, where, as in a work of art, a little counts for a great deal, lies in part in its conducing to the reassembly of one's scattered powers."

The winter beach-walker, unconsciously reassembling his "scattered powers," comes home refreshed, carrying a handful of shells, or a few sticks of driftwood to burn in the fireplace with colors lacking in land-logs.

Artists find wood oddly shaped by the action of sea and wind. One man, who gave up the great city to live in a Long Island seaside village, bought an ordinary, uninteresting small house and almost rebuilt it with driftwood. Wall panels, cupboard shelves, a coffee table, still have sand in the cracks. The soft gray of sea-weathered timber makes a fitting background for paintings.

THE WRECK MASTER

The almost-forgotten office of Wreck Master was instituted in New York State on February 16, 1787, by "An act concerning wrecks of the sea, and giving redress to merchants and others who be robbed, or whose goods be lost on the sea." Section Two provided for the appointment of wreck masters by the governor, "with the consent and advice of the Council of Appointment as . . . they may think necessary . . . in each of the counties bordering on the sea."

In those days, if goods were thrown overboard to lighten a vessel and get her off the bar, or if a ship went to pieces, the entire population of a village would be on hand to see what they could salvage. It was as natural for them to claim the property thrown up on the beach as it was for them to count fish and lobsters as their own. Bounty from the sea was part of their life.

From 1787 to 1799 the officer appointed to cope with this situation (not always successfully) was called Coastmaster or Coast Officer; then Wreck Master or Vendue Master (pronounced Van-dew) because he would often hold an auction or vendue of a ship's goods, rigging, or the vessel itself. In New Jersey these were called commissioners and were, in that state, appointed by the Court of Common Pleas for the seacoast counties.

This officer's duty was to see that nothing was disturbed or removed until the ship was either pulled off or sold by the insurance company. He also organized and directed the volunteer rescue work; identified and buried the dead; and reported all facts he could discover to his superiors. After 1820, when the Board of Underwriters of the Port of New York was organized to handle losses and report casualties, the Wreck Master cooperated with insurance people and customs inspectors. He was generally a leading citizen of his community.

The only counties in New York State that border on saltwater are Kings, Queens, Nassau, Suffolk, Richmond (Staten Island), and Westchester. There was no Nassau County until Queens was divided in 1899. New York City was in a class by itself.

At first only Kings, Queens, and Suffolk were considered as requiring a Wreck Master to "aid and assist all ships and vessels as may happen to be stranded on the Coasts in their Respective Counties." In 1787 Suffolk, having the most shipwrecks and the most territory, was given nine Wreck Masters, as against Kings County's five, and three for Queens.

The first such officers for Kings County were Rutger Van Brunt, Jan Titus, Walter Berry, Nicholas I. Stillwell, and Wilhelmus Van Nuys. In 1797 Stephen B. Williamson took the place of Van Nuys. Other early Wreck Masters for Kings include: John Bergen, 1802; Van Brunt Magaw, 1805; Cornelius Sloothoff, Matthew Jones, Jacobus Ryder, 1811; James H. Cropsey, 1817; John Van Dyke and Tunis Bergen, 1819; James Cropsey, George Suydam, Abraham Hunter, and Henry Fauble, 1821; Senter N. Giddings and Garrett S. Webb, 1848.

For Queens County: Nathaniel Seaman, Joseph Rock Smith, and Walter Jones were appointed in 1787; in 1788, Peter Smith. Governor George Clinton appointed in 1802 General Jacob Seaman Jackson of Wantagh (then called Jerusalem); also Jacob Raynor and Joseph Smith. In 1803 Benjamin Cornell was appointed; and in 1804, Nathaniel Seaman, Jr.

Other Queens Wreck Masters were: Daniel Beadle, 1806; David Richard Floyd-Jones, 1807; Stephen Wood, 1808; Samuel Mott, 1809; James Jackson, Joseph R. Smith, Thomas Tredwell, Oliver Hewlett, and Gilbert Durlin, 1810; Samuel Hallett, 1811; Nathaniel Berrian, 1818; Thomas Tredwell again in 1819; Oliver Hewlett, John Simonson, Jacob R. Smith, and James Bedell, 1820; Edmund Hicks, Stephen Wood, Daniel Bedell, Daniel Raynor, James Bedell, Noah Mason, George Hewlett, and William Riker, 1821. Governor Martin Van Buren appointed John Seaman, Benjamin Coles Jackson, and Robert Carman in 1829.

A recent historian of Richmond County (Staten Island, Borough of Richmond) doubted that Staten Island ever had a Wreck Master. But it did. There were several. The first was Cornelius Mercereau, in 1802. Then came Henry Perine, 1811; Samuel Holmes, 1819; Richard Dubois, Abraham Jones, and Mathias Burger, 1821.

The only Wreck Master found recorded for Westchester County was Gilbert Lyon, in 1821; yet there were others. In 1848 the state legislature provided for the appointment of fifteen Wreck Masters for Suffolk County; twelve for Queens; three for Kings; and two each for Richmond and Westchester. These positions were to be filled by appointment by the governor for two-year terms.

In 1869 the statutes regarding Wreck Masters were amended. In 1886 they were partially repealed. In 1890 all sections pertaining to Wreck Masters were finally taken off the books.

HEROIC WRECK MASTER

Captain Raynor Rock Smith of Freeport, Long Island, Wreck Master, risked his own life and the lives of his three sons, Zophar, James, and Oliver, along with the lives of three other volunteer crewmen, to bring ashore eight persons—all who were saved of 124 on board the bark Mexico, which foundered on Point Lookout, off Hempstead Beach, Long Island, on January 2, 1837. (See Chapter 5.)

Captain Smith's gallant conduct was the talk of the day. The Mexico's owner gave him a purse of $350, which he divided among his crew. On March 27, 1837, a dinner was given in his honor at Oliver Conklin's Hotel in Hempstead, at which he was presented with a silver tankard, suitably inscribed.

He died in 1869. On his gravestone, a small marble slab in Greenfield Cemetery, Hempstead, are the words:

> He gloried in heroic deeds,
> He acted well his part—
> His hand was opened to human needs,
> He had an honest heart.

In 1972, more than a century after his death, the Village of Freeport honored the memory of Captain Raynor Rock Smith by giving his name to a new recreation building at Hanse Park, Freeport.

THE FLYING SCUD

The American brig Flying Scud, bound from Malaga, Spain, to New York with a cargo of fruit, went ashore on Rockaway Beach on November 17, 1866. One life was lost. Others on board were brought ashore safely.

For days the beach was strewn with oranges, almonds, and other unaccustomed delicacies.

The Flying Scud was a clipper. She had once made the passage from New York to Melbourne in seventy-five days, a record.

THE ACARA

The British freighter Acara, of Liverpool, inbound for New York from China, is well known to present-day fishing and diving enthusiasts as the "Tea Wreck." She went on the bar east of Jones Inlet (Short Beach) in a heavy southwest gale on March 1, 1902. The Life Saving crews from both Zach's Inlet and Short Beach went to her. Seas were very high, but the Acara managed to launch two boats. One of them, with forty-four men, was able to land. The other, carrying seventeen, capsized in the breakers. The Life Savers rescued them all, and part of the tea cargo.

Freeport ladies saw to it that the crew of Malays, Hindus, and Chinese were clothed and fed. They were housed temporarily in the old Sand Hill Church, since destroyed by fire. It stood just west of Rockville Centre on the Merrick Road. The ladies were rewarded with tea.

The Acara broke in two, a loss estimated at $700,000. Fifty years ago the ship lay about 600 yards offshore, across a sandbar on the east side of Jones Inlet. She sanded up, was partly awash at low water. She has probably shifted again, but fishing captains of the region can find her.

PETER RICKMERS, *the "oil wreck," ashore at Short Beach, 1908*

THE PETER RICKMERS

Another favorite fishing spot is the "Oil Wreck," a sailing ship that stranded a mile and a half southeast of Short Beach station on April 30, 1908, in thick weather with a heavy easterly gale. She was the Peter Rickmers, a four-masted German square-rigger carrying 125,000 cases of crude and kerosene oil from Perth Amboy to Rangoon, Burma. Due to her great spread of canvas she carried a crew of thirty-three.

The Rickmers had hardly cleared New York Harbor when the south-easter struck. The ship, heavily laden, could not manage to get offshore. She stranded on the bar, losing topmasts and most of her yardarms on impact. Life Saving crews from Zach's Inlet, Short Beach, and Point Lookout tried to heave a boat through the surf, but failed. Then they fired five shots with the life-line gun, but the Rickmers was too far offshore. Captains Chichester of Short Beach and Seaman of Point Lookout, both experienced surfmen, decided the ship could never be refloated or saved. They recommended abandonment.

Captain George Bachmann refused. He insisted on staying aboard, hoping the storm would let up. Instead, it got worse.

Word was sent to New York. The revenue cutter Mohawk left Sandy Hook with two tugs and forty wreckers. The Life Savers had just brought the crew ashore when the Mohawk arrived.

The Rickmers continued to pound on the bar. By May 9 she had twenty feet of water in her hold, and seas were breaking over her as she settled deeper and deeper. She showed signs of breaking up. The captain and wrecking crew, still on board, threw cases of oil overboard, trying desperately to lighten the vessel. Shore dwellers were gathering up a rich harvest. But trouble broke out. The wreckers, acting (they said) under orders, began to punch holes in all drifting cargo. Thereupon the Long Islanders appealed to the government, on the ground that the liberated oil would destroy fish life.

It was May 15 before the captain agreed to leave his ship, after thirty-six hours of another easterly storm. The Life Savers managed to bring ashore, safely if uncomfortably, by breeches buoy, the captain and every one of his forty wreckers.

The beach was littered for miles. Kerosene lamps were still in common household use in 1908. Nobody along that part of the Long Island shore needed to buy either kerosene or crude oil for a long, long time. The kerosene cans were crated in good substantial wood. That was bounty, too. One Seaford man salvaged enough wood to completely reshingle his house. Those were the days when a dollar was a day's wages. Any gift from the sea was a help.

The square-rigger caught fire, below decks, after she was abandoned, and burned to the water's edge. The wreck, so fishermen say, has worked inshore and now lies less than half a mile from Short Beach. It is partly awash at low tide.

CATTLE DRIVE ON THE BATTERY

One disaster brought a Christmas season gift of livestock into New York City.

The North Star of the Eastern Steamship Corporation collided, on the night of December 8, 1915, with the double-decker cattle barge El Paso, which was in tow. The barge sank off the Battery. The captain, Wilfred Miller, and his crew were taken ashore. One hundred steers, calves, and sheep drowned.

Other animals struggling in the water were seized in the dark and carried away. Waterfront idlers were seen lassoing a dozen sheep, five calves, and a steer. A facetious report in a contemporary newspaper described the incident: "One-eyed Ben Blithers, a Battery post-polisher, got on the Staten Island ferry with a sheep over his shoulder. Bongo the Battery Dolphin started to walk to Harlem with two calves tied by ropes. His Christmas dinner was in sight. Honest Bill Quigley, Battery boatman, and Juniper Jerry, the pious junkman, were pulling about in a rowboat, rescuing animals. Others were salvaged by the Merritt-Chapman Wrecking Company."

THE CHARLES E. DUNLAP

Everyone in the vicinity of Arverne and the Rockaways ate coconut cake in the summer of 1919, after the wreck of the four-masted schooner Charles E. Dunlap, which stranded in a fog a few hundred feet off Far Rockaway Beach and became a total loss.

The 1,609-ton Dunlap, once called Forest City, valued at $293,000, was owned in San Juan, Puerto Rico. She left San Juan on July 5, 1919, bound for New York, with a crew of twenty-eight and a cargo of coconuts.

Her master, Captain Richard Cropsey, tried to enter New York Harbor. He bypassed Ambrose Channel and piled up on the shoal to the eastward at 3 A.M. on July 22. He flashed distress signals. Due to the heavy fog, these were not seen for three hours.

Louis P. Pearsall of Oceanside, Long Island, a surfman on watch at the Arverne Coast Guard station that morning, recalls: "The surf was mild that day. We used an open drill boat and went off to the Dunlap. The Long Beach crew went in a power dory. The captain invited us to dinner. He and the first mate carried revolvers in open holsters. We heard there were two stowaways. They had really made the stowaways work hard for being aboard.

The CHARLES E. DUNLAP, *"coconut ship," ashore at Rockaway Beach, 1919*

"The Dunlap was a rebuilt job. Under her former name she had got afire and burned to the water's edge. Then was rebuilt from the waterline up. A new vessel on an old bottom. On the way north she had a fire in her forward hold. When they put that out, the bottom began to leak. The Puerto Rican crew were not too happy. They had been obliged to work the pumps all the way to these waters. Then the grounding increased her leakage.

"What's left of her lies deep off the end of the East Rockaway breakwater."

LAND PIRATES

Lurid tales of "wrecking" have been published about Cape Cod, Block Island, Fire Island off Long Island's south shore, Barnegat, Hatteras, and the Florida Keys; tales of bad actors who would swing a light on the beach or build a bonfire to lure unsuspecting vessels onto a sandbar where they would sit, easy prey to salvagers.

An 1848 novel titled *The Wreckers: of the Ship Plunderers of Barnegat: A Startling Story of Mysteries of the Sea-Shore*, was written by one Charles E. Averill. It described Rodolf Raven, "chief wrecker" of Barnegat. That book was an added factor in arousing Congress at a time when the terrible Bristol and Mexico wrecks on the Long Island shore had initiated a movement to appropriate $10,000 for a Life Saving Service. Representative William A. Newell, who later became governor of New Jersey, urged such an appropriation to aid in the "preservation of life and property from wrecks on the New Jersey coast."

This piece of sensational fiction probably had some slight basis of fact. But to descendants of the whalers and fishermen of sailing-ship days, when

178

these terrible deeds were supposed to have occurred, it seems out of character.

The name of Fire Island has been said, in other "wrecker" stories, to have come from wicked bonfires set to lure ships onto the beach. The island is thought, by sober historians, to have derived its name from the perfectly innocent fires that were kept going all night under try-kettles for whale oil. From the early 1700's to a century or so ago, offshore whaling flourished at the Great South Beach. It was organized at first by white settlers, with Indian helpers.

Agreements concerning this arrangement have survived. Brookhaven, in Suffolk County, has crossed harpoons on its Town seal. Further west, Nassau County, which was then a part of Queens, had its own whaling operations. A whaling station was established in 1700 on the outer beach near the present site of Jones Beach, so named for Major Thomas Jones. He had been a loser in the Battle of the Boyne and the siege of Limerick. He escaped to France, obtained a ship, and turned privateer, until the British bottled him up in the West Indies. He arrived on Long Island in 1692, became High Sheriff of Queens, lived near Massapequa, and eventually acquired a total of 6,000 acres including the whaling site.

Whaling was good on the New Jersey coast, too, around 1700. Younger sons from eastern Long Island pioneer families removed to Elizabeth and Cape May, at that time, both for the whaling and for more land.

In 1848, when the "wreckers" novel was written, almost every family along Long Island's shores and nearby New Jersey had some member who had been to sea, or was actually so engaged at the time. Most were God-fearing. Men were raised then to "Do unto others. . . ." They could imagine themselves in a similar situation. Whatever washed ashore accidentally, they were likely to appropriate, cheerfully. But it does not seem possible that they would deliberately wreck a vessel.

Robert Greenhalgh Albion in his *Rise of New York Port* says, speaking of wrecks, "Long Islanders generally succored the victims . . . wild Jerseymen too often looted them."

The late Robert Carse, author of some forty books concerning the sea and a merchant mariner himself, had a more mundane explanation of why the Long Islanders were not "wreckers." He said: "Several times a year, the local people combed the beaches for the litter of cargoes cast up by the sea. They did not need false lights to divert ships from a correct course to destruction. The savage southeast, southwest and northwest gales that blew during the winter months drove the craft ashore. . . ."

15

UNDERWATER
TREASURE HUNTERS
AND EXPLORERS

Wᴇᴇᴋᴇɴᴅ divers who live in New York, nearby New Jersey, or on Long Island's west end are not treasure hunters as such. Some belong to serious diving groups interested in marine biology, maritime history, marine archeology, and undersea research. Others just enjoy skin diving as a sport demanding considerable skill and involving a certain amount of danger.

No one today expects to find valuables off the beaches of Long Island or New Jersey, or under the swirling waters at Hell Gate. The only treasure that Captain William Kidd ever buried in these parts, as far as can be proved, was dug up shortly after he left Gardiner's Island in 1699 for Boston, from whence he was transported to London and hanged, not as a pirate but for hitting an unruly sailor on the head with a bucket. The piracy charge would have caused embarrassment in high places.

The nearest thing to a real treasure ship sunk off the shores of New York State seems to have been the British pay-ship HMS Hussar, which went down in the East River in 1780 (see Chapter 3). She was said to have carried gold and silver worth from $2 million to $4 million. Spectacular attempts were made for years to salvage her, but the Hussar now lies completely buried under New York traffic.

HMS HUSSAR

Fruitless salvage operations were organized for nearly 150 years, trying to locate the treasure supposed to have been on the Hussar. In the early 1800's all sorts of homemade diving equipment and grappling devices were used to try to find the wreck on the river bottom. Her rudder was recovered on July 23, 1811. Eight years later several of the cannon were hoisted to the surface, along with some copper sheathing from the hull. Iron cannon balls and a few beer mugs bearing the seal of George the Third were also raised. A cannon from the Hussar, and one and a half pounds of grapeshot are now in the Museum of the City of New York. Four gold English coins, today worth about $50, and a few silver coins, were recovered.

In 1823 an anchor bearing the Hussar's name was brought up off Port Morris. The following year a company tried for several weeks to raise the Hussar. They did raise about forty feet of the ship's stern, after placing chains under her. But as she was moved from her bed she broke in two from keel to quarterdeck. Part of the ship slipped from the slings and settled down again on the rocks. Timber that had been embedded in mud was found perfectly sound; the remainder was worm-eaten and rotten.

In 1832 a British diving company brought over a London-made diving bell and also considerable data extracted from the British Admiralty. The tide pushed the bell around like a toy. After one of their divers was nearly drowned, the company gave up. Another attempt to recover the supposed sunken treasure was made in 1856. By this time parts of the ship had scattered over quite a large area of river bottom.

Whatever may have been lying in the mud where the Hussar went down in 1780 must have been well shaken up in 1876 when, on September 24, U.S. Army engineers (to quote Charles Giebelhaus in the Long Island *Forum* for February, 1960) "blew the worst features of Hell Gate straight back to hell." On that day 52,000 pounds of explosives were touched off at Hallett's Point.

In 1880, one hundred years after the pay-ship's sinking, a corporation called "Treasure Trove" was organized for the sole purpose, it was claimed, of salvaging the Hussar. The corporation's president, Captain George Thomas, had his crew open their operations each morning by uncovering and sending up long appeals to heaven for help. His petitions must have gone unanswered, for after several weeks the operation petered out. "Some financial finagling," Mr. Giebelhaus said, "overshadowed the salvage work."

As New York City grew, Stony Island, where Captain Pole had wanted his ship to take refuge, became Port Morris. Once almost an island, it was now filled in solid to the Bronx.

But the hopes for Hussar gold died hard. The New York *Evening Post* on March 3, 1930, carried a story about treasure hunters in general and about the latest hopeful. With the story the *Post* ran a picture of one Captain Simon Lake and his reconstructed submersible, Defender, in which he proposed to dive to the bottom of Hell Gate channel in a hunt for the foundered Hussar.

Captain Lake told the papers that Captain George Thomas of Orange, N.J., had sent a fortune down into the muddy water of the river to bring up the frigate but had failed, and had given his maps and plans to his successor for the submarine experiment. Captain Lake, with half a dozen helpers and a new chamber of his submarine that would allow his divers to walk out of it while it lay on the bottom, proposed to take up the job.

Lake took seven years to get around to it. He and another inventor, both past sixty, Harry L. Bowdion of Whitestone, Long Island, applied to the Federal government for the exclusive right to search for and recover whatever remained in the hulk of the British vessel. Bowdion had refitted the cable ship Telegraph, which he renamed the Salvor, with some wreck-finders, observation tanks, and other equipment to permit the blasting away of an entrance to the supposed strong room of the sunken ship. He had also invented a new type of diving suit to reach depths of 500 feet.

When this last recorded attempt was made, in 1937, Lake used the most modern gear ever tried up to that time. It included an underwater conveyor housed in a long steel tube.

But the attempt failed. Lake's final opinion was that the shore line had shifted so completely since the Revolution that the frigate might now be resting under dry land.

John S. Potter, Jr., underwater explorer and author of *Treasure Diver's Guide*, says: "Today, the wreck of the Hussar may lie between Locust Avenue and 134th and 135th streets, deep under the Riker's and North Brothers Island ferry, or under the Hell Gate power plant of the Consolidated Edison Company."

THE BLACK WARRIOR

Many other wrecks lie off Rockaway Beach, Long Island, where the Black Warrior went down in 1859. She lay there unidentified until two divers—Murray Seliger and Don Marchese—members of a group called the Oceanographic Historical Research Society, came up with some engraved silverware. Charles Dunn and Graham Snediker, founders of that group, have told the Black Warrior story.

She was built in New York in 1852 at a cost of $135,000, a fast United States mail packet of 1,556 tons gross weight. She was not only full-rigged with sails, but also powered by steam-driven side wheels. Most of her voy-

The BLACK WARRIOR, *before wreck on Rockaway Shoals, Long Island, February 20, 1859*

ages were between New York, New Orleans, and Havana, Cuba.

The Black Warrior nearly got us into a war with Spain in 1854. She was seized by the newly appointed governor of Cuba, fresh from Spain and not too fond of "gringos." Seizure was made on the basis of irregularities in her cargo manifest. She had Alabama cotton on board, which was not listed in the papers presented to Havana officials. Her captain stated that this was completely within regulations, for the cotton hadn't been unloaded in Havana and was not to be unloaded at any point in Cuba. Since this part of his cargo was being transshipped, he argued, it didn't have to be listed for the Havana customs people.

Nevertheless, on February 28, 1854, her commanding officer, Captain Bullock, was forced to leave his ship and cargo by order of Cuba's governor. Her crew and passengers were transferred to the American steamer Fulton, which was then loading in Havana, and her cargo was removed and confiscated.

This triggered a reaction in the States. The proslavery faction in Congress seized on the Warrior incident to back a demand for war with Spain, their hope being to annex Cuba as another slave territory. But calmer Northern heads prevailed. Because of the clamor raised in the States the Cuban government backed down, made full restitution for the confiscated cargo, and returned the Warrior to her owners.

The packet next made history in 1857, when her skipper and crew performed a feat of seamanship which, the veteran skin divers say, "belongs in all anthologies of astounding feats of the U.S. Merchant Marine."

She was under command now of Captain J. W. Smith, said to be the best "steam man" out of the Port of New York. She left New Orleans on January 11, 1857. She made Havana on the 13th, and left almost at once for New York. Her owners next saw her on January 26, mantled with snow, glazed with ice, stripped of masts, spars, bulwarks, lifeboats, and a good portion of her wheelhouse, heading up the North River for her dock. The thirty passengers and sixty crewmen on board told the story.

There were strong head winds the first three days out of Havana, but nothing special for that season. At midnight on January 17, while fifty miles from Hatteras, she began to run into heavy gales from the north, which by midmorning came around to the north-northeast. The ship began to pitch violently. It was snowing hard and ice formed rapidly in her rigging. By 3 P.M. on Sunday, January 18, it became impossible to keep her heading into the storm. It was decided to make as heavy a drag anchor as could be jury-rigged. They lashed together a six-pounder cannon, 600 pounds of grate bars, and all the spare masts and spars. This conglomeration was heaved over the side at the end of sixty fathoms of eleven-inch hawser.

The drag anchor worked well for a time. But as the storm increased, the ship started to plow right through the wave crests and fall off in the troughs, swept each time from bow to stern by walls of green water. It did not take much of this action to wash away most of her bulwarks, her lifeboats, and part of the wheelhouse. The violent motion of the Warrior then caused the fore topmast stay to part, with a report like a rifle shot. Then the masts began to fall like timber. Swift action with axes saved the situation temporarily; the packet seemed to ride better without her upperworks swaying with the wind.

At about 1 A.M. that Monday a short lull gave some hope of clearing weather. But soon the wind came roaring in again from the north-northeast, this time with near-hurricane force. Attempts were made to rig staysails, but these were torn to shreds. Finally all the spare sails were gone and every tarpaulin aboard ship was in ribbons. The engines were tried at regular intervals, but by now the Warrior was too iced up to answer her helm.

They drifted dead in the water for about two hours; then the wind slacked off enough finally to enable the ship to maneuver under steam. As she began to make headway northward, her chief engineer reported the bunkers almost empty of coal.

The crew scurried around the ship. They broke up furniture in the cabins and ripped wood paneling from cabin bulkheads. Even cargo holds were broken into. Crates of Havana oranges were brought topside, their contents jettisoned overboard and the wooden crates broken up for the hungry fires.

By 8 A.M. on Tuesday they had made it to within 200 miles of the mouth of the Chesapeake. Late that afternoon the wooded shore of Nag's Head came up over the horizon. Wood-cutting parties were planned, but on nearing land the mariners realized that nothing could get through that heavy surf. Then they began seriously to doubt the outcome of the voyage.

When they were off Cape Henry, the next day, pressure on the Warrior's boilers fell below requirements. The engines stopped. All anchors were let go. Then watching, waiting, and praying began. . . .

Early next morning, help came. They were towed to Old Point Comfort, Va. Captain Smith, who had been on deck for a sleepless seventy-two hours, was the hero of the day. Crewmen were suffering from frostbite. The passengers had behaved well through it all. Some coal was purchased locally, and officers and men of Fort Monroe donated more from their personal supply, until there was enough to take the ship to New York.

The rest of the voyage was uncomfortable, without the cabin furnishings, and plenty of ice floes about. But the battered ship finally made port. She was refitted in New York and resumed her regular route.

She left Havana again for New York on February 15, 1859. By 9 A.M. on February 20 she was off New York in a dense fog, in charge of a harbor pilot. Suddenly, without warning, she went hard aground on the Rockaway bar. The air must have turned blue with the lusty, pungent comments on his navigating flung at the pilot by long-suffering Captain Smith.

Mail and passengers were transferred immediately to the pilot boat George W. Blunt. The Warrior appeared to be sound and still tight. Skipper and crew remained aboard to work over the ship and guard $208,000 reposing in her safe.

Before long the steam tugs Achilles, Huntress, and Screecher arrived on the scene and began efforts to pull the Warrior off the bar. On February 22 the Screecher docked in New York with the specie, passengers' baggage, most of the crew, and a small part of the vessel's cargo.

The captain remained on board, with a wrecking crew under direction of the insurance company agent. By this time the hull had opened in several places and about ten feet of water was sloshing around in her holds.

She had run aground on a high tide, which meant that the salvagers could not count on high water to help get her off. Hope of pulling her free was abandoned. Her cargo was removed and much of her machinery dismantled and taken off on lighters. She was left to sink into sand and sea.

The wreck lies in about thirty-five feet of water just off Riis Park. Rockaway Inlet has moved far westward since 1859. The Black Warrior's boilers

Contents of sink in BLACK WAR-
RIOR's *galley, brought up in 1961
by divers after 102 years under
water*

were above water for many years; a buoy was put there when they rusted
away.

Until October, 1961, when the Oceanographic Historical Research
Society divers brought up some ironstone china and other items that appeared to have been in the galley sink when the Warrior went aground for
the last time, no one was sure what ship she was. They found silverware
which bore the imprint "Black Warrior—Officers." Rogers Smith & Co. had
made the tableware. Dating it was done by the International Silver Company of Connecticut. This "tipped" pattern was manufactured by one of International's predecessor companies. They made that line only from 1856 to
1858.

THE IBERIA

Another wreck that is a favorite of divers and fishermen is the freighter
Iberia, an old tramp of 943 tons, owned in Marseilles. She met her end at
Jones Inlet, three miles off Long Beach, on November 10, 1888. She lies in

186

about sixty feet of water, close to the East Rockaway Whistling Buoy, better known to fishermen as Buoy No. 6.

On September 28, 1888, the Iberia finished loading her cargo of wool, dates, hides, and coffee at hot, dusty Bussorah on the Persian Gulf, and cleared that port for New York. Captain Sagols had a very mixed crew of thirty, picked up on the waterfronts from Port Said to Singapore. The Iberia had almost reached New York when her tired old engines gave out. Off the south shore of Long Island she lay to, for almost three weeks, while her engineer tried to revive her for the short run into port.

Meanwhile in New York the Cunard liner Umbria, a 7,798-ton trans-Atlantic luxury liner built at Leith in 1881 and fresh from a complete refit, cleared for Liverpool on Saturday, November 10, at 10:45 A.M.

Captain William McMickan carried 215 first-class passengers, 67 second-class, and 429 in the steerage. November 10 dawned wet and hazy, with promise of fog. By 12:12 P.M. they had passed Sandy Hook. Fifteen minutes later the pilot was put over the side, and off went the Umbria at a good nineteen knots.

By 1 P.M. the fog had rolled in all along the coast. Word was passed to slow down the Umbria. At 1:15 a whistle was heard off the starboard bow. The captain ordered the ship to be slowed down even more. Again the whistle was heard, this time very close. The command was given to stop all engines. At 1:18 a small tramp steamer appeared through the fog, steaming slowly into the path of the Umbria, headed north.

The Umbria's engines were put in full reverse, but too late. Her sharp, straight bow sliced into the stern port quarter of the tired ship from Marseilles and took away fourteen feet of her fantail. The collision made so slight a shock that it went unnoticed by most of the Umbria's passengers.

The fog was now really pea soup—the ships could not see each other. The Umbria lowered boats to examine her own damage, which proved slight. The captain decided to return to New York for repairs. The Umbria then began to look for the Iberia. Twenty minutes later they found her, flying distress signals.

The two captains got together. The Cunard captain advised Captain Sagols to transfer his crew to the Umbria. The Frenchman refused, with some asperity.

Both ships dropped anchor and remained near each other the rest of that day and night. By the next morning the Iberia was noticeably lower by the stern. The French captain was finally convinced that his crew should be transferred. Once he got ashore, a great controversy started up as to where to place the blame. One report blames the Iberia entirely, saying she failed to keep a proper lookout.

A salvage crew was placed aboard the Iberia. They secured a boat to her side for a possible hasty exit, which proved necessary. Two tugs started out for her late that afternoon, but before they arrived a bulkhead collapsed and the Iberia went to the bottom.

Divers say: "She makes for an easy scuba dive and, if visibility is good, a very interesting one. She lies roughly in a northwest-southeast line about four miles off Long Beach. The sand has crept over a good portion of her center, but on a good day you can see thirty to thirty-five feet of her shaft back to the old squared-off propeller. Her sides are completely broken down and pieces of her deck plating are scattered about. . . ." They go on to give a detailed description of the poor old Iberia's innards.

POLICE DIVER

The New York City police force has a scuba unit. It is headed by Sergeant Robert Byrne, skin diver and marine historian. He went down to the USS San Diego, an armored cruiser torpedoed by the German submarine U-156 in July, 1918, with a loss of six lives. She lies on the ocean floor off Fire Island in 110 feet of water.

Sergeant Byrne says: "She lies bow to shore and upside down. One propeller is off on the sand and her anchors protrude from the ocean bottom. I have been through her upside-down officers' quarters, in which, of course, the admiral's brass bed rests on the overhead."

Sergeant Byrne has been diving for thirty years on such wrecks as Mohawk, Stolt Dagali, Gulftrade, and City of Athens.

THE WEEKEND DIVERS

Several years ago a Florida man directed a team that probed the sands and shallows of Florida's east coast. From the remains of the Spanish Plate Fleet that sank in a 1775 hurricane, they recovered some wonderful and valuable things—after years of toil. But the man said: "The money value seems almost meaningless. The real treasure lies in our having touched hands with history."

That is what some of the New York and western Long Island divers who have spent weekends under water have enjoyed most.

Graham Snediker of Jericho, Long Island, and Charles Dunn of New York were prime movers in assembling in 1958 the diving group incorporated in 1961 as the Oceanographic Historical Research Society. Each member was obliged to have already done several years of wreck-diving, and to possess some special skill or knowledge that would benefit the group. The society's primary activity was "to gather, verify, and catalogue information

188

concerning sunken vessels and other locations of historical interest in New York State waters."

They kept careful records of their operations. Their findings have been of considerable interest to naval historians and to the Smithsonian Institution in Washington. They have gone down to depths of 170 feet or more in their search for wrecked ships. They have positively identified many.

For several years that society had twenty members. But one of the group said recently: "We haven't done much diving since 1967—with growing families and growing waistlines. We sail, instead."

Graham Snediker said: "I got hooked on skin-diving more than twenty years ago . . . before most people knew that scuba means 'self-contained underwater breathing apparatus.' " His skill is far beyond that of the amateur. He was called to Napeague Beach, just west of Montauk, Long Island, in February, 1961, for salvage operations on an American Astro-Jet wrecked in the ocean there. When an American Airlines 707 jet plunged into the icy waters of Jamaica Bay, Long Island, he was called to assist in recovering the bodies of ninety-five victims.

Mr. Snediker, speaking of diving to the USS San Diego, says: "Entering a wreck such as that with a thousand-watt lamp that penetrates a scant six feet through the murk is not for people with claustrophobia."

Members of the Oceanographic Historical Research Society did not come back from their weekend expeditions empty-handed. They brought up color pictures of what they saw; and antique crockery, silverware, and other artifacts which they have presented to museums. Other divers have brought up bronze portholes, ships' bells, and deadeyes (the circular blocks of wood used for tying up ropes on old ships). The most valuable object I have heard of, brought up from a Long Island wreck, was a silver serving tray with a silver seahorse mounted on each corner. That was from the Iberia, the freighter that went down off Long Beach on November 10, 1888, after a collision with the Cunard liner Umbria.

The amateur divers' main interest seems to be just the adventure of exploring the silent, unknown world under the sea. And they often furnish valuable tips to skippers of fishing boats about hitherto undiscovered wrecks. As every fisherman knows, fish congregate around the hulls of sunken ships.

Another diving group was founded in the winter of 1958–1959 by five students from City College, New York. They called it the Club Sous-Marin of Long Island. Frederick P. Schmitt of Westbury, Long Island, said: "After reading *Ship Ashore* we set our sights on locating and raising relics from the HMS Culloden, the British 74-gun frigate wrecked at Montauk in 1781." Which they did. In 1958 some of her timbers could still be seen, at intervals when the tide was right. The young divers brought up artifacts that they thought proved the ship's identity. This resulted in a meticulously researched book, *H.M.S. Culloden*, written by Mr. Schmitt and his fellow club member, Donald Schmid, and published by the Mystic Historical Association.

Another, older group of scuba divers from New York and New Jersey came along a year or two after that. They photographed the last visible timbers from the Revolutionary War wreck. These were burned by picnickers shortly afterward. Now, sadly, the once beautiful, isolated shore with its beachplum bushes and pepperidge trees and green hills has been bulldozed bare and flat and covered with a housing development.

Both groups placed pieces of wood and metal thought to be from the Culloden in the East Hampton Town Marine Museum in Amagansett. But it was not until August, 1971, that two other weekend divers came up with positive proof. David Warsen of Hampton Bays, Long Island, and Bob Miller of Aquebogue, Long Island, brought up among other pieces a solid brass gudgeon, marked with the Culloden's name—from right where it was supposed to be.

16

WRECKS FOR FISHING

As every fisherman knows, there is no place like a wreck to find fish. A sunken ship, encrusted with barnacles, mussels, and seaweeds, is a haven for sea worms and other marine life on which fish feed; and it is a sheltered place for fish to breed.

The men who leave New York before dawn, on weekends, to board an open party-boat in New Jersey or on Long Island expect the captain to take them where the fish are. The captains have to keep posted. Private boat owners, too, make a study of the best fishing grounds in their area.

A few wreck-fishing spots have been named in print. More are being discovered all the time, due to modern fishing-boat installations such as decca, loran, sonar, and radar. But many such wrecks remain closely guarded secrets, known only to certain party-boat captains.

If a captain is first on a particular wreck where he finds the fishing good, it is a point of honor for no one on board to tell others where it is. Sometimes a location will be handed down from father to son. Or, if a fisherman seems to be having unusually good luck, a rival might sneak out and follow him.

Skippers with the latest instruments to locate wrecks take out divers as well as fishermen. The divers would not get on the offshore wrecks without the fishing boats. Usually the fishermen and the divers cooperate very well. The fish, however, do not always cooperate as well with the divers. Party-boat fishermen have noticed that when a skin diver goes down, the fish depart. But scuba divers, with their tanks of air and streams of escaping bubbles, not only allay the fears of the fish but quickly win them over as friends. Captain Jay Porter, now of Montauk, Long Island, who sailed for years out of Freeport, Long Island, says, "They seem to be lulled by bubbles."

WRECK SPECIALIST

Only a few of the open party-boat captains are interested in the history of the wrecks on which they fish. Captain Porter is well known as a wreck fisherman. He loves to explore and identify the sunken ships. He is just as interested in the wrecked vessel itself as he is in the fish he and his customers catch there.

He has a great ship's bell that he recovered from the Tennyson, a wreck he discovered in 1962 and identified through the bell which bore the name, and the date 1864. Through Lloyd's of London he found that the schooner was built in Bath, Maine. She was lost off eastern Long Island. Among other wreck souvenirs he has a plaque from the wheelhouse of the Cunard liner Oregon, which went down off Center Moriches, Long Island, in 1886; a mug from the steam tug Eureka, sunk seventeen miles south of Jones Inlet; dishes from a patrol boat 100 feet long with a gun mounted on its bow, sunk southeast of Jones Inlet (so far that wreck is unnamed; the china does not look like Navy or Coast Guard stuff). He has a square dish from the British tanker Coimbra, which went down twenty-seven miles south of Shinnecock Inlet in 1942.

"The first wreck I ever found," Captain Porter said, "was the Hilton Castle, a freight steamer that went down in February, 1886, off Fire Island. I found her in 1958, lying so close to the beach you can see ranges on her."

Speaking of wreck exploration, Captain Porter says the dream of his life is to locate the Savannah, first ship to use steam in crossing the ocean. She went down off Fire Island in 1821.

Frank O. Braynard, author, artist, and editor, knows more about that first Savannah than anyone living. He was instrumental in getting the first commercial vessel in the world to use atomic power, named for the old Savannah. His book, *S.S. Savannah: Elegant Steam Ship*, came out in 1963. He has been searching for the 1821 wreck for years, employing divers, a blimp, and helicopters, but so far without success.

He and Captain Porter have discussed it. Jay Porter thinks it is possible that a ship's water tank he found off Moriches Inlet may be a part of the old Savannah. But there are innumerable wrecks off Fire Island. The Savannah may remain one of the countless mysteries hidden by the inscrutable sea.

NAMING A WRECK

Most fishing captains, when they find a wreck where fish are plentiful, note the exact location and call it whatever they like. "The Dodger," name unknown, lies off Jones Inlet. It was so-called by the captain who found it on the day the Dodgers won the pennant. Captain Porter says he has brought up timbers from it.

Before all the new detecting gadgets came out, he says, he used to drag chains behind his boat and take bearings, from shore telephone poles, gas tanks, etc., when he had hit a wreck with his chain. He came across a wreck three miles south of the "Dodger" that he thought at first might be a light-ship, because it was so heavy. It had an iron propeller instead of the bronze usually found on active boats. It lies southeast of the Fire Island buoys. It turned out to be an old hump-backed barge.

What fishermen call "Nervous" is a wreck southwest of the jetty tip at Rockaway. It moves. Some days fishermen cannot find it. "Doll's Wreck," named for a fishing captain, lies at Rockaway, also a short distance from the southwest tip of the jetty.

Three coal barges snapped their tow in a storm in 1917 and settled on the bottom in an equilateral triangle, within five miles of shore, near the Iberia, the "Wire Wreck," and the Boyle. These are commonly called the "East Wreck."

Freddy Wrege, a western Long Island party-boat captain, discovered the wreck of a schooner off Fire Island the day Wolcott beat Joe Louis. He named it "Wolcott" after the champion. Another vessel, of whale-back design, which lies in ninety-six feet of water off the island's west end, is familiar to divers and fishermen, who call it "Wrege's Wreck." The "Benson," so-called from the captain who found it, is one of two barges and a tug, sunk crisscross off Rockaway Inlet. It moves westward, and may have gone down where Jones Beach is today.

Captain Porter tells how a large steel ship, apparently unknown to the government, got its name. It probably went down before World War II. He says: "Years ago, going out of Sheepshead Bay, I fished what I thought was a virgin wreck. That is, one never fished before.

"An Italian customer, thinking we had said 'Virginia,' remarked: 'Oh, I fished this years ago out of Sheepshead Bay.' So we named that wreck Virginia."

The captain continued: "There is a big ship upside down, forty-eight miles off Long Island's south shore. We don't know its name. . . . And near the ruins of the Texas Tower, fifty miles offshore, is the Bidevind, lying on its side." (The Texas Tower No. 4 went down off Long Island on January 15,

Perils of the Port of New York

1961, with a loss of twenty-seven lives.)

The Bidevind was a Norwegian freighter, a motor vessel built in 1938, 414 feet long and 4,956 tons. She was torpedoed and sunk on April 30, 1942.

THE ROCKAWAYS AND JONES BEACH

The Rockaways and Jones Beach are strewn with wrecks that have been fished for years. One of the old favorites for fishing captains and their anglers is the Black Warrior, lost in 1859 on Rockaway Shoals.

Charles Dunn and Graham Snediker, scuba divers who have made many visits to the Black Warrior, say: "Her midsection is filled with holes and crevices well tenanted by the local finned population. It affords plenty of refuge from predators. Fish roam about other portions of the wreck in search of food, but the concentration in the region of the engines is something to see."

Although there are plenty of porgies and sea bass down there too, they wander around, the divers say; but: "in general, the Warrior is now pretty much a summer resort for blackfish, and her midsection . . . has the heaviest concentration of them.

"The Black Warrior, having been under water for over 100 years and probably fished for 90, has on her decks and skeleton the largest collection of sinkers anyone has ever seen in one spot."

The British brig Mic Mac, 147 tons, bound from Cardenas to New York with a cargo of molasses, became a total loss on Rockaway Beach in a fog on January 3, 1873. . . . The James Lawrence, a schooner with a cargo of resin, went down a quarter-mile east of Rockaway Life Saving Station on January 24, 1877. . . . The schooner Mary E. Turner became a total loss one mile east of Rockaway Beach village on January 2, 1881. . . . The tragic Ajace, lost in 1881, is another Rockaway casualty known for its fishing. . . . The 135-ton Copia, a coal schooner bound from New York to Rockaway, sank off Rockaway Point on September 18, 1882. . . .

Fifty-odd years ago the French tramp steamer Iberia was called "the most popular, and probably the best of the fishing wrecks around New York." It is still rated high for blackfish and sea bass. The Iberia, which went down on November 10, 1888, lies about three miles south of Long Beach, Long Island, close to the East Rockaway Whistling Buoy.

A New York City scow, without cargo, went down on November 18, 1892, two miles southwest of Rockaway Point Life Saving station. . . . The schooner Robert A. Snow, known as the "Derrick Barge," was lost near the Black Warrior on February 8, 1899. . . . Three schooners were wrecked on

April 30, 1900, west of Rockaway Point: the Kenyon, the Evelyn, and the Boyle. All became notable fishing grounds.

What fishermen call the "Granite Wreck" is really the three-masted schooner Cornelia Soule, 306 tons, bound from Maine to Philadelphia with a cargo of granite slabs when she went down on April 26, 1902, a mile offshore of Rockaway Point and only a quarter-mile east of the wrecked Ajace. The Cornelia Soule's crew of six were rescued with difficulty by the Life Savers at Rockaway after a long, hard fight against a heavy sea and a hurricane-force gale.

Plenty of blackfish and fluke are found around the Roda. She was a British iron single-screw steamship, 315 feet long and 1,587 tons, bound from Huelva, Spain, with a crew of thirty. She lost her bearings in a fog, and went aground a hundred yards offshore at Jones Beach, halfway between Jones Inlet and Fire Island on February 13, 1908. A southeast storm washed over her and drove her still further up on the beach, where she broke up. The Life Savers made a heroic rescue of her crew. Captain G. W. Wilson of the fishing boat Alert retrieved part of her cargo. Not long ago a motor boat, fishing over the wreck, was caught in it and ruined.

Fishermen and divers are interested in the "Steel Wreck," or "Wire Wreck," which is actually a wooden vessel with a square mast, lying in seventy feet of water dead south of Jones Inlet. She was outbound, with a cargo of bedsprings and other wire products, about 1895. . . . The schooner Sabao, of Machias, Maine, bound from Delaware Breakwater to Providence, R.I., with a cargo of logwood on October 13, 1889, when she sank on the outer bar of New Inlet (now Jones Inlet) south of Freeport, Long Island. Her crew of six was saved. . . . The coal schooner Richard B. Chute, bound from Philadelphia to Plymouth, Mass., was lost on Jones Inlet bar at 2 A.M. on November 16, 1893.

The so-called "Howard" or "Scow" wreck was a steam-powered lighter attempting to salvage copper ore from the British steamer Roda. The "Howard" lies a quarter-mile southeast from the Peter Rickmers, or "Oil Wreck." About twenty-seven feet of water cover it at low tide.

The three-masted schooner H. R. Keene, bound from Cuba to New York, ran on the bar at Long Beach in May, 1901—the same bar where the Cavour was to strike nearly a year later. Good fishing is reported there.

The coal sloop Mary Seaman went down at Short Beach, Long Island, in 1902.

Two of the fishing wrecks off New Jersey are the Ramos, a 1,208-ton vessel sunk in 1933 three miles off Sandy Hook, and a nameless barge lying five miles off the Hook in sixty feet of water.

Since 1964, when the tanker Stolt Dagali was split in two by the

Israeli cruise liner Shalom off Long Beach, N.J., her stern has become a fishing spot (the forward part of the vessel remained afloat, was rebuilt, and is in business today).

SALVAGE AND CONSERVATION

In the winter of 1962 a great hubbub ensued when the salvage rights on the USS cruiser San Diego, sunk on July 19, 1918, by a German mine or torpedo about four miles off Fire Island, were sold to a professional salvage company. The company planned to blow up the 503-foot, 13,400-ton cruiser for its scrap metal. They paid an initial $1,200, plus another $1,200 for a performance bond. The company agreed to give up the job if they were compensated for $15,000 already spent on surveys, equipment, and negotiations.

Throughout 1963 there were meetings up and down the coast to protest the destruction of sunken ships by either amateur or professional salvagers. John Clark, president of the American Littoral Society, a nonprofit organization of skin-diving enthusiasts and anglers, urged legislation to bar unrestricted salvaging that causes "irreparable losses through the destruction of fish habitats." He said that the San Diego alone had become such a good fishing ground that it was responsible for $100,000 a year in revenue to party-boat owners and their suppliers, retailers of fishing gear, and other persons whose livelihood comes from deep-sea fishing. Mr. Clark is assistant director of the Sandy Hook Marine Laboratory, and has studied the relationship of wrecks to fish and other ocean life.

In September, 1963, the Atlantic States Marine Fisheries Commission heard a plea presented by the National Party Boat Owners Alliance that Commission backing be given to a drive to place important offshore fishing wrecks under state or Federal protection from opportunistic salvage or similar destruction. Paul Tzimoulis of Waterbury, Conn., told the Commission that there are some 750 wrecks on the east coast alone which are actual or potential fish-producers for various types of fishing craft.

Joseph Mitchell in his *The Bottom of the Harbor*, published in 1944, estimated that there were 800 or 900 old submerged hulks in New York Harbor alone. He spoke of the "Mudhole," a great fishing ground south of where Scotland and Ambrose lightships used to be, an area fifteen miles long and five to ten miles wide. The wrecks lying on the bottom of the approaches to the harbor are great shelters for fish. "The most popular party boats are those whose captains locate the fishiest wrecks and bridle them," he said. Bridling, he explained, means that if a wreck lies north and south, for instance, the party boat goes in athwart it and drops one anchor east and one west, so it cannot be slewed around by wind or tide.

Salvagers, however, are not the greatest threat to western Long Island and New Jersey fishermen in the New York area. The greatest threat is pollution. One fishing captain says: "At Sheepshead Bay there used to be five ex-subchasers, 100-footers, in the fishing business; two former PT boats, 85-footers; and twenty or twenty-five smaller boats. They would carry maybe 1,500 people a day. Today you're lucky if there are 200. Due to pollution— factories and such—you have to travel very far to get any fish."

He may be overly pessimistic, but certainly the metropolis is crowding out natural resources over a wider and wider area.

SOVIET FISHING PRACTICES

When he spoke of the Texas Tower, Captain Jay Porter showed a foot-square, dark brown piece of fish net—nylon, with a half-inch mesh. "That came off the Texas Tower ruin," he said. "It's Russian. A net like that will never deteriorate as the old nets did. And with that size mesh, nothing escapes. If one of those nets gets caught on a wreck, it spoils the fishing there.

"Fish caught in it die; they rot and pollute the water. Divers say they find no fish within fifteen or twenty feet of a wreck with one of those nets lost on it. We pay them to take the Russian nets off.

"That is just one thing the foreign fishing boats do to us. They are allowed to come twelve miles offshore—and I've seen them closer. Not only Soviets—East and West Germans, Poles, Norwegians—fish off here. They scare our customers on the party boats.

"Once, six of the Soviet boats put out nets in a circle all around us. They concentrate, to louse up our fishing. You never see a sea gull back of any of those boats, as you do with ours. We throw trash overboard.

"Once there used to be plenty of porbeagle sharks off here. You don't see them anymore. They are caught by foreign vessels and sold to Italy. Bring almost as much as our swordfish.

"Talk about American commercial fishermen depleting the sea! We don't have enough boats to do that."

ARTIFICIAL DUPLICATION OF WRECKS

The allure that any submerged junk has for fish has a scientific name— thigmotropism. Taking cognizance of the fact that fish tend to congregate around sunken ships and other wreckage, the United Nations Food and Agriculture Organization has recently suggested sinking wrecked or discarded automobiles, railway cars, tractors, or other industrial equipment in lakes and oceans to attract fish. Underwater "housing" for fish had been

encouraged prior to the United Nations' suggestion by only two nations—
the United States and Japan. The Japanese have put down trees, sunken
boats filled with trash, and concrete blocks to create fish colonies; they also
blast underwater reefs to provide nooks and crannies. Such recesses give
algae, sponges, and other marine life a place to grow. They also attract
lobsters and other valuable crustaceans who feed on primitive sea life.

Several years ago a group of sportsmen and boatmen, aided by New
York State, started an artificial reef off Fire Island to create a home for fish
and shellfish. Divers find shellfish, flounders, blowfish, and ling already in
residence.

17

PORT CASUALTIES
IN WARTIME

O_N July 12, 1776, Richard, Lord Howe, Admiral
of the British fleet, arrived in New York Harbor. His brother, General Sir
William Howe, had arrived on June 10 with authority to "negotiate peace in
the revolted colonies." The Lower Bay was immediately held by the British
Navy. Staten Island had been abandoned without resistance, thus surrendering the strong position of the Narrows. Governor's Island was still occupied
by the Americans, and American troops were massed on Brooklyn Heights.

Captain Henry Duncan, commanding HMS Eagle, flying the Admiral's
flag, was lying off Staten Island on August 12. He reported the arrival of 104
sail, including Hessian troops on transports, which joined the fleet of 130 to
140 ships already there. On August 22, after the British had crossed from
Staten Island to Gravesend Bay, the Long Island shore of the Narrows,
Washington withdrew from Governor's Island.

On August 25, Hessians landed on Long Island and were soon within
musket shot of American troops on Brooklyn Heights. Two days later the
Americans lost the Battle of Long Island. On September 14 the British captured the "town of New York," and for the duration of the war occupied all
of Long Island.

The British fleet played a cat-and-mouse game, waiting for French
ships to come down from Newport, R.I. British ships lay in Gardiner's Bay,
a commodious anchorage off the eastern end of Long Island, thirty or
forty miles from Rhode Island. On one occasion the fifty-gun ship Experi-

ment, Captain Sir James Wallace, was out in the open sea off Montauk Point when she was chased by the French fleet into Long Island Sound and was only able to reach safety at New York by way of the East River. The Experiment was the first ship of the line ever to pass through Hell Gate; that was on August 18, 1778.

Vice Admiral Marriot Arbuthnot kept his 161-foot long flagship, HMS Royal Oak, seventy-four guns, in Gardiner's Bay during the winter of 1780–1781. On April 14, 1781, the Royal Oak went aground on the rocks opposite Whitehall Street, New York City. She was hauled off.

WHALEBOAT WARFARE

After the Battle of Long Island, when the British occupied the Port of New York and the whole of Long Island, there was a great exodus of able-bodied men to Connecticut, where they joined Washington's forces, or began to organize raids to harass the British and capture supplies. This "whaleboat warfare" was carried on in small (twenty to thirty feet long), easily maneuverable boats, with swivel guns that could be carried or concealed.

Boatmen came from New Jersey, Staten Island, and all parts of Long Island for this purpose. The Tories retaliated by plundering patriot vessels. "Whaleboat warfare" finally degenerated into a free-for-all, since these miniature privateers were under no real authority; but in some degree it did help the Colonial cause.

Long Island was very valuable as a source of fuel, forage, and provisions to the British occupying New York City, but many a boat carrying these articles never reached Manhattan. It was said there were 150 boats on Long Island, east of Jamaica, engaged in this unofficial warfare.

Captains Adam Hyler and William Marriner of New Brunswick, N.J., annoyed the British troops so much that an armed force was sent to destroy their boats. The object was effected, but the cost was more than it was worth. New boats were built immediately.

Hyler and Marriner cruised between Egg Harbor, N.J., and Staten Island, and often visited Long Island. About nine o'clock one dark night in 1776, Captain Hyler with two whaleboats took a British corvette of twenty guns in Coney Island Bay.

The ship lay at anchor, about to leave for Halifax to complete her crew. Hyler had one of his boats, with muffled oars, rowed up close under the British ship's stern. The officers could be seen in the cabin, playing cards. There was no watch on deck.

The spy boat then fell astern to her consort, and reported. Orders were given to board. The boats were rowed up silently and the ship was boarded instantly on both sides. Not a man was injured. The officers were confined in the cabin, the crew below.

Captain Hyler ordered the British to be removed from the corvette, well fettered, and placed in the whaleboats. Then a few articles were taken from the ship, and she was set on fire. Captain Hyler left with his prisoners for New Brunswick.

A contemporary story says that the captain of the corvette wept as they were crossing the bay. He reproached himself for permitting one of His Majesty's ships to be surprised and taken "by two damned egg-shells." He added that there had been $40,000 in British money on the burning vessel. Whether this was true or was told to tantalize the patriot privateer, no one knows.

Hyler was pursuing a refugee, one Lip-
Hook captain and was wanted by Gen-
w York in his boat with his crew dressed
-war press-gang. He went ashore looking
was attending a cock fight, which would
him.

Whitehall, Hyler got as far as the Battery
p from the West Indies, loaded with rum,
l, cut her cable, set her sails, and with a
ethtown Point. Before daylight he had
. He then burned the sloop to prevent her

whaleboats entered the bay at Rockaway,
nd burn every vessel in sight. Three Tory
n alarm. They recaptured a seized sloop,
ty-three prisoners.

h boats were bound from New York to
ey were attacked by two Colonial whale-
's Point. Two of the British boats escaped.

venue, of twelve guns and fifty-two men,
ation off Hempstead, Long Island, by the
British ship C... le bilged, and her men were just able to make shore with their arms. They had no more than landed when a loyalist Queens County militia group came bearing down on them. After a skirmish, ten rebels and a boat were taken. Reinforcements of Tories arrived and all were taken. The privateer had been after cows and sheep.

The British packet ship Carteret, carrying a valuable cargo of goods, specie, and public papers, was driven ashore at Jones Beach by an American privateer. Tories of Hempstead helped the officers and crew to escape to New York with the papers and valuables, but the ship itself was left to the "mercy of the waves and the King's loyal subjects." It was looted, dismantled, and sold at auction for 100 pounds as it lay on the beach.

On August 26, 1781, HMS sloop Swallow, Captain Thomas Wells, master, was driven ashore by four American privateers, so British dispatches said, "on Fire Island, near Long Island, America." She was lost. Particulars have never been ascertained.

AIDED BY LONG ISLAND QUAKERS

In February, 1957, the Liverpool Nautical Research Society wrote to John L. Lochhead, librarian of the Mariners Museum in Newport News, Va., asking for information concerning the twenty-eight-gun British naval vessel Liverpool, supposed to have been wrecked on Long Island on February 11, 1778. The society wanted to know whether her crew set her on fire to prevent her falling into American hands; if her crew were made prisoners or picked up by another British ship; if she was driven ashore in a gale, or as a result of action by American forces.

Mr. Lochhead had no record of the Liverpool's loss.

According to a note found in the East Hampton (N.Y.) *Star* of February 2, 1917, it was weather that drove the Liverpool ashore. The officers and crew went from the vessel in small boats, some of which were swamped by the heavy sea. Residents came in wagons and took the men to their homes, dried and fed them. Admiral Harvey of the British Navy told Washington Irving, years later in Paris, that a Quaker family named Hicks provided for him liberally for several weeks. The Navy men had no pay but the King's allowance for such an emergency.

In the same Long Island weekly this item appeared on February 27, 1920: "Rockaway Beach residents are concerned over the appearance of an old wooden ship washed out of the sand in a recent storm. The craft is over one hundred feet long and firmly constructed with old-fashioned handmade spikes. Captain Joseph Meade of the Arverne Coast Guard station said it was probably an old British man-o'-war wrecked during the Revolution. Attempts will be made to dig the boat out of the sand when the weather moderates." That could have been the Liverpool.

PRISON SHIPS BURNED

Decommissioned, dismasted British ships of the line were anchored during the Revolution in Wallabout Bay, later the site of the Brooklyn Navy Yard. These rotting hulks were jammed with American prisoners. Conditions aboard the ships, according to historians, were terrible. The first vessel to arrive there, on October 20, 1776, was the Whitby; other early arrivals were the Stromboli, Scorpion, Hunter, Falmouth, Scheldt, and Clyde.

On a Sunday afternoon in October, 1777, one of the prison ships burned. It was reported that the fire had been set by prisoners, but no one knew exactly. A few prisoners were burned to death; the rest were removed to another vessel. In February, 1778, another prison ship suffered the same fate. Two months later, the infamous ship Jersey, largest of them all, was moored in the Wallabout and all prisoners (except the sick) were transferred to her. About 11,000 Americans—citizens and soldiers—who died on these floating prisons are buried near the Navy Yard.

TREASURE SHIPS

On December 26, 1777, the British frigate Mercury was wrecked in the North River (Hudson) off New York. An attempt was made to raise her in 1823. The Mercury, according to tradition, was carrying considerable specie for paying troops.

Some writers have claimed that the British ship Lexington, which sank in 1780 in the East River in sixty-six feet of water, off 138th Street, carried the equivalent of nearly $2 million. Details seem unavailable.

But there is no doubt that the story of the British frigate Hussar, which struck a rock and sank at Hell Gate on November 3, 1780, and became a total loss, is authentic. That is told in another chapter, 3.

THE WAR OF 1812

The first shot in the War of 1812 is said to have been fired six years before war was declared. On April 6, 1806, the British frigate Leander wantonly fired a cannon ball into a small, unarmed American trading vessel as it stood off Sandy Hook Lighthouse, coming out of the Port of New York. One seaman was killed.

War seemed imminent in 1807 when a fort called the Southwest Battery, equipped with twenty-eight cannons, thirty-two pounders, was built on a small island off the lower tip of Manhattan, connected with the main island by a bridge. Later it was called Fort Clinton, or Castle Clinton, after New York State's governor, DeWitt Clinton. Landfill made it part of the Battery itself, and it became Castle Garden in 1824, with a concert hall where the "Swedish Nightingale," Jenny Lind, made her American debut. From 1855 to 1892 Castle Garden was the reception center for immigrants arriving from Europe. Then the Port of Entry was moved to Ellis Island. From 1896 to 1941 Castle Garden was the site of the New York Aquarium. In the summer of 1968 work began on the restoration of the old fort.

A British fleet of 240 guns blockaded New York during the War of 1812, but it never attacked.

In 1811 another fort was added to the defense of New York Harbor. That was Fort William, or Castle William, which still stands on Governor's Island and is now headquarters for the United States Coast Guard, Third District.

In 1812 a fort with ninety-six gun emplacements, called Fort Diamond because of the shape of the tiny jut of land on which it rested, was begun. In 1823 it was renamed Fort Lafayette, to commemorate the service of the French general, the Marquis de Lafayette. The fort continued in harbor defense until 1861. During the Civil War it was used as a military prison for captured Confederates. The old fort was razed when the Verrazzano–Narrows Bridge was built. Hendrick's Reef, on which it once stood, now lies beneath the bridge's Brooklyn tower.

The declaration of war on Great Britain by Congress in June, 1812, followed years of harassment of American ships and seamen by both Great Britain and France. The Jeffersonian Embargo of 1807, forbidding all ships to leave American ports without the President's permission, had practically wiped out New York shipping for two years. Before that, in what was supposed to be a time of peace, the American coast had swarmed for years with British blockading fleets. In 1809 the Non-Intercourse Act, directed only against Great Britain and France, permitted a limited revival of commerce.

It was feared that the British might enter New York by way of Long Island Sound, so more forts were erected at Hell Gate and on Upper Manhattan. A blockhouse was built in 1814 on Mill Rock (so named because a mill had been built there in 1700) to defend the city at that point. Fort Stevens was built that same year on Hallett's Point, now Astoria, Long Island.

Cornelius Vanderbilt started on his way to fortune with his Staten Island ferry in the War of 1812. During this war he carried supplies to the New York forts.

War had not yet been declared on May 30, 1812, when the American ship Egeria, under command of Captain Cook, of and for New York from Copenhagen, was halted by the British cruiser Morgiana while crossing the Grand Banks. One of the Egeria's passengers was the secretary of the American Minister to Denmark. He bore dispatches from that minister to our State Department. The British captain ordered the secretary to board the Morgiana with his dispatches. The secretary refused, pointing out that this was an intolerable invasion of the law of nations. His dispatch boxes were then seized, broken open, and their contents read. After that the secretary was allowed to remain on the Egeria, but the other passengers were removed to the Morgiana.

The Egeria was declared a prize and ordered into Halifax, with a prize crew and prize master in charge. As she was bound from Denmark to the United States, there could be no pretense, in her case, that she was trading with France.

On June 10 the Egeria spoke a schooner from which the prize master learned that he had blundered 200 miles off his course. He was heading not for Halifax but for Long Island Sound. He altered his steering and turned northwestward. The next day, June 11, the former captain of the Egeria, held prisoner on board, observed that the seawater was discolored and, as he knew the coast well, went to the prize master and warned him that they were evidently close to shore and that he had better keep the ship off.

"You mind your business and I'll mind mine," the prize master replied. The next morning, June 12, they found themselves within musketshot of rocks. The prize master now tried to wear the ship offshore. He made a hash of this. The Egeria went on broadside and became a total loss.

The people on board cut away the masts and floated ashore. They found themselves in a region without food or shelter. At this crisis, a New York–Sandy Hook pilot boat arrived.

A NAUTICAL PAUL REVERE

Charles Edward Russell in *From Sandy Hook to 62°* related a proud chapter in the history of the New York–Sandy Hook pilots. He told how New York merchants, expecting a declaration of war, chartered the fastest of the pilot boats, holding her ready to sail at a moment's notice. That small boat saved an incalculable number of American ships and millions of dollars for our shipowners and merchants. She gave the first warning to American merchantmen abroad that a state of war with Great Britain existed. A courier who had ridden night and day from Washington reached New York at 9 A.M. on June 20, 1812, with the news. At the word, the New York pilot boat (name now unknown) hoisted sail and slipped out of the harbor.

A half-circle of British warships stood on guard outside Sandy Hook. The little pilot boat sailed right through them. Because she flew the blue ensign of her calling, she went unchallenged. She spoke all the American fishing vessels on the Grand Banks. She continued at top speed until she reached Gothenburg, Sweden, where many American merchantmen were congregated. She passed the word, then went from port to port, as far as Archangel in Russia, a transocean Paul Revere delivering the warning.

Two weeks later news of the war filtered through Europe by way of the regular channels. By that time every American skipper had gone home or laid up in a safe neutral port. The whole history of our country might have been different, it seems, but for that pilot boat's successful voyage.

PRIVATEERS

The War of 1812 was fought largely at sea, and largely by privateers, both British and American. Our Navy was in its infancy. Three New York pilot boats were armed and turned into privateers during the war. These were the Teazer, Jack's Favorite, and Black Joke. They were authorized to take, burn, sink, and destroy enemy commerce. They did.

The typical pilot boat of that time was a schooner, seventy-five feet long, of sixty tons, usually without a foretopmast. Her business in peacetime was to cruise outside harbor heads and keep up an intimate relation with ports and coasts, guiding vessels in.

The Teazer, Captain Charles W. Wooster, master, sailed through Hell Gate, stood up Long Island Sound, and sent in many prizes.

An article on "The Evolution of New York" in *Harper's New Monthly Magazine* for June, 1893, says that these American privateers, to the great profit of their owners, mowed a fairly broad swath through the English merchant marine. But public opinion about privateering "had suffered a decided sea-change in the course of the years which had passed since it had been so much in vogue in these parts." This "legalized piracy," which enriched a few free-booting New Yorkers, "did not take the place of the more moderate enrichment of all the merchants of the city by legitimate trade. While the war lasted, New York languished miserably."

The American privateer Mars, a large war vessel of fifteen guns and 100 men, left New York Harbor early in December, 1813, in quest of fortune. Captain Ingersoll took her to Newfoundland, off the coast of Africa, and to Portugal. She captured the brig Britannia coming out from Lisbon. She cruised to the Leeward Islands, destroying enemy vessels. She was chased on February 10, 1814, during a lively voyage to the West Indies, but made many captures.

On March 6 she was off Long Island when HMS Endymion, forty guns, under Captain Henry Hope, hove in sight. He gave chase. A British frigate and the sloop Rattler also appeared. Captain Ingersoll could not escape. He ran his ship ashore near Rockaway.

The captain and some of his crew managed to row ashore, chased by the boats of the British men-o'-war under command of First Lieutenant John Sykes of the frigate Belvidera. The rest of the American crew, seventy in all, were taken off and the ship burned. The captured crew were put on board the Endymion and taken to Bermuda, where they were well treated.

The British blockade of New York Port in the War of 1812 was described in a Long Island *Forum* article of April, 1961, by Frederick P. Schmitt. The United States frigate President tried to escape from New York to sea on January 14, 1815, while the British blockading squadron still lay off Sandy Hook. This was a month after the British–American peace negotiations had concluded, but before the news of peace had reached the United States. The President went aground on Sandy Hook bar. Crippled, she was overtaken by the British and captured after a stiff fight in which Captain Stephen Decatur was twice wounded and three of his officers were killed. The President, sister ship of the Constitution, had been built on the East River.

On February 11, 1815, the news of peace was brought to New York by an American Legation secretary and a British King's messenger, on the British sloop-of-war Favourite. There was great rejoicing.

American vessels were still barred from British ports, however, for many months. In January, 1816, the British brig Martha, bound from New York to Demerara in British Guiana with a cargo of horses and lumber, went ashore on Sandy Hook. The livestock had been brought to New York by sloop and transshipped to the British vessel.

THE CIVIL WAR

Marine losses from 1861 to 1865 were largely confined to southern waters or to the Arctic, where Captain James Waddell on the 790-ton Confederate raider Shenandoah burned practically the entire Yankee whaling fleet of some thirty vessels in June, 1865, three months after the war was over. The news had not yet reached the far north.

A curtain of ships to keep cotton from going out of the Confederacy to England and to prevent arms, ammunition, clothing, salt, medicine, and other supplies from going in, was an absolute necessity to the Northern war effort. "Strangling the South at sea" had much to do with the ultimate outcome.

There was virtually no Navy in 1861, at the outset of the Civil War. The Revenue Cutter Service was assigned the duty of blocking the Southern ports, leaving Northern ports unprotected. Anything that could be made to look like a cutter was pressed into service. In November, 1861, the "Rathole Squadron" of old whaleships loaded with stone was sent to stop up Southern port entrances against the British and Confederate blockade-runners. There were even a few Northern-owned blockade-running vessels.

According to an article in *Harper's New Monthly Magazine* for December, 1870, that blockade of the Southern coast was one of the wonders of the 19th century. A coastline of 3,549 miles, with a low, sandy shore pierced by

189 openings for commerce, was equally open for smuggling, with no end of internal water communication. It presented a terrific challenge. A capture meant that the captors were entitled to half the value of a blockade-running vessel and cargo, so "pride, patriotism and pocket were all appealed to." *Harper's* stated that "in the four years of the blockade, sixteen hundred captures of every description were made."

In 1862 the James Funck, Sandy Hook Pilot Boat No. 22, was sunk in the Narrows by the SS Union, and later raised. On August 12, 1864, the Funck was cruising, looking for incoming ships, when she came upon Pilot Boat No. 24, the William Bell, seventy miles southeast of Sandy Hook. The Bell was unwillingly piloting the Confederate privateer steamer Tallahassee. Both the Bell and the Funck were captured, used for a short time as tenders to converted rebel merchantmen, and as decoys. Then they were destroyed.

On April 25, 1862, the Federal ship Santiago de Cuba captured the Confederate blockade runner Isabel. She was renamed the Ella Warley and sent to New York. On February 9, 1863, the Ella Warley, bound for New Orleans, was sunk just below Sandy Hook in a collision with the North Star.

No one knows what happened to the schooner Sarah S. Bird, which disappeared mysteriously after leaving East Rockaway Inlet at some time during the Civil War. Her captain and crew of seven disappeared; her cargo and destination were unknown. It was thought she might have been trying to run through the Union blockade to the South.

The draft laws of 1863 set off trouble on the New York waterfront. The Conscription Act provided that draftees could avoid service by paying $300 for a substitute. This was understandably regarded as being unfair to the poor. During the riots a mob tried to wreck an ironclad ship, the Dunderberg, under construction in a city shipyard. The following year, several vessels in the Port of New York were set on fire by rebel agents.

As it turned out, New York City was never endangered by rebel ships during the Civil War. But Fort Totten was built in 1863 at Willett's Point overlooking Long Island Sound and Little Neck Bay to protect the approach to the East River from the Sound. Since 1964 it has been the headquarters of the Eastern Region, Army Air Defense Command.

WORLD WAR I

After the sinking of the Lusitania on May 7, 1915, by a German submarine ten miles off the coast of Ireland—with a total loss of 1,198 lives, of which 124 were Americans—whatever pro-German sympathy had existed in New York earlier in the war disappeared.

Great quantities of war supplies for transfer to Allied ships were concentrated on a peninsula called Black Tom, jutting out into the Hudson from

Jersey City just behind the Statue of Liberty. On the night of July 29–30, 1916, two million pounds of explosives were stored there in railroad cars, on piers, and in barges tied alongside docks.

At 2:08 A.M. on July 30 all two million pounds of munitions blew up.

For over three hours, shrapnel and shells burst into the sky like giant fireworks. Damage to windows and other property within a radius of twenty-five miles was estimated at $45 million. Seven lives were lost. Black Tom itself was demolished at a cost of $20 million. Investigations went on for fourteen years, but the suspected sabotage was never established.

War between the United States and Germany was declared at 3:12 A.M. on April 6, 1917. This country's first overt act of war was made by U.S. Coast Guard cutters stationed in New York and troops from Governor's Island. Eighteen minutes after the declaration of war, a battalion of infantry was ordered aboard several cutters to seize all German ships and their crews in New York Harbor. By noon the Coast Guard had taken all eighteen ships then in the Port of New York; five of them had been anchored in the Hudson off 135th Street. The vessels were interned. The enemy crewmen were put on Ellis Island.

New York Harbor during World War I became the busiest port in the world. Over one million troops were shipped overseas from there, as well as astronomical amounts of food, clothing, and munitions; even ninety-ton locomotives were sent to France, complete, so that within a few hours after a vessel's arrival they were on tracks, hauling trains.

A steel net was sunk across the Narrows to keep U-boats from entering the Upper Bay. Soon the German submarines planted mines around Sandy Hook, in the path of outbound ships. Sixteen tugs based at Staten Island were turned into minesweepers. Working in pairs, they swept the ocean every day for 100 miles out from Sandy Hook, finding and exploding a large number of floating mines.

During the two years of United States participation in that war, the Sandy Hook pilots, who alone knew the location of the hidden gate in New York's submarine net, guided through it 22,000 vessels under control of Allied governments, as well as 9,000 sailing under neutral flags. There were few serious mishaps.

The pilot boat Pilot, up from Maryland, entering the harbor bound for New York to take on coal and other supplies, tangled with the submarine net. It this predicament she was rammed and sunk on December 16, 1917, by the steamer Berkshire of the Merchants and Miners Line, inbound from sea. The Pilot went down in sixty feet of water. Her crew was rescued.

Ship casualties occurred up and down the Atlantic coast during World War I, but thanks to the Navy and the Coast Guard, not too many of them were in the vicinity of the Port of New York.

A spokesman for the Third Coast Guard District at the Governor's Island headquarters, New York City, says: "It is a little known fact that the United States Coast Guard suffered greater losses in proportion to its strength than any of the other United States armed forces in World War I."

WORLD WAR II

The worst year for marine casualties off the New York coast in World War II was 1942. Long Island's south shore beaches that summer were crusted with heavy oil from torpedoed vessels. Life preservers and life rafts washed ashore, along with timbers and other grim reminders of war at sea. Tankers were a favorite target for the submarines.

Only about a month after war had been declared, on January 14, 1942, the 6,007-ton tanker Norness, under Panamanian registry, was sunk in deep water between the New Jersey and Long Island shores. . . . The next day the British tanker Coimbra, 6,768 tons, not in convoy, was torpedoed by a German submarine and sunk seventy miles off Sandy Hook. Captain J. P. Barnard and thirty-five others were killed, and six were wounded. . . . On February 26 the American tanker R. P. Resor, owned by the Standard Oil Company of California, was torpedoed thirty-one miles due east of Barnegat, at 11:30 P.M. She was a single-screw ship of 7,451 tons, 435 feet long, built in 1935, on her way from Houston, Texas, to Fall River, Mass., with 78,729 barrels of fuel oil, a crew of fifty men—without escort. The first torpedo set her afire. There were two explosions. Only two men were saved, by the Coast Guard. Captain Fred Marcus went down with his ship. The Resor drifted in flames for two days, sending out billows of black smoke easily visible on shore. Then she turned turtle and went down. She still lies on the bottom, off Barnegat Light.

On March 10, 1942, the Gulftrade, 429-foot, 6,776-ton American fuel-oil carrier, Captain Torger Olsen, master, was torpedoed thirteen miles east-northeast of Barnegat Light. Of her crew of thirty-five, sixteen survived. She broke in two and lies in eighty-two feet of water.

On March 13, 1942, the Chilean freighter Tolten (the former Danish Lotta), 1,858 tons, bound from Baltimore to New York, was torpedoed east of Seaside Park, N.J. Twenty-four of the crew of twenty-seven were lost. . . . The Dutch freighter Arundo, bound from New York to Alexandria, Egypt, lies in 145 feet of water about fifteen miles south of where Ambrose Lightship was stationed at that time. She was torpedoed on April 28, 1942, by the German submarine U-136. Six lives were lost. . . . The American tanker Virginia, 10,731 tons and 501 feet long, was sunk off Baytown, N.J., on her way to Baton Rouge on May 12, 1942. Fourteen of her crew were lost.

Four or five enemy submarines lay in wait off New York at that time.

"Before the general blackout," retired Sandy Hook pilot E. W. Florimont says, "ships, silhouetted against the shore lights, were sitting ducks. The subs had a field day. Ships were sailing unescorted. It was midsummer before an antisubmarine cable was laid from inside Spermaceti Cove, N.J. (near Scotland Lightship) to Ambrose Lightship and ashore at Rockaway. Anything that passed over that charged cable registered at shore stations. Scout planes were alerted. If a challenged vessel did not reply, measures would be taken.

"The summer of 1942 was sweltering hot. I was assigned to the ship laying that antisubmarine cable. I wasn't really needed, but they had to have a pilot with local knowledge along. It took two weeks, working in daylight only, steaming along at two or three knots. Accommodations were meager. I slept on a locker fourteen inches wide, in a cubbyhole."

Asked what was his worst experience during World War II, Captain Florimont said: "I think that was sleeping on one edge for two weeks. But I was shocked when the tanker Norness, that I had brought out at 11 A.M. in January, 1942, was torpedoed four or five hours afterward. I had been aboard her overnight and that forenoon when she was anchored in Gravesend Bay, and got acquainted with her Norwegian crew. They were all lost. That was about the beginning of the submarine war off here."

On September 22, 1942, the British patrol boat HMS Pentland Firth, 500 gross tons, was torpedoed and sunk in seventy feet of water off Rockaway Inlet (six miles off Sandy Hook and three miles from Ambrose Lightship). . . . On December 1, 1942, the Greek freighter Ioannis P. Goulandris was sent to the bottom in the "Mudhole," ten miles off Ambrose. . . . Once, during that war, the Coast Guard cutter Harriet Lane had a gunfight with a submarine within sight of Ambrose Lightship. Captain Florimont called it a "Mexican standoff."

The normal track of incoming and outgoing vessels was changed when the convoy system was established; diversionary, zigzag courses were ordered. But that took time. At first there was considerable confusion between the military authorities and civilian agencies, which made difficulties with pilots, tugboats, port services, and anchorage. So many ships were crowded into New York Harbor that men in offices, charting positions, often forgot size and a vessel would not fit in. At one point in 1943 there were 543 oceangoing merchant ships in the harbor.

GUARDING THE PORT

An antisubmarine net was stretched from Norton's Point, on the west side of Coney Island and two miles below the Narrows, to where a guard boat and a net boat lay, at the gate maintained by the Navy. From the guard boat the net stretched, under water of course, to Hoffman Island, on the west side of the channel; on the other side of that island the water was too shallow for anything more than a pleasure boat to go through. Friendly vessels could enter or leave through the gate, between sunrise and sunset. At an alarm, the gate would be closed.

A pilot would bring orders as he boarded a ship. Each ship was assigned a code number to answer a challenge from the shore stations at Sandy Hook and at Fort Wadsworth, Staten Island, adjacent to Quarantine.

Captain Florimont says: "We had to be very careful not only to avoid confusion of signals but to watch tide conditions, running a convoy. Once we were bringing in on a flood tide a convoy of deeply laden tankers coming from south, to take on at New York a deckload of airplanes for Europe. Some smart aleck thought it a good time to have a drill at the net boat. But for an alert signalman on the Commodore ship, we would have had a terrible disaster. He passed the word astern. We were able to round-to, and avoid crashing the net and collisions.

"The crew of every merchant ship included some Navy or Coast Guard. The Navy had two forces: the signal crew around the bridge, and the gun crew on the fantail aft."

Many munitions ships were being sent up the East River to the relatively protected waters of Long Island Sound, rather than through the Lower Bay where submarines might be lurking. During that war there were twenty Hell Gate pilots—where today there is only one. All pilots were commissioned in the U.S. Coast Guard, rated from lieutenant to commander, according to license. Nearly 15,000 vessels were taken through the East River between Pearl Harbor and V-J Day; on the busiest day, Captain James H. Thombs, the last Hell Gate pilot, recalls that fifty-eight went through.

The inside waterways—Hell Gate and the Cape Cod Canal, then up the shoreline to Halifax—were the route for slow convoys bound for eastern ports or Europe. Fast ones went by Sandy Hook. Convoys went through Hell Gate on slack water. Currents there are dangerous for the slow ship. And there is very little slack water.

Captain George H. Seeth was president of the New York Pilots' Association when America entered World War II. Captain Seeth tells a story that involves the East River, City Island, and spies. ("Bud" Delano, he says, was president of the American Pilots' Association at that time, and Hilton Lowe was president of the New Jersey Association.)

One day the boatman who took pilots to and from ships at City Island telephoned Captain Seeth and said he had noticed a tall blond man spending many hours on the City Island beach, watching ships with a powerful pair of binoculars. The man usually wore bathing trunks and did not appear to be taking notes. He was picked up for questioning, and released with apologies. He seemed harmless. But one detail did not pass unnoticed. His driving license bore a different address than his home. His suspicions were not aroused, but all mail to both addresses was carefully examined. The license address proved to be a "drop." All the mail was tested for secret writing.

Captain Seeth heard no more about it until the war was over. Then he met his liaison in Naval Intelligence for luncheon in downtown New York. The Navy man said that the apparently harmless discrepancy of addresses had resulted in locating spies all the way to California, and radio stations on both coasts.

THE NORMANDIE

Both fire and water killed the Normandie, "dream ship," pride of the French Line, as she lay at her berth along Pier 88 in the Hudson River on February 9 and 10, 1942. The disaster was not war-caused but a result of "monumental carelessness."

The fire started with a spark from a welder's torch. Only one man was killed. But the ship's loss was a serious blow to the Allied war effort. It was said afterward: "Fires are, in effect, battles; and battles call for commanders. None was available here."

The United States government had taken possession in December, 1941, of the crack French liner (1,029 feet long, of 120-foot beam, 83,500 tons, with turbo-electric engines and capable of making a speed of over 30 knots; the world's largest and most beautiful ship when she was launched in 1935).

A rush job of converting her to a 15,000-passenger troopship was under way and she had been renamed the USS Lafayette. She was to have sailed in five days, when fire was discovered on the afternoon of February 9.

The late Commodore John S. Baylis, USCG Retired, was captain of the Port during the pre-war era. Captain Joseph Mazzotta, USCG Retired, was then a junior lieutenant on Commodore Baylis' staff. Captain Mazzotta was, in 1967, captain of the Port when he and Commodore Baylis were interviewed about the Normandie, New York's most spectacular ship disaster, then just twenty-five years past.

Commodore Baylis recollected that he was called to the fire shortly before 3 P.M. on February 9, a cold, windy day. "When I got to the pier," he said, "I couldn't find out who was in charge. I learned later that the first call to the New York City Fire Department wasn't put through until 2:49 P.M., or fourteen minutes after the fire aboard was first discovered."

Over 3,000 men were on the Normandie that day, including 500 who were to form the crew. They were unfamiliar with the ship's layout and had been assigned no duties in case of emergency. The guard was haphazard. A

French liner NORMANDIE *burning at Pier 88, New York City, 1942*

U.S. Coast Guard fire patrol of four petty officers and thirty-six enlisted men had been assigned to the ship, with nine on duty at a time. Civilian workers got no fire instructions.

The Normandie had a fine fire alarm system, an audible smoke-detector system, and firefighting apparatus with 504 hydrant outlets. But the French type of couplings did not fit the standard American type used by the New York Fire Department. A firm of fire engineers was in the process of changing over the hydrant and hose connections to American types. The work was not yet completed.

On February 9 at 2:30 P.M., 110 burners and welders were operating in the main saloon. Eleven hundred and forty bales of kapok life preservers had been stored there a week earlier. Men laying linoleum on that day had moved the bales from the center of the saloon to the port side, and piled them around the forward and after stanchions. It was there that the blaze started.

There was great confusion and lack of coordination in the early stages of the fire. No one seemed prepared to take full command. At 6:30 P.M. the fire seemed under control, but the vessel was listing ten degrees to port. The first three city fireboats at the scene had poured 3,500 tons of water into the burning liner. No water-ejector pumps were available. Finally, four of the

214

ship's double-bottom tanks were cut open from outside, but not enough to prevent the ship's keeling over at 2:45 A.M. on February 10. She sank into the mud.

For more than a year it was hoped that the Normandie might be saved. She became a diving school for Navy men who later were experts employed around the world during the war years. The Merritt-Chapman & Scott Corporation, under Commander W. A. Sullivan, U.S. Navy salvage chief, finally refloated the rusty hull—what was left of the Normandie—on September 15, 1943. On October 25, 1943, she was delivered to the Brooklyn Navy Yard. A naval commission decided that her restoration would not be justified by the cost. The $60 million vessel was sold on October 2, 1946, for junk—for $161,680.

COLLISIONS

Inevitably, there were collisions in and around the crowded wartime port. The Byron D. Benson, a tanker, collided with the freighter Continent off Scotland Lightship on January 10, 1942. The freighter sank, with one man lost. . . . The U.S. cargo ship Nathaniel Bacon and the M/V Esso Belgium were both damaged in a collision in New York Harbor on November 24, 1942. . . . The steam tanker John Worthington damaged the U.S. Naval minesweeper YMS #12, on December 16, 1942. The latter was one of three such vessels engaged in clearing the channel approaches to New York Harbor.

On February 15, 1943, the 506-foot freighter Lanarkshire, Captain Charles E. O'Byrne, master, collided in the Main Ship Channel, Upper Bay, with the 384-foot U.S. destroyer Hobby, Lieutenant Commander Ernest Blake, master. It was 1:10 A.M. Visibility was good. Both men were experienced, but they were navigating New York Harbor without a pilot and were unfamiliar with these waters.

The Cunard liner Mauretania, in service throughout World War II carrying troops to Australia, the Middle East, North Africa, Europe, and the Pacific, collided with the SS Hat Creek, a U.S. War Shipping Administration tanker, outside Ambrose Lightship on January 8, 1944. The Mauretania's starboard bow was damaged, but a fine rush job was done and she sailed in twelve hours.

A five-vessel collision occurred in a dense fog on September 20, 1944, when the inbound South American ship Choapa, fifth in a convoy of seven ships, collided with the tanker British Harmony, which was loaded and outbound in a convoy of three. The Choapa, not badly damaged, anchored. This happened in the wartime-swept channel approach to New York Harbor. The next day the tanker Voco hit the Choapa; then the 483-foot steam tanker

Empire Garrick, inbound, hit the already twice-damaged Choapa, sideswiping her stem. The Choapa sank stern first. Then the Garrick collided with the John P. Poe, a 441-foot liberty ship in a convoy about to leave.

On February 4, 1945, the M/V tanker Orville Harden of the Panama Transport Co., which had served throughout the war carrying fuel to both the European and Pacific combat areas, was sunk near Ambrose Channel in a collision with the outward-bound Netherlands flag tanker M/V Ena. The Harden, bound from Beaumont, Texas, to New York with a load of fuel oil, carried a Danish crew of forty-five and a U.S. Navy armed guard of twelve. One man was killed. The ship settled by the stern in ten minutes but was refloated two days later and her cargo saved.

The tanker Springhill, carrying 110,000 barrels of high-test aviation gasoline, burned in Lower New York Bay just off Bushwick Basin on February 5, 1945, following a collision that eventually involved two other tankers, a New York City fireboat, and a Coast Guard vessel.

The SS Clio had left Constable Hook, Bayonne, N.J., under ballast, for Venezuela. The anchorage was crowded. She turned right and headed southeast between two lines of anchored ships, making for an opening of about 1,000 feet in the outside line of vessels. She struck the forward side of the Springhill at 8:56 A.M. The Springhill's plating was broken. The high-octane gas ignited instantly. Fire enveloped the ship. "Hell and havoc broke loose," the newspapers said the next day. Wind drove the flames aft. Aircraft ammunition exploded. The flames were carried to the Vivi, a Norwegian tanker anchored astern of the Springhill.

Five men were trapped under the Springhill's gun mount. The fireboat William L. Strong, berthed at Bushwick Basin, nosed to the Springhill's stern, raised a twenty-foot ladder, and saved the five men. While this rescue was in progress, a Coast Guard vessel rammed the Strong. The Strong's crew sustained burns but they lived, and the fire was put out. The crew of the Strong were afterward cited for bravery.

The death toll from the Springhill was put at seventeen, with 122 injured. The cause of the disaster was ruled accidental.

FIREBOATS IN WARTIME

Few realized at the time what the Marine Division of the New York Fire Department was up against during the years of World War II. Immediately after the war started, fireboats were painted Navy gray. They patrolled their districts twenty-four hours a day. When the Coast Guard and Navy established a patrol along the waterfront, the fireboats were relieved of perpetual duty; however, they attended the arrival and departure of big transports, among many other activities.

New York had again become the largest port of embarkation in the world. Half of our armies sailed from here, and one-third of their supplies. It was the Army's rear echelon, the real base in America for European and Mediterranean operations. Its facilities were scattered over fifty-four miles of waterfront.

Between Pearl Harbor and V-E Day, the port moved over three million troops and their equipment—more than double the number of men shipped during World War I. It could handle 100,000 troops a day and sixty-three million tons of supplies. The North River Terminal at Twelfth Avenue and 46th Street, Manhattan, was the principal embarkation point.

The Brooklyn Army Base at First Avenue and 58th Street became the largest warehouse in the world. Supplies went out of Bush Terminal, Brooklyn. High explosives and ammunition were stored and loaded at Caven Point Terminal, Jersey City, the U.S. Army supply base. Howland Hook Terminal in Staten Island stored petroleum products refined across the river in Bayonne and Elizabeth, N.J.

Shipments of high explosives, bombs, ammunition, and jellied or liquid gasoline were loaded and cleared with prayers; 100 percent success was not always reached. Every fireboat had a set of plans for each ship in the district, with the location of the magazine where ammunition was carried. It was the Fire Department's job to make certain that fire was kept away from the magazines.

Sometimes a ship would arrive in sight of port with its hold on fire. No call for help could be given over the air in wartime. No radio could be used. Only a dispatch upon entering the harbor, and a telephone call after the fireboat had returned to its berth.

Early in the war, a catastrophe that could have been far worse than the Black Tom disaster of 1916 was averted by the combined efforts of the Coast Guard and two fireboats. The crews of the latter were decorated for a deed performed in the face of seemingly unavoidable death. That was the El Estero disaster.

EL ESTERO

A Panamanian vessel under charter by the U.S. Maritime Commission, El Estero, was loading ammunition for the war zone on April 24, 1943, at Caven Point Terminal, Jersey City, when a fire started in engine-room bilge. The flames chased the crew up on deck, licked hungrily at the bulkhead of the cargo hold, and went up through the engine-room and fire-room hatches.

Gasoline drums on deck were already afire when the crew swarmed ashore. El Estero had 1,400 tons of ammunition and bombs already on board. More lay on the pier.

Radio warnings were broadcast through the New York–New Jersey area in expectation of a holocaust. Meanwhile, at 5:30 P.M. the Jersey City Fire Department had notified New York. They asked for two fireboats. The Firefighter and John J. Harvey were dispatched to the scene. The ship had to be removed immediately from the waterfront. She might explode at any moment. Other ships at the pier, loaded with the same cargo, might have been set off, as well as the great oil tanks at Bayonne and Staten Island, severely rupturing the throat of New York Harbor.

El Estero was towed to Robbins Reef Light by two tugs. Even as they left the pier, tons of water from the fireboats' heavy nozzles swept the burning and exploding gasoline drums from the deck and rushing down the hatches of the giant burning bomb. The fire was finally extinguished by flooding the vessel and sinking it. It was submerged to the superstructure, about a half-mile east of Robins Reef Light. As the ship settled, explosions were heard from below.

Twenty-six members of the New York Fire Department were decorated for their work that night. Extraordinary bravery was shown by the men who went aboard El Estero when she was expected to "blow" at any minute.

THE USS TURNER

At dawn on January 3, 1944, the 348-foot, 1,700-ton destroyer USS Turner, one year old, just back from a convoy run to Casablanca, exploded as she lay at anchor north of Ambrose Channel Fairway buoy, "The Whistler," almost midway between the tip of Sandy Hook, N.J., and the Coast Artillery base at Rockaway, Long Island. Ammunition was being brought up from the magazines, preparatory to unloading that day.

To Coxswain Fred Williams, standing anchor watch aboard a Coast Guard 83-foot sub-chaser at the pier of the Sandy Hook Coast Guard station, she appeared to jump clear out of the water. A great ball of brilliant red fire hovered over the ship's midsection. A second or so later the sound of a terrific explosion rolled across the bay.

Williams' hand reached the General Quarters alarm. The crew came tumbling topside. Williams told the skipper what he had seen. The sub-chaser roared off toward the Turner.

Flames following the explosion were also seen from lookout towers at the Sandy Hook and Rockaway Coast Guard stations. Lieutenant Commander George F. Morin, USCG, skipper at Sandy Hook, immediately organized a disaster mobilization plan. All available floating equipment was ordered to get ready to go to the scene. Boat crews had warmed up their engines when the word to cast off was flashed. Sandy Hook's barracks and sick bay were made ready to receive victims and survivors.

One of the first rescue craft at the explosion was the 77-foot Coast Guard Reserve vessel Wanderer, attached to the Sandy Hook Pilot Command, ferrying pilots to their stations. The Wanderer threaded her way through debris surrounding the Turner, rescuing thirty-nine men from the water. Coast Guard boats circled the stricken ship, removing the wounded, dying, and dead. Throughout the rescue work, twenty- and forty-millimeter shells were exploding.

Rockaway Coast Guard station had dispatched all available craft to the destroyer. Units of the Coast Guard and the Captain of the Port Harbor Patrol Fleet were also speeded to the scene to act as a protective screen, warning commercial shipping to stand clear of the doomed destroyer and the rescue vessels.

The survivors were taken to Sandy Hook for medical attention. Blood plasma for the wounded was desperately needed. A Coast Guard helicopter from the Air Station at Floyd Bennett Field, Brooklyn, was dispatched to the Barge Office at South Ferry, Manhattan, to pick it up. Commander F. A. Erickson, USCG, commanding officer of the air station, delivered two cases of plasma in fourteen minutes, saving several lives. That was the first actual rescue mission the Coast Guard helicopter had ever made as part of the service's air arm.

Meanwhile, out in Ambrose Channel, fire raked the Turner's main deck. No officers could be seen. The enlisted men seemed unaware of the gravity of the situation, as if waiting for an officer to give orders.

Ensign Peter Chase of the C.G. 83-footer, whose coxswain had first seen the explosion, took over. He looked toward what was left of the Turner's bridge. It was a mass of burnt, twisted steel. He realized that the ship would plunge to the bottom in minutes—perhaps seconds. Chase gave the order for all hands on the Turner to abandon ship. The remaining crewmen on board went over the side, to be picked up by the flotilla of rescue boats. Forty-six men scrambled aboard the 83-footer, skippered by Chase, which was still tied to the blazing destroyer.

Two machinists' mates from the 83-footer boarded the Turner searching for injured men, but were forced to come away empty-handed. No one could be seen on the after end of the sinking ship. The lines were cast off. The sub-chaser backed clear. Minutes later, with another terrific explosion that sent debris flying all around the rescue ships, the destroyer settled deeper into the water. With a sudden hissing sound, she sank beneath the surface of the sea and there she lay, in forty-five feet of water, until July 4 of that year, when the submerged wreckage was blown up as a menace to navigation in New York Harbor.

One hundred and thirty-eight men—fifteen officers, including the ship's

Outward bound, Port of New York

commander, Lieutenant Commander H. F. Wygant, USN, and 123 enlisted men—lost their lives in that disaster.

The cause of the tragic explosion was never proved. It was set down as "of undetermined origin."

18

THE LAST
HELL GATE
PILOT

Captain James H. Thombs had been guiding ships through the dangerous "Gate" for over eighteen years. On a calm June day in 1968 he strolled from his City Island home to call on a retired Hell Gate pilot, Captain Albert Larsen. Captain Thombs is a tall, erect, deeply tanned, blond, powerful-looking man with sea-blue eyes and the confident air of a man who knows his job.

He said: "I am the last Hell Gate pilot. Once there were forty. In 1925 there were fourteen. When I went on in October, 1949, there were five.

"In November, 1967, the New York–Sandy Hook Pilots' Association was ordered to absorb the Hell Gate pilots. Since then I have rotated with a New York–Sandy Hook man until I retire, which is a good while yet. I will take every other ship that passes through. If I need help, the Pilots' Association can always send up one of their eleven men who are licensed for Hell Gate."

Captain Larsen was sunning himself on a bench outside his City Island boatyard overlooking the upper East River. He is a wiry, lively man with a great fund of reminiscences and salty stories. "I went to sea in 1918 in the merchant marine," he said. "I was a Hell Gate pilot from 1938 to 1958 and have been retired for ten years now."

He looked across the water. A tug with five barges was going by Stepping Stones Light station, a red Victorian building on a rock halfway between City Island and Elm Point on Great Neck, Long Island.

"The law says now not to exceed five," Captain Larsen remarked. "But I've seen as many as thirteen in the Gate. The little one at the end is the steering boat. Today most of the traffic consists of tugs and tows."

Records in a New York Admiralty law office show that tugs have been known to pull as many as twenty tows. On that June day, it seemed just as well not to tell the Hell Gate pilots that two eastern Long Island men, good sailors, had brought sixteen old Navy whaleboats through the Gate in one tow, from Newtown Creek, a few years before. They had bought the boats at an auction and wanted to take them home. They hired a sixty-year-old tug to take them through Hell Gate, the whaleboats strung two abreast. They made it without interruption, shortly after midnight.

Even the tugs and tows have diminished, Captain Thombs said. "For one thing, there's a building slump on. Few sand tows are going down through here, and fewer cargoes of crushed traprock are going up. Also, we are affected by the drop in shipping at the Port of Boston. They've been having stevedore trouble up there for five years. In the past couple of years, fifteen steamship companies have stopped going to Boston. They avoid it like the plague."

This comment was made before the long, disastrous tie-ups at all ports, including New York, in 1968–1969 and 1971.

Hell Gate is the back door to the Port of New York, its entrance from Long Island Sound. In the 19th century the Sound route had fully as much traffic as the ocean entrance to New York Harbor through Ambrose Channel. It was a shortcut to New England, and it took thirty-eight miles, or two hours' running time, off the route to England. It also eliminated the necessity for deep-draft ships to wait for the tide as they had to do then, in the shifting, shallow channel off Sandy Hook.

But Hell Gate has been described as "the most dangerous waterway that leads to any great seaport." There are fierce tides, cross currents, jagged rocks, whirlpools, and a narrow, twisting channel. The Triborough Bridge goes directly over it.

Captain Thombs said: "If you throw a block of wood into the water off Hallett's Point [opposite Gracie Mansion at 86th Street] it will remain quiet for just four minutes. That's all the slack water there is."

In the days when the East River was full of Sound steamboats, ferries, ocean freighters, coal schooners, and fishing smacks, flying every flag on earth, accidents were continual. In sailing-ship days vessels were forever ripping out their wooden bottoms on sunken reefs, or ramming into each other.

An item in the *Suffolk Democrat* for July 20, 1849, gives an idea of the volume of Long Island Sound and East River traffic in those days: "From a record kept by Benjamin Downing, keeper of the lighthouse on Eaton's

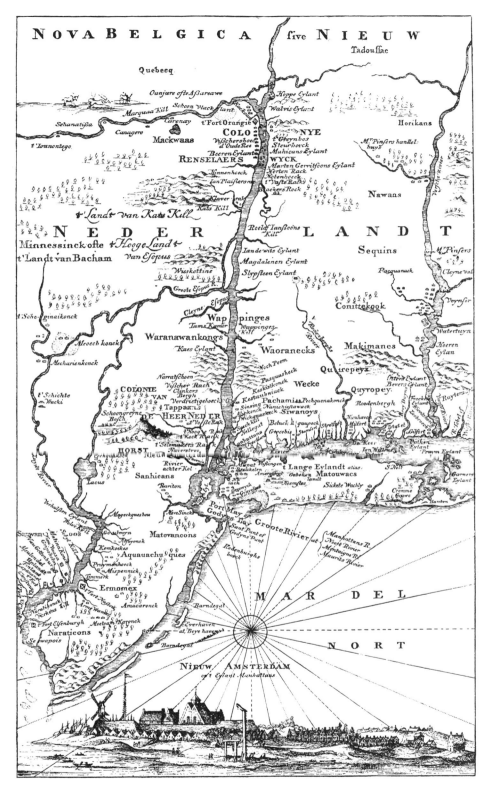

A Dutch map of 1656, by Adriaen Van der Donck

Neck [off Huntington, Long Island] it appears the following number of vessels passed Eaton's Neck by daylight during the week ending the 15th inst., viz: 3 ships, 25 brigs, 134 schooners, 262 sloops, 5 propellers, 56 steamboats: total 485."

In the early part of the 20th century there was still plenty of sail. During the Prohibition Era—from January, 1920, to December, 1933—rum-runners from Nassau in the Bahamas and from Nova Scotia used sail. Supply craft for the rum-running vessels and the American bootleggers caused an extra complication in the East River, running without lights after dark and pursued by the Coast Guard.

CITY ISLAND

City Island, part of the Bronx, has always been headquarters for the Hell Gate pilots. Fifty years ago City Island was a picturesque, mile-long, tree-shaded village where New Yorkers would go for a shore dinner of lobsters and clams at twenty-five cents and up. Recently it had a permanent population of only 5,709; some families have lived there for two or three generations. Like everywhere else in the urban periphery, it seems overcrowded now to the old-timers. There are piers on the river, and shipyards, and swarms of small pleasure boats. "Hardest Place to Get to in New York," an article in the New York *World* of May 25, 1913, called it. The trip then involved five changes—subway, train, elevated, monorail, and horse car— and the visitor finished up by walking. It still takes over an hour from midtown Manhattan.

City Island is where Long Island Sound and the East River converge, off Orchard Beach and Pelham Bay Park. To the south is Throg's Neck Bridge, where the East River joins the Sound through a narrow passage between Throg's Neck in the Bronx and Willett's Point in Queens, Long Island. The bridge is almost over Fort Schuyler, which once guarded the approaches to the East River and Manhattan. A steel tower and automatic red navigation beacon has replaced the Throg's Neck lighthouse. Still further south is the Bronx–Whitestone Bridge. Ships coming in from the Sound, going down river, pass many small islands—among them Riker's Island, occupied by city prisons; North and South Brother islands; Randall's and Ward's islands—before entering Hell Gate. The Triborough Bridge goes over Hell Gate from Astoria in Queens, across to Ward's Island, Randall's Island, then straight on to the Bronx, or, making a left turn, into Manhattan.

EXECUTION TO THE BATTERY

The Hell Gate pilot's route is from Execution Rocks, then ten miles to Hell Gate, and nineteen miles more to the Battery. "I never go below

Verrazzano Bridge, nor east of Execution Light," Captain Thombs said.

"Coastwise vessels are not obliged to use a pilot in Long Island Sound. But it's a good idea, to take on a Federal coastwise pilot who knows the rocks and wrecks. There are thirty-five Sound pilots now," he said.

"A vessel coming from South, if desired, has a Federal coast pilot as far as Ambrose Light Station, then a New York–Sandy Hook pilot brings it to Stapleton, Staten Island. If it is going further east, I take over from there. I also go from Staten Island to Yonkers, then a Hudson River pilot takes over for as far as Albany. Yonkers is my farthest run.

"All Navy ships proceeding through Hell Gate are required to take pilots.

"One time," Captain Thombs continued, "the captain of the Cape Drepanon, an old Liberty ship then under Greek ownership, undertook to cross the Sound steering by an Esso road map, rather than pay a Coast pilot's fee. I was waiting for him at City Island. He had left New Haven seven or eight hours earlier. It turned out the ship was piled up on Execution Rocks, the bottom ripped out of her, a total loss."

Asked about some tough spots he had been in, Captain Thombs said: "There was one about twelve years ago that took years off my life. I was taking the Ocean Alice, a Liberty ship, from the Communipaw, N.J., scrap dock to Bridgeport. Missed my tide. Had to fight it. Spent three hours and ten minutes trying to round Hallett's Point. Put the starboard anchor down three times and the port one twice. But made it. Very fortunate."

He went on: "On December 18, 1956, I was bringing the African Star of the Farrell Line from City Island to Staten Island. Every pilot and executive officer knows that between the Battery and Governor's Island on the Brooklyn shore are red and green range lights. Going down the East River you must range two over the stern, otherwise you will surely ground on Diamond Reef, between the Battery and Governor's Island.

"Well, I got the African Star past the Battery when the Alcoa Pilgrim hit me in the engine room. I sank. The Alcoa Pilgrim was in a hurry, going from the Army base in Brooklyn to Pier 9, Hoboken.

"There were no casualties. The general alarm was sounded in time or we'd all have drowned. The Pilgrim was damaged and the pilot on the up-bound ship—he is now retired—was suspended. We had a quarter of a million damage."

Captain Thombs feels that most accidents are man made due to mistaken signals, being in too great a hurry, not watching the tides, or not observing the rules of the road. "Sometimes it's not the fault of a pilot or a captain when a ship gets into trouble, but in the office of a dispatcher who doesn't understand and insists on sending a ship at a certain time, like a railroad schedule. I make my own time. Otherwise, it's too dangerous. When I'm assigned I look in my book and see just what I'm going to face in my passage through Hell Gate.

"One big trouble," he said, "is the lack of knowledge on the part of towboat captains as to positions that deep-draft vessels must maintain. It is the fly-by-night, underpowered, underequipped towboats who do not fully understand the range lights. (For instance, at the United Nations we must cut directly across the river toward Brooklyn to follow the deep-water channel.)

"This could be cleared up if the Coast Guard would compel towboat men to memorize the courses of all ranges, and why ranges are placed there. And a walkie-talkie should be compulsory for every commercial vessel that moves. That goes over Channel 13. All foreign ships now have them. This is a great added safety feature. I have used one for four years. It's a little thing, 8 by 3 by 1½ inches, with a range of thirty-five miles. Costs $770 and worth $700,000 to avoid accidents."

Pleasure boats in summertime, the captain says, are almost as great a menace as the Hell Gate tides.

The last Hell Gate pilot navigated the East River about twice a day, averaging sixty big cargo ships a month, mostly foreign, many of them over 700 feet long. But by 1972 that figure had dropped appreciably. He now works on a contract basis.

View of Brooklyn from United States Hotel, Fulton and Front streets, New York City

19

SHIP NEWS

THEY Don't Meet the Ships Anymore." That was
the headline on a story by Walter Hamshar, the last ship news editor on the
late New York *Herald Tribune*. Mr. Hamshar, now executive editor of the
Port Authority of New York and New Jersey, wrote the story in 1966 during
the long, disastrous New York newspaper strike. It appeared in the *Royle
Forum*, a New Jersey quarterly.

Ship news, of such importance to the public of a century and more
ago, is relegated today to a brief story or two in the back pages of *The New
York Times,* unless some great disaster occurs; and to the *Journal of Commerce*, which deals with the commercial aspect of shipping. The only ship
news editor left in the New York area—and his title is not Ship Editor but
Transport Editor—is George Panitz of the *Journal of Commerce*. He says:
"We don't go out much—unless it's a maiden arrival. There's no need."

Ship reporting began, in New York as in London, in the coffeehouses.
Bulletins were tacked on the walls. The Tontine Coffee House in New York
kept a registry of maritime and mercantile activity, as did Lloyd's of London. The Tontine burned down in 1804.

Lloyd's, a London coffeehouse founded in 1689 by one Edward Lloyd,
became a meeting place for businessmen engaged in marine ventures. Some
of them were willing to take out insurance against sea risks. Lloyd's gradually became a center for such insurance. Since 1734 Lloyd's has published
continuously Lloyd's List, devoted to shipping news from all over the world.
Lloyd's also publishes a Loss Book, commonly called the "Black Book,"
which reports sea casualties.

Perils of the Port of New York

Beginning in 1725, William Bradford in his two-page *Gazette*, first New York newspaper, gave lists of ships entered and cleared. So did the New York *Commercial Advertiser* later in the 18th century, along with very stale foreign news often taken from overseas newspapers brought in by ship captains. There was little local news. The ships brought news and made news. By 1820 the New York *Courier* and New York *Journal of Commerce* sent out small boats to collect news from incoming transatlantic packets off Sandy Hook.

These ships were often delayed by head winds or calms. The crossing took weeks, sometimes even months. Besides that, in the early days a ship would wait for a full passenger list and cargo before sailing. Regular schedules were an American invention. The Black Ball Line, with four packets, pioneered this in 1817.

In sailing-ship days the newspaper headline "Lost at Sea" or "Missing" —with its terrible uncertainty—would strike terror to families in and around New York City. Shipping intelligence was read avidly, not only for business reasons.

Headlines of those days, though, were more apt to read "Ship Ashore at . . ." or "Burned at Her Pier" rather than "Lost at Sea" or "Missing." As every mariner knows, a good stout ship is far safer in the open ocean than within sight of or surrounded by, land—or even tied up at a pier. Stranding, collision, and fire have been, and still are, major causes of marine catastrophes.

News, good or bad, was so slow in coming. It is now hard to realize how long a family left at home might be without word from husband, father, son, or sweetheart after he said goodbye at the wharves of South Street in Manhattan, or at Cold Spring Harbor, Greenport, or Sag Harbor on Long Island. Letters, sent when the whaleship or merchantman bound around Cape Horn for China, the South Seas, or Bering Straits, could be sent only when the ship "spoke" a homeward-bound vessel. These were so rare that families of the mariners cherish them to this day.

Such a voyage might keep a man away from home anywhere from two to four years. An oft-told incident supposed to have taken place at a Long Island Sound port concerns a weeping wife whose handkerchief had waved goodbye to her whaler husband until his ship was out of sight. "He didn't kiss me!" she sobbed. A ship owner on the wharf said: "What are you crying about? He's only going to be gone a year or two!" (That would probably have been a voyage to the South Atlantic whaling grounds, not around the Horn.)

As early as 1827 a New York editor recognized the importance to the city and to the country of news collecting. Robert Greenhalgh Albion in his *Square Riggers on Schedule*, published in 1938, quoted: "Nothing is more

important in mercantile business than system and certainty of transmission.
. . . While from this cause the amount of business brought to the hands of
our merchants is doubtless very great, it is also more completely establishing
our city as the center of commercial and political intelligence for the west, as
London is for the east." In 1830 the same editor said: "We take it for
granted that there is no place in the country where the business of collecting
ship-news is carried on with so much energy and industry as in the port of
New York." He doubted if any place in the world could rival it in this
respect.

Harper's New Monthly Magazine for July, 1868, said: "The collection
of shipping intelligence may be said to have been the beginning of news collecting in this country—the origin, in fact, for the present system of American journalism. It has only been within the last forty years that we first
began to collect news for the purposes of sale, and ship news was the first
that was supposed to have marketable value. . . . The papers that existed
before that time used to publish whatever came to hand, and made no effort
to collect news . . . they discoursed very learnedly and elaborately about
parties and politics . . . but as far as news was concerned the papers con-
tained only brief statements of what the editors happened to hear."

There was frantic competition for the freshest of foreign news from the
1820's onward. The *Journal of Commerce* in 1828 had a $3,000 clipper
schooner built expressly to scoop its rivals on marine news. Other papers
followed, sending newsboats as far out to sea as 80 or 100 miles to meet incoming vessels. When James Gordon Bennett founded the New York
Herald in 1835 he kept a yacht, the Owlet, berthed at South Ferry with a
crew of seamen and reporters always on duty.

Walter Hamshar's story, "They Don't Meet the Ships Anymore," told
how Bennett engineered in 1846 what he considered a remarkable scoop,
and credits Robert Greenhalgh Albion's *Square Riggers on Schedule* for the
details.

Bennett's competitors had sent a pilot boat all the way to England to
gather the latest news of Parliamentary discussions on Corn Law repeal. So
Bennett dispatched a newsboat to meet the Black Ball packet Yorkshire, then
fastest of her type, near Montauk Point—97 miles from Sandy Hook. She
had left Liverpool on May 5. On May 31 at 3 P.M. a *Herald* news force
boarded her. One of Bennett's reporters, after receiving the latest English
newspapers, landed at East Hampton at 4 P.M.

From there on, to an eastern Long Islander, the story goes a little
haywire—although Mr. Hamshar, who is well acquainted with that area and
is certainly well acquainted with ships, is positive that the *Herald* reporter
could have arrived in New York ahead of the Yorkshire by what seems a
very roundabout route.

Perils of the Port of New York

The East Hampton landing would have been made through the open surf—not easy. If he was lucky enough not to capsize there, he must have been driven seven sandy miles to Sag Harbor. Then three more miles to the Shelter Island ferry at North Haven. That ferry in 1846 might have been a rowboat, with sail. If so, he would have had to engage another rig to take him across Shelter Island to the Greenport ferry, which was probably much the same as the Sag Harbor one. That would land him close to the Long Island Rail Road terminal, as the larger ferry does today.

The Albion story goes: "After fording three streams and leaping several ditches, he secured a horse and wagon and drove across the island to Greenpoint [sic] where, at 9:45, he obtained a Long Island Railroad locomotive. The first thirty miles were covered in thirty-two minutes and the news was at Brooklyn Ferry at 12:30 A.M. By 1 A.M. it was in the hands of Bennett, who called it the 'quickest and most remarkable express ever run.' "

Ordinarily it would have taken the little wood-burning engine of 1846 four or five hours to pull its train from Greenport to the Brooklyn ferry for New York. The special locomotive bearing the "scoop" made it in less than three hours, which is about the same speed as today. Greenport, on Long Island's north fork, was the nearest railroad station to East Hampton in 1846. The Long Island had established rail service that far only in 1844. It was not until 1895, fifty-one years later, that it came through East Hampton and all the way to Montauk, on the south shore.

That 1846 news beat was one of the last to be delivered by packet from abroad.

A few years after that, steamships were delivering European papers to Boston, where their most sensational contents were quickly extracted and promptly relayed by Samuel Morse's new telegraph to New York. In 1866 the laying of the Atlantic Cable eliminated newsboats as transmitters of important foreign events.

Shipping intelligence gathered from the Morse operator in the office of the Atlantic & Pacific Telegraph Company at Sandy Hook, N.J., and from reports by arriving shipmasters about other ships met at sea, was of the utmost importance to New York ship owners, to businessmen, to families of mariners.

In the 1860's and 1870's an operator would sit for a twelve-hour shift overlooking the entrance to New York Harbor, his right hand at a Morse key and his left hand on a pair of binoculars. He could tell the nationality of a vessel by the shape of its hull or its rigging, in daylight, and could often identify it by name without using the reference books and records close at hand. The ship news office was warmed by an enormous stove in the center of the room. In winter gales, however, a pail of water on the floor, a few feet from the stove, would freeze solidly, and the ten-by-twelve office would

230

tremble on its foundations. At such times there might be shipping news of more drama than the ordinary arrivals and departures. The operator, uncomfortable as he was, felt himself far better off than the pilots aboard their schooners offshore, or the watch on the deck of a vessel clawing off a lee shore, perhaps off Sandy Hook itself.

Walter Hamshar, who was on ship news from 1935 to 1966, says: "The gathering of news from the ships could be divided into three periods: In the first period it was the news brought from overseas by the ship itself which was most important. Later, the celebrities sailing aboard the liners were the news—their opinions, their experiences abroad and their reasons for making the journey. And now, ship news consists of stories about the ships and the problems of shipping such as labor, legislation and economics. There is no longer a reason to go down the bay to meet all the ships to cover this type of news."

Frank Braynard, author, artist, and nautical historian, spent four youthful years on ship news for the New York *Herald Tribune*. He says: "Ship reporters had a good thing, and most of them had the grace to know it. Their papers joined in maintaining a butt-littered room at the old Barge Office at the Battery, near where the Aquarium used to be. Later it moved to 45 Broadway. There was always a poker game going, until the Western Union ticker reported the passage of a ship past Ambrose Lightship."

Until well after World War II, reporters, photographers, and newsreel men would ride down the bay to the Narrows on a Coast Guard cutter with the Customs, Immigration, and Health officers to meet an incoming transatlantic liner off Quarantine.

The ship newsmen were "gentlemen of the press," referred to as journalists, not mere reporters. They were brash, energetic, and talented; literary, and well versed in world economics and politics. Their job was a glamorous one. They would interview notables in the hour or so it takes to come up the bay and North River to the pier. Then they would race down the gangplank to the telephone.

The photographers were in a different category. They would take pictures of all the famous people they could find; and would persuade pretty girls to expose a good deal of leg. That came to be called "cheesecake" and a treat, in those far-off days.

George Horne, the last ship news editor on *The New York Times*, retired in 1969. He is a former president of the Ship News Reporters' Association of New York City. That was formed in the 1920's. By that time there was too much world news for any paper to cover individually, and costs were too high. So most of the New York papers and national news-distributing syndicates joined forces. In its early days the New York *Herald* and the *Journal of Commerce* were the only exceptions. They handled maritime events independently. The Association went out of existence early in 1968.

Werner Bamberger, who had worked with George Horne, is still on the *Times* staff and does an occasional ship story; but he does general news as well.

William Seabrook, new retired, went down the bay almost every day from 1931 to 1960. He remembers a time when half a dozen ships at once would be waiting their turn at Quarantine. He was press liaison for steamship lines. He regrets the passing of the transatlantic passenger ships, due to stiff competition from airlines, union trouble, etc. He agrees that air travel is uninteresting. But: "You suffer for six or seven hours—then enjoy yourself."

Frank Engle of *Women's Wear Daily* used to go out to the ships to meet fashion designers. He has since done freelance work for a Port of New York news service. Ernie Payne, former stringer for United Press International, still went down the bay on a freelance basis not long ago.

In the 1940's the ships themselves, and the problems of the shipping industry, became the news. Shipping has become too large and impersonal, like other city commerce—a mechanized and capital-intensive industry, and therefore not exactly story material. The ship news that was a big thing for some 250 years has all but disappeared in the newspapers.

Walter Hamshar, last New York *Herald Tribune* ship news editor, says: "I loved every minute of it. The maiden voyage of the superliner United States, in 1952, was perhaps my highlight."

South Street, Manhattan, waterfront, early 1800's

20

THE SEA AND
THE CITY

SHIPPING in New York and everywhere in America
has had its ups and downs. Before 1800, New York was a small city.
Nathaniel Dwight's *Geography of the World*, published in 1795, gives it
10,000 inhabitants in 4,000 houses. "It stands on a point of land which is
formed by the junction of the North and East Rivers, in the finest situation
for commerce in the United States," the worn old book says. As to the state
of commerce: "It is very flourishing and extended over the world; and the
inhabitants are distinguished by their industrious attention to business."
Jedediah Morse's *American Universal Geography,* published in 1806 when
New York was still the state capital, gives the city 60,489 inhabitants and
2,868 slaves. "This city is esteemed the most eligible situation for commerce
in the United States." However, New York was outclassed in shipping at
that time by both Boston and Philadelphia.

A few years later, New York led its American rivals—and has done so
ever since. American clippers sailed out of New York to China and the
goldfields of California; American whaleships sailed from New York, as well
as from Massachusetts, Connecticut, and Long Island ports. They rounded
Cape Horn and the Cape of Good Hope and penetrated the Arctic. America
led the world in maritime enterprise by the mid-1800's, and the Port of New
York led America.

Before 1860 the great fortunes of this country had come from the sea.
American ships and shipping were the most conspicuous feature of New

York's business life. The waterfront was the center of interest.

By the end of the Civil War our overseas merchant marine had all but disappeared. The shipping industry used foreign bottoms. At the onset of World War I, American shipbuilding revived. That happened again in 1939.

At the end of World War II, the United States owned three-fourths of the entire world tonnage of oceangoing liners. The American merchant marine was content to operate with war-built tonnage after that, while other maritime nations quickly entered postwar building programs to replace the war-built ships they had obtained from our government.

S. Kip Farrington, author of many books about the sea and fishing, wrote in *Ships of the U.S. Merchant Marine* (1947): "No nation has remained a leader among free peoples which did not maintain a strong position on the seas: for trade, travel, defense—the American Merchant Marine."

He cited the service of our merchant ships in World War II. They carried ten million men to war and home again. They carried 270,000,000 tons of cargo and billions of tons of gasoline and oil, during the war years.

Then, he said, "the Merchant Marine turned overnight from a wartime operation to a life-saving organization, bringing corn from our farms to the hungry peoples of the world; rushing domestic animals from our Western ranges to re-stock the ruined farms of Europe and many other lands; hauling coal from our mines and oil from our refineries to keep millions from freezing to death."

During the twenty-five years following Mr. Farrington's eulogy of our merchant marine, the shipping industry was confronted by almost insoluble problems. In December, 1971, a substantial diversion of European cargo from New York to Canadian ports was made, due to the striking New York longshoremen, and looked likely to become permanent. The manager of the New York Port Authority's trade development office for Continental Europe said that the strike was "doing a damn good job of killing the goose that lays the golden egg." Another reason for loss of tonnage for New York, he said, was the fact that the combined ocean and rail rate available for cargoes shipped to the United States via Canada are lower than for cargo routed through for New York. European exporters are anxious, he said, to find the cheapest route to the United States because of the upward valuation of their currencies and the 10 percent surcharge ordered by our government.

However, in the 1970's both city and Federal governments became deeply concerned about New York's waterfront. Along the Hudson it had become disgracefully dilapidated. It took five years of planning and negotiation between shipping lines, longshore labor, the City of New York, the Port Authority of New York and New Jersey, and the Federal Maritime Commission to begin a new consolidated passenger ship terminal late in 1971.

South Street, Manhattan, waterfront, about 1878

THE PORT AUTHORITY OF NEW YORK
AND NEW JERSEY

On April 30, 1921, the Port Authority of New York was created by a compact between New York and New Jersey. (In 1972 the agency's name was changed to include New Jersey.) The Port Authority is a self-supporting agency set up to plan and develop terminal and transportation facilities in the port district—an area of 1,500 square miles—and to protect and promote commerce in the port. Its twelve commissioners, six resident in New York and six in New Jersey, are appointed by the governors of their respective states. They serve without pay for six-year terms.

The Port Authority's World Trade Center for international business looms up in downtown Manhattan. Its two towers, 110 stories each, are the tallest buildings in the world: 1,350 feet high (the Empire State rises only 1,250 feet.)

The Port of New York has 650 miles of navigable waterways—395 in New York State, the rest in New Jersey. The port's central location, on the east coast, with a fine landlocked harbor, gives it the best geographical position of any American port. The only access to the Atlantic for New York

State, and its entire saltwater front, is along the shores of Manhattan, Staten Island, and Long Island, plus a bit of Westchester County.

FULTON FISH MARKET

The old Fulton Fish Market, just below the Brooklyn Bridge on South Street, has been scheduled for removal to the Bronx. The first market was built there in 1821. Some commercial buildings around the market date back to 1811.

From before dawn to noon on weekdays, the fish market is a hive of activity. Downtown businessmen join the fish brokers for lunch at Sweet's (established 1842) at 2 Fulton Street, or at Sloppy Louie's at 92 South Street, just across from the market. That dates back to 1914. Fish just out of the water at these places have a flavor unobtainable uptown.

An eastern Long Island captain of fishing boats who had brought cargoes to Fulton Fish Market under sail, up through the Sound, past Hell Gate, and down the East River, and later under steam by the ocean route, said in 1930: "I first saw New York at the age of fourteen. Father took me along when he went to call on commission merchants on Front Street, who bought and sold whalebone and whale oil. Father carried samples of bone from two whales that he had killed off Amagansett. He took a long, a medium, and a short slab of bone out of each right whale's mouth, lashed up the pieces in a snug bundle with hay-yarn. He carried four-ounce bottles of oil from each whale in his pockets. We must have looked funny going along the city streets: I an overgrown boy in homemade country clothes; Father with his long hair and long beard—they were snow white even then—carrying his bundle of hairy black whalebone taller than himself. People looked.

"We stayed at the United States Hotel and had our meals at Sweet's Restaurant.

"Father went the rounds of the commission merchants to get the best price for the Amagansett whales. He not only led the whale chase, but transacted the business connected with it for our village. Whale oil was used for leather tanning, then; the bone was not only used for women's underpinnings, for umbrellas, and for carriage whips, but scraped whalebone was used as stuffing for the best upholstered furniture. Like feathers or horsehair, it was very springy. That memorable trip to New York—100 miles from home—was in 1885."

THE STATELY SHIPS

The great liner United States made news again, some twenty years after the day that ship news editor Walter Hamshar called her maiden trip the "highlight of his career." In July, 1952, she had steamed into Le Havre with a broom lashed to her towering mast, to proclaim that she had established a new transatlantic speed record on her maiden voyage. In July, 1972, the United States, 990 feet long, of 243,000 horsepower, capable of 42 knots, and still the fastest passenger ship in the world, was being moved to the government reserve fleet in the James River, Va. She had been mothballed for three years due to heavy operating losses, primarily a result of higher American wages.

United States Lines was turning her over to the U.S. Maritime Commission. The government had bought the great ship for $12 million, to place her in reserve status for possible future use as a troopship in an emergency. Terms of the transfer would make her available for return to active duty as a passenger liner, but chances for that were considered very slim.

In July, 1972, not one passenger ship flying the American flag was making the transatlantic run; and very few foreign ones. Four United States flagships were still crossing the Pacific.

Werner Bamberger of *The New York Times* had written nostalgically in 1969: "Six stately ships of our once-esteemed passenger fleet sit rusting in tidewaters that lap gently at their hulls. . . . Foreign ships as well are finding it increasingly difficult to stay alive in the trans-Atlantic trade, but they have been helped to stay in business by a growing demand for cruises . . . a dismal outlook."

Before ships had the equipment to send out the Morse code SOS, a ship's flag would be run upside down as a distress signal. No distress signal was flown when the great American liner United States went out of business in 1969. But a laying-up can destroy a ship or a line as surely as a stranding, a collision, or a fire. It just takes longer. At least the United States will have care in her old age—which was not yet, in 1972. Twenty years is no great age for a well-built ship.

Now the Port of New York maintains its superiority through containerships and tankers. The greatest array of containerships of any port in the world is being offered to exporters and importers at the Port Authority Marine Terminals at Elizabethport and Newark, N.J.; also at two other terminals, one in Jersey City, the other on Staten Island.

Conventional freighters will be relegated to trade with the less-developed nations of the earth and those with ports where the traffic is unsuitable for containerization. By the new method, large amounts of cargo can be stowed in huge, standard-size boxes (or vans as they are called), at a factory inland. Locked and sealed, they can be sent as a unit by truck or rail to the ship. This mass production was intended to enable American manufacturers to meet competition here and abroad in the face of high production costs.

Port of New York, 1970's

Containerships and supertankers are great, graceless things, so different from the beautiful clippers and schooners of the past, or the doomed, majestic liners. Containerization is the shipping industry's technological answer to the cargo-carrying jets. Its purpose is to reduce shipping costs and improve service. Four containerships can replace fifteen or twenty breakbulk (conventional) freighters.

An even more recent breakthrough in naval architecture is the LASH type. LASH means Lighter Aboard Ship. Such vessels are really even more specialized containerships. They carry fifty or more 300-ton lighters, which can be hoisted aboard in seconds. Such vessels do not even need to go to a berth (or dock, as laymen say). They can stop offshore, meet their four or five loaded lighters, take them aboard, and be off. Half a dozen United States and foreign lines were operating or building LASH types by the early 1970's.

Future generations are no more likely, though, to grow nostalgic over today's containerships, when they are replaced by something even bigger and possibly even more utilitarian and impersonal, than this generation is over the fast-vanishing freight trains.

SOUTH STREET SEAPORT

The New York public is welcoming South Street Seaport, a memorial to the great days of sail and steam, from the 1790's through the 1870's. In 1966 a group of amateur historians and boat-lovers came up with a $42 million plan to convert a section of decaying lower Manhattan waterfront in the Brooklyn Bridge area into a working replica of the New York seaport of 150 years ago. In 1966 that seemed "the impossible dream."

Half a dozen years later, it was well on its way. A *New York Times* writer has called it "one of the most ambitious declarations of faith in the future of New York as a liveable city." It pledged the return of dignity to a once proud neighborhood. It is a salute to the kind of shipping which made New York great; a potentially magnificent and permanent recognition of those adventurous mariners, merchants, and ship-builders whose courage and vision turned the tiny Dutch fur-trading post of the 1600's into a mighty city. It reminds city dwellers of the sea around us; of the saltwater that cleanses, stimulates, and soothes at the same time.

On any mild day of any season, nowadays, people are visiting the first of a large collection of historic vessels; or sitting on benches on the piers just enjoying the sea air and sunshine. There is an outdoor theater, a galley, and a continuous program of special events.

The Seaport project comprises six city blocks, with two piers. A row of eighteen Federal-style buildings, called Schermerhorn Row, will be restored. Fulton, South, John, and Front streets are involved. High-rise buildings had been planned for this site, now declared Historic.

The collection of ships with a history includes the full-rigged, 279-foot Wavertree; the Ambrose, last New York lightship; the Alexander Hamilton, long a Hudson River dayliner; and many others. The Pioneer, a schooner-rigged boat, is used in summer for sea training. Groups of youngsters, once drug addicts, are taken out on two-week cruises throughout the summer by dedicated volunteers. The total change of environment, regular hours, and the discipline inherent in seafaring has produced good results.

The period 1790 through the 1870's was chosen for the South Street Seaport project because in the 1840's and 1850's that street was one of the most exciting thoroughfares in the world. Money came in over the bar at Sandy Hook with every tide. There was rum from the West Indies; whale oil and bone from all over the world; furs and flour; tea, silks, and spices from Canton; coffee from South America; cotton and molasses from New Orleans; lumber from Savannah. . . . When the American clipper Oriental reached London in 1850, the *Times* ran a warning editorial that referred to "our gigantic and unshackled rival" across the sea. For a brief period American ships may have moved more ocean tonnage than the whole British merchant marine, then so powerful. The American ships were newer, bigger, faster, and got full holds every trip. Most of these ships were owned and run from South Street. New York shipbuilding flourished.

South Street Seaport will be a mixed community of museum, craft, and commercial activity; a marine oasis in the steel-and-concrete desert that is

New York. The Seaport aims to combine beauty, history, and a feeling of space. It hopes to preserve one area of the metropolis that cannot be periodically torn down and hustled into oblivion. New York has been called "the capital of the wrecking-ball."

Peter Stanford, originator of the project, is its president. Jakob Isbrandtsen is chairman of the board. Frank Braynard is editor of its quarterly bulletin and program chairman.

Alan Villiers, Australian-born author and master sailor, wrote a letter to *The New York Times* in June, 1972, from Oxford, England. He said:

"I would like to add my voice to those commending to the citizens of New York the work and aims of their South Street Seaport Museum, which seeks to set up in the heart of old maritime Manhattan a monument in the shape of ships—sailing-ships, deepwater-men, the real thing—like the full-rigger Wavertree which is there now, slowly being restored.

"For such ships are a reminder of the long line of their gracious forebears sailing from this port, which went about their share of the world's work by grace of man's patiently acquired, long-nurtured skills—his use of aerofoils called sails set from spars on high masts to convert the understood ocean winds into successful long voyages. This was a skill, indeed.

"These ships sailed in peace under God. They consumed nothing they did not carry with them; they destroyed nothing; they polluted nothing. To reflect upon their worth and their achievement, as our eyes may catch the sight of the symmetry of their spars today, could be salutary indeed."

CHRONOLOGICAL LIST
OF VESSELS IN DISTRESS

Off the Port of New York, Western Long Island, and Nearby New Jersey, from 1614

Wherever possible, this list includes date of wreck, type and name of vessel, place of origin and destination, place wrecked, and results.

Jan. or Feb., 1614: Ship, TIJGER (TIGER) from Amsterdam; burned in New York Harbor; total loss.

1620: Dutch ship, name unknown; Sandy Hook; total wreck.

1632–33: Pinnace; cast away upon Long Island; all saved.

1636: Vessel, 50 tons, bound Connecticut to Virginia; wrecked on Long Island; 7 drowned, 2 killed by Indians.

1640: Pinnace MAKE SHIFT, bound southward; stranded on rocks off Long Island; crew saved.

1643: Pinnace, name unknown, carrying ministers from Connecticut to Virginia; bilged upon rocks at Hell Gate; lost.

March 9, 1657: PRINS MAURITS, wrecked on South Beach, Long Island.

1695: Ship, HALCYON, from West Indies to New York; wrecked Jones Inlet; crew escaped.

1741: Ferry boat THOMAS JONES, of Oyster Bay, L.I., upset in Long Island Sound; 4 men, 3 women, 6 horses drowned.

Feb. 27, 1749: JANE, lost at Sandy Hook.

Dec. 21, 1750: BILL SAVAGE, lost at Sandy Hook.

Nov. 13, 1752: CHARMING PEGGY, lost at Sandy Hook.

Dec. 16, 1755: Snow, JAMAICA PACKET, of New York City, bound for Surinam, wrecked at Rockaway, L.I. Capt. Richard Bennet, Isaac Halstead, mate, Thomas Gurney, seaman, Original Couch, seaman, Andrew Mersyer, boy, perished.

July 10, 1764: HM sloop CHALEUR, burned by mob in New York.

1767: Ship BRITANNIA, ashore Merrick Beach, L.I.; 5 lost, some passengers reached shore on raft; ship fell to pieces.

Dec. 26, 1768: FELICITY, wrecked off Sandy Hook.

Jan. 30, 1773: BETSEY, lost off Sandy Hook.

Dec. 27, 1774: ELIZABETH, total loss off Sandy Hook; had been ashore there Oct. 9, 1752.

1776: British corvette, name unknown; Capt. Adam Hyler and Capt. William Marriner of New Brunswick, N.J., captured corvette in Coney Island Bay, burned it, imprisoned its officers.

1776–1780: British packet ship CARTERET, driven on Jones Beach by American privateer; looted and dismantled.

1776–1780: American privateer REVENUE, 12 guns, 52 men, run ashore at Hempstead, L.I., by British ship GALATEA; vessel bilged.

1776–80: Sloop, name unknown, from West Indies with cargo of rum, captured and burned by Capt. Adam Hyler at Elizabethtown, N.J.

Dec. 26, 1777: British frigate MERCURY, possibly a treasure ship, wrecked in North River; attempt made to raise her in 1823.

Feb. 11, 1777 or 1778: LIVERPOOL, 28-gun British naval vessel, wrecked on Rockaway Beach, L.I. Admiral Harvey of British Navy on board; a Quaker family, Hicks, succored him.

1777–78: Prison ships anchored in the Wallabout Basin burned; possibly fired by American prisoners on board.

Aug. 4, 1778: British ordnance sloop MORNING STAR, blew up near New York coffeehouse; believed struck by lightning.

1779: Six American whaleboats entered Rockaway Bay, seizing, burning, and capturing every British vessel in sight; British retaliated.

During Revolution: Wooden ship, over 100 feet long, probably British man-o'-war, uncovered 1920 at Rockaway Beach, L.I.; possibly the LIVERPOOL.

1780: British ship LEXINGTON, sank in East River, N.Y., off 138th St., in 66 feet of water; loss reported at $1,800,000.

June, 1780: British boat, bound New York to Huntington, L.I., run ashore at Butler's Point and burned, in whaleboat warfare.

July 25, 1780: British man-o'-war BLOND, on rocks at Corlear's Hook.

Nov. 3, 1780: British frigate HUSSAR, 28 guns, struck rock at Hell Gate; total loss.

April 14, 1781: British flagship ROYAL OAK, Vice Admiral Arbuthnot on board, aground on rocks opposite Whitehall St., New York City.

Aug. 26, 1781: HMS sloop SWALLOW, Capt. Thomas Wells, master, driven ashore by four American privateers "on Fire Island, near Long Island, America." Lost.

1784: Ferry, Brooklyn to New York, upset when 5 horses shifted; 3 passengers, 2 ferrymen saved.

Jan. 15, 1784: New Jersey ferryboat, name unknown, damaged by ice and sank. Eight passngers climbed on cake of ice; one froze to death in East River.

Jan., 1785: Schooner DOLPHIN, bound New London, Conn., to New York, ran ashore Matinecock Point, Oyster Bay, L.I.; 3 saved; John Antony, Spaniard of New London, drowned.

1793: British frigate BOSTON, Capt. George W. Courtenay, challenged Capt. Bompard of French frigate L'AMBUSCADE to single-combat naval duel off Sandy Hook; French won; BOSTON much damaged and Capt. Courtenay killed.

Aug. 8, 1793: Packet sloop SOUTHAVEN, total loss off Long Island Sound; all saved.

Dec. 17, 1795: Ferry, name unknown, overset in East River; 1 man and 7 fat oxen drowned.

April 2, 1798: Ferry between Fly Market, Manhattan, and Brooklyn sank in East River; 7 drowned, 1 saved.

Aug. 20, 1798: Sloop, name unknown,

struck by lightning off west end of Long Island; 1 man killed.

Feb. 15, 1799: Sloop, name unknown, from Smithtown, L.I., upset in East River; boatmen drowned. A Miss Hawkins, passenger, climbed on vessel's side and remained there until boat drifted ashore.

Sept., 1800: THREE FRIENDS, from Massachusetts, total loss on "backside of Long Island."

May, 1801: Ferry, from Fulton Market ferry stairs, capsized in East River on way to Brooklyn; seven drowned, 6 saved.

Jan. 18, 1809: Ship TRIAL, Capt. Trask, wrecked on rocks off north shore of Long Island; sank; some of crew saved from rigging, 3 lost limbs, frozen.

Sept. 18, 1810: Schooner SALLY, Capt. Ebenezer White, bound for Barbados from New London, Conn., with cargo of horses; found on beam ends, south side of Long Island. Captain, mate, 1 seaman lost; 4 saved.

Dec. 24, 1811, Christmas Storm: BLACK ROCK, wrecked Manhasset, L.I.

Dec. 24, 1811: GENERAL GATES, ashore Governor's Island.

Dec. 24, 1811: MAYBELLE, wrecked north shore, Long Island.

Dec. 24, 1811: Seventy vessels driven on Long Island's north shore in gale and snowstorm; 42 at Cow Neck (Manhasset); brig and 6 sloops, Whitestone; 4 sloops, Oyster Bay; vessel stove in, Red Spring Point, captain and crew swam ashore; other vessels stranded at Oak Neck, Little Neck, and Flushing.

June 12, 1812: American ship EGERIA, Copenhagen to New York, total loss in northwest part of Long Island Sound.

March 7, 1814: American privateer MARS, 15 guns, 100 crew; captured and burned by British.

Jan. 14, 1815: U.S. frigate PRESIDENT, Commodore Rogers, aground on Sandy Hook bar trying to escape to sea; crippled, captured by British.

Jan., 1816: British brig MARTHA, bound New York to British Guiana with horses and lumber; ashore on Sandy Hook.

1818: Steamer OLIVE BRANCH, New Brunswick, N.J., to New York; racing, damaged.

Dec. 17, 1819: American schooner SALLY, said to have been attacked by a sea serpent off Long Island.

Sept. 3–5, 1821: Schooner GLORIAN and eight others sunk at Rockaway, L.I.

May 15, 1824: Steamer AETNA, Citizens' Line, bound New York from Washington, N.J.; Capt. Thomas Robinson; exploded in New York Harbor; 24 saved, 13 lost; ship complete wreck.

Dec. 13, 1824: Ship NESTOR, Capt. Place, from Liverpool to New York with salt, coal, and lead cargo; ashore off Hempstead, L.I.; bilged.

1827: Steamboat OLIVER ELLSWORTH, Hartford to New York, exploded near mouth of East River; 3 scalded.

March 19, 1828: Sloop ANN MARIA, New York to Providence, R.I.; collided and sank off Rock Lighthouse. Ten dollar reward for two casks Madeira wine, probably floated off.

June 4, 1829: U.S. steam frigate FULTON THE FIRST, blown up in Brooklyn Navy Yard; complete wreck; 33 killed, 29 wounded.

1830: Brig VINEYARD, cargo of cotton, sugar, and molasses, plus Mexican specie; scuttled and burned off Coney Island by pirates.

July 24, 1831: Schooner SPECULATOR, sank off Coney Island; Capt. Thomas Carman and Mate James Akerly drowned.

Dec. 4, 1831: Ship PRESIDENT, Charleston Line packet, Capt. Wilson; aground on Romer Shoals in storm; 20 persons saved after great distress.

1832: Ship, name unknown, wrecked at Hempstead, L.I.

July 6, 1832: Steamer OHIO, exploded, New York; five lost.

Nov. 12, 1832: Steamer MARTHA OGDEN, stranded, New York.

Dec. 1833: Sloop IRENE, Capt. J. H. Cook of Greenport, L.I., went to pieces on rocks at Hurl (Hell) Gate.

Aug. 23, 1836: Steam ferry boat GENERAL JACKSON, coming from Long Island to foot of Walnut St., Manhattan; run down and sunk by steamer BOSTON; 6 lost, 19 saved; 14 horses and wagons lost.

Nov. 21, 1836: American bark BRISTOL, carrying Irish immigrants, wrecked at Far Rockaway; 84 lost, 32 saved.

Jan. 2, 1837: American bark MEXICO, from Liverpool to New York, wrecked at Hempstead Beach; crew of 12 plus 112 passengers; 116 lost, 8 saved.

Nov. 1, 1837: Schooner ISABELLA, bound New York to Wilmington, N.C., foundered in gale near New York; 3 lost, 1 saved.

1838: Pilot boat FRANKLIN, driven ashore in gale; all on board lost.

1839: Many wrecks, Coney Island, in gale.

July, 1839: Pilot boat JOHN MCKEON of New Jersey; lost at sea in hurricane with all 6 hands.

July 4, 1839: Ferry boat SAMSON, wrecked between New York and Staten Island; 2 killed.

July 28, 1839: Pilot boat GRATITUDE, lost in hurricane with all hands: 4 pilots, 3 apprentices, 3 others.

1840's (probably): Tugboat, name unknown, Capt. David Havens; boiler blew up; the captain died; vessel wrecked.

March 12, 1841: British–American Steam Navigation Co. paddle steamer PRESIDENT, bound New York to Liverpool, disappeared in storm; first passenger steamship to founder on transatlantic run; all 136 persons aboard lost.

April 27, 1841: Steamer HENRY ECKFORD, exploded; one lost.

1842: Pilot boat SAN JACINTO, lost with all hands.

1843: Pilot boat FLY, lost with all hands.

Feb. 13, 1843: Sailing ship NORTH AMERICA, wrecked off Highlands Light Tower south of Sandy Hook.

Nov. 11, 1843: Liverpool packet SHEFFIELD, struck and heeled over on Romer Shoal entering New York Harbor; Capt. Charles W. Popham; 130 passengers, crew, and pilot on board; Capt. Oliver Vanderbilt on steamer WAVE saved passengers.

Sept. 28, 1844: Bark EUGENIA, leaving New York for Vera Cruz; in sinking condition in North River; saved.

Feb. 6, 1845: Schooner REESIDE, Boston for New York, stranded Lloyd's Neck, L.I.; embedded in ice. All on board perished.

Feb. 12, 1845: Liverpool packet SHEFFIELD of Hull, England, bilged on Gilgo Bar, Long Island; John E. Gillespie, Master; passengers and crew safe.

Feb. 13, 1845: Bark LA PLATA, from Philadelphia; Capt. Michaels; ashore in gale on southwest spit of Sandy Hook.

Feb. 18, 1845: pilot Boat MARY ELLEN, ashore in storm off Sandy Hook; all hands lost.

May, 1845: Sailing vessel REFORM, lost in gale off Sandy Hook.

June 1, 1846: Steamer OREGON, raced, considered very fast; aground on rocks called Gridiron at Hell Gate; repaired.

Nov. 1, 1846: Steamer RHODE ISLAND, Providence & Stonington SS Co.; Capt. S. Manchester; going to New York from Stonington, Conn. Lost rudder, anchored windward of Cow Neck, L.I.; 150 passengers saved.

Sept. 30, 1847: Packet ship AUBURN, New York to New Orleans; wrecked Long Beach, L.I.: 18 lost, including captain and first mate; 7 saved.

May 10, 1848: Sloop GENERAL MERCER, of Bridgeport, Conn., bound to Hartford with cargo of lime; disabled in storm and driven ashore; burned to waterline.

Oct. 25, 1849: Hudson River day liner NEW WORLD, reversed too suddenly opposite Fort Washington, walking beam dropped, connecting rod snapped and pushed through bottom of boat; sank; passengers saved by steamer OHIO.

Oct. 12, 1849: Steamer SPITFIRE, burned at New York.

Nov. 1849: Sloop DISPATCH of Cold Spring Harbor, L.I., struck Pot Rock going through Hell Gate; Capt. John Mahan killed by blow from tiller.

1850: Screw-propeller tugboat RESOLUTE, blew up at foot of Wall St., Manhattan; all aboard killed.

Jan. 12, 1850: Immigrant ship AYRSHIRE grounded in storm off Squam Beach, N.J.; volunteers used all-enclosed metal lifeboat to save 201; 1 lost.

Feb. 10, 1850: British Brig MINERVA, from Halifax, N.S., for New York; Capt. Delany; 6 passengers, cargo of fish; total wreck 7 miles west of Fire Island; 4 drowned.

March 4, 1850: Steamer CHARTER OAK, burned, New York City.

Nov., 1850: Schooner EXTRA, Capt. Terrell, bound for New York with cargo of wood; ashore on flats off Crane Neck, L.I.; total wreck.

Winter, 1851: Pilot boat SYLPH, foundered at sea in blizzard; New Jersey pilot McKnight Smith drowned.

Aug. 7, 1851: Steamer TROJAN, burned, New York; 4 lost.

1852: Pilot boat COMMERCE, lost with all 9 on board.

July 28, 1852: Side-wheel Hudson River steamer HENRY CLAY, racing with ARMENIA; on fire near Sing Sing; run aground at Riverdale; 60 lost.

Sept. 3, 1852: Day liner REINDEER, New York to Albany; exploded and burned 40 miles below Albany; 31 died.

Dec. 3, 1852: Pilot boat YANKEE, struck wreck 35 miles east of Sandy Hook;

sank; pilots Henry Budd and Robert Curtis lost, with 2 others; 5 saved by pilot boat E. K. COLLINS.

1853: Pilot boat SARAH FRANCIS, ashore at Sandy Hook; lost.

March 29, 1853 British ship CLYDE, total loss at Sandy Hook.

Aug. 26, 1853: Coastwise steamer, New York to New Orleans, burned at wharf, New York; no lives lost.

Nov. 4, 1853: Steamer JAMES RUMSEY, burned at New York.

Dec. 27, 1853: Clipper ships GREAT REPUBLIC and WHITE SQUALL, and New York–Liverpool packet JOSEPH WALKER, burned at piers in East River, New York.

1854: Pilot boat JACOB BELL, sunk in gale off Sandy Hook; all hands lost.

Jan., 1854: Caloric engine steamer ERICSSON, built by John Ericsson who built the MONITOR, famous ironclad of Civil War, capsized in squall, North River; $50,000 insurance paid.

May 15, 1854: Black Ball Line packet MONTEZUMA, with 500 immigrants from Liverpool; wrecked in storm on Jones Beach; all saved by tugs.

June 29, 1854: Steamer BUFFALO, foundered off New York.

Nov. 15, 1854: Many vessels wrecked in storm.

1855: Pilot boat WILLIAM G. HAGSTAFF, wrecked off Sandy Hook; built 1841 by George Steers, it was then fastest vessel afloat.

1856: Steamer SHEPHERD KNAPP, burned, New York.

Jan., 1856: New York–Staten Island ferry COLUMBUS, Vanderbilt-operated; hull crushed by ice off Battery; passengers crossed ice to Governor's Island; one horse drowned in harness.

Feb. 14, 1856: Bark, New Orleans packet, JOHN MINTURN, Capt. Starke; wrecked off Squam Beach, N.J.; 60 lost. N.Y. pilot Thomas Freeborne froze to death after giving his coat to the captain's wife.

March 20, 1856: LEVIATHAN, total loss off Sandy Hook.

Dec. 22, 1856: Steamer KNOXVILLE, burned at wharf, New York; total loss.

1857: J. W. HARRIS, wrecked Long Island Sound; 14 lost.

1857: Pilot boat THOMAS H. SMITH, ashore on N.J. beach in gale, lost with 3 pilots and crew.

Jan. 10, 1857: Pilot boat SYLPH, lost off Fire Island with all on board (6 pilots, 5 crew, 1 passenger).

Jan. 18, 1857: Pilot boat WASHINGTON, sunk at sea; N.Y. pilot Thomas Orr and 6 sailors lost.

Feb., 1857: PILOT, total loss off Sandy Hook.

April 14, 1857: JOHN FREDERICK, total loss off Sandy Hook.

Aug. 21, 1857: Steamer SPLENDID, burned at Jersey City, N.J.

March 18, 1858: Fall River liner EMPIRE STATE, westbound, sunk in Long Island Sound; passengers saved. Had history of disasters. Raised.

April 20, 1858: Pilot boat WESTERVELT, wrecked; Pilot John O'Keefe lost.

May 14, 1858: Tow boat (steam) HERCULES, burned at Sandy Hook dock.

Nov. 6, 1858: Propeller PETREL, exploded, North River, N.Y., opposite foot of Jay St.

Feb. 20, 1859: Side-wheel steamer BLACK WARRIOR, total loss at Rockaway Inlet, L.I.; 65 saved.

Nov. 1, 1859: New Haven–New York steamer CHAMPION, collided off Matinecock Point, Glen Cove, L.I.; 41 saved; 4 lost.

Jan. 28, 1860: Tapscott Line clipper ship, Liverpool packet, JOHN J. BOYD, burned at Pier 8, North River, New York; $60,000 loss.

March, 1860: Sloop SPRAY, Capt. Leete of Guilford, Conn.; collided with sloop LUCINDA four miles north of Barnegat Light. Made port. Captain and brother disappeared; murder suspected; Chinese, John Low, arrested.

March 7, 1860: Pilot boat VIRGINIA, lost in fog and gale ten miles east of Rockaway Shoals.

March 21, 1860: Sloop E. A. JOHNSON, Capt. George Burr; abandoned between Sandy Hook and Coney Island; 3 murdered; mate, murderer, caught.

March 21, 1860: Schooner JOHN B. MATHER of Dennis, Mass., Capt. Nickerson; damaged in collision with sloop E. A. JOHNSON off West Bank.

Summer, 1860: Bark, BRITISH BANNER, Capt. W. Thomas, said to have been attacked at sea by sea serpent.

July 4, 1861: Hudson River day liner NEW WORLD, sunk off Stuyvesant shore on way to Albany; no lives lost. Ended up as Civil War hospital ship.

Oct., 1861: JOSEPH A. SMITH, former Sag Harbor–New London ferry, cargo of stone; sank in head of Long Island Sound; Capt. Ryan and 3 lost.

1861–65: Schooner SARAH S. BIRD, left East Rockaway Inlet; captain and crew of 7 disappeared with vessel.

1862: Pilot boat EDWIN FORREST, lost off Long Island.

1862: Pilot boat JAMES FUNCK, sunk in Narrows, New York, by SS UNION; raised. In 1864 was seized by Rebel privateer TALLAHASEE, used as tender and decoy, destroyed.

Feb. 9, 1862: Steamer ELLA WARLEY, once the ISABEL; ex-blockade runner for Confederacy; sunk in collision with steamer NORTH STAR, below Sandy Hook.

Oct. 16, 1862: Steamer UNION STAR, burned, New York.

1863: Pilot boat WILLIAM J. ROMER, struck submerged wreck and sank; 1 pilot lost.

Sept., 1863: Steamer AUGUSTA, stranded Hell Gate, New York.

Oct. 22, 1863: Steamer OREGON, collided with CITY OF BOSTON, sunk in New York Harbor.

Dec. 5, 1863: Steamer ISAAC NEWTON, starboard boiler exploded opposite Fort Lee, N.J., in Hudson River;

burned to water's edge; 9 died, 17 scalded.

Aug., 1864: Sloop (yacht) UNKNOWN, actual name; Capt. Morrell; racing with yacht DAISY, capsized 3 miles east of Sands Point, L.I.; 8 saved.

Aug. 12, 1864: Pilot boat WILLIAM BELL, captured by Confederate privateer TALLAHASSEE, 70 miles s.e. Sandy Hook; used for short time, then destroyed.

Dec. 8, 1864: Schooner WILLIAM PENN of Port Jefferson, L.I., on run New Haven, Conn., to New York; capsized Hell Gate; Capt. Wesley Havens drowned.

Feb. 12, 1865: Pilot boat GEORGE STEERS, lost with all 5 on board off Barnegat, N.J.

March 16, 1865: Schooner DANIEL C. HIGGINS, of New London, from New York to Port Royal; ashore at Rockaway, L.I.

April 2, 1865: Sloop REPORT of Sag Harbor; hit near Blackwell's Island, East River, by lumber schooner; carried away bulwarks and bowsprit.

May 10, 1865: Steamer E. L. CLARK, New York to Philadelphia; burned at foot of Fifth St., East River, New York.

Aug. 4, 1865: Steamer ARROW, ferry between Haverstraw, Nyack, and New York; Capt. Isaac Smith; exploded off 30th St., New York, killing several persons.

Aug. 13, 1865: Sloop PLANTER of Sag Harbor, Capt. Williams; cargo bone dust; total loss on Hallett's Point at Hell Gate; crew escaped.

Nov. 3, 1865: Schooner CHIEF from Rondout for Nantucket; run into at Hell Gate, sunk.

Nov. 27, 1865: Boston schooner, W. CARLETON, from Baltimore for Cohasset Narrows; collided with steamer off Smith's Point; sunk.

Dec., 1865: Steamship ALLEGHANY of Baltimore, ashore at Gilgo Beach, Hempstead, L.I.; total loss.

Dec. 5, 1865: Steamer NEPTUNE, Balti-

more & Liverpool S.S. Co.; wrecked on Long Island.

Dec. 16, 1865: Bark NIFADELOS, Havana to New York, collided with steamer ALABAMA, sunk in New York Harbor.

Dec. 23, 1865: Steamer IDAHO, stranded at Barnegat, N.J.

Dec. 28, 1865: T. J. HILL, wrecked at Sandy Hook.

1866: EVENING STAR, out of New York, foundered at sea; 100 lost.

Jan. 3, 1866: Schooner JOHANNA WARD, bound Virginia to New York with cargo of oysters; total loss at Far Rockaway, L.I.

Jan. 3, 1866: Steamer NEPTUNE; exploded off Sandy Hook; 1 lost.

Jan. 8, 1866: Steamer MARY A. BOARDMAN, stranded, Romer Shoals.

May, 1866: Schooner COMMODORE of Lubec, Maine; stranded Glen Cove, L.I.; got off, arrived New York, May 13; took fire at steamboat dock and sunk.

July 3, 1866: Schooner EXCHANGE, from Rondout to Providence, R.I.; home port Brookhaven, L.I.; wrecked at Hell Gate.

Oct. 1, 1866: Steamer TEMPEST, burned, New York.

Nov. 12, 1866: Steamer T. A. KNICKERBOCKER; exploded, New York.

Nov. 16, 1866: Bark RHINEHARD, bound New York from Bremen; ashore near Rockaway in gale; damaged; 300 (all) saved.

Nov. 17, 1866: American brig FLYING SCUD, clipper, from Malaga to New York; cargo fruit; stranded Rockaway Beach, L.I.; 1 lost.

Dec. 1, 1866: British steamship SCOTLAND, of National Steam Navigation Co., bound Liverpool to New York, collided 10 miles from Fire Island with sailing ship KATE DYER, of Portland, Maine, bound Callao to New York with cargo of cotton. Both vessels sank; lightship named for SCOTLAND.

247

Perils of the Port of New York

Dec. 7, 1866: Steamer J. D. SECOR, burned at Blackwell's Island, New York.

Dec. 27, 1866: Danish bark CHRISTIANE, Capt. Cornelius Isbrandtsen, from Rio de Janeiro for New York; rammed by outgoing steamer NORTH AMERICA off lightship below New York; 12 on bark lost, also Pilot Joseph Fredell; 4 saved.

1867: GRANITE STATE, beached after striking rock at Hunter's Point; sank; later raised.

1867: Pilot boat NETTLE, run down by steamship and sunk.

Jan. 22, 1867: Steam tug ENTERPRISE, boiler exploded, North River; 3 hurt.

Feb. 10, 1867: Ship DASHING WAVE, Capt. Carlton, San Francisco to New York; sunk at southwest spit, New York Harbor; raised, arrived at city Sept. 13.

April 2, 1867: Schooner H. A. BARNES, New York to New Bedford; run down and sunk off Riker's Island, New York.

April 29, 1867: Brig HOUND of Halifax; from Kingston, Jamaica, to New York; ashore at Rockaway, L.I.

May 2, 1867: Ship HIBERNIAN, Allan Line of Liverpool; bound New York for Liverpool; burned at Fulton Ferry, New York.

June 21, 1867: Schooner REAPER, sunk in East River.

July 23, 1867: Sloop VIENNA, Elizabethport, N.J., to Norwich, Conn.; sunk at Hell Gate.

July 28, 1867: Schooner L. R. OGDEN, of Camden, N.J., from Port Johnson; sunk at Hell Gate.

Aug., 1867: Bark HENRY TROWBRIDGE, found derelict s.e. Atlantic Highlands by pilot boat NETTLE; bodies of 3 men, drowned, in hulk; on way north from West Indies.

Oct. 9, 1867: Steamship HOME, between New York and Charleston, S.C.; struck buoy on Gedney Channel, New York Harbor; floated; two nights later went to pieces 6 miles north of Oglethorpe Light; all 80 hands drowned.

Nov. 16, 1867: Steamer KING PHILIP, burned, Jersey City, N.J.

Dec. 13, 1867: Sloop MARIA, Capt. Harris, Montauk to New York; wrecked on David's Island, Long Island Sound; 2 saved, 2 lost.

May 15, 1868: Schooner E. C. KNIGHT, Elizabethport, N.J., to Boston; sunk at Hell Gate.

May 24, 1868: Stonington Steamship Co. steamer OCEANUS, bound Providence to New York; burned, New York.

July 3, 1868: Schooner T. S. GRIER, New York to Delaware, run down and sunk by steamer COLUMBIA, 12 miles north of Barnegat.

Sept. 5, 1868: Schooner WASHINGTON, Capt. Tiffany; South Amboy, N.J. to New Bedford, Mass.; sunk in Hell Gate.

Sept. 20, 1868: Sloop ETHAN ALLEN, sunk off Blackwell's Island, New York.

Oct. 25, 1868: Steamer KINGS COUNTY, burned, Hunter's Point, New York.

Oct. 25, 1868: Brig LORD HARTINGTON, bound New York for Cork, Ireland; burned, Hunter's Point, New York. Raised Nov. 7.

1869: Pilot boat A. T. STEWART, sunk by steamer SCOTIA while acting as station boat; all saved.

1869: British steamship RUSSIA, rammed and sank an Austrian ship at anchor off the Battery, New York.

March 6, 1869: Pilot boat JOSIAH JOHNSON, run down and sunk by schooner WANATA in bay; all saved.

May 8, 1869: Schooner SALLIE SMITH of Fall River, Mass.; Connecticut to New York; sunk 8 miles off Huntington Light, L.I.

Oct. 3, 1869: Sloop, name unknown, cargo lumber; capsized off Fox Island (what is now Lattingtown, L.I.).

Jan. 20, 1870: Schooner STATESMAN. wrecked at Rockaway, L.I.; 2 lost.

Jan. 30, 1870: Ferry UNION, Hoboken to Manhattan; oceangoing tug crashed into port side, cutting deep gash below waterline; salvaged.

Sept. 24, 1870: Schooner MONITOR, New York for Wareham, Mass.; struck on point of North Brother Island, N.Y.; June 26, 1873, cut down to water's edge by schooner JOSEPHINE of Bridgeport; made it to New London.

1871: Fall River liner PROVIDENCE, Capt. Brayton; aground. Aug. 3, 1871, collided in Long Island Sound with schooner WILLIAM MCCOBB and unknown schooner. Dec. 8, 1871, grounded on reef off Delancy St., New York; Oct. 15, 1872, collided with drilling machine at Hell Gate, badly damaged; Dec. 10, 1907, Capt. George F. Chase, collided with ferry BALTIC in East River, 1 ferry passenger drowned; PROVIDENCE damaged.

Jan. 26, 1871: Schooner ALFRED HALL and bark KATE SMITH lost off N.J.; 14 died.

March 18, 1871: Pilot boat JOHN D. JONES, run down by SS CITY OF WASHINGTON, Inman Line; all saved.

May 5, 1871: Brig OMEGA of Sydney, Cape Breton, struck on Brigantine Shoals, N.J., in fog; went to pieces; crew saved.

May 31, 1871: Norwegian bark RHEA, Capt. Andersen, bound Rotterdam for New York, collided with North German Lloyd steamer HANSA. RHEA sank; her captain and 7 crewmen lost; 2 mates, 5 seamen saved.

July 8, 1871: Schooner M. A. LONGBERY, Elizabethport to Bridgeport, sunk at Hell Gate.

July 12, 1871: Schooner ELLA, Rondout for Boston; struck by lightning in North River; damaged.

July 18, 1871: Schooner OSCAR C. ACKEN, Westport to New York; run into at Hell Gate by steamer ELM CITY; ACKEN sunk.

July 23, 1871: Schooner JENNY; cargo in hold exploded; burned to water's edge, off N.J. flats.

July 29, 1871: Sloop THOMAS RANSEN,

Elizabethport to New Haven; cargo coal; ashore on Holmes Rock, Hell Gate.

July 30, 1871: Staten Island ferry WESTFIELD, boiler explosion, at dock in New York; 400 passengers; 104 lives lost.

Aug. 3, 1871: Fall River liner PROVIDENCE collided in Long Island Sound with schooner WILLIAM MCCOBB and an unknown schooner.

Aug. 21, 1871: Schooner JUNO of Rockland, Maine; cargo lime; ran on Gridiron, Hell Gate; took fire; total loss.

Aug. 28, 1871: Schooner C. D. HALLOCK, Elizabethport to Portsmouth, N.H.; foundered, Long Island Sound.

Aug. 31, 1871: Schooner KATE CHURCH, from Port Johnson for Gardiner, Maine; struck reef off Ravenswood, L.I.; sunk.

Sept. 14, 1871: Schooner SARAH of New Bedford, bound Philadelphia to Portsmouth, N.H., cargo coal; ashore Romer Shoal off Sandy Hook; went to pieces; all hands saved.

Sept. 14, 1871: Schooner SARAH ELIZABETH, Harlem to Weehawken, N.J.; in North River, ran afoul of bark CERES at anchor; schooner's stern torn away; bark lost her jibboom.

Sept. 17, 1871: Schooner, name unknown, bound Elizabethport, N.J., to Providence, R.I.; collided at Hell Gate with schooner ACKLAM of Amboy, N.J.; badly damaged.

Sept. 28, 1871: Steam tug DELAWARE, struck by Astoria ferry WILLIAMSBURG, sunk in Pot Cove; port side stove in, pilot house carried away.

Sept. 29, 1871: Schooner D. C. HULSE, bound New York from Brookhaven, L.I.; sunk at Astoria.

Oct. 4, 1871: Schooner, pilot boat MOSES H. GRINNELL, run into by Norwegian bark URSA MINOR off Governor's Island; had been run into by steamer UNION on Outer Middle Ground, Oct. 11, 1863, and cut to water's edge; crew stayed by and saved her.

Oct. 16, 1871: Ship WILD ROVER, Capt. Nichols, ashore near Jones Inlet; bilged, went to pieces.

Nov., 1871: Brig ALFARETTA of Dorchester, New Brunswick, for New York; cargo of stone; ashore on Gridiron, Hell Gate; filled.

Nov. 1, 1871: Fall River Line steamer BRISTOL, ashore on Gridiron, Hell Gate; got off; burned at Newport, R.I., dock, 1889.

Nov. 25, 1871: Bark J. H. MCLAREN, cargo coal, New York to Aspinwall; sunk in Lower Bay off Staten Island; probably total loss.

Dec. 8, 1871: Sloop J. DURYEA, in tow, East River; run into by steamer ELM CITY, cut through amidships; crew rescued.

Dec. 8, 1871: Fall River liner PROVIDENCE grounded on reef off Delancey St., New York City.

Dec. 8, 1871: Steam tug WILSON D. REED, run into off Pier 8, East River, by unknown steamer; cut down to waterline, starboard side; sank.

Dec. 17, 1871: British bark SYDENHAM, Bremen to New York; ashore near Jones Inlet.

Jan. 15, 1872: Sloop G. J. DEMOREST, Oyster Bay to New York; cargo bricks; sunk Hell Gate.

Jan. 31, 1872: British ship LA GLOIRE, New York for Antwerp; grounded Swash Channel; part of crew mutinied.

Feb. 5, 1872: British ship LEPENSTRATH, Demerara to New York; driven eighty miles s.e. from Highlands in storm; damaged; chief officer James Robertson fell overboard, drowned.

Feb. 5, 1872: Schooner MATTHEW KINNEY of Darien, Ga., for New York; in Narrows, bow port stove in by ice; vessel filled.

March 12, 1872: Steamer CITY OF BOSTON, collided, Long Island Sound, with unknown schooner; damaged; several other casualties, 1863, 1874, 1881.

March 13, 1872: Schooner CLARA BELL, New York for Boston; wrecked Highland, N.J., Light.

April 1, 1872: Schooner BELLE of Rockport, Mass., bound for New York; ashore at Gridiron, Hell Gate; filled.

April 8, 1872: Schooner MORNING STAR, New York to Camden, Maine; passed Hell Gate March 17; did not arrive at destination.

April 9, 1872: Schooner BREEZE, cargo oysters; ashore Far Rockaway; vessel lost, crew saved.

April 9, 1872: Bark NARRAGANSETT, Savannah to New York; collided with brig ANNA of Bermuda off Highlands, N.J., in fog and gale; badly damaged; all on board ANNA taken off; brig abandoned.

April 15, 1872: Schooner ABBY MORTON, Elizabethport to Plymouth, Mass.; cargo coal; ashore at Hell Gate; filled.

May, 1872: Sloop GLYDE of Hoboken for Cow Bay, L.I.; cargo coal; sank off Fort Schuyler bar.

May 1, 1872: Schooner HENRY COLE, South Amboy for Providence, R.I.; cargo coal; ashore on Hog's Back, Hell Gate.

May 2, 1872: Schooner WILLIAM R. KNAPP, run into by steamer CITY OF HARTFORD, between Hell Gate and Astoria, L.I.; sank; cook drowned.

May 4, 1872: Cunard steamer BATAVIA, New York for Liverpool; collided with SS ATLANTIC, Collins Line, New York for Liverpool; West Bank, N.Y.; repaired.

May 6, 1872: Schooner TRIMMER, Albany to Hartford, Conn.; cargo lumber; struck Hell Gate; filled; beached by steam tug JOE at Astoria.

May 10, 1872: Schooner WILLIAM BUTMAN, Elizabethport for Boston; struck reef at Hell Gate; sunk.

May 19, 1872: British bark LAKEMA, of Windsor, Nova Scotia; New York for Antwerp; cargo petroleum; ashore in fog, Jones Inlet; cargo removed.

May 27, 1872: Steamer HARRY BUMM, exploded, New York; 3 lost.

June 9, 1872: Steam tug N. S. STARBUCK, collided off Battery with British SS CITY OF LONDON, New York to Liverpool; STARBUCK badly damaged.

June 12, 1872: Schooner FLORENCE, New York for St. John's, New Brunswick; general cargo; struck by lightning off Captain's Island, Long Island Sound; two injured, vessel badly damaged.

June 22, 1872: Baltischer Lloyd steamer of Stettin, FRANKLIN; on fire at Pier 12, North River; damaged.

July 20, 1872: Schooner DIADEM, Newburgh, N.Y., to Fall River, Mass.; cargo coal; run into, Hell Gate, by steamer GALATEA; sank off Ward's Island Bluff.

July 30, 1872: Steamer SENECA, burned, New York.

July 30, 1872: Fire in Standard Oil Yard at Hunter's Point, N.Y., destroyed British bark EDWARD, of Halifax, Nova Scotia, cargo oil; also destroyed brig ROSLYN, Capt. Tuthill, bound for Trieste, which caught fire from burning canal boat. Brig MAX and Norwegian ship ELPIS, bound for Baltic, burned.

Aug. 18, 1872: Schooner BLACK DIAMOND, Elizabethport for Providence; cargo coal; Hell Gate; struck on North Brother Island; sank.

Aug. 21, 1872: Canal steamer CATHCART, cargo coal; collided at Hallett's Point, Hell Gate, with government scow; ashore at College Point.

Aug. 23, 1872: Sloop BRANDYWINE, Haverstraw for College Point, L.I.; cargo brick; collided with government scow at Hell Gate; sank on Pot Rock.

Aug. 24, 1872: Sloop GEORGE B. BLOOMER, Hartford to New York, cargo brownstone; capsized, Negro Head; got off by Wreck Master Brown, put on Astoria beach.

Aug. 25, 1872: Sloop NORMA, cargo tallow; ashore on Gridiron, Hell Gate; filled; got off.

Aug. 28, 1872: Schooner C. L. HULSE, Rondout to Providence, cargo coal; collison Hell Gate, sunk.

Aug. 29 or 30, 1872: Long Island Sound steamer METIS, sunk after collision in Sound, bound New York to Providence, R.I.; 50 lost.

Aug. 31, 1872: Steamer NARRAGANSETT, New York to Stonington, Conn.; collision with schooner SPARKLING SEA in Sound; injured.

Sept. 3, 1872: Steamer CITY OF LAWRENCE, first Sound steamer with iron hull; New York to New London; collided in East River with schooner EMPIRE STATE; slightly damaged.

Sept. 17, 1872: Schooner V. M. BARKALEW, New York to Greenport, L.I.; cargo lumber; sunk at Hell Gate; raised.

Sept. 20, 1872: Schooner FLAGG, Greenwich, Conn., to New York; struck wreck of schooner DIADEM, Hell Gate; capsized; crew rescued by Wreck Master W. E. Brown of Astoria.

Sept. 21, 1872: Schooner JUSTICE collided with yacht EMILY at Hell Gate.

Sept. 29, 1872: Schooner ALIDA, New York to Newport; ashore on Hog's Back, Hell Gate; got off.

Oct., 1872: Brig VILLAGE BELLE, of Demerara, anchored off Battery, N.Y.; run into by steamer WESTERN METROPOLIS; damaged.

Oct. 15, 1872: Fall River liner PROVIDENCE collided with drilling machine at Hell Gate, badly injured.

Nov. 14, 1872: Schooner INDIANA, Tiverton, R.I., for Hunter's Point, N.Y.; cargo coal; collided at Hallett's Point, Rock, Hell Gate; filled.

Nov. 29, 1872: Schooner PEARL of St. George, Maine, for Brooklyn; collided in snowstorm with unknown vessel; sunk off City Island, Long Island Sound; 2 seamen lost; others saved by schooner EVERGREEN.

Dec. 9, 1872: Schooner ABBIE K. BENTLEY, damaged at Hell Gate.

Dec. 9, 1872: Ship SONORA of Boston, inbound from Manila; damaged in squall off Sandy Hook.

Dec. 11, 1872: Schooner ADELINE EL-WOOD, New York to Boston, in tow of tug JACOB SINEX, run into by CAMBRIDGE, bound Boston to N.Y.; damaged.

Dec. 20, 1872: Steamer ANDREW FLETCH-ER, burned to water's edge; Quarantine landing, Staten Island.

Jan. 3, 1873: British brig MIC MAC, bound Cardenas to New York, cargo molasses; ashore Rockaway Beach; total loss.

Jan. 25, 1873: Schooner CHARLES A. GRAINER, Port Johnson, N.J., for Providence; sunk at Hell Gate.

March 10, 1873: Pilot boat MARY E. FISK, run into by brig PRAIRIE ROSE; cut down almost to waterline.

April 2, 1873: Pilot boat JANE, ashore on West Bank, N.Y.; filled; all saved.

April 25, 1873: Schooner ALEXANDRIA, Philadelphia to New Haven; cargo coal; on rocks at Hell Gate; sunk; raised.

April 28, 1873: Sloop, name unknown, Southport to New York; collision off Ward's Island, N.Y.; Capt. Marshall killed; sloop cut to water's edge.

May 13, 1873: Steamer HOPE, run into by steamer AMERICUS at Hell Gate; HOPE cut in two; 4 drowned.

May 15, 1873: Lighter SEA, capsized Hell Gate; raised by Wreck Master Brown.

May 26, 1873: Schooner JACOB LORIL-LARD, Hoboken to Bridgeport; struck by steam tug in East River; sunk; raised.

June, 1873: British bark CURAÇAO of Windsor, Nova Scotia, from Curaçao to New York; sunk by collision, lower New York Bay; raised.

June 17, 1873: Schooner TABITHA & HAN-NAH, New York to Hartford; cargo salt; ashore Hell Gate; sunk.

June 18, 1873: Schooner S. H. CADY, of Providence, R.I.; bound Philadelphia for Boston; cargo coal; ashore Long Island; all saved; vessel lost.

June 23, 1873: Schooner CHALLENGE of Gardiner, Maine, bound for New York; cargo lumber; run into by unknown schooner, Hell Gate.

June 25, 1873: Schooner A. J. SIMONTON, Savannah to Boston; collided off Long Island with schooner RESTLESS; damaged.

July 8, 1873: Schooner PATRON, of Riverhead, L.I., bound for New York; ashore on Little Mill Rock, Hell Gate; stove; filled.

July 29, 1873: Belgian steamer C. F. FUNCH, White Cross Line, Antwerp to New York; run into by Italian bark BORZONE in East River; damaged.

July 30, 1873: British steamer EASBY; from Sydney, Cape Breton; cargo coal; struck on rock off 17th St., East River; sank.

July 31, 1873: Schooner SEA LARK, of Calais, Me.; loading pig iron at Hoboken; took fire; scuttled by crew.

August, 1873: Bark JOSIE MILDRED, of Boston, from Caibarien, Cuba; anchored lower Quarantine, N.Y.; run into by steamer GENERAL MEADE of New Orleans; cut through from waterline up.

Aug. 5, 1873: Australian brig OSCAR, loading oil, Hunter's Point, for Queenstown; set on fire by burning barge; burned.

Aug. 5, 1873: German bark TONI; loading oil, Hunter's Point; for Stettin; caught fire; badly damaged.

Aug. 14, 1873: Schooner BRITON COOK; cargo bricks; run into by steamer C. VANDERBILT, in North River off Hoboken; sunk.

Aug. 19, 1873: Schooner pilot boat DAVID MITCHELL, run into by pilot boat W. H. ASPINWALL; e.s.e. of Sandy Hook Lightship; damaged.

Aug. 23, 1873: Schooner ALPHA of Boston; from St. John, New Brunswick; cargo lumber; ashore on Gridiron, Hell Gate; filled; got off by Wreck Master Brown; beached at Astoria, L.I.

Sept. 7, 1873: Steam tug VIXEN, run into by SS GRANITE STATE, Hell Gate; cut in two; sunk; Capt. Perkins drowned, engineer badly hurt.

Oct. 11, 1873: German Bark A. J. POPE of Stettin, run into by SS SAN SALVADOR, bound for Savannah in North River; damaged.

Oct. 22, 1873: Schooner SHEPARD A. MOUNT, of Brookhaven, L.I., bound for Elizabethport, N.J.; run into off City Island by steamer ISAAC BELL, bound Virginia from New York; badly damaged.

Oct. 25, 1873: Schooner pilot boat ARIEL PATTERSON, struck sunken wreck s.e. of Highlands, N.J.; badly damaged.

Oct. 25, 1873: Schooner LEON, Derby, Conn., to New York; struck Gridiron, Hell Gate; sank.

Nov. 14, 1873: Sloop GOLD LEAF, New York to New Haven, run into by Houston St. ferry, East River; stove in port side; sunk on Ravenswood Reef, Astoria.

Nov. 18, 1873: Schooner F. V. TURNER, Honduras for New York; cargo coconuts; struck Stratford Reef, Conn.; drifted across Sound to Lloyd's Neck; capsized; steward and two crewmen drowned, Capt. Groves and wife saved.

Nov. 23, 1873: Steam tug RESCUE, burned Sandy Hook bar; crew saved.

Feb. 7, 1874: Steamer CITY OF LAWRENCE collided with lighter in East River; starboard side stove in; wrecked, 1907.

Feb. 13, 1874: Schooner RODNEY PARKER of New Haven, bound Baltimore to New York, Capt. Parker; cargo coal; ashore Romer Shoals; bilged; abandoned.

Feb. 18, 1874: Barge JOSEPH E. DOW from New Haven; cargo ice for Brooklyn; ashore on Gridiron, Hell Gate.

March 10, 1874: Schooner BENJAMIN REED of Booth Bay, Maine; from Mexico for New York; cargo mahogany; driven ashore West Bank, Sandy Hook.

March 11, 1874: Steamer AMOS C. BARSTOW, New York for Providence; ran ashore on rocks, Blackwell's Island; Coast Wrecking Co. and divers hauled her off.

March 19, 1874: Steam tug R. S. CARTER, run into by ferry BALTIC, East River; sunk.

March 20, 1874: Schooner ELIZABETH B.; cargo coal; Elizabethport to Providence; ashore Hallett's Point, Hell Gate; filled.

March 22, 1874: Brig A. R. STORER, Cardenas to New York, ran into German bark CHRISTEL, Bremen to New York; in North River; both damaged.

April 3, 1874: Schooner ABBY WELD, Belfast to New York; cargo ice; ashore on rocks, Hell Gate; damaged.

April 17, 1874: Ship PURITAN of Boston, bound Manila to New York; struck on Outer Middle, a sandbar s.s.e. from East Beacon at Sandy Hook; Pilot Isaac Campbell mistook buoys in gale, thick weather.

April 27, 1874: Bark ALFRED; cargo coal, bound Delaware breakwater for St. John, New Brunswick; dismasted in storm; rescued 13 days later by pilot boat GEORGE W. BLUNT.

May, 1874: Schooner C. J. ERICKSON, Providence to Hoboken; aground on Gridiron, Hell Gate; got off by Wreckmaster Brown.

May, 1874: Schooner LIZZIE, for New York in ballast; collided off Oyster Bay, L.I., with schooner SARAH W. BLAKE; LIZZIE sank.

May 17, 1874: British brig PRINCESS BEATRICE, at New York from Point-a-Pitre, Guadelupe; collided with Norwegian bark ODD, bound New York to Helsingfors; brig's bowsprit, etc., carried away.

May 24, 1874 Schooner ARROW, New Bedford to New York; foundered off Glen Cove, L.I.; two lost.

June 13, 1874: Lighter OHIO; cargo tobacco; collided in East River with ferry WINONA; sank.

June 18, 1874: Steamer CITY OF NORWICH collided, East River, with brig TORRID ZONE; returned for repairs.

June 24, 1874: Sloop CAROLINE of Greenport, L.I.; cargo coal; run into off Battery by steamer PROVIDENCE; stern knocked off; filled, sank.

July 12, 1874: Schooner ALLIE BICKMORE; cargo corn; ashore Long Branch, N.J.

July 13, 1874: Schooner CHINA; cargo oak timber; run into in East River; sunk off Williamsburg.

Aug. 9, 1874: Schooner V. M. BARKALEW, ashore Eaton's Neck, L.I.; went to pieces.

Aug. 22, 1874: Schooner MARTHA JANE, Port Jefferson to New York; Capt. Henry Mott; struck rock in Hell Gate; ashore, filled, 1 lost.

Sept. 3, 1874: Steamer RIVER BELLE of N.J., Southern R.R. & Steamboat Line; burned and sunk at Pier 8, North River; raised and floated.

Oct., 1874: Schooner R. M. CLARK, of Middletown, Conn.; collided with schooner TRISTRAM DICKENS off Eaton's Neck, L.I.; cargo corn; was sunk and raised.

Oct. 14, 1874: Schooner JOHN RANDOLPH run into by steamer NEW YORK, cut to water's edge; towed and grounded by steamer.

Oct. 24, 1874: British steamer ADRIATIC, New York for Liverpool; collided in New York Bay with steamer PARTHIA, also for Liverpool; damaged.

Oct. 29, 1874: Bark J. SARGENT; N.Y. pilot James M. Clark drowned from her.

Nov. 17, 1874: Steam tug LILLY, blew up and sank, Hell Gate.

Nov. 29, 1874: Schooner ANTHONY BURTON, Providence for Elizabethport; struck on Flood Rock at Hell Gate in squall; damaged; ashore Cow Bay.

Nov. 30, 1874: Schooner WEBSTER KELLY of Deer Isle; cargo coal; bound Philadelphia for Boston; ashore east of Jones Inlet; bilged, filled.

Dec., 1874: Schooner FANNY FERN, previously sunk at Hell Gate; raised, taken to Astoria; was towing in Hell Gate alongside tug D. S. STETSON, slewed onto Middle Ground, hole knocked in bottom. Tug cast off towlines and refused to assist; FANNY FERN sank.

Dec., 1874: Steam tug MAY QUEEN, towing schooner BRANDYWINE, on fire off Hart's Island; burned on Cow Bay Flats.

Dec. 11, 1874: Steam tug L. MARKLE, blew up and sank off Randall's Island.

1875: Pilot boat G. W. BLUNT, lost on Long Island shore about 30 miles from Sandy Hook lightship; crew saved.

1875: Pilot boat J. W. ELWELL, driven ashore in gale at Sea Girt, N.J.; wrecked.

Winter, 1875: Yawl, capsized in gale; N.J. pilot William Lucy drowned.

Jan. 4, 1875: Steam tug WILLIAM MORGAN, run into by unknown vessel, towed into Horse Shoe, Sandy Hook; foundered.

Jan. 16, 1875: Steam lighter SENTINEL, crushed by ice; sank at Peck Slip.

Jan. 18, 1875: British ship ROSLIN CASTLE, from Calcutta for New York; struck by field of ice in New York Harbor; carried to Brooklyn.

Feb., 1875: Steamer E. A. WOODWARD, ashore Faulkner's Island, Feb. 7–10; got off; fast in ice again Feb. 15, distress signals flying.

Feb., 1875: Schooner OAKWOOD; cargo coal; Perth Amboy to Narragansett; frozen in two weeks at Whitestone; CITY OF LOWELL, aiding her, cut into side; OAKWOOD sank.

Feb. 7, 1875; Schooner ELIZA PHARO; cargo coal; Port Johnson for Providence; forced ashore Bedloe's Island by ice; sunk.

Feb. 10, 1875: British ship AMBASSADOR, New York to London; driven ashore by ice near Bedloe's Island; some damage.

Feb. 11, 1875: Steamer ACAPULCO, anchored Gravesend Bay; damaged by ice.

Feb. 14, 1875: British steamer CORNWALL, Great Western Steamship Line; from Bristol, England, entering East River; ice caused her to be stranded off Castle William, Governor's Island; later hauled off.

Feb. 15, 1875: Lighter JACOB L., cargo cotton; afire at Peck Slip.

March, 1875: French brig RAPIDE, bound New York to London; anchored off Robbins Reef; cut into by ice; filled; later raised.

March 11, 1875: Barge GLADIATOR, bound for New York, sunk at Execution Rocks; crew saved by tug.

March 12, 1875: Schooner AMELIA of St. John, New Brunswick; cargo, melhado and honey from Matanzas for New York; ashore on Hog Island, near Rockaway; filled; went to pieces; crew saved.

March 15, 1875: Steam tug MARY, collided with Harlem passenger boat SHADY SIDE, New York; MARY sank; crew saved.

March 17, 1875: Brig AMELIA EMMA, for Puerto Rico, collided off Governor's Island with British brig GLADIATEUR; both damaged.

March 17, 1875: Schooner SUSAN WRIGHT, Matanzas for New York; sunk in collision off Squam, N.J.

March 30, 1875: Steamer THOMAS E. HULSE, damaged by ice, New York.

April 2, 1875: Schooner ACARA from St. John's, Puerto Rico; deckload of molasses washed overboard at New York.

April 14, 1875: German bark AEOLUS from Antwerp, caught by ice off Battery; collided with British brig ANNIE WHARTON; both damaged.

April 30, 1875: Swiftsure Line steamer VULCAN, Hartford for Philadelphia; cargo machinery; struck rock between Robbins Reef and Bedloe's Island; sank.

June 30, 1875: Steamer W. W. COIT, Long Island Rail Road service between eastern Long Island and New York; run into by Stonington Line steamer RHODE ISLAND in Hell Gate; damaged.

Nov. 30, 1875: Steamer MARIGOLD, burned, New York.

Feb. 27, 1876: Pilot boat CAPRICE, run down in Narrows by steamer NEW ORLEANS; sunk; had series of six disasters; lost 3 men at sea, Jan., 1881; junked, 1890.

March 20, 1876: MAGGIE M. WEAVER; cargo coal; Philadelphia to Saugus, Maine; total loss off Sandy Hook; 6 lost.

July 20, 1876: Yacht MOHAWK, from Brooklyn Yacht Club, capsized in bay near New York; lost; Capt. Oliver P. Rowland exonerated.

Oct. 7, 1876: German bark EUROPA; fire in hold at New York; 6 burned.

Nov. 20, 1876: Sloop W. E. HULSE, from Great River, L.I., to New York; capsized Jones Inlet Bar; 2 lost, 1 saved.

Dec. 12, 1876: Schooner KATE GRANT, lost east of Long Beach, L.I.

1877: Schooner JENNIE C. RUSS; cargo coal; sunk at Hell Gate.

Jan. 24, 1877: Schooner JAMES LAWRENCE; cargo resin; total loss one-fourth mile east of Rockaway Life Saving station.

March 17, 1877: Belgian Red Star Line steamer RUSLAND, Antwerp to New York; blown ashore south of Staten Island; plowed into sunken wreck of Dutch freighter ADONIS (sunk 1859 carrying grindstones); sank; ship total loss; all 204 saved by Life Savers and citizens ashore.

Nov. 27, 1877: Steamer C. H. NORTHAM, Capt. Aaron Hardy; burned to water's edge at East River pier; 3 lost. Later disasters: 1881, 1898, 1899.

Dec. 6, 1877: Schooner GENERAL CONNOR, bound Turks Island to Boston; cargo salt; stranded east end of Long Beach, L.I.; total loss; 8 rescued.

Jan. 28, 1878: Steamer WILLIAM E. CHENEY, boiler exploded in North River; 1 lost.

Jan. 31, 1878: Schooner NELLIE BLOOM-FIELD; cargo brick; New York to Greenwich, Conn.; wrecked off City Island, N.Y.; 2 lost.

Feb. 11, 1878. Brig CARRIE WINSLOW, Montevideo to New York; cargo wool and hides; wrecked New York Bay; 2 lost.

Feb. 23, 1878: Steam ferry CASTLETON, collided in New York Bay off 13th St., with steamer JAMES FISK, JR.; CASTLETON partial wreck; one lost on each vessel.

June 1, 1878: DR. J. P. WHITBECK, Brooklyn to New York, wrecked in East River; two lost.

Oct., 1878: German bark ERNA, foundered in storm 50 miles s.e. of Sandy Hook; crew rescued by pilot boat JESSE CARLL.

Oct. 17, 1878: Schooner GREENBURY WILLEY, of Seaford, Del.; cargo phosphate rock; total loss at Rockaway, L.I.

Nov. 5, 1878: Schooner GAZELLE of Patchogue; sank outer point of Jones Inlet bar, L.I.; 3 rescued.

Dec. 7, 1878: GENERAL SCOTT, total loss, Sandy Hook.

Dec. 10, 1878: Steamer EMILY B. SOUDER, foundered at sea out of New York; 9 passengers, 28 crew lost.

Dec. 15, 1878: Steamer UNION burned, New York; lives lost.

Dec. 19, 1878: Schooner ELIZA A. HOOPER of Camden, N.J., stranded south of Jones Inlet; 5 rescued.

1879: Pilot boat ABRAHAM LEGGETT, becalmed in lee of SS NAPLES; steamship rolled over, crushed her; all saved.

Jan. 14, 1879: GEORGE T. OLIPHANT, Wall St. Annex ferry; ran into Grand St.

ferry WARREN, off Broome St., OLIPHANT'S bow broken; sank; 70 passengers removed.

May 17, 1879: Pilot boat ISAAC WEBB; N.Y. pilot Fred Baudier drowned from her.

Nov. 20, 1879: Schooner L. V. OSTRUM of Patchogue; aground south of Freeport, L.I.; 3 saved.

Nov. 21, 1879: Schooner HECTOR, bound Philadelphia to Boston; cargo coal; wrecked Jones Inlet bar; 8 saved.

Jan. 17, 1880: Bark THOR of Oster-Risoer, Norway; bound St. Nazaire, France, to New York; stranded Hog Island Shoals off Rockaway, L.I.; 13 safe.

Feb. 2, 1880: Schooner MARY E. NASON of Provincetown, Mass.; bound Virginia to Boston; cargo oysters; stranded Jones Inlet bar; all saved.

Feb. 3, 1880: British brig GUISBOROUGH foundered on Crab Meadow, L.I.; 3 lost.

Feb. 3, 1880: Brig CASTALIA of Bath, Maine; bound Galveston, Texas, for New York; cargo cotton; ashore Highlands, N.J.; 11 saved.

Feb. 3, 1880: Schooner KATE NEWMAN, southbound, rammed by STEPHEN HARDING off Sandy Hook; all lives lost but one.

Feb. 3, 1880: Three-masted coastal trading schooner STEPHEN HARDING of Damariscotta, Maine, Capt. Stephen Harding; bound Florida to New York; cargo lumber; collision off Sandy Hook with KATE NEWMAN; ship and cargo lost; captain, wife, crew of 6 saved.

April 20, 1880: Pilot boat WILLIAM H. ASPINWALL, total loss, w. Fire Island.

June 11, 1880: Steamer NARRAGANSETT collided with SS STONINGTON at Cornfield Point; fire, sunk; 27 lost.

June 23, 1880: Steamship CITY OF NEW YORK of Alexandre Line; burned with cargo, East River; sunk.

June 28, 1880: Steamer SEAWANHAKA, New York to Glen Cove and Sea

Cliff; burned in East River; vessel total loss, 24 to 50 of some 300 passengers died.

Oct., 1880: Steamer P. W. SPRAGUE, burned, New York.

Oct. 8, 1880: Catboat BRIDE OF THE MINE, of Sayville, L.I.; went to pieces, Jones Inlet bar; crew of 3 saved.

Oct. 24, 1880: Bark W. A. HOLCOMB, of Bath, Maine; bound from Iloilo, Philippines, to New York; cargo sugar; total wreck at Long Beach, L.I.; all 17 saved.

Jan. 2, 1881: Schooner MARY E. TURNER, of Norfolk, Va.; bound Smithfield, Va. to New York; cargo pine wood; vessel total loss east of Rockaway Beach, L.I.; all saved.

Jan. 9, 1881: Schooner NEVINS FLOYD; cargo coal; Elizabethport, N.J., to Greenport, L.I.; total wreck at Great Neck, L.I.; crew saved.

Jan. 21, 1881: Ship SACHEM of Boston; broke moorings in East River, careened over, took fire, righted.

Jan. 22, 1881: G. BROTHERS, canal boat, in tow of six; five boats went down 4 miles off Sandy Hook; 2 men missing; off South Amboy, N.J.

Jan. 27, 1881: British bark BELLA MUDGE, Halifax to New York; arrived Feb. 12 badly damaged.

Feb., 1881: Schooner JOHN ROACH of Greenport, L.I., wrecked on South Shoal, Absecon, N.J.; went to pieces.

Feb. 8, 1881: Steamer HENRY L. FISH cut through by ice off Execution; rudder gone; towed to Bridgeport in sinking condition.

Feb. 10, 1881: California clipper ship DAVID CROCKETT, collided with brig STARLIGHT off Sandy Hook Lightship; badly damaged.

Feb. 17, 1881 British ship STAR OF INDIA, Capt. Bailey; New York for London; damaged by ice in East River; ashore near Bedloe's Island.

March 1, 1881: German bark AUGUSTE, bound Havana to Boston, cargo sugar; ashore on Romer Shoals, Lower Bay, New York.

March 1, 1881 Schooner CARRIE S. WEBB of New York, from Puerto Rico; cargo sugar and molasses; sank alongside AUGUSTE; wrecked; crew saved.

March 2, 1881: Steam tug H. G. LAPHAM, collided with steam tug AMOS BARSTOW, East River; LAPHAM cut in two, sank; crew rescued.

March 3–4, 1881 Italian bark AJACE, Antwerp to New York; wrecked Rockaway Shoals (Coney Island); 1 saved, 13 lost; vessel total loss.

March 4, 1881: Sloop J. R. BROWN, sunk at Barren Island, Rockaway Bay.

March 23, 1881: Norwegian bark ALBION, bound New York from Hull; damaged in hurricane.

April 19, 1881 British steamer TITANIA, at New York from Dundee; collided in Narrows with bark HYPATIA of St. John, New Brunswick.

Nov. 4, 1881: Schooner RICHARD MORRELL; cargo stone; wrecked between Greenwich, Conn., and New York; 1 lost.

Dec. 30, 1881: Schooner COMMANDER, Baltimore to New York; cargo coal; sank at Sandy Hook; 9 saved.

1882: ROTTERDAM, Holland–America Line, run down by Wilson liner LEPANTO; damaged; 2 lost.

Jan. 11, 1882: Barkentine J.H.M. of Milford, England; bound New York to Portugal; cargo petroleum; ashore Jones Beach; damaged; seven saved.

March 23, 1882: Sloop DISPATCH, of Cold Spring Harbor; cargo brick; foundered two miles south of Scotch Cap, Rye, N.Y.; 2 lost.

April 12, 1882: Schooner THOMAS W. H. WHITE, bound Virginia to New York; cargo wood; ashore n.n.e. Sandy Hook Station, N.J.; 4 saved.

April 17, 1882 Sloop, name unknown, pleasure trip; total loss off Sandy Hook, N.J.; 4 saved.

Sept. 18, 1882: Schooner COPIA; cargo

coal; total loss off Rockaway Point; 4 saved.

Oct. 15, 1882: Schooner ADA TAYLOR, of Jersey City, N.J.; pleasure trip; total loss, Sandy Hook Point; 4 saved.

Oct. 18, 1882: Sloop ADA RHAME, Capt. Pearsall; bound East Rockaway to New York; stranded west side Hog Island Inlet; got off.

Oct. 21, 1882: Sloop HANNAH ANN of Huntington Harbor, L.I.; cargo hickory wood; on rocks at Hell Gate; total loss.

Dec. 1, 1882: Brig JENNY PHINNEY of Portland, Maine; cargo sugar from Cardenas, Cuba, for New York; stranded Jones Inlet; 10 saved by breeches buoy.

Dec. 11, 1882: Steamer SALIER of Bremen, Germany; bound to New York; ashore Sandy Hook; all 341 on board saved.

Feb. 16, 1883: Steamer CITY OF RICH-MOND, Inman Line of Liverpool; bound to New York; ashore s.e. Sandy Hook station; 425 aboard, all saved.

Aug. 20, 1883: Steamer RIVERDALE, boiler exploded in Hudson; sank with loss of life.

Sept. 13, 1883: Steamer INDEPENDENTE, of Palermo, Italy; bound to New York; cargo sulphur and fruit; stranded e. Short Beach, L.I.; all saved.

Dec. 3, 1883: Pilot boat COLUMBIA, run over by steamer ALASKA; all lost (4 pilots, 4 sailors, and cook).

Dec. 13, 1883: Ferry GARDEN CITY; on fire as left berth at James Slip for Long Island City; 30 passengers and ferry hands saved; 4 horses burned; rebuilt.

1884: Pilot boat WASHINGTON, run down off Sandy Hook by SS ROMA.

Jan. 1, 1884: Schooner JULIA, sunk Hog Island Shoal; 2 saved.

Jan. 19, 1884: MARY MATHESON, total loss at Sandy Hook.

March 23, 1884: Schooner HENRIETTA

COLLYER, New York to Bridgeport; cargo iron; capsized near Sands Point, L.I.; damaged; 1 life lost.

April 19, 1884: Guion Liner OREGON (became Cunard, July 1884); Liverpool to New York; ashore two miles n.e. of Sandy Hook Station; 713 saved.

May, 1884: Fall River liner PILGRIM, hit uncharted rock, Blackwell's (now Welfare) Island; gash in bottom; double-hulled, so made dock unaided.

July 31, 1884: Schooner WASHINGTON, sunk with stone ballast, three miles e.s.e. from Sandy Hook.

Nov. 14, 1884: Schooner ALEXANDER HARDING of Philadelphia, bound Baltimore to Portsmouth, N.H.; cargo coal; sunk Hog Island Inlet Shoals; total loss; 7 men saved.

Nov. 19, 1884: GUADELOUPE, Mallory Line, New York to Galveston; wrecked on Barnegat Shoals, N.J.; no lives lost.

1885: Pilot boat MARY E. FISH, run down by schooner FRANK HARRINGTON 40 miles off Barnegat; all saved.

1885: Pilot boat MARY AND CATHERINE, sunk off Absecon, N.J., by SS HAVERTON; all saved.

Jan. 24, 1885: People's Line side-wheel steamer ST. JOHN, night boat to Albany; destroyed by fire at winter quarters, Canal Street.

Sept. 9, 1886: Steamship EMPIRE STATE, aground on Sandy Hook; 560 passengers; little damage.

Nov., 1886: Schooner LONG ISLAND; cargo coal; found drifting off Sea Cliff, L.I., sails set, no one aboard; signs of murder; Capt. Thomas D. Carpenter, at wheel previous day, disappeared; deck hand arrested.

1887: Pilot boat J. F. LOUBAT sunk by steamer SANTIAGO; raised.

Jan. 3–4, 1887: Bark LOTUS, of Windsor, Nova Scotia, from Forney, England, to New York; cargo china clay; ashore on outer bar between Long Beach, L.I., and Point Lookout; total wreck; crew of 10 saved.

Jan. 24, 1887: Pilot boat FRANCIS A. PER-KINS, struck wreck on Barnegat Shoals, N.Y.; pilot Walter A. Reddin and 1 seaman lost.

March 19, 1887: Schooner A. W. THOMP-SON, collided near Willett's Point; 1 man lost, vessel total loss.

April 10, 1887: Schooner R. S. LINDSAY, sank s.w. of Rockaway Life Saving station.

July 10, 1887: Sloop MYSTERY, capsized in Jamaica Bay; 24 drowned.

Aug., 1887: Pilot boat HOPE, lost 3 in storm; history of disaster (1871, 1876, 1887, 1888, 1890); total loss off Sandy Hook.

Oct., 1887: Tug AMERICAN EAGLE, collided with steamer GEORGE W. BEALE, New York Harbor; 1 killed on BEALE; AMERICAN EAGLE damaged.

Dec. 24, 1887: Schooner GEORGE TEMPLE of Mystic, Conn., ashore on Romer Shoals; 8 saved.

1888: Schooner LAMARTINE of Rocky Point, L.I., lost in East Bay, New York.

March 11–12, 1888: Pilot boat CALDWELL H. COLT, damaged in blizzard.

March 11–12, 1888: Pilot boat CENTEN-NIAL, ashore in Horseshoe, Sandy Hook, wedged in ice; lost.

March 11–12, 1888: Pilot boat CHARLES H. MARSHALL, thrown on beam ends, driven 100 miles before storm but came in safely.

March 11–12, 1888: Yacht CYTHERA, never seen again after blizzard.

March 11–12, 1888: Pilot boat EDMUND BLUNT, lost at Horseshoe, Sandy Hook.

March 11–12, 1888: Pilot boat EDMUND DRIGGS, ashore at Bay Ridge, hole in bottom; ice; lost.

March 11–12, 1888: Pilot boat EDWARD COOPER, wedged in ice at Horseshoe, Sandy Hook.

March 11–12, 1888: Pilot boat EDWARD F. WILLIAMS, sunk inside Horseshoe, Sandy Hook; men saved.

March 11–12, 1888: Pilot boat ENCHAN-TRESS, went down off Barnegat with all hands (5 pilots, 3 seamen, and cook).

March 11–12, 1888: Pilot boat EZRA NYE, hammered to pieces at Manhattan Beach railroad pier; men escaped.

March 11–12, 1888: Tugboat GOVERNOR, sunk between Rockaway Point and Swash Channel.

March 11–12, 1888: Schooner MARY HEITMAN, last seen going through Narrows.

March 11–12, 1888: Pilot boat PHANTOM; lost in storm with 2 pilots, boat-keeper, 4 seamen, and cook.

March 11–12, 1888: Barge, name un-known, wrecked at East Neck; 1 lost.

March 11–12, 1888: Pilot boat W. W. STORY wrecked on Horseshoe, Sandy Hook.

March 11–12, 1888: Pilot boat WILLIAM H. STARBUCK, collided with fruit ves-sel from Mediterranean, the JAPA-NESE; damaged; 4 men lost.

March 28, 1888: North German Lloyd steamer SAALE, bound from New York to Bremen; ashore Swash Chan-nel, a mile and a half from Sandy Hook Station; all saved.

Aug. 11, 1888: Steamer BAY RIDGE of Glen Cove, L.I.; New York to Sea Cliff, Roslyn, Glen Cove, etc.; burned at dock; total loss; 1 died.

Nov. 10, 1888: Freight steamer IBERIA, in-bound from Persian Gulf, collided with outbound Cunard liner UMBRIA at Jones Inlet; slight damage to UMBRIA; IBERIA sank (wreck known as good fishing ground).

March, 1889: Steam freighter WINGATE; cargo rags and bones; broken crank shaft, drifting in gale; picked up, towed to New York by Bermuda steamer ORINOCO.

March 3, 1889: Ferry KILL VAN KULL; burned, Elizabethport, N.J.

March 18, 1889: Pilot boat CHARLOTTE WEBB, run down and sunk e.s.e. of Sandy Hook Lightship by French

Line steamer LaNormandie; Pilot Albert C. Malcomb and boatkeeper lost.

April 15, 1889: Pilot boat BATEMAN; N.Y. Pilot John Handran lost.

July 12, 1889: Steamer THOMAS S. BRENNAN, rammed and sunk rowboat off Randall's Island; 1 lost.

Sept. 16, 1889: Steamer VERTUMMIS of London, from Jamaica, West Indies, to New York; cargo fruit; wrecked Long Beach, L.I.; all aboard saved.

Oct. 12, 1889: Pilot boat JESSE CARLL, stranded in gale on outer bar abreast of Zach's Inlet, L.I.; 9 saved.

Oct. 13, 1889: Schooner SABAO of Machias, Maine; cargo logwood; from Delaware Breakwater to Providence, R.I.; sank south of Freeport, L.I.; vessel almost total loss; crew of 6 saved.

Nov. 19, 1889: Bark BEECHDALE of Liverpool, bound Havana to New York; ashore e. of Point Lookout station, L.I.; partly wrecked; crew saved.

Dec. 26, 1889: Schooner DAVID CROWELL, bound New York in ballast; capsized, Hell Gate.

1890's: Name unknown; sunken wreck two and a half miles n.e. from Ambrose Channel Lightship; found 1893 by VESUVIUS.

Jan. 22, 1890: Bark EDWARD CUSHING; N.Y. Pilot John J. Canvin of CHARLES H. MARSHALL washed overboard; New York.

Feb. 19, 1890: Steamer JOHN A. HADGEMAN, burned, New York.

April 3, 1890: French steamer PANAMA, bound Bordeaux to New York; general cargo; ashore Jones Inlet; 30 saved.

April 12, 1890: KATE MARQUISE, total loss off Highlands, N.J.

April 14, 1890: Steamer ANN JANE LAUGHLIN of New York; on fire, adrift, Sandy Hook Bay; total loss; 6 saved.

May 25, 1890: Yacht YEADA, wrecked, New York Bay.

Aug. 20, 1890: Steamer DANIA, Hamburg–American Line; Hamburg to New York; general cargo; Jones Inlet Bar; vessel got off by wreckers; all 437 on board saved.

Oct. 24, 1890: Yacht CATARINA, bound Newport to New York, on rocks at Glen Cove; 33 safe, $100,000 damage.

Oct. 6, 1890: Schooner SCOTIA of New London; total loss off Sandy Hook; 10 saved.

Oct. 28, 1890: Brig EUGENIE, bound Brazil to New York; cargo sugar; total loss, Jones Inlet Bar; 7 saved.

1891: Schooner EXPEDITE, wrecked Sands Point, L.I.

Feb. 18, 1891: Bark MASCOTTA, wrecked in collision, New York Harbor.

Feb. 20, 1891: Steamer JAMES RUMSEY, sunk, New York.

March 5, 1891: CITY OF RICHMOND, of N.Y. & Hartford Steamship Co., burned at New York wharf; remains rebuilt, renamed WILLIAM C. EGERTON; later renamed GLEN ISLAND.

March 13, 1891: Italian Bark UMBERTO I, bound Argentina to New York; cargo hides and wool; on Romer Shoals; 12 saved, $112,000 loss.

March 24, 1891: Brig JOSEPH BANNIGAN, ashore near Long Beach Life Saving station; 1 life lost.

Aug., 1891: Double-decked passenger barge REPUBLIC; upper deck collapsed in storm; 12 killed, 40 injured. Rebuilt, sailed two years later as the COLUMBIA; New York to Lloyd's Neck, Cold Spring Harbor.

Oct. 7, 1891: Schooner ETNA of Portland, Maine; bound New Brunswick to Chester, Pa., with lath; total loss, Sandy Hook; 7 saved.

Oct. 11, 1891: Sloop THREE SISTERS of New York; wrecked s.e. Sandy Hook Station; 7 saved.

Nov. 24, 1891 Schooner ADELE TRUDELL, from Cape May, N.J., to New York with sand; total loss, Romer Shoals; 8 saved.

1892: Pilot boat EBEN D. JORDAN, sunk off Barnegat, N.J., by SS SAGINAW, in fog.

Jan. 24, 1892: Fireboat NEW YORKER collided with fireboat ZOPHAR MILLS; damaged.

Feb. 27, 1892: Pilot James Smith drowned while boarding steamer VAN DYK from pilot boat EDWARD COOPER.

Sept. 28, 1892: Steamer ROSEDALE, New York to Bridgeport, Conn. Collision; 1 lost.

Dec. 2, 1892: Bark PRINCE FREDERICK of Christiania, Norway; bound New York to Antwerp; cargo petroleum; ashore False Hook, Sandy Hook station; 19 saved.

Dec. 25, 1892: Pilot boat EDWARD COOPER, wrecked and sunk at sea; crew saved by Wilson Line freighter MARENGO.

1893: Pilot boat JAMES GORDON BENNETT, forced ashore off Barnegat by drift ice; all hands taken off by breeches buoy.

1893: Wooden double-ended side-wheeler SHACKAMAXON, ferry Ellis Island from Whitehall St., New York; damaged in three collisions.

Feb. 6, 1893: Schooner GLENOLA of Windsor, Nova Scotia; bound Haiti to New York; sunk, Jones Inlet Bar; 6 saved.

Feb. 19, 1893: Schooner JAMES BUTLER, Perth Amboy to Sandy Hook; cargo coal; sank, Sandy Hook; 4 saved.

Aug. 29, 1893: Schooner C. HENRY KIRK, bound New York to Virginia; sunk Point Lookout, near Long Beach, L.I.; total loss; 7 saved.

Aug. 29, 1893: American bark MARTHA P. TUCKER, from Tampa, Fla., to Carteret, N.J.; cargo phosphate rock; driven ashore south of Freeport, L.I.; 11 saved by breeches buoy; 1 lost.

Sept. 17, 1893: Schooner DAVID CARLL, total loss off Point Lookout, L.I.; 7 saved.

Nov. 16, 1893: Schooner RICHARD B. CHUTE of New London, Conn., bound Philadelphia to Plymouth, Mass.;

cargo coal; sunk Short Beach, L.I.; total loss; 6 saved.

Feb. 14, 1894: Steamer OLIVER A. ARNOLD, burned, New York.

Spring, 1894: Steamer I. N. SEYMOUR, Connecticut to Glen Cove, L.I.; cargo lumber; passengers; many lost.

March 7, 1894: Sloop MARY F. DARRUA, drifted into Jamaica Bay, spars cleared away, sails dragging; master in cabin, dead.

July 26, 1894: Sloop MABEL EMMA, fishing trip, capsized in squall, East Rockaway Inlet; total wreck; Life Saving station keeper, 1 volunteer, rescued entire 17 with yawl.

Oct. 9, 1894: Steamer CITY OF ALBANY, burned, New York.

Nov. 9, 1894: Four-masted schooner MASSASOIT, bound Newport News, Va., to Fall River, Mass.; cargo coal; wrecked Long Beach, L.I.; 11 saved.

Nov. 22, 1894: Schooner F. GREENVILLE RUSSELL, bound Portland to Philadelphia; cargo stone; total loss, Romer Shoals; 6 saved.

Dec. 4, 1894: Schooner CLARA E. SIMPSON, Maine to New York; granite paving blocks; collision Long Island Sound; 3 lost, 3 saved.

Dec. 26, 1894: Sloop E. A. WILLIS, Port Eaton, N.Y., to Jersey City; cargo gravel; lost in Long Island Sound off Dosoris Creek, L.I., with crew of three.

Jan. 14, 1895: Schooner-rigged coal barge SETH LOW, wrecked near Short Beach, L.I.; three rescued; Capt. Oliver Dottridge's son and cook lost.

Feb. 5, 1895: Pilot boat GEORGE H. WARREN, lost at sea, with 6 pilots and crew of 5.

March 7, 1895: North German Lloyd steamer HAVEL, bound Bremen to New York; ashore n.e. Sandy Hook; 680 passengers safe.

March 12, 1895: Tug F. W. VOSBURGH of New York, on Romer Shoals; all 7 saved.

Aug. 5, 1895: Steam canal boat JOHN LANG, Bridgeport, Conn., to New York; wrecked Long Island Sound; 1 lost.

Sept. 18, 1895: Steamer GENERAL A. E. BURNSIDE, burned, New York.

Nov. 11, 1895: Steamer F. A. SHARP, aiding IRRAWADDY wrecked off Asbury Park, N.J.; aground on Sandy Hook; 6 saved.

Nov. 23, 1895: Schooner CORNELIA M. KINGSLAND of Greenport, L.I., bound from Fire Island to New York with fish; total loss, Romer Shoals; 9 saved.

Jan. 25, 1896: ST. PAUL, of American Line Steamship Co., bound from Southampton, England, for New York; ashore near Brighton Hotel, Long Branch, N.J.; damaged; passengers taken off, crew remained on board; refloated.

Sept. 5, 1896: SAXON, total loss at Sandy Hook.

1897: Side-wheel steamer CATSKILL, going north, rammed and sunk by steamer ST. JOHNS coming down North River; several lives lost.

1897: Wooden steamer JAMES B. SCHUYLER, burned at East River dock, New York.

Jan. 19, 1897: British steamship ALVENA, New York to Haiti, run down and cut through by British freighter at entrance Gedney Channel, off Sandy Hook; beached; passengers and crew rescued by pilot boat WALTER ADAMS.

May 25, 1897: Steam tug GEORGE L. GARLICK, owned 1883 by Michael Moran's agency; wrecked Coney Island; 10 saved.

July 15, 1897: Sloop FAWN, from Virginia; foundered off Sandy Hook Lightship; crew of 3 rescued by pilot boat ALEXANDER M. LAWRENCE.

Aug. 15, 1897: Scow FRANKLIN and others, bound Barren Island, N.Y., to New York City; FRANKLIN total wreck, Rockaway Inlet; 3 saved.

Oct. 26, 1897: Wooden side-wheeler ferry KINGS COUNTY, ran from James Slip and East 34th St. to Long Island Rail Road terminal, then at Long Island City; burned at Hunter's Point.

Nov., 1897: Steamboat JOHN E. MOORE, Capt. Morrell, 150 on fishing excursion; aground Romer Shoal; filled; passengers saved by pilot boat WALTER ADAMS.

1898: U.S. armored cruiser COLUMBIA sank British freighter FOSCOLIA off Fire Island; held liable; masked lights.

1898: Schooner CYNTHIA JANE, Capt. Peter Muller, wrecked Gowanus Creek.

1898: Sloop FIRE ISLAND, sunk in Gowanus Creek; total loss.

1898: British freighter FOSCOLIA, sunk by U.S. cruiser COLUMBIA, off Fire Island.

1898: Schooner FRANK BEATTIE, lost, Astoria Cove, L.I.

1898: Schooner J. G. PARSON, lost at Crab Meadow, L.I.

1899: EAGLE WING, total loss at Sandy Hook.

Feb., 1899: Steamer RED JACKET, Cardiff, Wales, for New York; ashore near Long Beach, L.I.; refloated.

Feb. 8, 1899: Schooner ROBERT A. SNOW, total wreck at Rockaway Inlet; cargo fertilizer.

Feb. 13, 1899: Brooklyn fireboat DAVID A. BOODY, sank in East River returning from a fire; raised; retired Dec. 17, 1914.

June 13, 1899: Old Dominion liner HAMILTON, outward bound, collided with incoming Ward liner MACEDONIA, cargo sugar; off Seabright, N.J.; both vessels sank; no lives lost.

Oct. 14, 1899: Bridgeport–New York propeller steamer NUTMEG STATE, burned near Execution Rock, Long Island Sound; vessel total loss; 13 lost; 30 rescued.

Dec. 1899: Fall River liner PLYMOUTH, grounded Riker's Island, East River; damaged; 600 passengers taken off.

April 30, 1900: Schooners BOYLE, EVELYN, and KENYON, wrecked west of Rockaway Point, L.I.

June 30, 1900: North German Lloyd liner BREMEN, destroyed by fire, Hoboken; 74 lives lost.

June 30, 1900: North German Lloyd liner KAISER WILHELM DER GROSSE, about to sail burned, Hoboken; visitors saved.

June 30, 1900: North German Lloyd liner MAIN, Hoboken, destroyed by fire, 135 lives lost.

June 30, 1900: North German Lloyd liner SAALE, about to sail for Bremen, by fire at Hoboken; estimated 150 lives lost.

July, 1900: Coal schooner CHARLES L. DAVENPORT, Philadelphia for Bangor, Maine; spontaneous combustion fire; off Sandy Hook; saved.

Aug. 11, 1900: Bark ABIEL ABBOTT, of New York; cargo sugar; bound Puerto Rico to New York; wrecked Jones Inlet; 11 saved.

Sept. 3, 1900: Steamer MOSQUITO, Point Lookout; 110 saved.

Oct. 30, 1900: Schooner VALENTINE KOON of Patchogue; ashore Jones Inlet; 3 saved.

Nov. 9, 1900: Schooner GROVER CLEVELAND of Port Jefferson, L.I.; cargo lumber; sunk Sandy Hook; 4 saved.

Nov. 14, 1900: Schooner MARGARETTA, sunk off Riker's Island.

1901: Schooner BALTIMORE, of Port Jefferson, L.I.; collided in New York Harbor; wrecked; taken to Gowanus.

Jan., 1901: Sound steamer IDLEWILD, New York–Glen Cove route; burned in winter quarters, Brooklyn; 8 lost; history of disasters.

March 26, 1901: Norwegian steamer GWENT, bound Cuba to New York; cargo fruit; passengers; stranded Long Beach, L.I.; all saved.

May, 1901: Three-masted schooner H. R. KEENE, Cuba to New York; went to pieces on bar, Long Beach, L.I.; cargo cedar; 7 saved.

May 2, 1902: Sloop MARY SEAMAN, total loss, Jones Inlet Bar, L.I.; cargo coal.

May 28, 1901: Sloop BAY QUEEN, of Patchogue, L.I.; cargo oysters; total loss, Long Beach, L.I.; 2 saved.

June 14, 1901: U.S. Army transport INGALLS, toppled over in dry dock, Erie Basin, Brooklyn; 185 on board; 1 killed, 32 badly injured; later raised and floated.

June 14, 1901: New York–Staten Island ferry NORTHFIELD, rammed, sunk, New York Harbor by ferry MAUNCH CHUNK; 5 of 995 passengers killed.

July 18, 1901: Ship COMMODORE T. H. ALLEN, on fire, drifted ashore, abandoned by crew; pilot boat NEW YORK put men on board, pulled her off; fire extinguished next day.

July 19, 1901: Sloop yacht VENITZIA, foundered near Captain's Island, Long Island Sound; 5 lost.

Aug. 17, 1901: Pilot boat JAMES GORDON BENNETT, cut in two by Hamburg–American liner ALENE, off Scotland Lightship; 3 pilots and one steward lost; 2 pilots saved.

Oct. 22, 1901: Steamer ELIZABETH, burned, New York.

Jan. 31, 1902: Steamer CAVOUR, Lamport & Holt Line, of Liverpool; Buenos Aires to New York; cargo coffee, hides, tallow, wool; grounded Long Beach, L.I. in snowstorm; all saved.

Feb. 2, 1902: Tugs E. S. ATWOOD and JOHN E. BERWIND, foundered 11 miles e. of Sandy Hook Lightship, taking provisions to CAVOUR; crew of 7 on each vessel saved by German steamer BARCELONA.

Feb. 3, 1902: Full-rigged American merchant ship L. SCHEPP, Hong Kong to New York; cargo spices, tea, etc.; on shoals at Point Lookout, Long Beach, L.I.; damaged; crew saved.

March 1, 1902: British steamer, freighter ACARA, inbound from China; cargo tea; on Short Beach; total loss; crew of 61 saved.

March 21, 1902: Barkentine PERSIA, struck Long Beach, L.I.

April 26, 1902: Three-masted schooner CORNELIA SOULE, Maine to Philadelphia; cargo granite; sank off Rockaway Point, L. I.; all 6 crewmen rescued; fishermen call it "Granite Wreck."

Aug. 26, 1902: Steamer DUCHESS, burned, New York.

1903: Schooner EDWIN COLLYER; cargo sand; sunk, Gravesend Bay.

June 2, 1903: Hamburg–American liner DEUTSCHLAND, bound New York to Hamburg; carrying gold for Paris and Berlin markets; stranded at Gedney Channel; hauled off by tug I. J. MERRITT.

Jan. 23, 1904: British schooner ALEXA, total loss, Rockaway Point, L.I.

Jan. 31, 1904: British steel crew steamship BOSTON CITY, of Bristol City Line, collided in Lower Bay, New York, with COLORADO of Wilson Line, bound Hull to New York. BOSTON CITY damaged; no lives lost.

June 15, 1904: Excursion steamer GENERAL SLOCUM, about 1,500 passengers, burned at Hell Gate, East River; 1,021 lost.

Nov., 1904: Ferry COLUMBIA, rammed and sunk in East River by CITY OF LOWELL.

Nov. 20, 1904: British Prince Line ship SICILIAN PRINCE, grounded Long Beach, L.I.; damaged.

Dec. 25, 1904: British tramp steamship DRUMELZIER, outward bound for Le Havre and Dunkirk, grounded near Jones Beach; cargo steel and copper; total loss; crew saved by tugs CATHERINE MORAN and I. J. MERRITT.

1905: Sloop ANNIE E. LEETE, "died at Flushing under the ministry of Captain Stummey."

1905: Schooner GLIDE of Staten Island; lost at Rockaway, L.I.

Aug., 1905: Schooner CAROLINE AUGUSTA of Baldwin, L.I.; fishing; ashore at Neponsit, Rockaway Beach, L.I.

Oct. 2, 1905: Steamer NANTASKET, owned by Long Island Rail Road; New York–Glen Cove route; struck schooners LAWRENCE HAYNES and HARRY PRESCOTT; damaged HAYNES, which sank; steamer also damaged.

Dec., 1905: Coastwise steamer, Savannah Line's CITY OF ATLANTA, outward bound; crashed into submerged scow in Swash Channel; damaged; carried cavalry for Fort Oglethorpe.

Dec., 1905: Schooner, name unknown, sunk off Bayville, L.I.; cargo lath.

Dec., 1905: Starin Line steamer GLEN ISLAND, burned in Long Island Sound off Dosoris (Glen Cove); wreck drifted ashore; 10 burned to death.

Dec. 27, 1905: Schooner BESSIE WHITING, struck two barges in tow of tug JOHN FLEMING; sank them in Swash Channel.

Dec. 27, 1905: Clyde Line steamer COMANCHE, inbound from Jacksonville, Fla., struck submerged wreck, Swash Channel; damaged.

About 1906: Schooner LEJOK, of Ellsworth, Maine, run down by four-master off Highland Light, N.J.; abandoned by crew.

1906: Schooner SHAMROCK, sunk at entrance to Oyster Bay, L.I.

Feb., 1906: YAWL from pilot boat NEW YORK caught under stern of pilot boat; smashed; 2 saved.

Nov. 13, 1906: M. P. GRACE; cargo coal; sunk off Long Island shore at 40–50.8 n.; 72–26.8 w.

Dec., 1906: Italian liner LIGURIA, Genoa, Naples, to New York; incoming; collided in New York Bay with PECONIC, outward bound.

Dec. 15, 1906: Pilot boat HERMIT, cut in two and sunk by Ward Line steamship MONTEREY off Sandy Hook Lightship; all saved, but N.J. pilot Frank Neilson later died of injuries.

1907: EDMUND PHINNEY, total loss, Sandy Hook.

July 15, 1907: Montauk Steamboat Company's SHINNECOCK, hit sunken reef at Hart's Island, end of Long Island Sound; passengers taken off.

Dec. 2, 1907: Freight steamer BUNKER HILL, Boston to New York; collided with New Haven Rail Road tug TRANSFER NO. 3 in East River; both vessels sank; 1 lost on each.

Dec. 10, 1907: East River ferry BALTIC, rammed by Fall River liner PROVIDENCE in fog; 1 drowned, ferry damaged.

Dec. 14, 1907: Yawl, from pilot boat NEW YORK, capsized; pilot Thomas Shields lost.

1908: Schooner C. H. MALLISON, ashore, lost, Hempstead, L.I.

1908: "HOWARD" or "SCOW" wreck, steam-powered lighter; cargo copper ore; Jones Inlet; good fishing spot.

Feb. 13, 1908: British steamship RODA, inbound from Spain to New York; cargo copper ore; became total loss off Jones Beach; heroic rescue of crew.

April 16, 1908: Ward Line steamship MONTEREY, for Havana and Mexico, rammed into Danish ship UNITED STATES, in main New York ship channel; MONTEREY damaged; UNITED STATES holed, flooded, run aground to prevent sinking.

April 30, 1908: Four-masted square-rigger German ship PETER RICKMERS; cargo kerosene; ashore Short Beach (called "Oil Wreck"); total loss; crew rescued.

Nov., 1908: Metropolitan Line steamer H. M. WHITNEY, sunk, Sunken Meadow; raised later.

Nov. 22, 1908: United Fruit Co. steamship ADMIRAL DEWEY, inbound from Jamaica, West Indies; smashed into steamer MOUNT DESERT off Coney Island; mad rush for safety.

Nov. 26, 1908: Panama Railroad Co. steamer FINANCE, outward bound for Colón, Panama; collided off Sandy Hook with White Star freighter

GEORGIC; FINANCE sank; 3 passengers, 1 officer lost. GEORGIC unhurt.

Dec. 18, 1908: Steamship DAGHESTAN, collided with SS CATALONE, s.e. of Gedney Channel buoys; CATALONE sank; no lives lost.

Feb. 22, 1909: URBANUS DARK, sank, Sandy Hook.

April 7, 1909: Munson Line freighter CUBANA; cargo sugar from Matanzas; rammed by inbound Ward liner HAVANA, at anchor at Quarantine, Staten Island; hole stove in side; HAVANA unhurt.

May 27, 1909: North German Lloyd steamship PRINZESS ALICE, outbound for Bremen, in fog with 1,720 on board, grounded on sand ledge off Fort Wadsworth, S.I.; refloated.

Aug. 17, 1909: Schooner ARLINGTON, of Boston, outbound from New York; carrying pea coal; wrecked off Long Beach, L.I.; 8 saved, 1 drowned.

1910: FRANKLIN D. NELSON, wrecked Sandy Hook.

May, 1910: Tug JOHN T. PRATT, burned to water's edge off Glen Cove, L.I., captain and crew of 6 escaped.

Dec. 30, 1910: Four-masted schooner MARTHA E. WALLACE, ashore off Lookout Shoals, L.I.; captain and crew of 8 rescued by Life Savers.

March 7, 1911: Steam lighter HOWARD, wrecked near Jones Beach, L.I., taking copper out of hold of RODA; snowstorm; 9 saved.

May 13, 1912: Pilot boat AMBROSE SNOW, rammed and sunk by Clyde Line SS DELAWARE, in Lower Bay; all saved.

May 29, 1912: French Line HUDSON, inbound from Bordeaux with 83 passengers; rammed by freighter BERWIND, of New York–Puerto Rico Line, in New York Harbor; HUDSON's bow stove in, began to sink, panic.

Dec. 19, 1912: JOHN H. MAY, total loss, Sandy Hook.

March 13, 1913: Steamer SS WYCKOFF, collided with HEROINE, New York; 2 lost.

Oct. 13, 1913: Schooner CHARLES ATKINSON, foundered Matinecock Point, L.I.; 3 saved.

Oct. 13, 1913: Steam screw ROBERT RODGERS, burned off New York; 6 saved.

Oct. 21, 1913: Gas screw MARTHA J., struck by lightning in Jamaica Bay; burned; 3 saved.

November, 1913: Fall River liner PLYMOUTH struck rock, Hell Gate; gashed bottom.

Nov. 9, 1913: Schooner A. J. MILLER, foundered, Long Island Sound; 4 saved.

Nov. 21, 1913: Steam screw BUFFALO, burned off Staten Island; 3 saved.

Jan. 12, 1914: Five-masted coal schooner FULLER PALMER, foundered in storm off Highland Light, N.J.

Jan. 24, 1914: Five-masted schooner GRACE A. MARTIN; cargo coal; foundered in storm off Highland Light, N.J.

Jan. 24, 1914: Steam screw WILLIAM DINSDALE, in collision with SS CONCHO, New York Harbor; 2 lost, 1 saved.

Feb. 16, 1914: LIZZIE HARVEY, sank, Gowanus Canal.

March 16, 1914: Ferry ITHACA, collided with N.J. Central car float; 3 lost.

July 10, 1914: Pilot boat NEW JERSEY, sunk in collision with SS MANCHONEAL, fruit ship, off Ambrose Lightship; never raised.

About 1915: Ferry, wrecked 100 yards west of Execution Light.

June 19, 1915: Ferry NASSAU, hit pier; 1 killed, 3 hurt.

July 23, 1915: British steamer CRAGSIDE; cargo sugar; bound from Kingston, Jamaica, to Gibraltar, possibly Dardanelles; loading at West 23rd St. pier; fire; suspect bomb.

Sept. 28, 1915: Steamer ISABEL, New York to South Norwalk, Conn.; struck obstruction and sank off Shippan Point.

Oct. 6, 1915: Schooner BROWNSTONE, foundered in Long Island Sound; Capt. Pease and wife dead.

Dec. 8, 1915: Cattle barge EL PASO, sank off Battery after collision with SS NORTH STAR: 100 cattle drowned on EL PASO.

Dec. 17, 1915: Barge VIRGINIA, carrying horses for French government; sank in Hudson River; probable sabotage.

March 1, 1916: FIRE ISLAND LIGHTSHIP, struck by SS EASTERN CITY, outbound for St. Nazaire, France; damage slight; EASTERN CITY reported sunk.

May 8, 1916: FIRE ISLAND LIGHTSHIP, reported sinking after collision with SS PHILADELPHIAN; crew removed.

Nov. 16, 1916: J. R. BODWELL, total loss, Sandy Hook.

Dec. 17, 1916: Brazilian bark NETHTIS, lost in storm off N.J. coast; 12 abroad.

1917: DOVERFJELD (originally RHODE ISLAND), six-masted schooner; sank in New York Harbor; raised, broken up.

1917: "EAST WRECK," three coal barges in triangle; fishing spot.

1917: Wooden City of Brooklyn fireboat SETH LOW, sank at dock.

April 13, 1917: Ferry EVELYN, wrecked in explosion.

July 7, 1917: Tug JOHN E. MCALLISTER, sunk in East River.

July 13, 1917: Sloop EDNA, lost 4 miles west of Long Beach, L.I.

July 14, 1917: Standard Oil launch DELIVERY, sunk in East River by lighter VALVOOVIAN; 2 lost.

July 14, 1917: Lighter VALVOOVIAN, sunk launch DELIVERY; 2 lost.

Oct. 1, 1917: MOHAWK, USN revenue cutter, lost in collision off New York.

Dec. 3, 1917: MCCALL, U.S. destroyer, collided with Clyde liner COMANCHE, below Narrows in high wind; at fault.

Dec. 15, 1917: Schooner RUTH E. PEMBA, struck submerged wreck off N.J.; total loss.

Dec. 16, 1917: Pilot boat PILOT from Maryland, caught in submarine net off New York; rammed, sunk, by steamer BERKSHIRE, Merchants and Miners Line; crew rescued.

Dec. 27, 1917: Tug JUANITA, sunk in collision, New York Bay.

1918: Red Star tug WESTCHESTER, towing coal barge, capsized coming out of Pot Cove, East River; 2 men lost.

April 25, 1918: Liner ST. PAUL, rolled over at pier; 3 lives lost; refloated in September.

May 2, 1918: Schooner HENRIETTA, broke up 3 miles east of Arverne, L.I.

July 19, 1918: USS SAN DIEGO torpedoed by German submarine off Fire Island.

Aug. 22, 1918: Motorboat NONESUCH, and tow of 17 canoes; capsized west end Rockaway Beach; 18 drowned.

Sept. 6, 1918: ALMIRANTE, sunk in collision off New Jersey coast; 5 lost.

Sept. 30, 1918: Motor boat BERNADETTE, total loss, Rockaway Beach.

Oct. 16, 1918: British steamer PORT PHILIP, rammed by USS PROTEUS, Ambrose Channel; 6 saved, 49 lost.

Oct. 18, 1918: Transport AMERICA sank at pier, Hoboken; 2 lost.

Feb. 28, 1919: Freighter LORD DUFFERIN, sunk in New York Bay by AQUITANIA; 1 killed.

March 17, 1919: Tug JAMESON, sunk in East River by LEXINGTON of Colonial Line, inbound from Providence; tug sank, crew rescued.

March 17, 1919: Freighter WAUBESA, U.S. Shipping Board; cargo grain for England and Holland; collided with ferry MAYOR GAYNOR in fog; also with ferry QUEENS; WAUBESA sank, New York Harbor; ferries damaged.

June 12, 1919: Hamburg–American steamer GRAF WALDERSEE; rescued two boatloads men from steamer sunk in collision 15 miles s.e. Rockaway Beach.

July 22, 1919: Four-masted schooner CHARLES E. DUNLAP from Puerto Rico for New York; cargo coconuts; total loss, Far Rockaway; crew saved.

Oct. 6, 1919: Colonial Line steamer LEXINGTON, New York to Providence; rammed at Hell Gate by U.S. submarine O-7.

Oct. 20, 1919: CHICAGO CITY, sunk in collision off Staten Island.

Nov. 25, 1919: Motor boat MAMIE K., total loss 4 miles w. of Rockaway Beach.

Nov. 29, 1919: White Star liner ADRIATIC, rammed ST. MICHAEL at anchor in fog, off Statue of Liberty.

Dec. 5, 1919: Schooner MARY E. LYNCH, sunk by tug in North River; 4 dead.

Dec. 13, 1919: British freighter GRANGE PARK, aground off Freeport, L.I.; total loss.

Dec. 14, 1919: Yawl from pilot boat NEW YORK, capsized by Japanese SS TAIYO MARU; 1 saved; George Beebe, Jr., drowned.

1920's: Morgan Line EL SOL, inbound, New York Harbor; collision in fog with outbound steamship SAC CITY; EL SOL sank; lay between Narrows a long time; both at fault.

Feb., 1920: Freighter PEQUONNOCK, imprisoned in ice at Execution Rocks.

Feb. 4, 1920: MAINE, of Providence & Stonington Steamship Co., encountered floating ice; total loss on Execution Rocks; passengers, horses marooned three days.

Feb. 6, 1920: PRINCESS ANNE, Old Dominion Steamship Co., total loss, Far Rockaway; all saved.

Feb. 7–17, 1920: Steamer LAKEVILLE, stranded in snowstorm in Jones Inlet; 34 aboard.

Feb. 8, 1920: Schooner B. F. JAYNE, adrift three weeks, East River.

Feb. 14, 1920: Steamer MALDEN, total loss, Jones Inlet Bar; 45 saved.

April 28, 1920: Fishing schooner NORMA, total loss near Point Lookout, L.I.; 19 saved.

Dec. 29, 1920: Lighter JOHN C. CRAVEN, sunk by NIEW AMSTERDAM, off Battery; two crewmen lost.

Nov. 30, 1921: Schooner THOMAS R. WOOLEY, adrift two days, Jones Reef; 3 saved.

Jan. 12, 1922: Five-masted auxiliary schooner MARIE DE RONDE, collided with barges off Staten Island; damaged; turned into towing barge in 1933.

Jan. 18, 1922: British motor schooner BERTHA A., rum-runner from Bahamas; collided at Quarantine with British steamer SHEAF FIELD; damaged; rum-runner captain arrested.

Feb., 1922: Tug TALISMAN, sunk off 52nd St., Brooklyn.

Feb. 2, 1922: Ferry BRONX collided in fog, Quarantine, with ferry QUEENS, then with coal tow.

Feb. 2, 1922: British steamship EMPRESS OF SCOTLAND, explosion at Pier 59, North River; 8 badly burned.

Feb. 8, 1922: Steamship CORSON, Hamburg to New York, drifting out of fuel, 140 miles s.e. Ambrose Lightship; towed to New York.

Feb. 9, 1922: Lighter MARY A. KENNY; cargo sugar; on fire Erie Basin, Brooklyn; cargo destroyed; fire extinguished by fireboats.

Feb. 10, 1922: Barge WHITEHAVEN, collided with steamer EL VALLE from Galveston; barge sank off Red Hook.

Nov., 1923: Rum-runner sloop CLARENCE, being towed through East River by enforcement authorities; prisoner tried to ram Long Island Sound steamer to destroy evidence.

1924: Side-paddle-wheel steamer MISTLE-TOE, burned off Rockaway Beach, close to BLACK WARRIOR wreck.

1924: Steamer OLD GLORY, Montauk Steamboat Co.; destroyed by fire; New York.

April 25, 1924: Steamboat GRAND REPUBLIC, destroyed by fire in winter quarters, Hudson River.

April 25, 1924: Excursion steamer HIGHLANDER, burned in winter quarters, Hudson River.

April 25, 1924: Excursion steamer NASSAU, burned and wrecked in winter quarters, Hudson River.

1925: CLINTON D. BARRY; cargo lumber; sank off Glen Cove, L.I.

June 1, 1926: WASHINGTON IRVING, Hudson River Day Line, collided with barge SEABOARD OIL NO. 415; passengers and crew landed in Jersey City, but 2 lives later lost; sank right over where Holland Tunnel was being built.

June 17, 1926: SCOW 0-21, towed by O. L. HALLENBECK, sank on dumping grounds off Scotland Lightship.

Feb. 23, 1927: Tanker BLACK SEA, on fire, exploded in Lower Bay; fireboats JOHN PURROY MITCHEL and WILLIAM L. STRONG went to her aid; MITCHEL caught fire; STRONG saved ship; captain and 3 men of BLACK SEA fatally burned.

May 21, 1927: Three-masted schooner WILLIAM H. BABCOCK, once in China trade, sank at mooring, Bensonhurst, Brooklyn.

July 3, 1927: RELAX, total loss, Highlands, N.J.

Oct. 13, 1927: Gas yacht ONRUST, burned, Bayside, L.I.

Dec. 30, 1927: Tug SENECA, total loss, Hoboken.

April 27, 1928: Ferry BRONX, nearly capsized; 3 drowned.

April 28, 1928: Steamer ATLANTIC BEACH PARK, beached by gale; 3 lost as lifeboat capsized.

April 30, 1928: Tug JAMES A. COX sank, Jamaica Bay; Capt. W. H. Southard drowned; 5 saved.

May 7, 1928: U.S. dredge NAVESINK, collided in New York Harbor with barge in tow of tug AUBURN; sunk; 18 lost.

Aug., 1928: CHESTER W. CHAPIN, Fall River Line, inbound from Providence, collided in Hell Gate with tug VOLUNTEER; one lost from VOLUNTEER, which sank.

Oct. 17, 1928: Steamer N. B. STARBUCK, burned, New York.

Jan. 6, 1929: Barge BELFAST, foundered off Frying Pan Shoals; crew rescued.

Feb. 1, 1929: Sloop HENRIETTA, supposed rum-runner, capsized in squall off Point Lookout, west of Jones Inlet;

1 of 4 on board survived; 3 bodies not drowned.

Feb. 17, 1929: Tug MANUT, collided with Lackawanna R.R. tug, East River, 1 drowned.

April 30, 1929: Tug MUTUAL, collided with ferry YOUNGSTOWN, sank.

Aug. 31, 1929: Auxiliary schooner ABACENA burned off Belden Point, City Island, N.Y.

Sept. 7, 1929: Cabin cruiser CLUNY exploded, City Island; 1 dead.

Oct., 1929: New London–New York steamer NEW HAMPSHIRE; rammed dredge, East River; 70-foot gash near waterline.

Dec. 18, 1929: ALGONQUIN, Clyde Line; rammed and sunk SS FORT VICTORIA in Ambrose Channel; all saved.

Dec. 18, 1929: Furness Line FORT VICTORIA, on Bermuda run; sunk by ALGONQUIN at entrance to New York Harbor; pilot boats NEW YORK and SANDY HOOK rescued 400 passengers and crew.

About 1930: RUTH SHAW, sunk Rockaway Inlet.

Jan. 3, 1930: Tug THOMAS J. HOWARD, sank after crash in East River.

Feb. 11, 1930: MUNCHEN, North German Lloyd, Bremen to New York; badly damaged by fire in New York; rebuilt in 1931, renamed GENERAL VON STEUBEN.

March 7, 1930: Pure Oil Co. TANKER NO. 5, exploded in Kearney, N.J.; 3 missing.

April 1, 1930: Barge NORTH RIVER, rammed by lighter PILOT LIGHT, sank, East River; 12 saved.

May 31, 1930: Schooner M. J. TAYLOR, rammed fishing launch off City Island, N.Y.; 1 missing.

Sept. 5, 1930: POCONO, total loss, Atlantic Highlands, N.J.

Nov. 19, 1930: Steamship OVIDIA, sank off Ambrose Lightship; crew saved by MAURETANIA.

Feb. 10, 1931: Motor boat EWSCRAY, burned and sank near Romer Shoals, lower New York Bay.

March 4, 1931: British auxiliary schooner JOHN MANNING, rum-runner; foundered s.e. Ambrose Channel Lightship; crew removed in speedboats, landed Barnegat, proceeded Halifax by train.

March 7, 1931: Tug JOYCE CARD, exploded in Erie Basin; 5 killed; tug sank, total loss.

March 17, 1931: Drill boat NORTH RIVER, sank Hell Gate; removed.

March 18, 1931: New York–Norfolk steamer ARMINDA; collided in Narrows with British motor vessel SILVERYEW, bound from Manila via Boston; both damaged.

April 13, 1932: U.S. Coast Guard cutter MANHATTAN, collided with freighter GUAYAQUIL, New York; 1 drowned, 6 hurt.

May 9, 1932: Steamer SEA BIRD, burned, New York.

Aug. 25, 1932: Barge RED FOX, sank, Perth Amboy, N.J.; Capt. H. Carlsen drowned.

Sept. 9, 1932: Wooden steamer OBSERVATION, exploded, East River; 39 dead; 72 injured; 8 missing.

1933: RAMOS, sunk 3 miles off Sandy Hook; fishing ground.

Jan. 26, 1933: Yawl from pilot boat went to SS BLACK GULL; storm, 3 lost.

Jan. 29, 1933: Steamship MALCHACE, grounded, Execution Light, Long Island Sound.

May 10, 1933: EXPRESS, later MANDALAY, sank at Manhattan Beach.

May 11, 1933: Steamer LOUISE, foundered, Brooklyn.

Nov. 17, 1933: SS DEUTSCHLAND, rammed SS MUNARGO off Statue of Liberty; MUNARGO beached at Bedloe's Island.

Nov. 22, 1933: SS OHIOAN collided with SS LIBERTY, Ambrose Channel; settled down on shoals; crew rescued.

Nov. 22, 1933: Ship, name unknown, rammed off Coney Island; sank on Craven Shoals.

Sept. 8, 1934; Pilot boat NEW YORK acted as rudder as MORRO CASTLE was towed ashore by other craft after fire off New Jersey; 125 lives lost.

Sept. 8, 1934: Tug W. J. TRACY, foundered in Narrows; 2 missing.

Oct. 14, 1934: SEA HAWK; total loss, Sandy Hook.

About 1935: Hudson River Day Line IROQUOIS, burned, foot of 13th St., New York.

Jan. 2, 1935: Arrow Line freighter JANE CHRISTENSEN of San Francisco, rammed Colonial Line's SS LEXINGTON, bound New York to Providence; LEXINGTON sunk; 7 lost.

Jan. 2, 1935: Sailing ship JOSEPH CONRAD, owned by Alan Villiers, ashore on flats at Bay Ridge, Brooklyn.

Jan. 11, 1935: Trawler ALERT, sank after collision with scow off Sandy Hook.

Jan. 25, 1935: Liner MOHAWK, outbound, collided with Norwegian freighter TALISMAN off Sea Girt, N.J.; 45 drowned; ship total loss.

Feb. 1, 1935: Cabin cruiser; cargo Cuban alcohol; ashore Jones Beach; total wreck; crew escaped.

Feb. 16, 1935: Tug ALLENTOWN cut barge NIMROD in two, New York Harbor; 1 hurt.

March 11, 1935: SS ABANGAREZ, collided in fog, Gravesend Bay, with SS CHEROKEE.

May 16, 1935: Freighter CHARLES H. CRAMP, collided in Kill Van Kull, Staten Island, with tanker LEONARD; 1 died.

Aug. 22, 1935: Fishing boat ATLANTIC swept by huge wave, Jones Inlet; 3 lost.

Aug. 31, 1935: Launch, name unknown, sunk in collision with hit-run oil tanker, at Eastchester Bay, S.I.; 1 killed, 2 rescued.

Sept. 17, 1935: SS SANTA BARBARA collided with Ambrose Lightship.

Oct. 28, 1935: Fishing boat BARRACUDA rammed, sunk, by SS PENNSYLVANIA off Barnegat, N.J.

Dec., 1935: Towing barge MARIE DE RONDE; cargo coal; burned 10 miles off Fire Island; sunk.

May 3, 1936: Fishing boat M. J. R. III, sunk by freighter ANGELINA outside Sheepshead Bay, L.I.

Jan. 10, 1938: Freighter SOUTHLAND, beached after collision with PANAMA CITY, New York Bay.

May 14, 1938: Auxiliary schooner QUITA, sank, City Island, N.Y.; 1 dead, 2 missing; others rescued.

May 28, 1938: Excursion steamer MANDALAY, rammed and sunk by liner ACADIA, New York Bay; passengers saved.

Aug. 11, 1938: Fishing boat SCUD, capsized, Sandy Hook; 1 missing, 2 saved.

Jan. 22, 1939: Tug S&H NO. 6, with towing scows BOUKER NO. 65 & 70; overturned East River; 65 lost from scow; tug raised; Coast Guard saved all hands.

Jan. 23, 1929: British motor ship SILVER ASH, burned, Brooklyn; sunk; raised.

Feb. 5, 1939: Erie ferry YOUNGSTOWN, rammed ferry MEADVILLE, Jersey City; both damaged.

Feb. 9, 1939: Ferry MISS NEW YORK, crashed into ship at Battery.

Feb. 27, 1939: American ship LILLIAN, from Fajardo for New York; cargo sugar; sunk after collision in fog with German SS WIEGLAND off Barnegat Lightship; crew saved.

March 11, 1939: Ferry GOLD STAR MOTHER, collided in fog with tanker NEWBERNE; 5 hurt.

March 26, 1939: Steamship CITY OF BIRMINGHAM in collision off Execution Rock.

April 27, 1939: N.J. pilot boat SANDY HOOK collided with Norwegian ship OSLOFJORD, one mile north of Ambrose Lightship; sank; all saved.

May 28, 1939: Cruiser BILOT, capsized, East River; 3 lost, 25 saved.

Sept. 15, 1939: LEHIGH VALLEY RR BARGE,

sank, Jersey City; cargo British flour; possible sabotage.

Nov. 11, 1939: DERRICK BARGE; cargo two bombers for Great Britain; sank, New York Harbor; salvaged.

Jan. 30, 1940: Tug HARRY R. CONNORS, collided in East River with tug MEX-PET; fire; 1 dead, 7 hurt.

Feb. 5, 1940: Tug S. H. 5, sunk at Brooklyn by ice floes; 1 dead, 1 saved.

Feb. 18, 1940: Tug AMY KELLER, sinks; one missing; Hoboken, N.J.

June 30, 1940: Schooner SCARLET II, in collision with unidentified barge, East River; 1 missing, 4 saved.

Aug. 5, 1940: Lighter DENVILLE, capsized off Stapleton, S.I.

Aug. 30, 1940: Ferry MISS NEW YORK, rammed by tanker MAGNOLIA, New York harbor; 5 hurt.

Dec. 13, 1940: Tug J. A. REYNOLDS, collided with SS SHAWNEE, sunk, New York Harbor; crew saved.

May 15, 1941: U.S. launch Q 11, collided with freight float, East River; sunk; 3 drowned.

Aug. 18, 1941: American freighter PANUCO; cargo sisal; destroyed by fire; 34 lost.

Aug. 22, 1941: Finnish freighter AURORA, burned in Hudson; 1 lost.

Aug. 30, 1941: Fishing schooner SCHULA, capsized in Jones Beach Inlet; 3 drowned, 2 hurt, 3 rescued.

Nov. 11, 1941: Lighter J. J. RUDOLF, sank at Atlantic Basin Pier, Brooklyn; Capt. W. C. Nelson hurt.

Nov. 13, 1941: Fishing boat RUTH LU-CILLE, sank after collision with collier CHARLES O'CONNOR off Sandy Hook; all saved.

Jan. 10, 1942: Tanker BYRON D. BENSON, collided with freighter CONTINENT off Scotland Lightship.

Jan. 10, 1942: Freighter CONTINENT, sank after collision with tanker BYRON D. BENSON off Scotland Lightship; 1 lost.

Jan. 14, 1942: Panamanian tanker NOR-NESS, with Norwegian crew; lost by enemy action off Fire Island.

Jan. 15, 1942: British tanker COIMBRA, assigned to patrol approaches to New York; Capt. J. P. Barnard; torpedoed, sunk, 70 miles off Sandy Hook; captain, 35 others killed; 6 wounded.

Feb. 9, 1942: French liner NORMANDIE, on fire and sank at New York City pier; 1 lost.

Feb. 15, 1942: Tanker POINT BREEZE, aground off Belden Point, Long Island Sound; explosion; 1 dead, 1 missing.

Feb. 25, 1942: Lighter LIBERTY, sank after ice smashed bow, North River; crew safe.

Feb. 26, 1942: Oil tanker R. P. RESOR, torpedoed 31 miles off Barnegat Light; 48 of 50 crewmen died.

Feb. 28, 1942: U.S. destroyer JACOB JONES, torpedoed by submarine off Cape May, N.J.; of 150 men, only 11 were saved.

March 10, 1942: Oil tanker GULFTRADE, inbound form Port Arthur, Texas; torpedoed 13 miles e.n.e. of Barnegat Light; 19 lost, 16 saved.

March 13, 1942: Chile freighter TOLTEN, from Baltimore to New York; torpedoed, sunk, off New Jersey; 24 of crew of 27 lost.

April 28, 1942: Dutch freighter ARUNDO, outbound New York to Alexandria, Egypt; torpedoed by German submarine U-136, 15 miles south of Ambrose Lightship; 6 lost.

April 30, 1942: Norwegian motor vessel BIDEVIND, torpedoed and sunk off New York.

May 12, 1942: American tanker VIRGINIA, torpedoed and sunk off Baytown, N.J.; 14 crew lost.

Sept. 22, 1942: British patrol boat HMS PENTLAND FIRTH torpedoed and sunk, Rockaway Inlet in 70 feet of water.

Nov. 24, 1942: U.S. cargo ship NATHAN-IEL BACON, and M/V ESSO BELGIUM damaged in collision, New York Harbor.

Dec. 1, 1942: Greek freighter IOANNIS P. GOULANDRIS, torpedoed and sunk 10 miles off Ambrose Lightship in "Mudhole."

Dec. 16, 1942: U.S. Naval minesweeper YMS #12 damaged in collision, New York Harbor.

Feb. 15, 1943: Freighter LANARKSHIRE, collided in Main Ship Channel, Upper Bay, with U.S. destroyer HOBBY; both without a pilot.

March 3, 1943: Schooner AMERICA, collided with tug JOHNSON CITY, East River; 1 dead, 2 hurt.

April 24, 1943: Ammunition ship EL ESTERO, loading at Caven Point Terminal, Jersey City; fire in engine room; fireboats showed extreme bravery; flooded vessel, sunk it.

Oct. 1, 1943: Coal barge ALICE SHERIDAN, sunk in New York Harbor after collision with SS CURAÇAO.

Jan. 3, 1944: U.S. destroyer TURNER, exploded, caught fire, and sank three miles from Ambrose Lightship; 138 lost; wreckage towed out to sea and blown up, July 4, 1944.

Jan. 8, 1944: Cunard liner MAURETANIA, collided with SS HAT CREEK outside Ambrose Lightship; damaged.

March 7, 1944: Barge WESLEY BELLIS, rammed by Navy landing ship in fog, East River; barge captain, H. Kroeger, lost.

May 11, 1944: Steamer VALLDEMOSA, collided in fog with SS WOODROW WILSON, approaching New York.

May 24, 1944: Tanker PETERSBURG, exploded, Constable Hook, N.J.; 1 dead, 13 hurt.

July 9, 1944: DEL RIO, of Eastern Transportation Co., with tug AGNES MORAN, collided near Hell Gate Bridge with barges LUTHER HOOPER and CHARLES T. RYAN, in tow of tug GOLIAH; GOLIAH and tugs damaged.

July 22, 1944: U.S. Navy escort vessel, exploded, Tompkinsville, S.I.; 2 dead, 1 hurt.

Sept. 14, 1944: Ferry RICHMOND, capsized in hurricane, Bay Ridge, L.I.

Sept. 20, 1944: South American ship CHOAPA, inbound; collided in fog in channel approaching New York Harbor with tanker BRITISH HARMONY; CHOAPA anchored.

Sept. 21, 1944: CHOAPA hit by tankers VOCO and EMPIRE GARRICK, which collided with JOHN P. POE; CHOAPA sank.

Jan. 2, 1945: Tanker SUNOCO, exploded and burned off Sandy Hook; 3 dead, 7 missing, 6 hurt.

Feb., 1945: Steamer COLONEL CLAYTON, sank at College Point, L.I.; raised after four months.

Feb. 4, 1945: M/V tanker ORVILLE HARDEN, Panama Transport Co., sunk by collision with Netherlands flag tanker M/V ENA near Ambrose Channel; 1 killed; others saved in lifeboats.

Feb. 5, 1945: SS CLIO, outbound for Venezuela, collided in New York Harbor with SS SPRINGHILL and Norwegian tanker VIVI.

Feb. 5, 1945: Tanker SPRINGHILL, on fire off Bushwick Basin; fireboat WILLIAM L. STRONG to rescue; SPRINGHILL exploded, burned, after collision with CLIO; 17 lost, 122 injured.

June 11, 1945: Freighter AYURUOCA, sank following collision with freighter GENERAL SS FLEISCHER off Ambrose Light; 1 missing, 60 saved.

1946: Barge, name unknown, 5 miles off Sandy Hook; good fishing.

Jan. 14, 1946: Tanker PEQUOIT HILL, on fire following explosion; Bayonne, N.J.; 1 dead.

July 6, 1946: Schooner ESCAPE, sank following collision off Ambrose Lightship; 2 died; 3 rescued.

Dec. 11, 1946: MILL ROCK, U.S. Army launch; sank, East River, following collision with tug EDWARD J. BERWIND; 2 missing.

Jan. 31, 1947: Tanker WELLESLEY VICTORY, collided with tanker ESSO SPRINGFIELD off Ambrose Lightship.

Feb. 2, 1947: Kayak, upset, Little Neck Bay, L.I.; E. H. Henning drowned, son E. H. Henning, Jr., rescued by Patrolman S. H. Biekunt.

March 7, 1947: Motorship JOHN ERICSSON, burned at Pier 90, North River, shortly before sailing; total loss.

March 18, 1947: Tug INVADER, capsized East River; 1 missing, 3 saved.

March 20, 1947: Army transport GEORGE WASHINGTON; on fire at Jersey City pier; put out by fireboats, Coast Guard, N.J. Fire Department.

Nov. 23, 1947: Tug ST. VINCENT, damaged in New York Harbor in collision with freighter; 1 missing, 1 hurt.

Dec. 31, 1947: Tanker PORT REPUBLIC, loaded, going through Hell Gate with two tugs, ST. JOHN and ST. CHARLES; struck by ST. CHARLES; aground at Steep Rocks.

Jan. 9, 1948: Ferry DONGAN HILLS, damaged in collision with ferry KNICKERBOCKER off St. George, S.I.; 2 hurt.

Oct. 1, 1948: Tug ANN MARIE TRACY, sank after collision with freighter ELIZA J. NICHOLSON, Hudson River; 6 dead, 3 missing.

Jan. 19, 1949: U.S. Coast Guard icebreaker EASTWIND, collided with tanker GULFSTREAM in fog off Barnegat, N.J.; fire; icebreaker burned for seven hours; 13 killed; 21 injured.

Dec. 16, 1949: Swedish motor vessel EKEFORS, inbound, collided at Narrows with SEATRAIN TEXAS; badly damaged.

1950: Munition barges, South Amboy, N.J., exploded; 30 dead.

Jan. 13, 1950: AMBROSE LIGHTSHIP NO. III, "brushed" in heavy fog by unidentified vessel.

March 18, 1950: Scow SEA WAVE, capsized off Ambrose Lightship; 1 believed lost.

March 28, 1950: AMBROSE LIGHTSHIP, rammed in heavy fog off Sandy Hook by Grace liner SANTA MONICA; hull punctured.

May 8, 1950: Small boats, Long Island Sound, capsized in heavy winds; 3 drowned.

June 19, 1950: Small boats, Long Island Sound, capsized; 9 missing.

June 27, 1950: Danish motor vessel COLOMBIA, run into by American Export Line's EXCALIBUR, in Bay Ridge Channel; both damaged; all safe; EXCALIBUR grounded on Gowanus flats.

July 2, 1950: Dredge SANDCRAFT, collided with collier MELROSE, New York Harbor, entrance to Narrows; sank, abandoned; crew saved.

Oct. 21, 1950: Victory ship PELICAN STATE, plowed into side of motor ship ERRIA, south of Ambrose Lightship; damaged; all safe.

April 15, 1951: Fishing craft, name unknown, capsized Long Island Sound; 6 missing.

July 28, 1951: Fishing boat BETTY B., exploded and sank in lower New York Bay; 1 missing, 4 rescued.

Aug. 22, 1951: USS WISCONSIN, freed after grounding on mud flats, New York Harbor. (May 7, 1956: badly damaged in collision with destroyer EATON in fog off Virginia.)

Sept. 5, 1951: Yacht CHARMTER, sank after hitting reef near Cockenoe Island, Long Island Sound.

Sept. 10, 1951: Cabin cruiser IDLE TIME, capsized off Rockaway Point; 1 drowned.

June 10, 1952: Excursion boat NEW YORKER, rammed bulkhead, Hudson River; 32 hurt.

July 19, 1952: Norwegian freighter BLACK GULL; cargo zinc, tin, castor oil; afire from naphthalene; abandoned 65 miles s.e. of Montauk Point; towed to Lower Bay, New York; fireboats put out fire; she sank; 7 killed, 8 hurt; refloated then scrapped.

July 19, 1952: POLING BROS. NO. 18 tanker exploded, burned, East River; 1 lost.

Dec. 4, 1952: QUEEN ELIZABETH, collided with tug in New York Harbor; slightly damaged.

1953: Tanker GULFTRADE, collided off

Barnegat Lightship with Brazilian freighter LORDE PANAMA; 1 died.

Jan. 5, 1953: Freighter AMERICAN VETERAN, collided in fog off Governor's Island with ferry GOLD STAR MOTHER; 12 hurt.

Jan. 15, 1953: Freighter AMERICAN LEADER, collided with freighter CHICKASAW, New York Harbor, fog.

May 15, 1953: CITY OF CALCUTTA, Ellerman Lines, anchored; hit by tug BROOKLYN and three scows, s.s.e. of Craven Shoal buoy; last scow sank.

Sept. 17, 1953: Fireboat GEORGE B. MCCLELLAN, explosion, East River; marine engineer killed.

Oct. 11, 1953: Motorboat FREDA M. of Sayville, L.I., overturned on Jones Reef, L.I.; 1 lost; swept east to Turtle Cove, Montauk, by heavy seas, onto rocks; 6 saved.

Nov. 6, 1953: Small boats, many sunk in full gale.

Jan. 14, 1954: Tanker VERDON, collided in East River with freighter BETHCOASTER; VERDON sank.

Jan. 20, 1954: Ferry VERRAZZANO, rammed freighter NORLINDO off Bedloe's Island; 7 hurt.

May 22, 1954: Small boat disasters; 17 fishermen rescued.

May 30, 1954: Small boat disasters; 100 disaster calls, City Island to Jones Inlet.

June 1, 1954: Tug BROOKLYN, sank at Battery; 1 drowned; tug raised.

Sept. 4, 1955: STAR OF THE SEA (former ANNIE C. ROSS), fore-and-aft-rigged schooner used as training ship; sank at anchor off Glen Cove, L.I.

Sept. 7, 1954: Steam lighter EXPRESS, burned off Bedloe's Island.

Sept. 27, 1955: Tug F. A. CHURCHMAN, rammed by barge, sank, Arthur Kill, New York Harbor; 2 missing; others saved.

Oct. 18, 1955: USS WISCONSIN, aground one hour, East River; no damage.

Nov. 4, 1955: CORNELL, former CHARLIE LAWRENCE, workboat; capsized, Tappan Zee, lost.

May 20, 1956: Cabin cruiser ESCAPE II, run into by tanker M. J. DERBY II, East River; capsized; 1 died, 5 safe.

July 23, 1956: American freighter FAIRISLE, collided with Panamanian tanker SAN JOSÉ three miles south of Ambrose Lightship; fog; both damaged; 2 injured.

Aug. 8, 1956: Excursion boat SIGHTSEER IX, rammed Madison Avenue bridge; 33 hurt.

Nov. 8, 1956: AGDA, gutted by fire off Long Island; sank; 5 saved by USN submarine and destroyer.

Dec. 3, 1956: New York City fireboat FIRE FIGHTER, fighting blaze on Luckenbach pier, Brooklyn; explosion; fireboat damaged, men hurt.

Dec. 18, 1956: Farrell Line's freighter AFRICAN STAR, collided with freighter ALCOA PILGRIM, New York Harbor; both damaged; no lives lost; AFRICAN STAR sank; PILGRIM damaged.

Jan. 19, 1958: Tug JIM STEERS, run over by tug towing oil barge near Stepping Stones Light; 3 lost.

Feb. 8, 1958: Tanker TYNEFIELD, collided off Staten Island with ferry DONGAN HILLS; both damaged; 30 hurt.

March 31, 1958: SS ALBION VICTORY, collided with scow SEA PRINCE off Sandy Hook; barge sank; barge captain, Rudolf Lauritsen, lost; SEA PRINCE faulted.

June 25, 1958: Tanker EMPRESS BAY, collided in East River with outbound Swedish Trans-Atlantic Steamship Co. freighter NEBRASKA; explosion and fire; fireboats did heroic work; 2 killed, 35 missing on EMPRESS BAY; 31 injured on NEBRASKA.

Jan. 6, 1959: Tanker ATLANTIC PRINCE, bound Stapleton, S.I., to Linden, N.J.; collided in Kill Van Kull with tanker OTCO BAYWAY; damaged; both faulted.

Jan. 26, 1959: Tanker NORTH DAKOTA, collided off Bayonne, N.J., with loaded U.S. Army dredge ESSAYONS, inbound from Port Arthur, Texas, to Bayonne; faulted.

March 1, 1959: Tanker JALANTA, collided with liner CONSTITUTION in fog outside New York Harbor; both damaged.

March 26, 1959: Cruise ship SANTA ROSA, American Grace Line; rammed tanker VALCHEM east of Atlantic City, N.J.; fires on both; 1 dead, 3 missing on tanker; liner towed tanker to New York.

June 26, 1959: Tanker NORTH DAKOTA, rammed tanker SEVEN SKIES, south of Ambrose Lightship; both damaged; NORTH DAKOTA faulted.

June 26, 1959: Yacht LORD JIM, sunk Long Island Sound; 7 saved.

July 29, 1959: Freighter AMERICAN HUNTER, collided in fog in Lower Bay with QUEEN ELIZABETH; both damaged; none hurt.

Sept. 6, 1956: Excursion boat SIGHTSEER VIII, hit Madison Avenue Bridge swinging span; 87 hurt.

Oct. 29, 1959: Freighter AMERICAN PRESS, collided in New York Harbor with liner ISRAEL; 1 missing; ISRAEL towed to Todd Yard, Brooklyn.

June 24, 1960: Freighter GREEN BAY, States Marine Lines, outward bound, hit RELIEF LIGHTSHIP NO. 505 on Ambrose Station, in fog; lightship sank; crew rescued by GREEN BAY; wreck site marked, but moved.

July 15, 1960: Tanker ALKAID, ripped open by submerged object, East River; beached, in tow.

Aug. 29, 1960: Ferry CHATHAM, collided in fog in New York Harbor with SEATRAIN GEORGIA; 13 hurt.

Aug. 30, 1960: Tug DEVON, Red Star Line, collided in Hell Gate channel with tanker CRAIG REINAUER; sunk; all saved.

Dec. 15, 1960: Ferry CORNELIUS J. KOLFF, crashed Staten Island slip; 20 hurt.

Dec. 19, 1960: U.S. aircraft carrier CONSTELLATION, under construction, Brooklyn Navy Yard; fire; CAROL

MORAN aided; 50 lives lost, 267 injured.

Winter, 1961–1962: U.S. Coast Guard lightship, Ambrose Channel, disappeared.

Jan. 15, 1961: TEXAS TOWER NO. 4, collapsed; all 27 lost.

June 23, 1961: Tug JULIA C. MORAN, collided in fog with U.S.N. service cargo vessel COMET, inbound from St. Nazaire, France; COMET faulted.

Jan. 1, 1962: Tug GWENDOLINE STEERS, New York to Northport, L.I.; lost west of Eaton's Neck; 9 lost.

May 10, 1962: Fireboat GOVENOR ALFRED E. SMITH, caught fire going to explosion in Brooklyn Mill Basin.

Sept. 18, 1962: Tug RUSSELL NO. 18, capsized in Elizabeth Port channel; 3 drowned; unexplained.

Sept. 28, 1962: Motor vessel RIO JACHAL, burned Pier 25, Manhattan; five-alarm fire.

March 14, 1963: U.S. Coast Guard cutter TAMAROA, sank in dry dock; Coast Guardsman court-martialed; damage $1 million; all crewmen escaped.

Sept. 7, 1963: Red Star Line tug FLUSHING, capsized between Triborough Bridge and Hell Gate Bridge; 4 lost.

Sept. 23, 1963: Ferry VERRAZZANO, damaged in collision with coastal tanker POLING BROS. NO. 8, off St. George, S.I.

About 1964: Schooner HERITAGE, sank on rocks, Stepping Stone Light; no cargo; 2 rescued.

April 10, 1964: Excursion boat TERESA, aground New York Harbor; 1 hurt; 1 passenger killed earlier by rock falling from Manhattan Bridge.

June 21, 1964: Freighter SANTA ANNA, burned in Hoboken, N.J., shipyard.

Nov. 26, 1964: Israeli liner SHALOM, collided with Norwegian tanker STOLT DAGALI, cargo oils and solvents from Manila for New York; south of Long Beach, N.J.; SHALOM unhurt; STOLT DAGALI cut in two, stern sunk, 19 crewmen lost.

Perils of the Port of New York

Dec. 28, 1964: Tug NEWPORT, Red Star Line; fire, off Glen Cove, L.I.

Fall, 1965: ALEXANDER HAMILTON, Hudson River Day Line; log jammed in one of two paddle-wheels; drifted; tugs NANCY MORAN and CAROL MORAN to rescue off Spuyten Duyvil; removed 1,350 passengers.

Oct. 31, 1965: Unknown craft—11 barges, 40 pleasure boats—at docks, Edgewater, N.J.

Jan. 12, 1966: Tanker MORANIA MARLIN, collided with tugs PATRICIA MORAN and DIANA L. MORAN; Kill Van Kull, off Bayonne, N.J.; bow damage to tanker; 6 rescued, 4 lost on PATRICIA MORAN; 4 dead, 6 saved on DIANA L. MORAN.

Jan. 23, 1966: British tanker CHELWOOD BEACON, with 30,000 tons of crude oil, ran aground on shoal near Sandy Hook Light; damaged; crew rescued.

Feb. 11, 1966: Tanker ATLANTIC ENGINEER, aground at entrance to Kill Van Kull, S.I., hauled off by tugs.

Feb. 11, 1966: Tanker CARBIDE CITY, aground Sandy Hook Channel; refloated.

March 3, 1966: Liner SANTA ISABEL, empty, rammed Raritan River drawbridge; damaged ship; $250,000 damage to bridge; bridge machinist had fatal heart attack.

June 9, 1966: Japanese freighter KAMIKAWA MARU, collided in fog with Norwegian freighter NORDVIND, near Ambrose Lightship; suit against pilots.

June 16, 1966: British tanker ALVA CAPE, collided in Kill Van Kull between Staten Island and Bayonne, N.J., with tanker TEXACO MASSACHUSETTS; three tugs were also involved: TEXACO LATIN AMERICAN, ESSO MASSACHUSETTS, and ESSO VERMONT; explosion, fire; 33 dead.

June 28, 1966: More explosions on the ALVA CAPE; 4 killed, 12 injured.

Sept. 7, 1966: Hamburg–American liner HANSEATIC, about to leave for Cherbourg; burned, New York Harbor; all safe.

Sept. 9, 1966: Tug DOROTHY MCALLISTER, towing oil barge BURCHARD, struck N.Y. Central railroad bridge linking Manhattan and Bronx; closed access to Harlem River for two weeks.

Dec. 29, 1966: Tanker PASSAIC SUN, beached Rockaway, L.I.; total loss; crew safe.

March 23, 1967: Norwegian freighter FERNFIELD, New York from Bangkok, Thailand, via Suez Canal; cargo rubber, pepper, sisal; on fire at pier, Clifton, S.I.; pier and most of cargo destroyed.

Dec., 1967: Tanker SOCONY-VACUUM, sank, New York Harbor; refloated.

Dec., 1967: Mobil Oil Corp. tanker WANETA, Panamanian flag; inbound from Venezuela; ashore at Northville, L.I.

Dec. 11, 1967: Mobil Oil Corp. tanker WAPELLO, aground New York Harbor; freed Dec. 13 by Moran Towing & Transporation Co. tugs.

Dec. 25, 1967: Norwegian freighter DIANET; cargo sugar; on fire in Hudson River; 3 crew dead, 18 hospitalized.

Dec. 23, 1968: Tanker MARY A. WHALEN; cargo 150,000 gallons of oil; aground at breakwater, Rockaway Point, L.I.; crew safe.

Dec. 27, 1968: RUSSELL BARGE NO. 4; cargo fuel oil; collided in Kill Van Kull with TEXACO BARGE NO. 802, both in tow; RUSSELL exploded, beached.

Dec. 28, 1968: Barge ESSO 31, on fire off Rosebank, S.I.; Capt. David Cloughsey burned.

Feb. 18, 1969: Liberian tanker WORLD JUSTICE, on fire near Hudson, N.Y.; 1 crewman burned.

March 3, 1969: Swedish tanker DAN BOSTROM, struck underwater obstacle off Port Newark, N.J.; damaged.

March 12, 1969: Tug OCEAN QUEEN, Red Star Line, sank off Queens shore after

276

collision in Hell Gate with tanker FOUR LAKES; 4 saved, 1 missing.

March 15, 1969: Barge MICHAEL B., on fire Arthur Kill, off Port Reading, N.J.; 2 missing, 2 burned.

June 2, 1969: Tug GENE POPE, Bronx Towing Line; sunk in Hell Gate, 5 rescued.

July 8, 1969: Oil exploration ship ATLANTIC SEAL, on fire from welder torch, Atlantic City, N.J.; burned three hours.

July 13, 1969: Tanker TULLAHOMA, outbound for New Orleans, hit fishing boat AMBERJACK III off Long Branch, N.J.; AMBERJACK sank; 47 saved by Coast Guard; 1 missing.

Feb. 9, 1970: Tanker DESERT PRINCESS, Liberian flag, southbound; aground on Mill Rock, East River.

April 30, 1970: Tug METROPOLITAN NO. 2, towing two scows, overturned in channel between Staten Island and Elizabeth, N.J.; 1 lost, 2 missing.

Jan. 10, 1972: Tanker MARTHA R. INGRAM, split in two at dock, Port Jefferson, L.I.; cause not ascertained.

Jan. 20, 1972: Tanker ATLANTIC PRESTIGE, hit submerged object in Arthur Kill, near Carteret, N.J.; damaged.

DATES UNKNOWN:

ADELPHI, built 1863, burned on Harlem River.

ANASTASIA, wrecked off New Jersey; magnetic course of 140 degrees.

BENJAMIN BIGLOW, schooner, Boston for New York, sunk on Execution Rock.

"BENSON," one of three wrecks, Rockaway Inlet; good for fishing.

CAPE DREPANON, Greek-owned, total loss on Execution Rock.

CAROLINE, brig, sunk near Ellis Island; cut by ice in North River.

CECILIA M. DUNLAP, sunk below Sandy Hook; magnetic course 185 degrees.

CHARLES, British schooner, sunk 8 miles west of Fire Island.

D. R. STOCKWELL, brig, Montevideo to Bangor, burned in East River.

"DERRICK BARGE," Rockaway Inlet; fishing spot.

"DODGER," Jones Inlet, fishing spot.

"DOLL'S WRECK," Rockaway; fishing spot.

"EDWIN DUKE," off Jones Inlet; fishing spot.

EMILY M. WELLS, schooner, lost at Cow Bay, L.I.

EUREKA, steam tug, sunk 17 miles south of Jones Inlet.

"GOLDEN NUGGET" wreck, west of Rockaway Inlet; fishing spot.

HANNAH WILLETS, schooner, sunk off College Point, L.I.

HARRIET FOSTER, sloop, sunk off Point Comfort, S.I.

HARRY AND NED, schooner, wrecked Crab Meadows, L.I.

HARRY FISHER, of New London, Jones Inlet; total loss; 2 drowned.

ISLE OF PINES, schooner, total loss, Hell Gate.

JACOB BELL, tug, wreck off Fort Lee, Hudson River.

JACOB W. MORRIS, schooner, total loss off Battery.

"JOE WRECK," Jones Inlet; fishing spot.

JUDGE HITCHCOCK, schooner, ashore Long Beach, L.I.; total loss.

LEONIDA, sloop, total loss off Astoria, L.I.

"LOUIE'S PIER" wreck, off end of last pier at Rockaway Point; fishing spot.

MARY HAMILTON, schooner, foundered in Long Island Sound; all lost.

MASSACHUSETTS, Providence & Stonington Steamship Co., aground North Shore, L.I.; scrapped.

MAZEPPA, sloop, Capt. Wilbur Newton, lost in Hell Gate.

"NERVOUS," fishermen's name for wreck at Rockaway, L.I.

QUICKSTEP, American bark, run down by outward-bound steamer; buoy placed on spot to mark shoal.

"ROCK BARGE," Jones Inlet; fishing spot.

"ROCKAWAY STEAMER," in bay off Bennett Field, L.I.

S. J. LINDSAY, schooner, Capt. Wit Baker, lost on Rockaway Shoals.

SCOW WRECK NO. 2, inshore from "Oil Wreck"—Peter Rickmers; good black-fishing.

"STEEL WRECK" or "WIRE WRECK," wooden vessel, square mast; 70 feet water; good fishing.

STONE BARGE, in 55 feet water; good for lobsters.

SUBWAY ROCKS WRECK, on magnetic course of 134 degrees; fishing spot.

T. V. ARROWSMITH, steamboat, sister ship of SEAWANHAKA; burned; salvaged.

TIBOR, Rockaway; on beach, can walk around bow on low moon tide.

TREMONT, fire at New York; Joy Line; trained lions for vaudeville act on board; suffocated in cages.

UNKNOWN, patrol boat 100 feet long, gun on bow; sunk s.e. Jones Inlet.

UNKNOWN, sunken wreck 6 miles south, one-half mile east Scotland Lightship; spars blown up 1890.

UNKNOWN, southeast Fire Island buoys; had iron propeller instead of usual bronze one.

UNKNOWN, 20 miles off Sandy Hook, in 69 feet of water.

UNKNOWN, vessel 1920 vintage; charted as obstruction; five miles off Sandy Hook, in Ambrose Channel; 40 feet water.

UNKNOWN, 5 miles off Sandy Hook, in 60 feet of water.

VERMILLION, sank about 1920 in 58 feet water; lat. 41.05.5; long. 71.45.7.

"VIRGINIA," large steel ship probably wrecked before World War II.

WILLIAM M. CLARK, schooner of Fort Monmouth, N.J.; lost in Gravesend Bay.

"WOLCOTT," schooner, off Fire Island; fishing spot.

"WREGGE'S WRECK," vessel of whale-back design; in 96 feet of water.

YANKEE, single-screw freighter; in 120 feet water off Long Island.

ALPHABETICAL LIST
OF VESSELS IN DISTRESS

C. L. Hulse (1872), 251
Caldwell H. Colt (1888), 259
Cape Drepanon (date unknown), 225, 277
Caprice (1876), 36, 255
Carbide City (1966), 276
Carolina Augusta (1905), 264
Caroline (date unknown), 277
Caroline (1874), 254, 277
Carrie S. Webb (1881), 257
Carrie Winslow (1878), 256
Carteret (1776–1780), 201, 202, 242
Castalia (1880), 256
Castleton (1878), 167, 256
Catalone (1908), 40, 265
Catarina (1890), 260
Cathcart (1872), 251
Catskill (1897), 262
Cavour (1902), 86, 195, 263
Cecilia M. Dunlap (date unknown), 277
Centennial (1888), 37, 259
Chaleur (1764), 241
Challenge (1873), 252
Champion (1859), 246
Charles (date unknown), 277
Charles A. Grainer (1873), 252
Charles Atkinson (1913), 266
Charles E. Dunlap (1919), 177, 178
Charles H. Cramp (1935), 270
Charles H. Marshall (1888–1889), 36, 259
Charles L. Davenport (1900), 263
Charlotte Webb (1889), 259
Charming Peggy (1752), 241
Charmter (1951), 273
Charter Oak (1850), 245
Chatham (1960), 275
Chelwood Beacon (1966), 67, 68, 276
Chester W. Chapin (1928), 25, 268
Chicago City (1919), 267
Chief (1865), 247
China (1874), 254
Choapa (1944), 215, 216, 272
Christiane (1866), 145, 146, 248
City of Albany (1894), 261
City of Atlanta (1905), 146, 264
City of Birmingham (1939), 270
City of Boston (1872), 250
City of Calcutta (1953), 274
City of Lawrence (1872), 251, 253
City of New York (1880), 256

City of Norwich (1874), 254
City of Richmond (1883), 258
City of Richmond (1891), 260
Clara Bell (1872), 250
Clara E. Simpson (1894), 261
Clarence (1923), 268
Clinton D. Barry (1925), 268
Clio (1945), 216, 272
Cluny (1929), 269
Clyde (1853), 245
Coimbra (1942), 192, 210, 271
Colombia (1950), 273
Colonel Clayton (1945), 272
Colorado (1904), 264
Columbia (1883), 36, 258
Columbia (about 1898), 262
Columbia (1904), 264
Columbus (1856), 160, 245
Comanche (1905), 146, 264
Commander (1881), 257
Commerce (1852), 36, 245
Commodore (1866), 247
Commodore T. H. Allen (1901), 263
Constellation (1960), 135, 136, 275
Constitution (1959), 152, 275
Continent (1942), 215, 271
Copia (1882), 194, 257
Cornelia M. Kingsland (1895), 262
Cornelia Soule (1902), 195, 264
Cornelius J. Kolff (1960), 275
Cornell (1955), 274
Cornwall (1875), 158, 255
Corson (1922), 268
Cragside (1915), 266
Cubana (1909), 265
Culloden (1781), 189, 190
Curacao (1873), 252
Cynthia Jane (1898), 262
Cythera (1888), 259

D. C. Hulse (1871), 249
D. R. Stockwell (date unknown), 277
Daghestan (1908), 40, 265
Dan Bostrom (1969), 276
Dania (1890), 260
Daniel C. Higgins (1865), 247
Dashing Wave (1867), 248
David A. Boody (1899), 142, 262
David Carll (1893), 261

New Yorker (1952), 273
Newport (1964), 276
Nieuw Amsterdam (1920), 267
Nifadelos (1865), 247
Nonesuch (1918), 267
Nordvind (1966), 276
Norma (1872), 251
Norma (1920), 267
Normandie (1942), 213, 214, 271
Norness (1942), 210, 211, 271
North America (1843), 244
North Dakota (1959), 274, 275
Northfield (1901), 167, 263
North River (1930), 269
North River (1931), 269
North Star (1915), 177, 266
Nutmeg State (1899), 120, 121, 262

Oakwood (1875), 158, 254
Observation (1932), 269
Ocean Queen (1969), 85, 276
Oceanus (1868), 248
Ohio (1832), 244
Ohio (1874), 254
Ohioan (1933), 269
"Oil Wreck" (1908), 195, 265
Old Glory (1924), 268
Olive Branch (1820), 243
Oliver A. Arnold (1894), 261
Oliver Ellsworth (1827), 243
Omega (1871), 249
Onrust (1927), 268
Oregon (1846–1863), 244, 246
Oregon (1884), 37, 192, 258
Orville Harden (1945), 216, 272
Oscar (1873), 119, 252
Oscar C. Acken (1871), 249
Otco Bayway (1959), 274
Ovidia (1930), 269

P. W. Sprague (1880), 257
Panama (1890), 260
Panuco (1941), 130, 271
Passaic Sun (1966), 276
Patricia Moran (1966), 85, 276
Patron (1873), 252
Pearl (1872), 251
Pelican State (1950), 273
Pentland Firth (1942), 211, 271

Pequoit Hill (1946), 272
Pequonnock (1920), 160, 267
Persia (1902), 264
Peter Rickmers (1908), 176, 177, 195, 265
Petersburg (1944), 272
Petrel (1858), 76, 246
Phantom (1888), 37, 259
Pilgrim (1884), 24, 258
Pilot (1857), 246
Pilot (1917), 209, 266
Pinnace (1632–1633), 3, 241
Planter (1865), 247
Plymouth (1899), 24, 262
Plymouth (1913), 266
Pocono (1930), 269
Point Breeze (1942), 271
Poling Bros. 18 (1952), 131, 273
Port Philip (1918), 267
Port Republic (1947), 273
President (1815), 207, 243
President (1831), 54, 243
President (1841), 244
Prince Frederick (1892), 261
Princess Anne (1920), 64, 65, 66, 67, 110, 111, 267
Princess Beatrice (1874), 253
Prins Maurits (1657), 5, 6, 241
Prinzess Alice (1909), 265
Prison ships (1777–1778), 203, 242
Providence (1871), 22, 23, 249, 250
Providence (1872), 251
Providence (1907), 265
Pure Oil Co. tanker (1930), 269
Puritan (1874), 253

Q11 (1941), 271
Queen Elizabeth (1952), 273
Quickstep (date unknown), 146, 277
Quita (1938), 270

R. M. Clark (1874), 254
R. P. Resor (1942), 210, 271
R. S. Carter (1874), 253
R. S. Lindsay (1887), 259
Ramos (1933), 195, 269
Rapide (1875), 158, 159, 255
Reaper (1867), 248
Red Fox (1932), 269
Red Jacket (1899), 262

INDEX OF PEOPLE AND PLACES

Index of People and Places

Beaumont, Texas, 216
Beaven, Capt. W. J., 109, 110, 111
Bebensee, Capt. Charles, 61
Bedloe's (Liberty) Island, 134, 254, 255, 269, 274
Beebe, F. C., 107
Beebe, Capt. F. H., 120
Beebe, George, Jr., 39, 267
Beebe, Theophilus, 46
Beekman's Slip, Wharf, 19, 165
Belden Point, City Island, 271
Bell, Joseph H., 103
Bellevue Pier, 128
Bellport, L.I., 99, 103
Bendiksen, Capt. Kristian, 154
Bennet, Capt. Richard, 241
Bennett, Elijah M., 103
Bennett, James Gordon, 229, 230
Berg, Capt. Samuel H., 129
Bering Straits, 228
Bermuda, 118, 206, 250
Biekunt, S. H., 273
Black Tom, N.J., 208
Blake, Lt. Comdr. Ernest, 215
Block, Adriaen, 1, 2, 17
Block Island, 2, 103, 178
Blue Point, L.I., 103
Bompard, Captain, 242
Booth Bay, Maine, 253
Bordeaux, France, 260, 265
Boston, 48, 63, 76, 233
Bowdion, Harry L., 182
Bradford, William, 228
Brandow, Everett, 127
Braynard, Frank O., 154, 192, 231, 240
Brayton, Captain, 23, 118, 249
Breitenfeld, Capt. Harry, 48
Bremen, 59, 122, 258, 265, 269
Bricksburg, N.J., 104
Bridgehampton, L.I., 99, 103, 107
Bridgeport, Conn., 22, 120, 225, 244
Brigantine Shoals, N.J., 249
Bristol, England, 158
Bronx, 19, 164, 236
Brookhaven, L.I., 247, 249
Brooklyn (Heights, Navy Yard), 70, 118, 159, 163, 164, 165, 166, 202, 203, 226, 230, 243, 268, 270, 275
Brooks, Capt. Charles M., 121
Brown, Captain, 53
Brown, Capt. Richard, 35
Brown, Wreckmaster W. E., 22, 251, 252
Brownrigg, John, 90, 91
Bucking or Buckins (also Ellis, Gibbet, Oyster) Island, 89
Buckport, Maine, 23
Budd, Pilot Henry, 245
Buenaventura, Colombia, 141
Buenos Aires, 86
Bullock, Captain, 183

Bunker, Capt. Elihu S., 19, 20
Burr, Capt. George, 94, 95, 96, 246
Bushwick (Basin, Terminal), Brooklyn, 216
Bussorah, Persian Gulf, 187
Butler, Capt. Frank, 89
Butler's Point, L.I., 201, 242
Byrne, Sgt. Robert, 188

Caibarien, Cuba, 252
Calais, Maine, 252
Calcutta, 254
Callao, 247
Camden, N.J., 248
Campbell, Pilot Isaac, 253
Canton, 239
Canvin, Capt. J. J., 38, 260
Cape Ann, 76
Cape Antonio, 89
Cape Cod, 2, 48, 178, 212
Cape Henry, 185
Cape Horn, 118, 228, 233
Cape May, N.J., 179
Cape of Good Hope, 233
Captain's Island, L.I. Sound, 251, 263
Card, William P., 103
Cardenas, Cuba, 194, 252, 258
Caribbean, 154
Carlsen, Capt. H., 269
Carlton, Captain, 248
Carman, family, 111
Carman, Capt. George, 67
Carman, Robert, 65
Carman, Capt. Thomas, 243
Carpenter, Capt. Thomas D., 258
Carse, Robert, 179
Carteret, N.J., 61, 62
Casablanca, 218
Casino Beach, 125, 127
Castle Garden, 203
Castle William, 158, 204, 255
Catherine Ferry, 94, 165
Cavanagh, Edward F., Jr., 135
Caven Point Terminal, Jersey City, N.J., 217
Cedarhurst, L.I., 72
Center Moriches, L.I., 37, 192
Chapelle, Howard I., 70
Chapman, William E., 82
Charleston, S.C., 53, 78
Chase, Capt. George F., 23, 24, 249
Chase, Ensign Peter, 219
Cherbourg, 276
Ches-Del Canal, 48
Chichester, Captain, 146
China, 175, 228, 233
Christiania, Norway, 261
Church, Aaron, 90
City Island, 153, 212, 221, 222, 224, 225, 251, 253, 256, 269, 270, 274
Clark, Pilot James M., 254
Clark, John, 100, 196

Index of People and Places

Index of People and Places